VIỆT NAM
A LONG HISTORY

NGUYỄN KHẮC VIỆN

VIỆT NAM
A LONG HISTORY

Tenth edition

THẾ GIỚI PUBLISHERS
HÀ NỘI - 2015

English translation
First edition 1987
Eighth edition 2012
Ninth edition 2014
Tenth edition 2015
Printed in Việt Nam
VN - TG - 12-103 - 1
ISBN: 978-604-77-0962-5

National Library of Vietnam Cataloguing in Publication Data

Nguyen Khac Vien
Việt Nam : A long history / Nguyen Khac Vien. - H. : The gioi, 2015. - 410p. : phot., m. ; 24cm

1. History 2. Vietnam
959.7 - dc14

TGF0045p-CIP

CONTENTS

PUBLISHER'S NOTE

Việt Nam, A Long History was written by Nguyễn Khắc Viện in French and first published in Việt Nam in 1976. Later, it was translated into English, Russian, German and Spanish. In 1999, L'Hamartan in France re-printed the French edition published by Thế Giới in 1993.

The fact that the book has up to now been re-published nine times proves its attractiveness to foreign readers. It was awarded the State Prize in 2001 by the Vietnamese government as a distinguished work in Social Sciences and Humanities. Earlier, the author Nguyễn Khắc Viện was awarded the Grand Prix de la Francophonie by the French Academy of Science in 1992 for this book, together with many of his works written in French.

Over the past 30 years, many foreigners have read *Việt Nam, A Long History* and shown a high appreciation of it. However, they have also often raised questions why the author's analyses of the Nguyễn Dynasty and the period after 1975 are not as exhaustive as expected.

Vietnamese scholars have a different attitude towards the Nguyễn Dynasty because the Nguyễn kings contributed much to the development of the nation. At the same time, they could be blamed for their narrow-minded policy of governance. Thus, Nguyễn Ánh, the founding-king of the dynasty, twice turned to foreign powers for support in his effort to suppress the progressive Tây Sơn uprising led by Quang Trung. At first, he sought help from the Siamese court. However, his forces and 50,000 Siamese troops were defeated by the Tây Sơn at Rạch Gầm – Xoài Mút (presently Mỹ Tho province) on 19th January 1782. Later, he sent his son to France as surety in an attemp to entreat the French to provide him with military personnel and materiel. Then, upon his enthronement Nguyễn Ánh sought cruel revenge on the participants

in the Tây Sơn uprising. Among Nguyễn Ánh's successors there were some who pursued a closed-door policy, opposing any idea of renovation. Thus, the nation remained backward and vulnerable to the invasion by French colonialists. As a consequence, Việt Nam became a colony of France for about 100 years.

Effectively, the Nguyễn ruled over Việt Nam for 81 years (1802-1883). From 1883 to 1945 their rule was only nominal. They made significant contributions to the development of the country in some aspects. For example, they fostered agriculture, organized land reclamation, built sea dykes, canals and drainage systems, and introduced reasonable land distribution allotment mechanism and taxes. In 1815, King Gia Long promulgated the *Dynastic Penal Code* composed of 22 tomes. King Minh Mạng carried out administrative reforms in 1831 and 1832 with a view to unifying the country. He divided the country into 30 provinces: 10 big, 10 medium-sized and 10 small; the number of levels of administrative authority was reduced to four; and the mandarinate was re-structured. At the same time, King Minh Mạng also carried out reforms in the education system with a view to selecting talented people for the court.

Possibly, the socio-political context of the 90's of the last century did not allow Nguyễn Khắc Viện as well as other Vietnamese scholars to have a fair judgment of the faults and merits of the Nguyễn kings in Việt Nam's contemporary history.

The post-period 1975 was marked by socio-economic upheavals. Devastated by the 30 years' war, Việt Nam started its economic recovery and national development according to the Soviet model, which eventually led the country into a serious socio-economic crisis. However, the renewal of thinking and numerous trials in economic development in the 80's served as an impetus for the emergence of a new policy line known as *đổi mới* (renewal) in late 1986. It is understandable that Nguyễn Khắc Viện needed time to gather facts and figures and to see how effectively the new policy would impact on social life, before he could present any judgment or analysis of his own. His work on the book finished in 1993, four years before his death and as a result he could not cover the *đổi mới* period.

Twenty years have elapsed since the beginning of renewal. Việt Nam has gained outstanding achievements in its *đổi mới* effort, which are recognized world-wide. And some personages and facts in Vietnamese history are now considered from an angle different from Nguyễn Khắc Viện's. However, this book retains its value with

approaches characteristic of Nguyễn Khắc Viện's time and as a reference source in foreign languages for readers who are interested in Vietnamese history.

We welcome any comment from readers for improving subsequent editions.

Hà Nội, Autumn 2015

Thế Giới Publishers

PART ONE

TRADITIONAL VIỆT NAM

Chapter I

ORIGINS

FROM THE STONE AGE TO THE BRONZE AGE

Paleolithic and Neolithic

Việt Nam is located in Southeast Asia, where the early appearance of anthropoids has been noted in many places.

In August 1965, in a cave in the area of Tân Văn commune, Lạng Sơn province, the discovery was made of the remains of two anthropoids closely related to *Sinanthropus*. These remains are still being studied, but the date of their appearance may be put, according to preliminary estimates, at the Middle Pleistocene, about half a million years ago.

The first traces of a real human industry were found in November 1960, on Mount Đọ in Thanh Hóa province. On a site 20-30 metres above the level of the surrounding rice fields were found thousands of stone splinters from cutters and scrapers. Among these were almond shaped hand-axes, carefully smoothed on both faces and typical of the Chellean period. The existence of an Earlier Paleolithic in Việt Nam was thus confirmed[1].

In many caves in Yên Bái, Ninh Bình and Quảng Bình provinces, where bones from post-Pleistocene fauna have been unearthed, teeth and jaw-bones from *Homo Sapiens* have also been discovered.

And so man had thus continued to exist over a long period, gradually improving his tools, albeit very slowly.

Towards the end of the Paleolithic, the Red River delta had not yet completely silted up. Humans had settled in the limestone hills bordering the plains, in spacious habitable caves located near rivers and forests where fish and game abounded. Tools were made from pebbles found in

1. A number of Vietnamese archaeologists dispute this

the streams. In Hòa Bình and Bắc Sơn, centres of Stone Age culture have been discovered in caves, with the remains of tools, utensils and hearths, even ashes, and traces of food preparation, particularly shells and bones.

Tools were made of roughly chipped stone, were ellipsoid, disc, or almond-shaped, and included cutters, scrapers and rectangular axes. Pebbles served as pestles for crushing nuts and grain. Gradually the so-called Bắc Sơn axe of polished stone made its appearance. Tools made of animal bones and horn have seldom been found. It is probable that bamboo was widely used to make stakes, arrows, cutters and so on. A section cut from the trunk of bamboo could serve as a vessel or even a cooking pot (still the case in the highlands), as could coconuts, gourds and calabashes. Pottery made its appearance in the Bắc Sơn period. Clay was first kneaded into a soft mass, and then molded into the shape of containers whose inner or outer surfaces were then polished. Traces have been found of a kind of spatula tied together by a piece of grass with which the clay was patted while still wet. In general, earthenware was still rough and fired at a fairly low temperature.

Hunting and food gathering were the main activities. No traces of agriculture and no remains of domestic animals, except perhaps for the dog, have been found.

In the same period, along the coast of Trung Bộ humans lived mostly from fishing. Shells from molluscs, which had been eaten, accumulated in enormous mounds, five or six metres high and several thousand square metres in area, the most typical having been found in Quỳnh Lưu (Nghệ An province). These mounds also contained the bones of mammals (deer, buffalo and dog) and pestles with hollowed-out stones used to crush grain. Many stone tools have been unearthed.

Under a heap of shells in Quỳnh Văn, several tombs have been found grouped together. The dead were buried in a sitting position with their knees bent, along with a few tools and adornments made of shell, bone and stone, small perforated beads of baked earth, and pottery with decorative motifs. On the walls of a cave in Hòa Bình, a drawing has been found of a creature with the body of an animal and a human head but with horns. The presence of shells in caves far from the coast and of stone tools in coastal areas where stone was not available seems to be evidence of some sort of exchange between regions.

It is reasonable to assume that at the end of the Neolithic Era, about 5,000-6,000 years ago, most of the primitive human beings living on the territory of present-day Việt Nam were entering into the era of rice cultivation. Recent archaeological discoveries have found evidence of this everywhere, from north to south, from highlands to lowlands, and from littoral areas to islands off the coast. Besides well-known Neolithic sites in the Red River delta and the basin of the Mã River, traces of the Hạ Long culture have been found along the coast of Quảng Ninh province, a culture that succeeded the Bắc Sơn culture. Farther south and also on the coast in the southern part of Bình Trị Thiên area, the Bàu Tró site can be regarded as a more developed stage of the Quỳnh Văn tradition. During the same period in the highlands in southwest central Việt Nam, open-air dwellings have been found chiefly in Gia Lai-Công Tum and Đắc Lắc, where the axes, knives, polishers, stone hoes and pottery found show no similarities in manufacturing techniques with those of articles found elsewhere in Việt Nam.

Farther south, in the basin of the Đồng Nai River nearly 50 Neolithic sites have been discovered in ancient or more recent alluvial layers of islands, the most representative being Cầu Sắt in Xuân Lộc district. This region flourished 4,000 years ago, with relatively important centres of human habitation. The Đồng Nai culture was an upland one whose inhabitants practised dry, rather than wet rice cultivation, in low-lying areas of the plains. This tradition developed without interruption up to the Iron Age and may have given rise to the Óc Eo culture in the low-lying western region of the Mekong River delta.

Polished stone implements became more and more specialized. Axes and shoulder axes (those with tenons) were well polished, in various sizes and with regular geometrical shapes, and set in hafts. Men knew how to saw and drill, and to use various tools to fell trees, clear large expanses of land, build boats, make wooden and bamboo implements, scrape tree-bark and hides, and make rings, bracelets, earrings and beads out of bone, shell or stone.

Pottery making reached a high level. The use of the potter's wheel and kiln made it possible to obtain items of good quality and varying size and shape, mainly pots and vases decorated with geometrical patterns. Bone needles, spinning wheels and shuttles of baked earth prove the existence of weaving and garment-making. Along the coast and near rivers and streams, sinkers of baked clay have been discovered as well as projectiles of the same material used in hunting with blowpipes.

The existence of agriculture and livestock breeding has been confirmed by the discovery of hoes, large earthenware grain containers,

---

1. Quảng Bình, Quảng Trị and Thừa Thiên - Huế provinces.

and pig and buffalo bones. It appears that rice was grown in burnt-out forest clearings on hill-slopes and in submerged fields on the plains. Indochina is one of the regions in the world where rice growing made its earliest appearance.

While humans continued to live in caves in mountainous regions, in recently discovered sites on the plains traces have been found of houses made of wood and bamboo, their size seeming to indicate that they were communal dwellings. The remains of such structures are scattered over tens of thousands of square metres, an area equivalent to that of the present-day village. Innumerable artifacts found here indicate the presence of thousands of people, comprising tribes made up of many clans. Houses were probably built on stilts as among present-day mountain-dwelling ethnic minorities. Historical records state that our ancestors built elevated houses to ward off attacks by tigers.

The large-scale manufacture of implements and large quantities of jewelry and decorated pottery show that the division of labour had reached a high level. The dead were buried together with implements, ornaments and pottery, and often in communal graves. Such equality in death shows that class differentiation among the living had not yet appeared.

*

* *

Skulls found in Hòa Bình, Bắc Sơn, Quỳnh Văn and Minh Cầm suggest that the people belonged to the Australo -Negroid group. However, Mongoloid elements appeared at a very early date. Intermarriage between Mongoloids coming from the north and Australo-Negroids gave birth to a southern Mongoloid group, which at first coexisted with the others but finally became predominant. Ethnic groups now living in Việt Nam all belong to this group, but have fairly definite Australo-Negroid features. Interracial mixing took place, from which sprang an autochthonous group that developed its own culture; as opposed to massive migration bringing in an external civilization. The study of stone tools and pottery from various Neolithic and Mesolithic sites has proved the continuity of an internal evolution occurring on the spot with its own unique features.

The Bronze Age

In the middle of the second millennium B.C., bronze first made its appearance together with stone tools. Sites dating back to the early Bronze Age were mostly concentrated in the uplands and the Red River delta. The most representative site is Phùng Nguyên (Phú Thọ province) discovered in 1958, where the objects found - finely polished working tools and ornamental items - testify to a high level of stone-working. This work was achieved mostly by cutting, making it possible to produce objects of precise and sometimes complicated form with a minimum of raw materials. Bronze appears to have become more and more common in the whole range of tools as well as weapons. The Phùng Nguyên culture at the beginning of the Bronze Age gave rise to the Đồng Đậu period (second half of the 2nd millennium B.C.), then to the Gò Mun period (early in the 1st millennium B.C.), finally reaching a peak with the Đông Sơn culture. Named after the eponymous site, this was the most important Bronze Age site and was discovered in 1924 in Thanh Hóa province. Archaeologists have now identified 96 Đông Sơn sites yielding a rich collection of items (at least 56 types) scattered throughout most of northern Việt Nam, mainly in the deltas of the Red, Mã and Cả rivers.

The first copper, and later bronze, objects appeared beside polished stone implements and earthenware, still Neolithic in nature. Sandstone moulds for manufacturing axes, spears and knives have been found in many places. The quality of the bronze and of their shaping improved little by little, eventually resulting in the remarkable creations of Đông Sơn. This evolution took place over many centuries. While it was marked by external elements, these were not decisive as has been claimed by European archaeologists.

On the basis of inadequate information and inspired by colonialist feelings, some European archaeologists have even put forward the theory that the art of bronze-casting in Việt Nam came originally from Europe.

Recent discoveries have revealed three important facts:

- The art of bronze casting appears to have been based on the Neolithic industry;

- It underwent a long period of development leading to the remarkable creations of Đông Sơn;

- It spread throughout all of modern-day Việt Nam, and recently discovered sites have revealed a unique civilization[1].

1. Excavations undertaken by Vietnamese archaeologists since 1959 have been principally at the following sites: Thiệu Dương in Thanh Hóa province; Cổ Loa near Hà Nội, Việt Trì, many sites in Phú Thọ province; Đào Thịnh in Yên Bái province, Sơn Tây, Hà Đông, Hà Tĩnh, Hòa Bình and Bắc Giang provinces. They have unearthed many Bronze Age relics. These discoveries have given rise to many studies by and debates among Vietnamese historians. Since 1975, many excavations have been made in the South.

The bronze artifacts discovered are extremely varied in nature: production implements such as ploughshares, axes, scythes, scrapers, chisels for wood-working, needles and fish-hooks; domestic utensils such as large containers, pots, basins and jars; weapons such as arrowheads, spears, sabres, knives, halberds and armour; musical instruments such as bells and drums; and works of art such as bracelets and statuettes.

The most remarkable objects are without doubt the bronze drums. They have been found in many places in Southeast Asia and China, but it is generally recognized that the finest were discovered in Vietnam. The drum found at Ngọc Lũ is 63 cm high, 79 cm in diameter, and cylindrical in shape. In the middle of the upper surface is an image of the sun with radiating beams, and 16 concentric circles with varied decorations: geometrical patterns, herds of deer and aquatic birds, and human figures, playing musical instruments, pounding rice, or beating drums. The men are clad in garments made from the feathers of aquatic birds, which give them the appearance of birdmen, probably indicating a totemic significance. They dance to the rhythm of clappers. There are also small buildings and houses on stilts and, on a curved edge below the top, boats and warriors carrying axes, spears and arrows.

These drawings and decorations are both realistic and stylized, testifying to the artistic talents of their creators. Most bronze artifacts were also highly decorated or finely shaped. This unquestionably shows a specific and unique civilization. The bronze drums were used during important festivals and ceremonies, especially those invoking rain.

Bronze ploughshares, scythe and sickle blades, and drawings on implements representing rice plants or people pounding rice, all testify to the development of agriculture. While cultivation in burnt-out forest clearings continued, wet rice planting was also developing. Fishing in oceans and rivers was widely practised. Handicrafts, pottery making and bronze casting, having reached a high level, began to be separated from agriculture. On pottery vessels, traces of plaited bamboo ties can be seen; basket-making must also have reached a high level of development.

Drawings on the bronze drums represent large houses on stilts and junks, some with towers, evidence of great progress in woodworking.

Overseas exchanges, especially with certain regions in southern China and Indonesia, have been proved by the discovery in tombs of various objects and weapons from the Warring Kingdoms Period (5th-3rd centuries B.C. in China), while bronze drums of Đông Sơn manufacture were sold in far-away lands.

While material civilization and art reached their peak at the end of the first millennium B.C. in the north, there appeared on a narrow strip of coastal land from south of the Ngang Pass (18th parallel) to the basin of the Đồng Nai River, another brilliant civilization related to the Đông Sơn culture. This was the Sa Huỳnh culture, named after the site where it was first discovered on the coast of present-day Quảng Ngãi province. Its principal distinguishing characteristic is a large number of funeral jars (usually 0.6 metres high) containing human remains, ornaments made of bronze, precious stones and glass and bronze or stone tools. These artefícts reveal a cultural tradition that had evolved without interruption for a thousand years from the beginning of the Bronze Age to the beginning of the Iron Age (4th-1st millennia B.C.).

The study of items collected leads us to assume that the economic basis of the Sa Huỳnh culture was the cultivation of rice and grain crops on varied terrain comprising high hills, low-lying plains and alluvial land along the coast. The people of Sa Huỳnh also practised sea-fishing and had a close relationship via the sea with the inhabitants of the Red River delta in the north and islands in the south. Their burial remains came within the framework of a wider cultural tradition whose range of influence spread over upper Laos, Thailand, the Philippines and Indonesia. The Sa Huỳnh culture may have given rise to the formation of ancient Malay-Polynesian states on the coastal plains of central Việt Nam in the 1st century A.D.

The Hùng Kings and the Kingdom of Văn Lang

Archaeological discoveries, especially the unearthing of a series of Neolithic sites along the Red River between Phú Thọ province and the suburbs of Hà Nội, legends recorded in historical annals, and observations in ancient Chinese books have supplied fairly precise information, which tallies closely on the beginning of Vietnamese history.

Early Chinese historians used the term Bách Việt (the Hundred Yues) to designate people living south of the Yangtze River. This was in fact a generic term covering various ethnic groups, among them the Lạc Việt, who lived on the plains and coastal regions of present-day northern Việt Nam and part of present -day Guangdong province in China.

The Lạc Việt then comprised 15 tribes, each with a fixed area of habitation. They practised rice growing in flooded fields, tattooed their bodies with images of aquatic animals, chewed betel, lacquered their teeth black, and pounded rice using hand-pestles.

A series of significant legends relate to this period. Lord Lạc Long Quân married Âu Cơ, who bore him 100 sons. One day he said to his wife: "I am a dragon, you are a fairy. We can't remain together." He took 50 of his sons with him to the plains and coastal regions, while the others followed their mother to the mountains. One of Lạc Long Quân's sons inherited his throne and was the founder of a dynasty of 18 rulers known as the Hùng Kings. Legends put the beginning of the Hùng dynasty as early as 4,000 years ago.

The kingdom was called Văn Lang, and it was made up of 15 tribes, the main one being the Mê Linh living in Bạch Hạc near present -day Việt Trì. The Hùng Kings ruled through *lạc hầu* (civilian chiefs), *lạc tướng* (military chiefs) and *bồ chính* (subaltern officials). The throne was hereditary; so were, in all probability, the functions of the *lạc hầu* and *lạc tướng*. Thus an aristocracy came into being, while primitive communes still existed in which social differentiation gradually increased. Wars between various groups supplied slaves.

The last of the Hùng Kings had a daughter of great beauty. Two suitors presented themselves - Sơn Tinh, the mountain genie, and Thủy Tinh, the water genie. The king promised he would give his daughter's hand to whoever came first with the required wedding gifts. Sơn Tinh arrived first with the gifts, married the princess and took her to the mountains to live with him. The frustrated Thủy Tinh unleashed his waters against Sơn Tinh, but the latter proved the stronger of the two. However, at the same period each year, the struggle resumes between the genies, ending invariably in the victory of Sơn Tinh. This legend reflects the struggle waged by the people against the floods caused each year by rivers in spate at the time of the summer monsoon. It is certain that, right from the dawn of their history, the Vietnamese people have had to organize themselves to bring the waters under control, hence the necessity for them to come together and build a centralized organization, gradually consolidated as the deltas of the great rivers were conquered.

The Âu Lạc Kingdom

While the Lạc Việt became organized on the plains and in coastal regions, they maintained interchanges with the Tây Âu (or Âu Việt who lived in the mountain regions of the present-day Việt Bắc and also in some parts of present -day Kwangsi in China). The Tây Âu were the ancestors of the Tày, Nùng and Zhuang, who now live in northern Việt Nam and southern China. They made up a federation of tribes, whose centre was in present-day Cao Bằng province. Wars also broke out from time to time between the Tây Âu and Lạc Việt.

Towards the end of the 3rd century B.C., King Thục Phán of the Tây Âu defeated the last of the Hùng Kings and merged the territories of the Tây Âu and the Lạc Việt to form the kingdom of Âu Lạc in the year 258 B.C. He took the royal title of An Dương and set up an embryonic state, with a court and an army which was, according to tradition, several hundred thousand strong. The territory of Âu Lạc comprised present - day northern Việt Nam down to the Hoành Sơn spur, excluding the mountainous areas south of the Red River and mountainous western parts of Thanh Hóa and Nghệ An provinces.

After his victory over the Hùng Kings, King An Dương transferred the capital from the hilly regions to the plains, to Cổ Loa. Cổ Loa citadel is the most important historical relic from ancient Việt Nam. It comprises three rings of walls, the outer ring measuring about 8,000 metres in length, with walls 12 metres thick (25 metres at the base) and 3-4 metres high. The earth walls were protected by baked earth ramparts in some places, by deep, wide moats linked to the Hoàng Giang River, and by watchtowers and other defenses. In 1959, at a site 300 metres from the southern ramparts, a stock of several thousand bronze arrowheads was unearthed. Soon afterwards, around the citadel stone and bronze axes and arrowheads were discovered. In 1966, three bronze ploughshares were found.

Cổ Loa citadel was a very important work of defence built using sophisticated techniques. Any assault from outside would run into a complex series of defensive installations. Communication between the citadel and local rivers made it possible to combine land and water operations. The volume of earth moved in order to build the citadel was about 2 million cubic metres.

The construction of the citadel was probably not all plain sailing; the people, pressed into service to build it, must have risen in revolt many times. Legend has it that "demons" disrupted the building work until the Golden Tortoise genie came and offered his help. When the citadel was completed, the genie presented the king with a magic claw which, used as a trigger on a crossbow, would give it devastating power against any enemy.

The size of Cổ Loa and the presence of significant stocks of bronze arrowheads point to the existence of a professional army and an embryonic state apparatus. The Âu Lạc kingdom was created at the peak of the Bronze Age around the 3rd century B.C. We have seen above how agriculture and handicrafts had flowered, presupposing a relatively complex division of labour.

What was the nature of the state and society in the kingdom of Âu Lạc? Opinion is divided among Vietnamese historians. Some think that Âu Lạc society was a state with slaves, a fairly sophisticated economic organization, and a well-developed regular army, as evidenced by the Cổ Loa citadel and the stocks of arrowheads. Inter -tribal wars are thought to have supplied most of the slaves who served as domestic servants, participated in agricultural and handicraft work, or were employed in the building of large defence works. The primitive commune remained solid, however, although some of its members may have become slaves.

Other scholars, while admitting the existence of slaves in Âu Lạc society, think that overall, it was not a society dependant on slaves. Production forces, although relatively developed, were not sufficient enough to allow the emergence of an exploitative class or a class-based state. One should not be fooled by the terms used at the time to designate the "king", the "nobility" and "functionaries." Works such as dykes and fortresses could have been built even by primitive communes. By and large Âu Lạc society remained one where the primitive commune, albeit on the way to disintegration, was predominant.

It must be said that neither thesis is definitively supported by archaeological research or the documentary evidence amassed thus far. A number of facts seem to confirm the slave hypothesis, but give no precise indication as to the way of life and numbers of people in either the ruling classes or slaves, the economic, political and legal relationships between them, and the functioning of the state. Research and archaeological excavations are still continuing, and we hope that more facts will emerge to shed light on this important period of Vietnamese history.

However, from the archaeological research available, the following facts have been established:

- The existence of man on Vietnamese territory as early as the Paleolithic;

- The continuous development of human society from the Stone Age to the Metal Age following a unique pattern which depended essentially on internal rather than external factors (the latter assuming greater or lesser importance according to the period);

- The flowering of a brilliant Bronze Age civilization which proved that society had emerged from its primitive state in the few centuries preceding the present era;

- The need to build installations to bring water under control, which implied a centralized organization;

- The continued existence of rural communes and the long-delayed appearance of private land ownership.

The well-established and crucial fact is that towards the end of the 1st millennium B.C., there appeared a unique and vigorous civilization, especially in the deltas and surrounding areas, which was soon to be confronted by a decisive challenge: confrontation with Chinese feudal expansion. The greatest proof of its strength and uniqueness is that it did not allow itself to be assimilated, and following a long resistance, was to become an independent national culture.

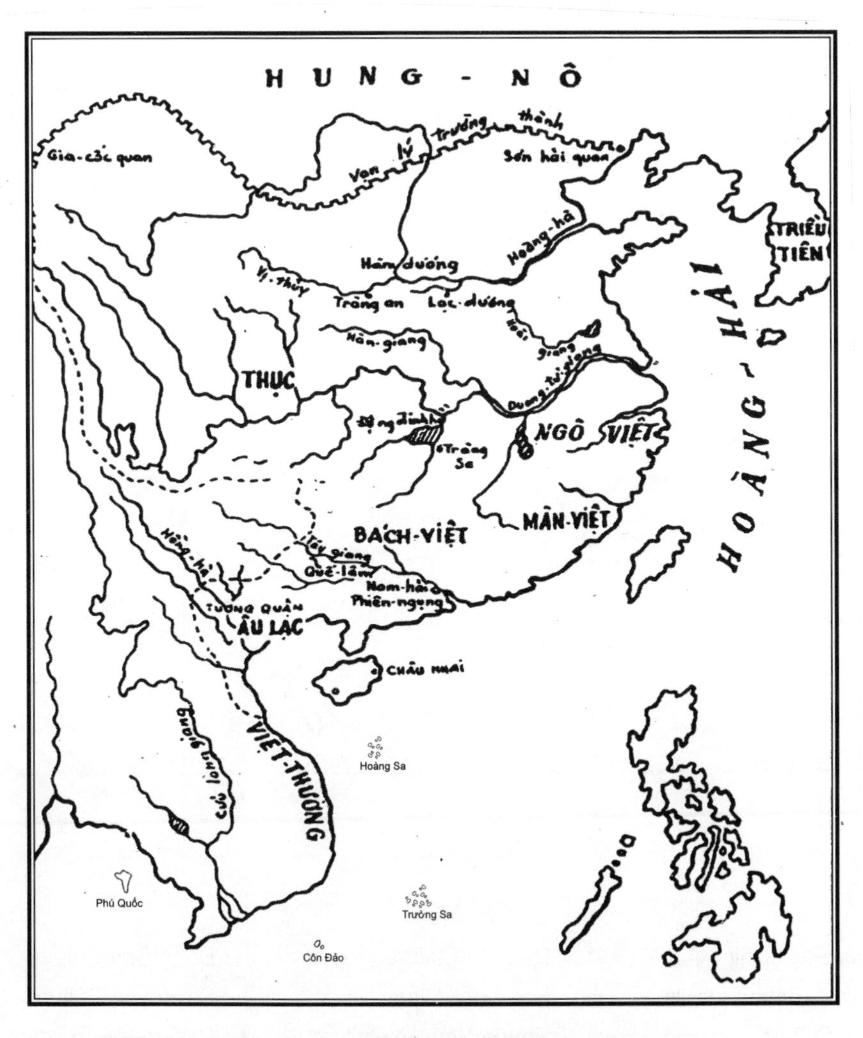
HUNG - NÔ
Vạn lý trường thành
Sơn hải quan
Hoàng-hà
Hàm dương
Tràng an
Lạc-dương
Hán-giang
THỤC
NGÔ
VIỆT
MÂN-VIỆT
BÁCH-VIỆT
Quế-lâm
Nam-hải
Phiên-ngung
TƯỢNG QUẬN
ÂU LẠC
CHÂU NHAI
TRIỀU TIÊN
HOÀNG - HẢI
VIỆT-THƯỜNG
Hoàng Sa
Trường Sa
Côn Đảo
Phú Quốc

ÂU LẠC STATE DURING THE QIN DYNASTY

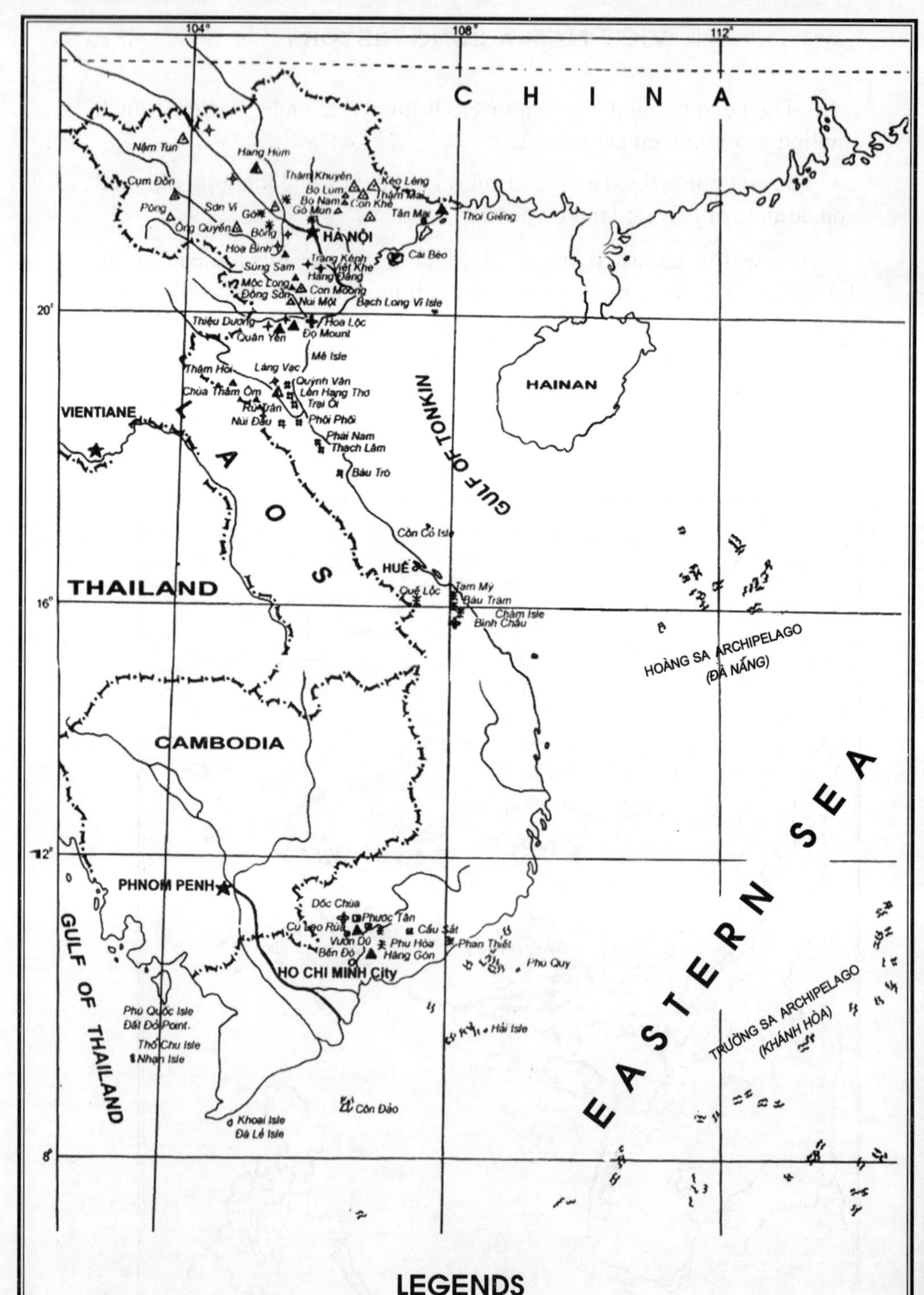
104°
108°
112°
20°
16°
12°
8°
CHINA
Nậm Tun
Hang Hùm
Thẩm Khuyên
Kéo Lèng
Cum Đồn
Bó Lúm
Thẩm Mai
Bó Nam
Con Khê
Pông
Sơn Vi
Gò Mun
Tân Mai
Ông Quyền
Hòa Bình
HÀ NỘI
Thoi Giếng
Cái Bèo
Tràng Kênh
Việt Khê
Sũng Sàm
Hang Đăng
Móc Long
Con Moong
Đông Sơn
Núi Mội
Bạch Long Vĩ Isle
Thiệu Dương
Hoa Lộc
Quán Yên
Đọ Mount
Mê Isle
HAINAN
Thẩm Hoi
Làng Vạc
Quỳnh Văn
Chùa Thẩm Ồm
Lèn Hang Thơ
Rú Trăn
Trại Ổi
Núi Đầu
Phôi Phối
VIENTIANE
Phái Nam
Thạch Lâm
Bàu Tró
GULF OF TONKIN
LAOS
Cồn Cỏ Isle
HUẾ
THAILAND
Quế Lộc
Tam Mỹ
Bàu Trám
Chàm Isle
Bình Châu
HOÀNG SA ARCHIPELAGO
(ĐÀ NẴNG)
CAMBODIA
EASTERN SEA
PHNOM PENH
Dốc Chùa
Phước Tân
Cù Lao Rùa
Cầu Sắt
Vườn Dũ
Phú Hòa
Phan Thiết
Bến Đò
Hàng Gòn
Phú Quý
HO CHI MINH City
GULF OF THAILAND
Phú Quốc Isle
Đất Đỏ Point.
Thổ Chu Isle
Nhạn Isle
Hải Isle
TRƯỜNG SA ARCHIPELAGO
(KHÁNH HÒA)
Côn Đảo
Khoai Isle
Đá Lẻ Isle

LEGENDS

- Inferior Paleolithic
- Grotto of Human fossils
- Sơn Vi Culture
- Hòa Bình Culture
- Bắc Sơn Culture
- Hạ Long Culture
- Bàu Tró Culture
- Hoa Lộc Culture
- Phùng Nguyên Culture
- Đồng Đậu Culture
- Gò Mun Culture
- Đông Sơn Culture
- Sa Huỳnh Culture
- Period of Bến Đò
- Pre-Đông Sơn
- Pre-Sa Huỳnh

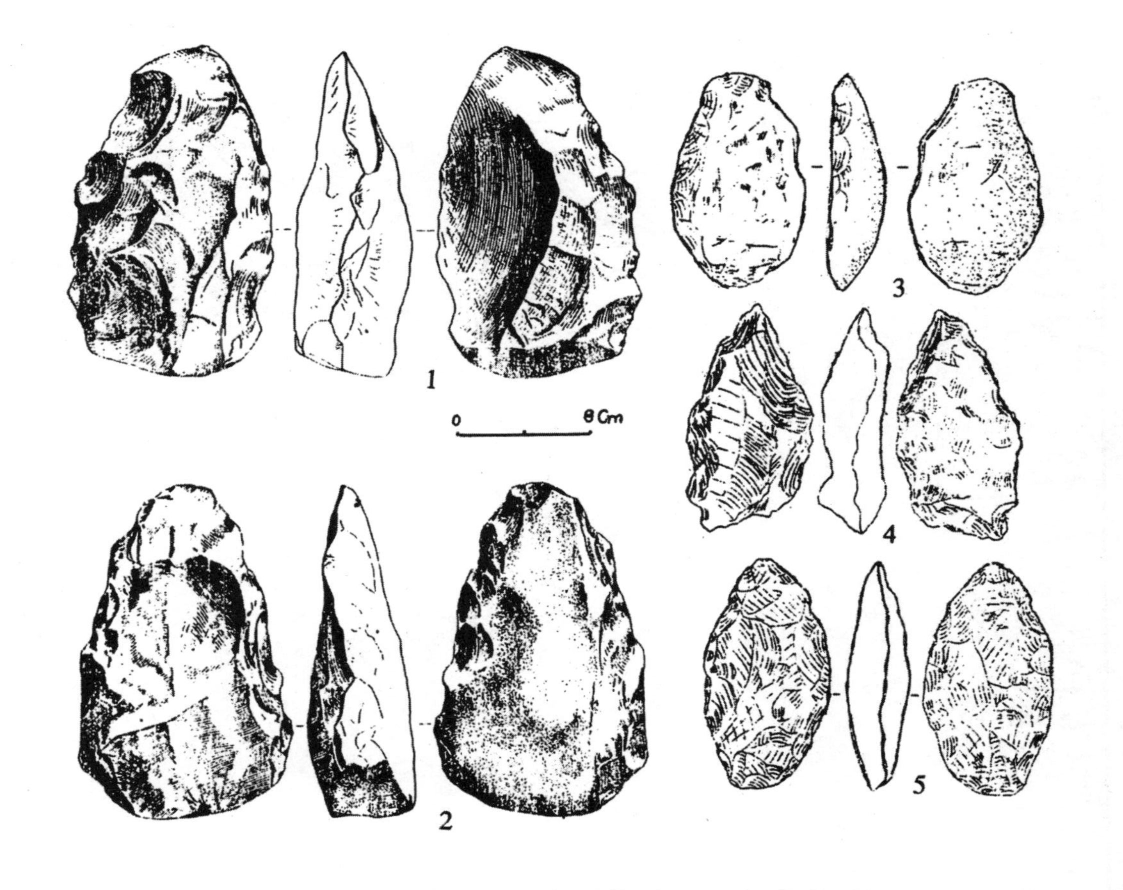
1
2
3
4
5
0
8 Cm

ARTIFACTS OF THE EARLY PALEOLITHIC
(1-2. ĐỌ MOUNT; 3-5 EASTERN NAM BỘ)

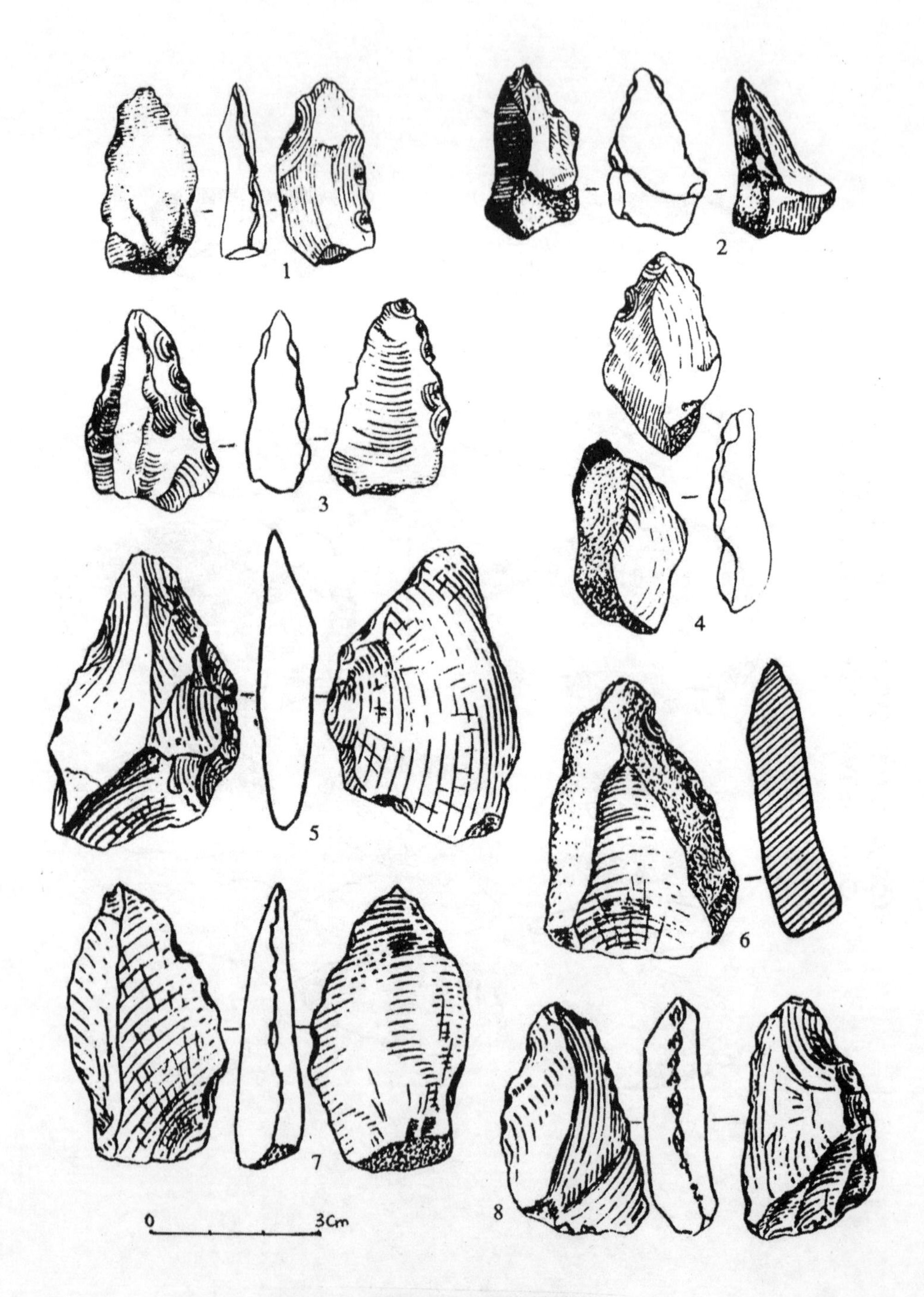
1
2
3
4
5
6
7
8
0
3Cm

STONE ARTIFACTS
(MIỆNG HỔ CAVE)

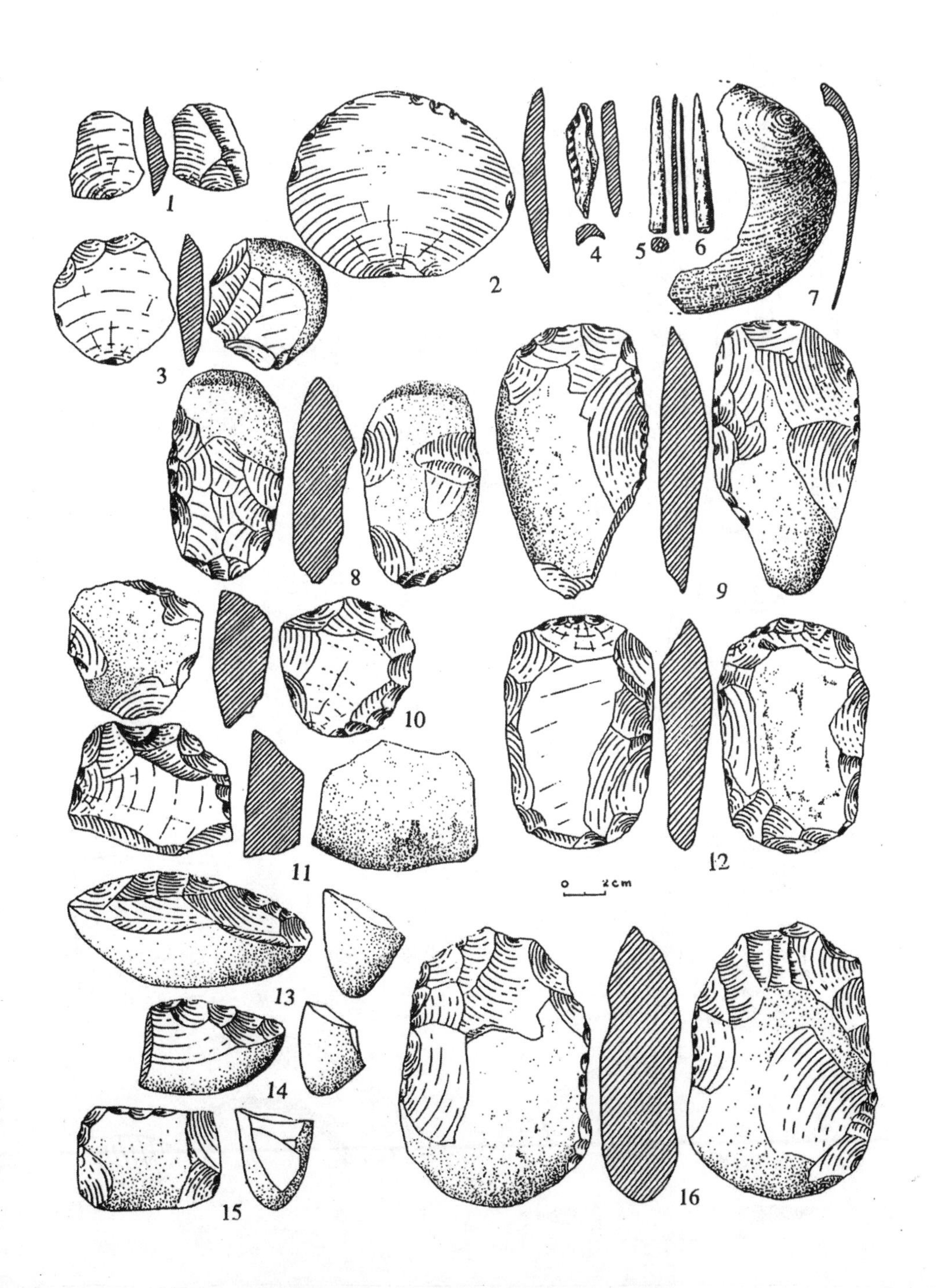
1
2
3
4
5
6
7
8
9
10
11
12
13
14
15
16
0 2cm

ARTIFACTS FROM CON MOONG CAVE
(1-12. TOOLS FROM HÒA BÌNH CULTURE; 13-16. TOOLS FROM SƠN VI CULTURE)

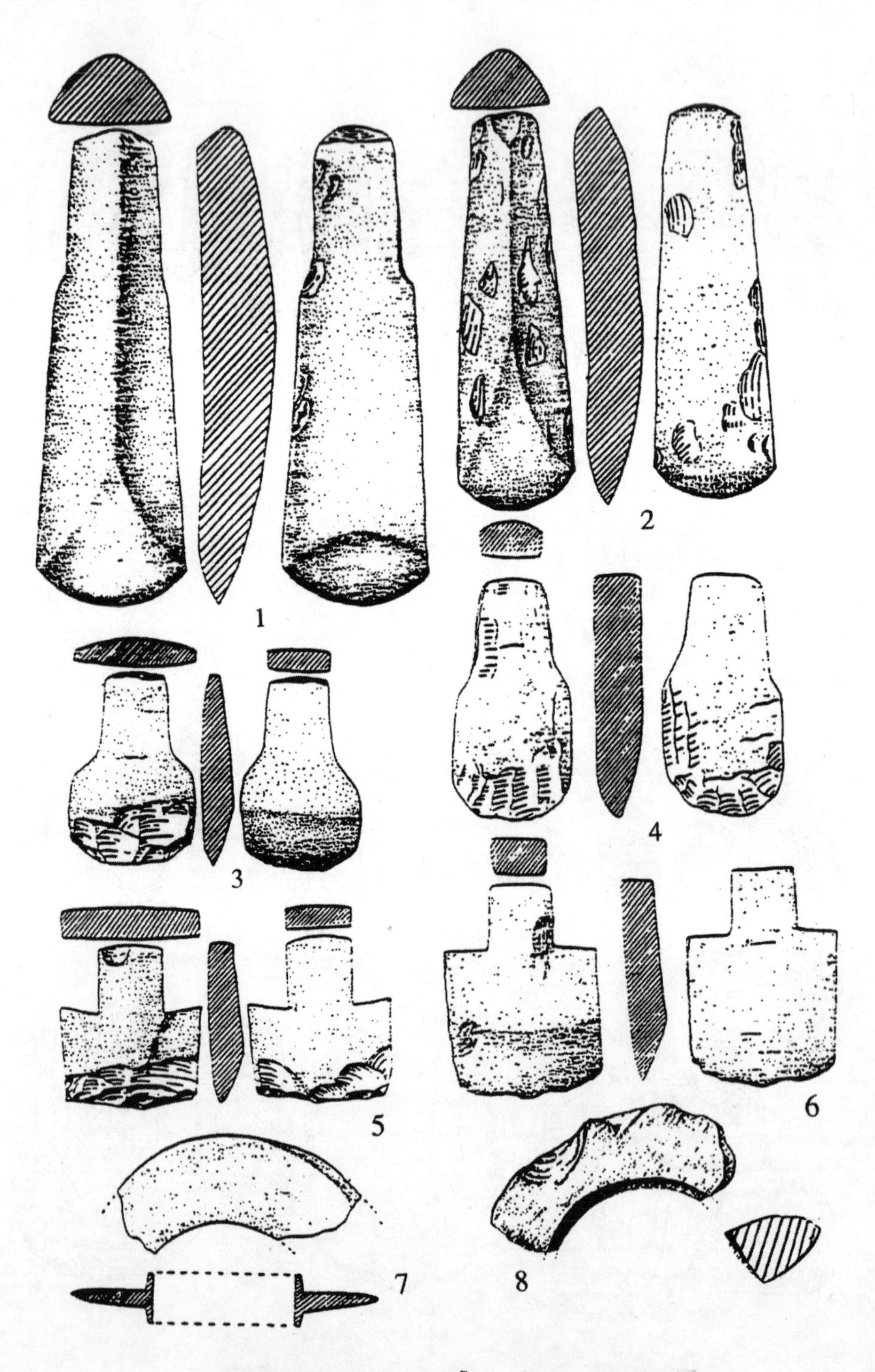
1
2
3
4
5
6
7
8

STONE TOOLS OF BIỂN HỒ CULTURE
(1-6. WORKING TOOLS, 7-8. STONE JEWELRIES)

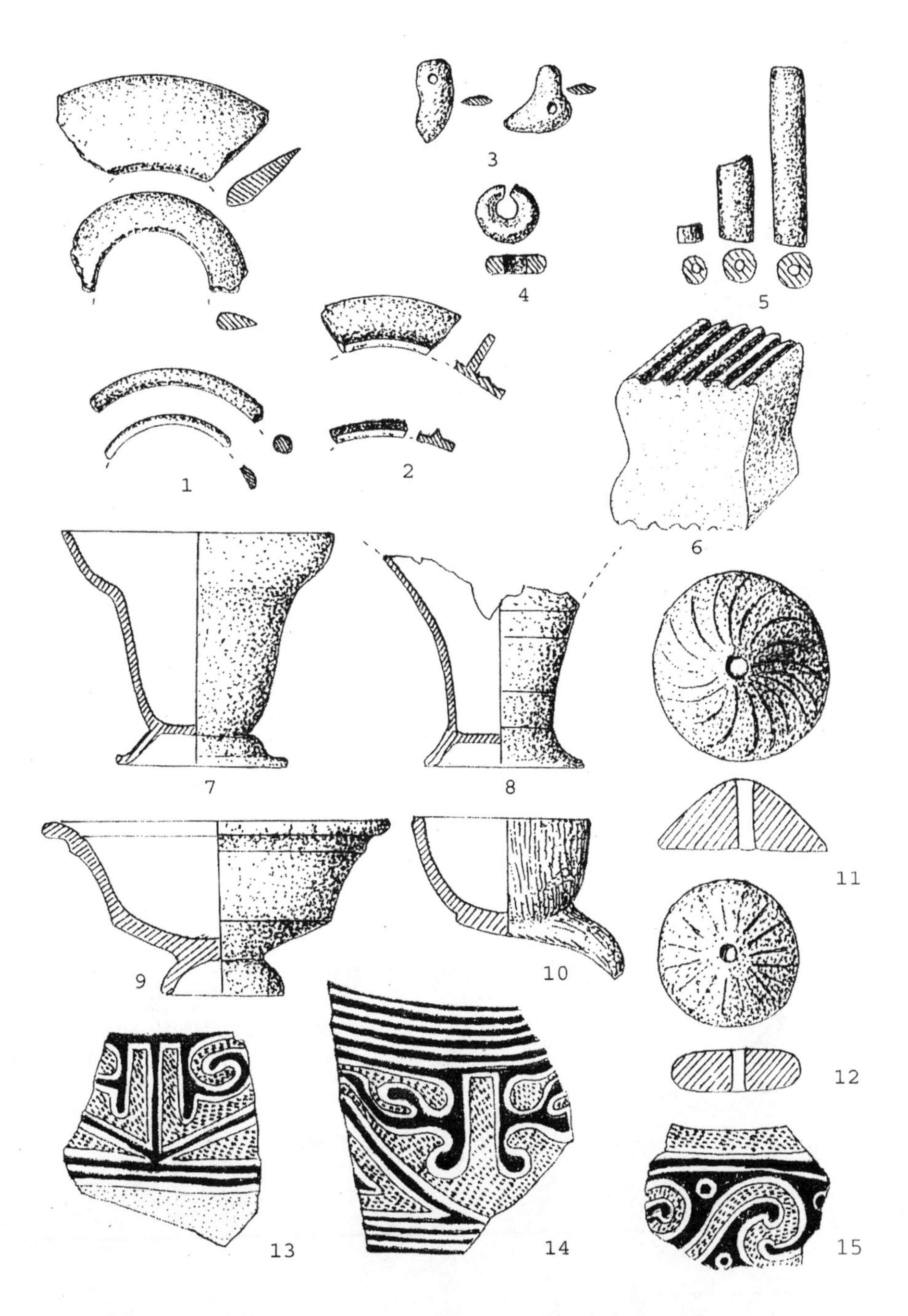
1
2
3
4
5
6
7
8
9
10
11
12
13
14
15

PHÙNG NGUYÊN CULTURE (PRE - ĐÔNG SƠN CULTURE)

Stone tools: 1-5: Jewelries; 6: Stone artifact

Ceramic tools: 7-9: Containers; 10: Ceramic hook

11-12: Plumbs

13-15: Patterned ceramic shards

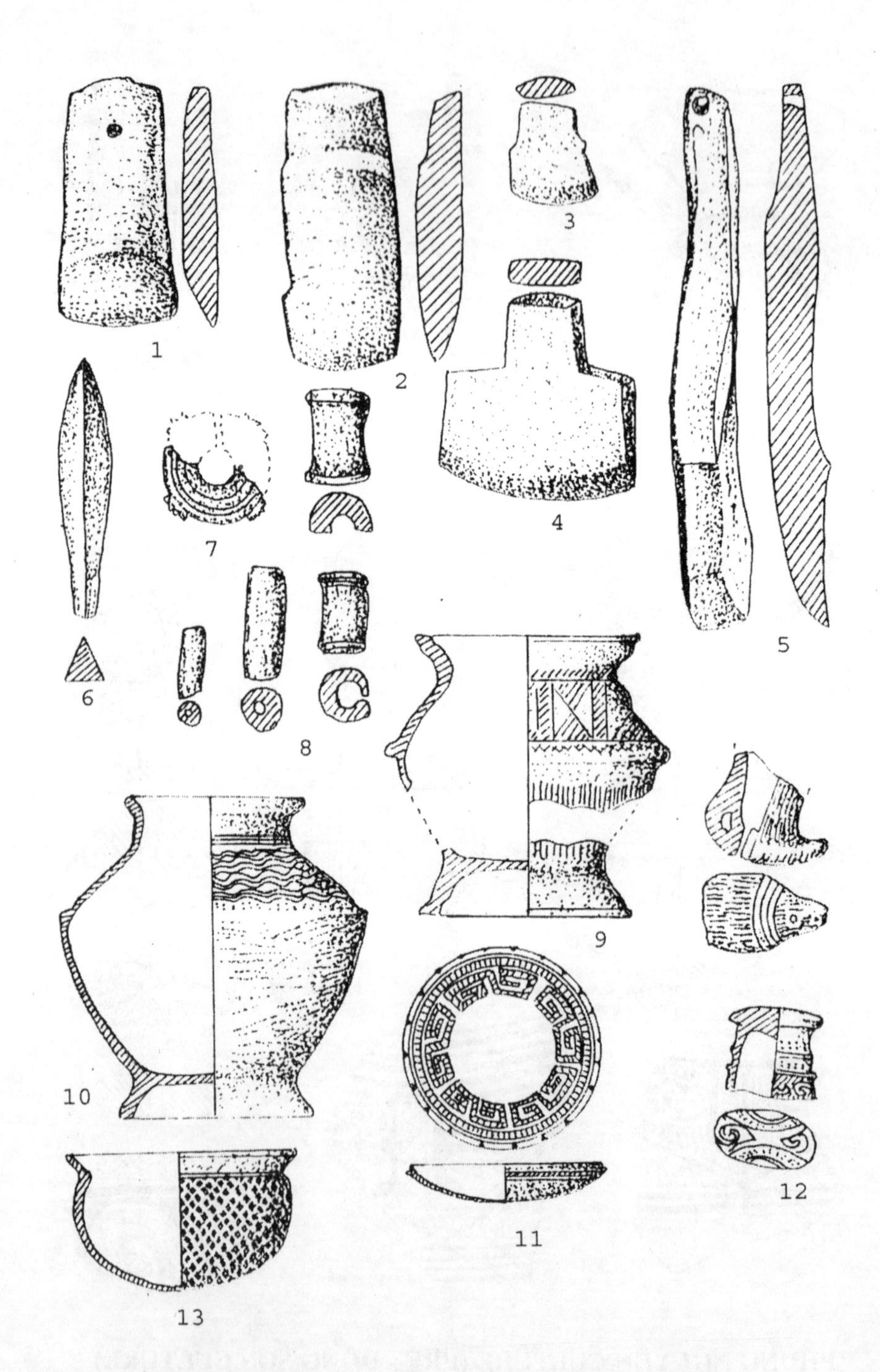
1
2
3
4
5
6
7
8
9
10
11
12
13

GÒ MUN CULTURE (PRE - ĐÔNG SƠN CULTURE

Stone tools: 1-4: Axes; 5-6: Stone artifacts; 7: earring; 8: beads
Ceramic tools: 9, 10, 11, 13: Containers, cooking utensils;
12: Ceramic hook

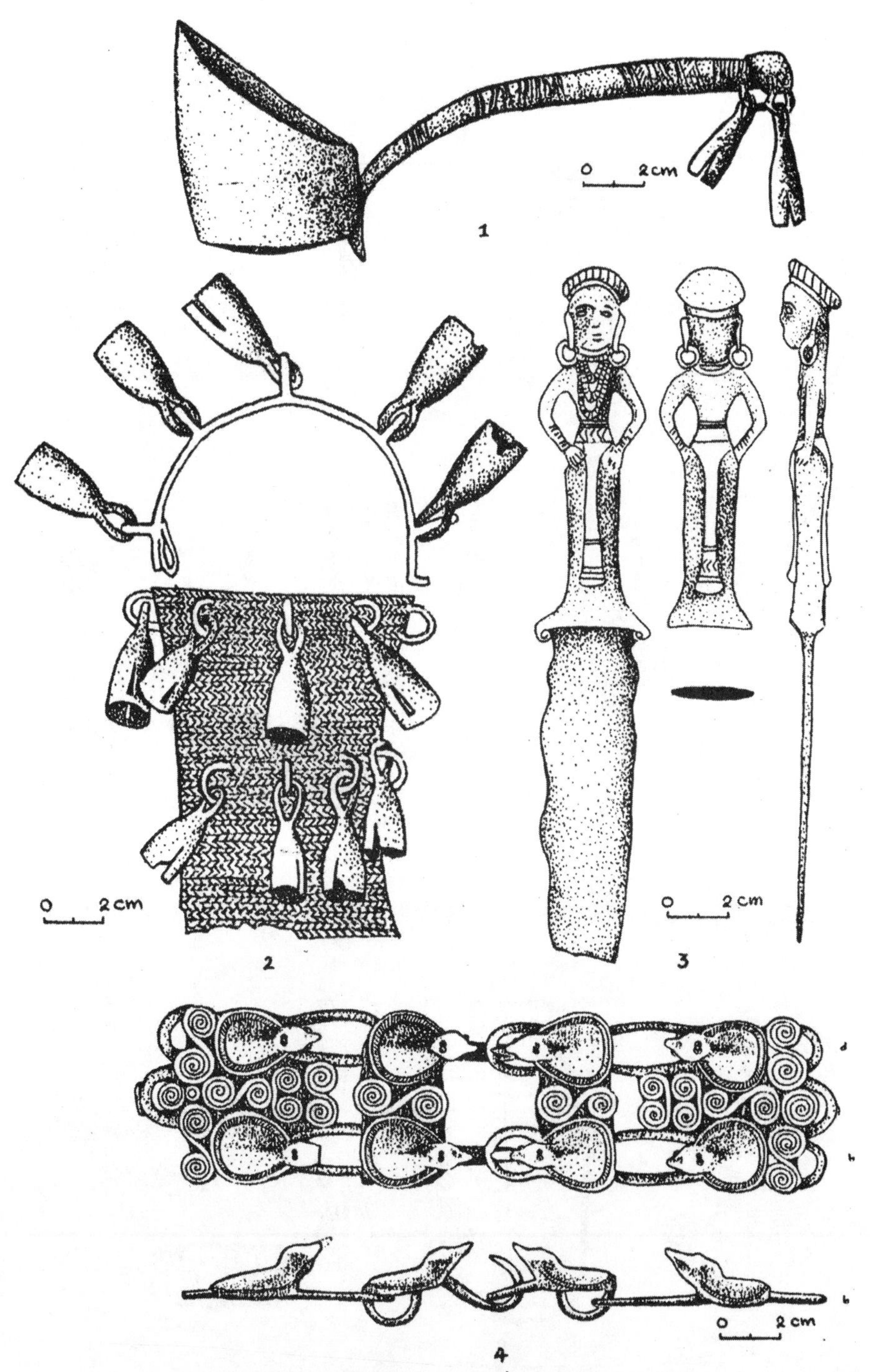

0 2cm
1
0 2cm
2
0 2cm
3
0 2cm
4

CERAMICS FROM SA HUỲNH CULTURE

1-11: Containers, cooking utensils

12: Ceramic actifacts

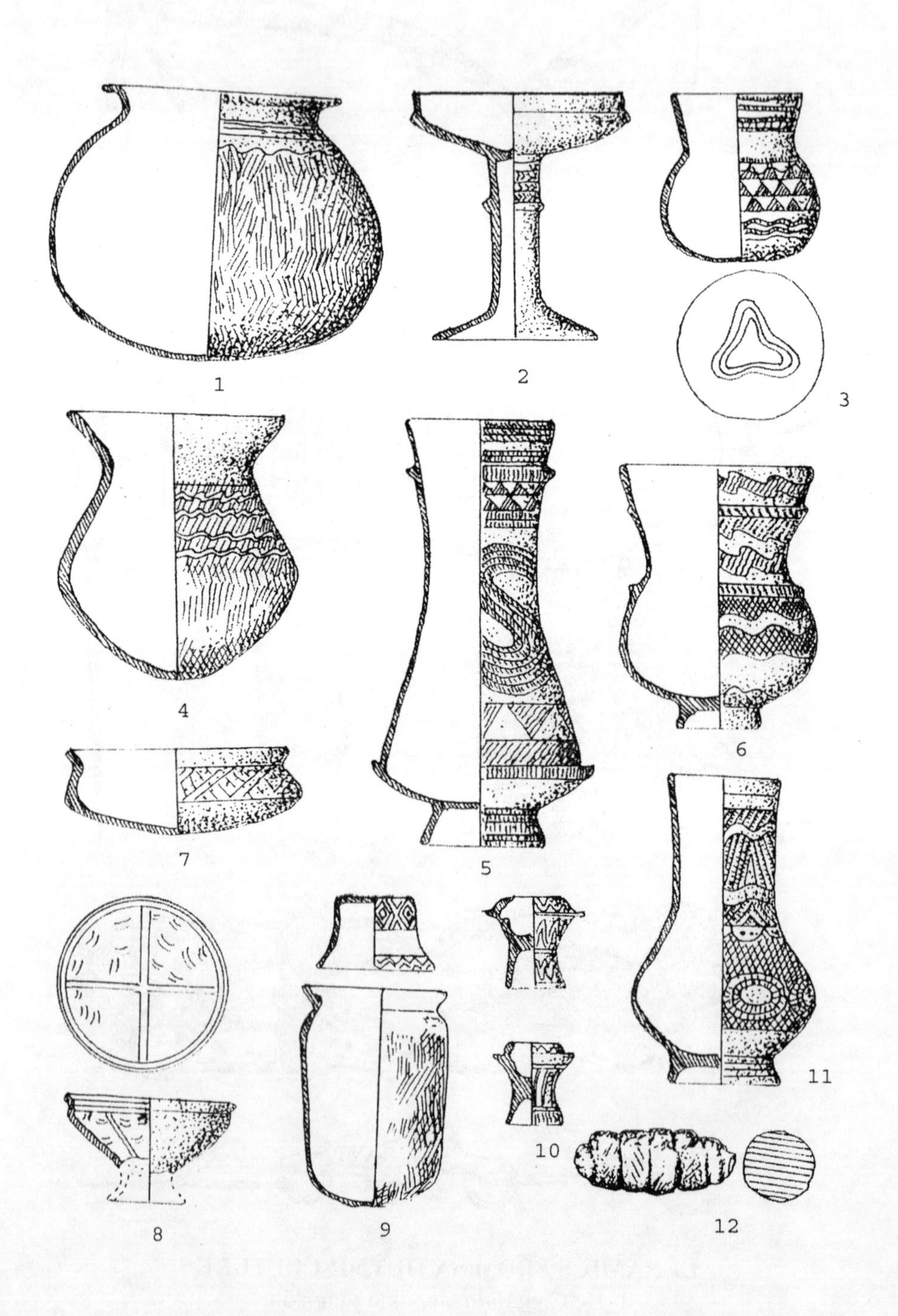
1
2
3
4
5
6
7
8
9
10
11
12

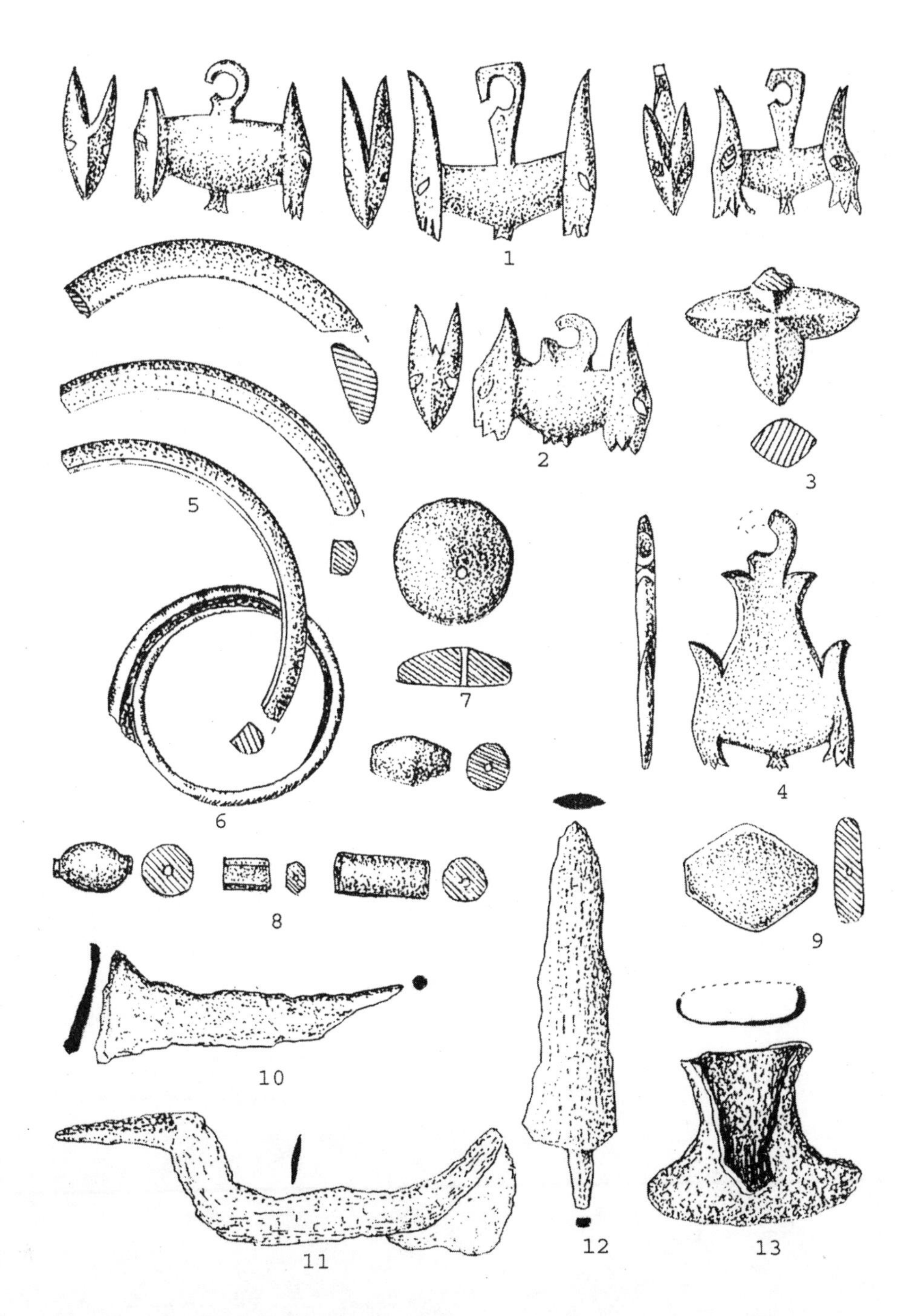
1
2
3
4
5
6
7
8
9
10
11
12
13

ARTIFACTS OF THE METAL AGE IN EASTERN SOUTH VIỆT NAM
1, 2, 4: earrings; 3, 5, 8, 9: bracelets
10, 11, 12: Instruments; 12: Spear; 6: Jewel

Chapter II

THE LONG MARCH TO INDEPENDENCE

(1st century B.C. - 10th century A.D.)

In the 3rd century B.C., the Han people, whose birthplace was in the Yellow River basin, unified China, merging into a centralized empire that comprised various ethnic groups who lived in southern China to the south of the Yangtze River. This feudal empire soon spread southwards. In 111 B.C., the Han dynasty sent an expeditionary corps to conquer the kingdom of Nam Việt established by Chao To, who had brought together under his rule the kingdom of Âu Lạc and several territories in southern China.

The Han integrated Âu Lạc into their empire, creating the commandery of Chiao Chih, which was divided into provinces and districts. The three provinces, which constituted present-day northern Việt Nam as far as the 18th parallel then, had a population of 981,375 according to Han documents. From then on, the history of Việt Nam evolved under the combined influence of two contradictory factors. On the one hand, a policy of economic exploitation and cultural assimilation, and on the other, a steadfast popular resistance marked by armed insurrection against foreign domination. This resistance, after many centuries, led to the preservation of the Vietnamese people's identity, the emergence of a national consciousness and the establishment of the independent state of Việt Nam. While keeping its unique character, the nation's culture assimilated quite a few elements of Chinese culture. Ten centuries of foreign occupation resulted in a thorough transformation of Vietnamese society.

The Imperial Policy of the Han

At first, the Han retained for their own benefit the established system of *lạc hầu* and *lạc tướng*, the civilian and military chiefs of the early communities. Little by little however, they replaced them with their own functionaries, appointed by the court, who administered the country down to province and district levels (there were three provinces and 56 districts). Presiding over each district was a mandarin, protected by an armed entourage. The rural communes, which contained most of the population, escaped their direct rule, so that this administration only very slowly expanded its network throughout the country while coping with a stubborn popular resistance. The imperial functionaries came from China, accompanied by an entourage of scribes, agents and family members, and many of them settled in the country for good.

The population had to make a double contribution: a tribute to the imperial court and taxes, duties and corvée to maintain the administration and military apparatus. The tribute paid to the court was mostly comprised of valuable tropical products such as ivory, mother-of-pearl, pearls and sandalwood, which Chinese documents of the time described as abundant and varied products from the southern territories. Tropical fruit, various handicraft items, fabrics, gold or silver engraving, and mother-of-pearl inlay work were also required. A certain number of craftsmen were exiled to work for the court, while part of the population was compelled to hunt for elephant and rhinoceros in forests or dive into the sea to gather pearls or coral.

Each inhabitant had to pay a head-tax and a land tax on each plot; the population was also forced to supply corvée labourers to dig canals and build roads and citadels. Chinese documents describe many revolts due to this systematic exploitation, and to extortion by imperial functionaries.

At the same time, the feudal Han carried out a policy of systematic cultural assimilation, the empire having to be unified in all aspects. The first concern was to impose veneration of the emperor, Son of Heaven, and use of the ideographic script was enforced as a vehicle for the official doctrine, Confucianism. At the centre of human obligation was absolute loyalty to the monarch, who ruled not only human society but also the kingdom of the gods. A tightly-woven network of obligations and rites bound societal and individual life, strictly governing relationships between parents and children, husband and wife, between friends, and between subjects and the imperial administration which tried to replace old customs with laws and rites inspired by Confucian doctrine.

Socio-Economic Transformation

Economic exploitation by the occupiers hampered the development of productive forces but could not check them. Excavation of tombs dating from the 1st to the 6th centuries has revealed the progressive diffusion of iron tools, production implements and weapons already known in the previous era. Iron cauldrons, nails and tripods appeared while objects in bronze became less common, but the making of bronze drums continued for centuries.

In the 1st century, furrowing with iron ploughshares or wingploughs drawn by oxen or water buffaloes step by step replaced cultivation in burnt-out clearings. In particular, hydraulic works, canals and dykes ensured control over water and the use of fertilizer facilitated more intensive farming, such as the practice of growing two crops a year on well-irrigated fields. The growing of tubers such as sweet potato, sugar cane and mulberry was already known, as well as that of various vegetables and fruit-trees. Mulberry growing and silk worm raising took pride of place; there was also betel, areca-nut trees, medicinal plants, bamboo and rattan, which supplied raw materials for basket making. Thus, from the earliest centuries, there was a diversified agriculture which, gradually improved, would last for a very long time.

Handicrafts also reached a relatively high level. Many tools of iron and bronze were forged; to the already flourishing pottery of the previous era was added ceramics with enamel coatings. The remains of citadels, pagodas and tombs showed that brick- and tile-making was thriving — some also being coated with a layer of enamel.

The most prosperous handicraft occupations were weaving and basket-making. Fabrics in cotton and silk, and baskets of bamboo and rattan were highly sought-after items. In the 3rd century, paper began to be made using imported Chinese techniques. From China and India, glass-making techniques also came to Việt Nam. To meet the need for luxury goods for the court and local functionaries, the making of objects in engraved gold and silver underwent new developments, the quality improving through the use of Chinese techniques. Lacquer was already a known and practiced trade. It could be said that, on the whole, Vietnamese handicrafts established themselves during this period.

If the economy as a whole remained autonomous, certain products supplied markets in administrative centres such as Long Biên which had trading quarters. River and sea transport was carried out using sampans or junks - some of which had barges and several score oarsmen. The Red River and the road running along it led to Yunnan and Sichuan, and hence to Central Asia as well as Myanmar. Communication with China was achieved by both sea and land, and the road was dotted with many relays. Chiao Chih served as a port of call for junks from Java,

Myanmar, Iran, India, and even the Roman Empire on their way to China. In large centres, there were a number of foreign residents such as Khmers and Indians. The vessels carried local products, valuable timbers, ivory and handicrafts, and also took part in the trade in slaves. This foreign trade was entirely monopolised by the occupiers.

The Han policy of cultural assimilation benefited from the prestige of Chinese civilization, which was then at a high level, but it was confronted with a stubborn resistance. The Vietnamese language was largely borrowed from Chinese, but the words had been Vietnamized to become part and parcel of the language which was progressively enriched without losing its identity; popular literature kept its vigour while beginning to develop and erudite literature written in Han (classical Chinese). Despite Confucian rites and precepts, many local traditions continued the veneration of founding fathers or patriots, participation by women in patriotic activities, and the making and use of bronze drums during great ceremonies. Relics found in the tombs of that era show stronger Han civilization influence; the indigenous upper classes came under greater foreign influence than the population at large or rural communities. However, Đông Sơn art was still clearly seen with its decorations and statuettes.

Together with Confucianism, Buddhist and Taoist doctrine also made its way into Chiao Chih. Buddhism coming from India by sea and from China by land was conspicuous from the 2nd and 6th centuries, with the town of Luy Lâu having 20 towers, 500 bonzes and 15 already-translated sutras. Taoism integrated itself with local beliefs, giving rise to magical, medical and ascetic practices. The main characteristic of these religions was that they did not encourage fanaticism nor exclude one another, thus helping preserve unity within the national community.

With the conquest by the Han, Vietnamese society gradually turned into a feudal society. De jure, land belonged entirely to the emperor, while all members of the population became his subjects, bound to pay taxes, corvée and other duties. Nevertheless, the communes stayed more or less autonomous. To ensure domination, the Han feudalists advocated the creation of "military colonies". Military men, political or common-law prisoners and destitute people coming from China were recruited, together with destitute Vietnamese and landless peasants, to reclaim and exploit the land under the direction of officers or functionaries. At the same time, private domains were built by Chinese functionaries who settled for good in the country, or indigenes loyal to the administration (members of the former ruling classes or notables from rural communities). After the 2nd century, a certain number of Vietnamese who had received a good education, had access to mandarin posts and hence could set up private domains. Slaves worked in these military colonies and domains. The tombs of that era often reveal models in baked earth of domains with outer areas dotted with watchtowers, houses, granaries and stables. As time went by, the Chinese functionaries and their descendants living in the country became "Vietnamized." With indigenous functionaries and landowners, they constituted an indigenous ruling class with feudal characteristics.

Shaped in a country subject to the harsh domination of the Han imperialists, this feudal class was opposed in some aspects to the court and sided with the population. Internal disturbances in China, caused mostly by peasant revolts, created favourable conditions for an open struggle against Chinese imperialist domination for secession - first temporary, then permanent.

Insurrections and the Struggle for Independence

The grim resistance by the population against Chinese imperialist domination, which persisted century after century, time and again broke out in the form of armed insurrection. The most important was that of the two sisters, Trưng Trắc and Trưng Nhị, born into a family of military chiefs in the district of Mê Linh. Between 40 and 43 A.D. the Trưng sisters launched a vast movement throughout Chiao Chih led by women in many places. Trưng Trắc was made "Queen" and Chinese imperialist domination overthrown. The Han emperor, then at the peak of his power, had to send to Chiao Chih his best general, Ma Yuan "Tamer of Waters". By the end of the year 43 A.D., the insurrection was crushed but left an indelible imprint on the history of the country.

However, Chinese annals kept deploring that "the people of Chiao Chih, relying on remote inaccessible areas, liked to rebel". The resistance movement in the Red River valley spread to the south, where military posts and the domains of imperial functionaries were attacked. Another young woman, Lady Triệu, launched in 48 A.D. in the province of Chiu Chen (present-day Thanh Hóa) a large-scale movement against foreign domination. She said: "I'd like to ride storms, kill the sharks in the open sea, drive out the aggressors, recapture the country, undo the ties of serfdom, and never bend my back to be the concubine of any man." Riding an elephant, she led the way to the battlefield. She was however, unable to put up a very long resistance against the Chinese imperial army.

Other insurrections marked the 4th and 5th centuries, including one in the year 412 when Chinese peasants who had risen in revolt and been driven out of China coordinated their efforts with Vietnamese patriots. The 6th century was marked by a major insurrection led by Lý Bí, a notable from Long Hưng in present -day Thái Bình province. His movement was launched in 542, and proceeded to sweep away the Chinese administration, defeat a counter-offensive by the imperial army in 543 and an attack by the Chàm in the south. In 544, Lý Bí made himself king of Vạn Xuân kingdom and established a national administration. However, he was defeated by the Chinese imperial army in 545-546 and died in 548, handing over command to one of his aides, Triệu Quang Phục. The movement's new leader mustered his troops in the swampy areas of Dạ Trạch, from where he carried out guerrilla raids and made himself king after Lý Bí's death. In 550, taking advantage of internal disturbances in China, he took back a sizable part of the nation's territory. However, the Vietnamese feudalists did not get on together and the last decades of the 6th century were marked by their rivalry, which enabled China's Sui dynasty to reconquer the country in 603.

The Sui dynasty moved the administrative capital to Tống Bình. In 618, the Tang dynasty took power in China; China's economy and culture saw unprecedented development as the empire experienced its greatest ever expansion. For the Tang dynasty, Chiao Chih (Việt Nam) was not only a colony for exploitation, but also a starting-point for expansion into Southeast Asia. In 679, they instituted the "Protectorate of Annam (Pacified South)"; the term then came to be used for the country itself. The Tang dynasty extended their administrative network to cover villages and mountainous regions; the annual tribute to the Court and the various taxes, corvée and duties were increased. However, agriculture, and handicrafts in particular, continued to develop, as well as land, river and maritime communications. The three doctrines - Confucianism, Taoism and notably Buddhism - spread nationwide, without doing away with local beliefs. The veneration of local genii, often patriots or founders of villages, remained widespread. In order to stifle deep-rooted national sentiment, the Chinese imperialists used geomancy in an attempt to drain the "veins of the dragon" running through Vietnamese soil resulting in resistance from the people. In society, more and more of those obtaining high positions in the administration through education or bribery were those who obtained important domains.

Under the Tang dynasty, the country faced several invasions from the south; that of the Champa, Java and Malaya, and from the kingdom of Nan Chiao (present-day Yunnan). In 863, Nan Chiao troops reached the capital at Tống Bình and destroyed it. The Tang Court had to send General Gao Pian against the Nan Chiao. Becoming governor after defeating the Nan Chiao, Gao Pian tried to suppress the nationalist movement that had continued to develop after the Tang dynasty took power.

The Recovering of Independence

Many insurrections took place under the Tang dynasty: that of Lý Tự Tiên and Đinh Kiến in 687, of Mai Thúc Loan in 722, of Phùng Hưng (766-791) and Dương Thanh (819-820). By the end of the 9th century, internal disturbances, particularly the insurrection of Hwang Chao (874-883) in China, shook the Tang reign and China entered a long period of anarchy from the start of the 10th century. In 905, the last governor sent by the Chinese imperial court to Việt Nam died.

Taking advantage of the disturbances in China, a notable from Cúc Bồ, Khúc Thừa Dụ, made himself governor, and in 906 the Tang Court was forced to recognize this fait accompli. Khúc Thừa Dụ's son, Khúc Hạo, tried to set up a national administration, but in 930, the Southern Han dynasty, which had taken power in Southern China, again invaded the country. In 931, however, a patriot, Dương Đình Nghệ, took up the fight and made himself governor. After Dương Đình Nghệ died, murdered by one of his aides, the fight was led by Ngô Quyền, who in 938 clashed with a Southern Han expeditionary corps approaching by sea. The Southern Han fleet entered Việt Nam via the Bạch Đằng estuary (the mouth of the river which flows into Hạ Long Bay) where iron-tipped stakes had been sunk into the riverbed by Ngô Quyền. At high tide a Vietnamese flotilla attacked the enemy, pretended to escape, and lured the Southern Han boats into the estuary beyond the stakes still covered by the tide. At low-tide, the entire Vietnamese fleet counter-attacked, forcing the enemy to flee and sink, impaled on the barrage of stakes.

The Bạch Đằng victory in 938 put an end to the period of Chinese imperial domination. In 939, Ngô Quyền proclaimed himself king, established his capital at Cổ Loa (previously a capital in the 3rd century

B.C.) and set up a centralized government. It was the first truly independent Vietnamese State.

Domestically, the main obstacle to the founding of a centralized power structure capable of assuming direction of the economy - management of the dyke system in particular - and of successfully resisting foreign aggression was the existence of feudal lords who each ruled an area of territory. On the death of Ngô Quyền in 944, 12 warlords divided the country among themselves and began to fight one another.

Starting from Hoa Lư in present -day Ninh Bình, Đinh Bộ Lĩnh defeated them all one after another, and unified the country in 967. The next year he made himself king, named the country Đại Cồ Việt, established his capital at Hoa Lư, reorganized the army and administration, and appointed renowned Buddhist monks as advisers. The murder of Đinh Bộ Lĩnh in 979 brought to the throne a six -year-old child. Meanwhile, the Sung dynasty had taken power in China where order was restored. A Sung expeditionary corps was sent to reconquer Việt Nam, which was also being attacked from the south by the Chàm. To deal with this danger, the Court and army appointed a talented general, Lê Hoàn. The latter defeated the Sung invaders on both land and water, thus saving the country (981). The next year, an expedition led by Lê Hoàn invaded Champa and conquered its capital Indrapura (now in Quảng Nam province), effectively removing the threat of invasion from the south for many years to come.

Thus was born a national, independent and stable state in which the subsequent dynasties gradually set up the usual institutions. In this framework, the economy and culture developed, and the transfer of power from one dynasty to the next no longer affected the stability of the national independence.

In 1009, the Lý dynasty took power, beginning a long period of independence and prosperity.

Chapter III

THE CENTRALIZED FEUDAL STATE

The Lý and Trần Dynasties (11th to 14th centuries)

Following the recovery of their national independence from the Chinese empire, the country gradually turned towards creating a centralized monarchy. This process became necessary by two factors: the construction of great hydraulic works, particularly dykes and canals for the development of agriculture, and the safeguarding of national independence against attempts at invasion by the Chinese imperial court.

However, before a well-organized monarchical state could be set up, the country had gone through a period of instability during which tendencies towards feudal domination still persisted. It was only with the establishment of the Lý dynasty in 1009 that the monarchy was able to gain a secure hold on power. The Trần, who succeeded the Lý in 1225, continued this work of unification and nation building until the end of the 14th century. During this 400-year period the country experienced vigorous development in many areas.

The Economic, Social and Political System under the Lý and the Trần

After his accession to the throne, Lý Công Uẩn, whose royal name was Lý Thái Tổ, ordered the transfer of the capital to Thăng Long in 1010. Thăng Long was to remain the capital until the 19th century. He decreed a general amnesty for prisoners and the destruction of all instruments of torture. In 1054, his successor, Lý Thánh Tông, renamed the country Đại Việt. Under the Lý and Trần dynasties, the regime underwent continuous consolidation, and it was only at the close of the 14th century that great transformations would take place.

Economic Development under the Lý and the Trần

The king owned all the land by right. The state, however, directly utilized only a small portion of this land, some of which was distributed to members of the royal family and high-ranking dignitaries as fiefdoms and personal domains, and taxes were levied on land owned by villages and individuals. There was thus an agrarian regime with several sectors:

- Land used by the state;
- Fiefdoms and domains;
- Communal land; and
- Private land.

Land distributed to nobles and high-ranking dignitaries was divided into two categories. There were fiefdoms whose beneficiaries had at their disposal both the land and people; the peasants had obligations only to their local lord, and were not required to pay taxes or provide labour to the state. In the great domains, the peasants paid rent and taxes to the owner and at the same time, had obligations to the state, and remained directly subject to the monarchy. Marshal Lý Thường Kiệt, for instance, received in appanage 4,000 peasant households, but his domains comprised another 10,000 households. Appanages and domains remained the property of the king. When a lord died, his heirs could inherit his land, but could also be dispossessed by the king.

Appanages and domains greatly increased in number under the Trần, when nobles and dignitaries endeavoured to reclaim new lands, then taking possession of them. Some used their power to seize land belonging to villages and individuals. On these appanages and domains, the peasants were in reality serfs, while the lords kept a large number of domestic slaves. The Lý had forbidden the traffic of young men to be used as slaves, but the order was rescinded under the Trần.

The slaves were usually former criminals, insolvent debtors, and prisoners of war. During periods of famine, children were sold by their parents as slaves. Some lords owned thousands of serfs and slaves. These people could not own property or gain access to public positions. Under the Trần in particular, the nobles had their own armed forces.

Buddhist monasteries also constituted large domains with serfs and slaves.

The great societal movement for the liberation of these serfs and slaves was to shake the regime to its foundations.

The majority of the land, however, belonged to the villages, which paid rent and taxes to the royal administration. The village population

was periodically required to provide labour for the construction of roads, dykes and canals, and to do military service. Communal land was periodically distributed among the villagers, under the direction of notables, naturally in a manner profitable to the latter.

Land appropriation by individuals became increasingly frequent under the Lý; as early as the 11th century, the Lý had to promulgate legislation on the sale and purchase of land. A class of peasant -owners thus appeared to challenge the lords with their larger domains.

The Lý and Trần kings attached great importance to agriculture. At the beginning of each year, continuing a tradition inaugurated by Lê Hoàn, the king himself made a symbolic gesture by ploughing a plot of land, following a ceremony in honour of the god of agriculture. In 1038, when King Lý Thái Tông was advised by a mandarin not to demean himself through such an action, he said: "If I myself do not do some ploughing as an offering to the god, how can I set an example for the entire people?"

Those who stole or killed buffaloes were severely punished under the law.

The dykes were given particular attention, and mandarins were held responsible for their maintenance. The construction of numerous dykes and other hydraulic works is recorded in the annals, for instance the Cơ Xá dyke in 1108, and the digging of the Đản Nãi canal in 1029, the Lẫm canal in 1050, and the Lãnh Kinh canal in 1089. The Trần, on several occasions, had dykes repaired and canals dredged. In 1382, they ordered the digging of several canals in Thanh Hóa and Nghệ An provinces, and in 1390, the Thiên Đức canal. Dykes were built along the Red, Thái Bình, Mã and Chu rivers. Every year, following the harvest, the mandarins inspected the dykes and directed maintenance and repair work. In August 1315, when the waters rose to a dangerous level, King Trần Minh Tông personally directed the work. A mandarin advised him against such work, saying, "It becomes virtue, not to devote himself to small things." Another dignitary, supporting the king's actions, retorted by saying, "When the country is threatened by a major flood or severe drought, it is a king's duty to take part directly in carrying out the necessary measures. This is the best way to show great virtue."

Dykes were also built along the coast so as to bring into production new land formed by silt accumulating at the mouths of rivers.

With administrative centralization, internal peace and the safeguarding of national independence, agriculture, the cornerstone of the economy, was able to develop further. Historical records note few severe famines under the Lý and the Trần. The kings sometimes decreed a reduction in taxes in order to encourage the peasants.

Handicrafts also saw rapid development. Cotton, silk and brocade weaving reached a high level. Multi-coloured brocades were exported or presented to the Chinese imperial court. The development of silver, gold, tin and lead mining gave birth to numerous metal-working trades and jewelry-making. The state minted copper coins and set up workshops for the manufacture of weapons, religious objects and court attire. Bronze smelting, for the making of bells in particular, and pottery with high-quality enamels, made great progress. The bricks, tiles and ceramic statues made in the Lý period were famous.

Printing from engraved wooden plates contributed to the development of education and the dissemination of Buddhist literature.

The development of handicrafts led the Trần kings to divide the capital into districts, each of which specialized in a particular trade. In the 13th century, the capital had 61 districts, each of which was occupied by a guild.

The growing shipbuilding industry was able to produce large junks with as many as one hundred oars. The capital Thăng Long became the country's great commercial centre, and markets were established in many places. A Mongolian ambassador, who visited the country in the 13th century, wrote that village markets were held twice a month, with "plenty of goods," and on the highways a market was situated every five miles. There were also inns established by the authorities, where travelers could rest.

Trading between the delta and mountainous regions flourished, the plains exchanging salt and iron tools for forest products. Trade with China was effected at special places near the frontier or the ports. In exchange for fabrics, the Chinese obtained essential oils, ivory, salt and other minerals. The silk trade was subject to rigorous regulation by the state, which itself sometimes engaged in commercial operations. Javanese and Siamese vessels came to the port of Vân Đồn to buy Vietnamese goods.

In 1280, King Trần Nhân Tông instituted a uniform unit of measurement for wood and textiles.

Commerce thus began to develop, but merchants were not held in high esteem, and external trade was tightly controlled by the state.

Society under the Lý and the Trần

At the top of the social structure was the king and his royal family, who lived in the royal palace situated in what is now Ngọc Hà district.

The columns and woodwork were painted red and decorated with images of dragons, phoenixes and gods. At the main palace gate stood a pavilion with a large bell.

Anyone wishing to present a request or petition to the king would ring the bell. The king often wore a dark yellow robe and red coat. In mid-autumn, he would preside over a water festival (probably on the Great Lake) with hundreds of gondolas and various forms of entertainment, most notably the water puppet shows. From the middle of the lake a huge golden tortoise would emerge, bearing on its back three platforms on which dancers performed.

Besides the royal family, the feudal class comprised of mandarins, court dignitaries, holders of large domains, and landowners belonging to prominent families. Higher office was reserved for members of the great aristocratic families; only the sons of such families and of mandarins had access to the mandarin competitions. Buddhist bonzes should also be counted as members of the feudal class, since the monasteries constituted large domains worked by serfs.

The ordinary classes comprised peasant owners, merchants, free peasants in the villages, artisans, serfs and domestic slaves. The law forbade them to dress and wear ornamentation like that of the privileged classes. Slaves could only marry within their own class.

Administrative, Military and Judicial Organization

From the beginning of their reign, the Lý endeavored to consolidate the state apparatus. The country was divided into 24 provinces entrusted to close relations of the royal family. The centralized monarchy governed with the assistance of this aristocracy. Princes of the blood had their personal appanages and their own armed forces. The court hierarchy was a strict one with a twin body of civil and military mandarins. These mandarins received no salaries, and lived on the money from rents and taxes paid by the population under their administration. But a mandarin bureaucracy gradually came into being, paid by the monarchy through taxes on landholdings, handicrafts, forest products, and market sales. Little by little, the administration lost its family-based character.

Bonzes played an important role as advisers to the king. The founder of the Lý dynasty was put on the throne with the help of a prominent bonze superior, Vạn Hạnh. The bonze Viên Thông received honours reserved for the heir to the throne.

In 1242, a village administrative apparatus was instituted by the Trần. Up to that time, the royal administration had covered only province and district levels.

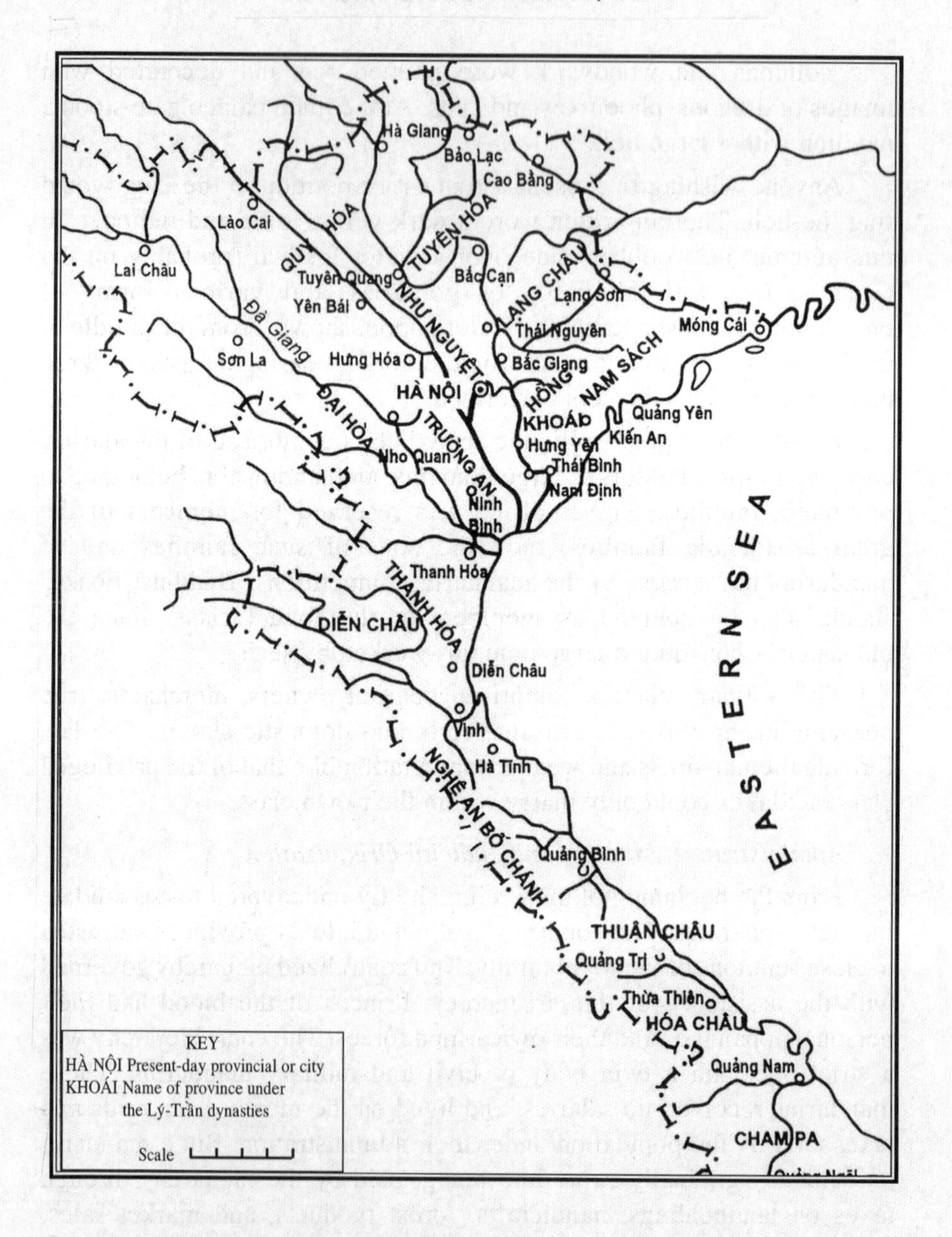
Hà Giang
Bảo Lạc
Cao Bằng
Lào Cai
Lai Châu
QUY HÓA
TUYÊN HÓA
Tuyên Quang
Bắc Cạn
LẠNG CHÂU
Lạng Sơn
Yên Bái
NHƯ NGUYỆT
Thái Nguyên
Móng Cái
Sơn La
Đà Giang
Hưng Hóa
Bắc Giang
NAM SÁCH
HÀ NỘI
HỒNG
KHOÁI
Quảng Yên
Kiến An
ĐẠI HÓA
TRƯỜNG AN
Hưng Yên
Nho Quan
Thái Bình
Nam Định
Ninh Bình
Thanh Hóa
THANH HÓA
DIỄN CHÂU
Diễn Châu
EASTERN SEA
Vinh
Hà Tĩnh
NGHỆ AN
BỐ CHÁNH
Quảng Bình
THUẬN CHÂU
Quảng Trị
Thừa Thiên
HÓA CHÂU
Quảng Nam
CHAMPA
KEY
HÀ NỘI Present-day provincial or city
KHOÁI Name of province under the Lý-Trần dynasties
Scale

The monarchy gave special attention to the building of a powerful army. Serfs were not recruited into the army, and positions of command were reserved for members of aristocratic families, with the highest posts for members of the royal family. For the protection of the king and the royal palace there was a special guard. Military service was extended to cover the whole population except serfs. Conscripts underwent a period of training, then returned to their villages to continue their work in the fields. This peasant-soldier policy made possible the mobilization of large forces whenever necessary. Training was regularly undertaken and, according to a Chinese ambassador of the time, was of a high level. Under the Trần, the princes and lords who owned large domains had their own armies made up of serfs and slaves. The sons of prominent families were trained in the art of war in a military school. Trần Hưng Đạo, who defeated the Mongols, wrote a handbook on military tactics for his officers' use.

The Lý also introduced written laws. In 1042, King Lý Thái Tông ordered his mandarins to "amend the laws and regulations so as to adapt them to the present circumstances, to classify them, and to compile them into a penal code which can be easily understood by all". It is reported in the annals that the code, when completed and made known to the population, was welcomed by all. The rehabilitation of delinquents and criminals was instituted; very severe punishment was decreed for the "ten capital crimes", particularly that of rebellion. Under the Lý, it was forbidden to sell 18-year-olds as slaves; there were laws for the protection of draught animals and on the mortgaging of land. Mandarins prescribed penalties against piracy and extortion. This legislation was then perfected by the Trần. It should be noted that the law paid special attention to the prevention of rebellion.

Ethnic Minorities

While the delta had a homogeneous Việt (or Kinh) population, the mountainous regions were inhabited by numerous ethnic groups, and the relationship between the central government and these mountain populations constituted a particularly difficult issue for the monarchy. The historical relationship between the Việt majority and minority groups was one of both integration and antagonism. On the one hand, the delta and highlands were integrated economically and needed each other; they were also closely bound by the need for mutual defence against foreign aggressors. The different groups were, therefore, moving towards progressively uniting as a single nation. On the other hand, the Việt feudalists, particularly the monarchy and mandarins, sought to exploit and oppress the minorities, leading to frequent revolts and the ensuring reprisals.

In the 11th century, when the Lý dynasty was founded, the frontiers of Đại Việt in the north and northwest had not yet been clearly delineated. Particularly important was the frontier with China in the north and northeast; these regions were inhabited by Tày and Nùng people whose allegiance was of prime importance for the Đại Việt kingdom. It was vital to incorporate them into the nation.

The Lý king often sought alliances with local chiefs by giving them princesses in marriage or by marrying their daughters. These alliances made it possible to constitute a zone of defence along the Chinese frontier. However, this policy of alliances was accompanied by military operations, and during each king's reign, one or more expeditions were conducted against mountainous regions, some led by the king in person.

The revolt led by Nùng Trí Cao in Cao Bằng province was the most important. The Nùng formed an ethnic group related to the Thái and Tày, living on Đại Việt territory and in southern China. In 1036, a Nùng chief proclaimed himself king, repudiating the suzerainty of the Lý. He was defeated and captured that same year by King Lý Thái Tông. His son Trí Cao succeeded in 1041 in carving out for himself a new area of territory, which he named the Đại Lịch kingdom. But he too was captured by Lý troops, and King Lý Thái Tông then made him chief of the region. Later he also rebelled and seized areas of southern China to set up another kingdom. Only with great difficulty were Chinese imperial troops able to defeat him at last in 1053. Whenever he was pursued by Chinese troops Trí Cao would request assistance from the Lý, who, however, did not dare send troops to China.

Despite repeated failures, Chinese imperial dynasties had not given up hope of reconquering Đại Việt. The great achievement of the Lý and Trần dynasties was their success in defending the nation's independence - the Lý against the Sung in the 11th century, and the Trần against the Mongols in the 13th century.

The Struggle against the Sung: Lý Thường Kiệt

Frontier incidents between Đại Việt and the Chinese empire were restarted by Nùng Trí Cao's revolt, which also revealed the weakness of

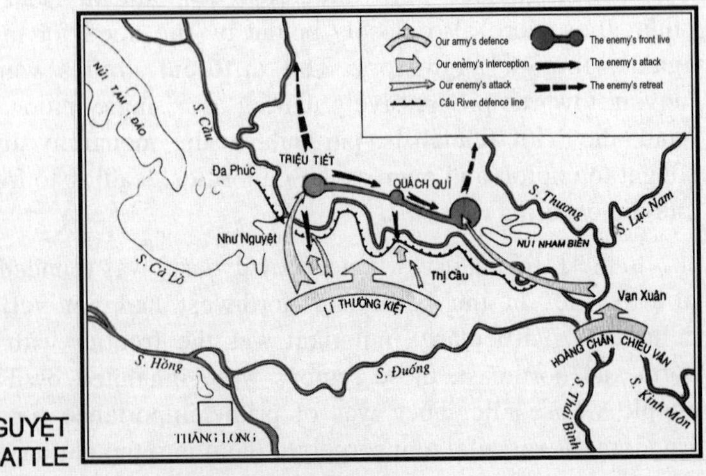
Our army's defence
Our enèmy's interception
Our enemy's attack
Cầu River defence line
The enemy's front live
The enemy's attack
The enemy's retreat
NÚI TAM ĐẢO
S. Cầu
TRIỆU TIẾT
Đa Phúc
QUÁCH QUỈ
Như Nguyệt
S. Cà Lồ
S. Thương
S. Lục Nam
NÚI NHAM BIỀN
Thị Cầu
LÍ THƯỜNG KIỆT
Vạn Xuân
HOÀNG CHÂN
CHIÊU VĂN
S. Hồng
S. Đuống
S. Thái Bình
S. Kinh Môn
THĂNG LONG

NHƯ NGUYỆT BATTLE

the Sung in southern China. The Quảng Nguyên district, rich in valuable minerals, was claimed by both sides, but the Lý kings, as we have seen above, had practically incorporated the region into their kingdom through a clever policy of alliances.

At the Chinese court, there still existed a faction that advocated the invastion of Đại Việt. In 1069, in an attempt to find the remedy to a serious economic and social crisis, the Sung emperor gave full powers to a bold reformer named Wang Ngan-che. When the reforms proved a disappointment, Wang Ngan-che, to save the Sung's prestige and seize Đại Việt's wealth, decided to send a great expedition against the Lý. In 1074, the provinces of southern China received the order to strengthen their armies, arm combat junks, and stop trading with Đại Việt.

At the Lý court, given that the reigning king was only ten years old, all power was concentrated in the hands of General Lý Thường Kiệt, who decided to take the offensive in order to forestall the Sung.

Two army corps totalling 100,000 men were sent to China in 1075, one overland under the command of Tông Đản, a Nùng chief, the other by sea, under the command of Lý Thường Kiệt himself. General Kiệt cleverly exploited the discontent of the Chinese population with Wang Ngan -che's reforms, and appeared as the liberator of the peoples of southern China. Placards were put up denouncing the reformer and proclaiming that Lý Thường Kiệt's only desire was to ensure the welfare of the people. The Lý troops were enthusiastically welcomed by the population and easily occupied many localities. The general attacked the Yung -chow stronghold, which fell, after a siege lasting 43 days, on March 1, 1076. The citadel was razed to the ground; other strongholds suffered the same fate.

The Sung prepared for a counter-offensive by forming a coalition with Champa and the Khmer kingdom. In April 1076, having attained his objective, which was to destroy the Chinese staging posts, Lý Thường Kiệt withdrew his troops from Chinese territory. Early in 1077, the Sung troops, having forced their way through the frontier passes, were facing the Lý army across the Như Nguyệt River. Fierce fighting ensued and the Sung army was unable to cross the river. It was in the course of this battle that Lý Thường Kiệt composed a poem and had it recited during the night, making his men believe that the river god was speaking:

Over the southern mountains and rivers, the Emperor of the South shall reign,
This was written down in the Book of Heaven.
How dare those barbarians invade our soil?
They will surely meet with defeat.

Its morale higher than ever, the Lý army repelled the attackers, who were also being decimated by disease. Lý Thường Kiệt then made a peace proposal, which included the ceding of five frontier districts (now Cao Bằng and Lạng Sơn provinces). The Sung accepted. This was in 1077. Two years later through negotiations, the Lý recovered the ceded territory.

Lý Thường Kiệt was the architect of the victory. An outstanding strategist, he was also a great politician who knew how to win the hearts of the people and inspire his troops with enthusiasm. The stability of the regime established by the Lý was confirmed by this brilliant victory over the Chinese imperial armies. The Trần further strengthened the country's armed voices, enabling them two centuries later to repel a Mongol invasion.

The Glorious Resistance Against the Mongols

At the beginning of the 13th century, Gengis Khan, having unified Mongolia, started a war of conquest against China. In 1253, Kubilai conquered the Đại Lý kingdom (now Yunnan province), thus reaching the Vietnamese frontier. The Mongols demanded passage through Đại Việt in order to attack the Sung from the south (1257), but the Trần refused. A Mongol army invaded Đại Việt, smashed its defences, and seized the capital Thăng Long, which was put to the sword and burnt to the ground. The Trần king left the capital, which was also abandoned by its inhabitants. The Mongol army was not able to obtain food and fared badly in the tropical climate. A Vietnamese counter-offensive drove it out of the capital. In retreat, the enemy was attacked by local partisans from an ethnic minority group living in the Phú Thọ region.

This was the first Mongol defeat.

Once they had become the overlords of China, the Mongols grew more and more demanding towards Đại Việt. Despite concessions by the Trần, the Mongol court remained intransigent, dreaming of conquering both Đại Việt and Champa. Relations between the two countries remained tense, and Mongols envoys behaved with arrogance at the Trần court. But the Trần were not inactive, and made serious preparations for the country's defence.

In 1281, Trần Di Ái, a member of the royal family, was sent as an envoy to China. The Mongols persuaded him to accept his investiture by them as king of Đại Việt. He returned to the country with an escort of 1,000 soldiers to ascend the throne, but the Mongol escort was beaten and he was captured.

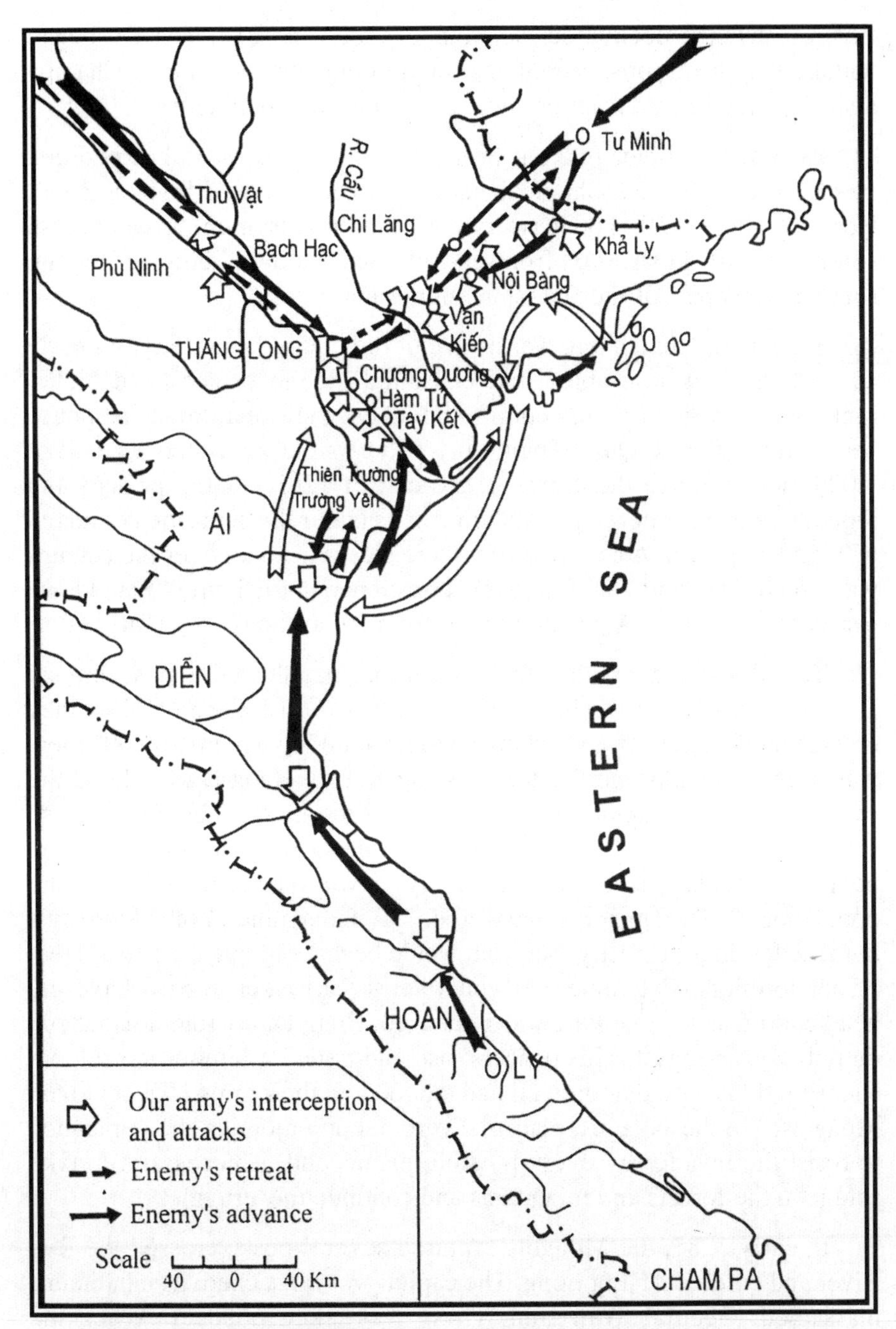
Tư Minh
R. Cầu
Thu Vật
Chi Lăng
Khả Ly
Bạch Hạc
Phù Ninh
Nội Bàng
Vạn
Kiếp
THĂNG LONG
Chương Dương
Hàm Tử
Tây Kết
Thiên Trường
Trường Yên
ÁI
EASTERN SEA
DIỄN
HOAN
Ô LY
CHAM PA
Our army's interception and attacks
Enemy's retreat
Enemy's advance
Scale
40 0 40 Km

Second war of resistance against the Mongols (1285)

In the meantime, the Mongols had completed preparations for an expedition by sea against Champa. At the end of 1282, a Mongol general, Toa Đô (Gogetu), landed in Champa, and seized its capital in 1283. But

Chàm resistance decimated the Mongol army. In 1284, Toa Đô began withdrawing his troops, regrouping them in the northern part of Champa near the Vietnamese frontier, awaiting further developments.

Kubilai had been making preparations for a powerful expedition against Đại Việt and Champa; under the command of his son Thoát Hoan (Toghan), 500,000 cavalrymen and infantrymen were to rush southward to push the frontiers of the Mongol empire to the southernmost part of the Indochina peninsula.

King Trần Nhân Tông was aware of the enemy's strategy. As early as 1282 he had assembled and consulted all the princes and high - ranking dignitaries on the action to be taken; their unanimous response was to fight. Prince Quốc Toản, only 16 years old, recruited a guard of 1,000 men to go to the front. At the end of 1283, all the princes and dignitaries were ordered to put their troops under the supreme command of Trần Hưng Đạo. A congress of village elders from all over the country was convened, and the following question put to them: "Should we capitulate or fight?" A great cry rose from the assembly: "Fight!"

The Mongols demanded that their troops be allowed to pass through Đại Việt territory for the invasion of Champa. At the close of 1284, they crossed the frontier. The Vietnamese force, totalling a mere 200,000 men, was unable to withstand the first onslaught. Trần Hưng Đạo ordered the evacuation of the capital and was asked by the king: "The enemy is so strong that a protracted war might bring terrible destruction down upon the people. Wouldn't it be better to lay down our arms to save the population?" The general answered: "I understand Your Majesty's humane feelings perfectly, but what would become of our ancestors' land, of our forefathers' temples? If you want to surrender, please have my head cut off first". The king was reassured. Hưng Đạo wrote a handbook on military strategy for his officers' use and issued a famous appeal that so inspired his men that they all had tattooed on their arms: "Death to the Mongols!" In the villages, placards were put up enjoining the population to resist the invader by every possible means and, if necessary, to take refuge in the forests and mountains and continue the struggle.

In early 1285, the Mongols captured several posts, crossed the Red River and entered Thăng Long. The capital was ransacked, its inhabitants massacred. General Trần Bình Trọng was taken prisoner. When the enemy tried to win him over, he said, "I would rather be a ghost in the south[1] than a prince in the north[2]," and was subsequently executed. The

1. Viz Vietnam
2. Viz China

Mongol general Toa Đô left Champa to join up with the army led by his colleague Ô Mã Nhi (Omar). A Vietnamese army under the command of Trần Quang Khải was beaten off when it tried to block his way in Nghệ An province. The Mongol fleet was sailing up the Red River. Many princes and nobles, among them Lê Tắc and Trần ích Tắc, betrayed their country. The Trần court had to take refuge in Thanh Hóa province. The Mongols controlled the greater part of the Red River delta and of Thanh Hóa and Nghệ An provinces, i.e. the majority of the country's territory.

However, in the process the Mongols were forced to distribute their forces among a multitude of vulnerable posts and patrols whose task was to keep communications open. In the first months of 1285, local chiefs in the uplands inflicted losses on the Mongols while in the delta the population, leaving a vacuum before the enemy, denied them all access to supplies and put them in a most difficult position. The determination of the Trần command was thus able to be brought into full play.

From Nghệ An province, Toa Đô's troops, harassed by guerrillas, tried to move up the Red River and join the Mongol army stationed farther north. The Trần sent 50,000 men to intercept them, and the Mongols suffered an overwhelming defeat at Hàm Tử (Hưng Yên province). Fired up by this victory, Trần Hưng Đạo's troops dashed towards the capital. Chương Dương, an outpost 20 km south of Thăng Long, was taken. And when the Trần king with his troops left their Thanh Hóa refuge to advance toward the capital, the population rose up, harassing the rearguard of the Mongol armies. Enemy troops evacuated Thăng Long and withdrew north of the Red River. The bulk of the Vietnamese forces threw themselves into battle against Toa Đô's army, which was crushed at Tây Kết in July 1285; the Mongol general was killed and 50,000 of his men captured.

After posting troops along the route taken by the enemy as they retreated towards China, Hưng Đạo staged a frontal attack on the Mongol army. As the latter drew back, it fell into ambushes. Thoát Hoan, the Mongol commander-in-chief, escaped by hiding in a bronze cask. By August 1285, the whole country had been liberated, and the Mongol army of half a million strong defeated.

Kubilai was forced to abandon plans for an invasion of Japan in order to make preparations for a revenge expedition against Đại Việt. As the Trần princes sought to recruit new troops, General Trần Hưng Đạo said to them: "The strength of an army lies in its quality, not numbers". And to the anxious king he said, "Our troops are now better trained, while the enemy, having suffered a defeat, has lost morale. Victory will be easier".

In late 1287, Thoát Hoan again crossed the frontier with 300, 000 men while a Mongol fleet of 500 vessels headed for the Vietnamese coast. The Trần King again left the capital. The Mongol general Ô Mã Nhi sent him this warning: "Even if you fled to the sky, I'd go after you. I'd pursue you to the bottom of the seas, to the heart of the forests, if necessary!" The Mongols sought to occupy more and more territory, but found only deserted areas around them. The Yuan (name of the Mongol dynasty) annals record that, "The Chiao Chih (Đại Việt) population hid their rice and fled". The invading army ran short of supplies. Thoát Hoan ordered the capital set on fire, then withdrew north of the Red River; during that time his troops were constantly harassed by the Trần army and the population.

At Vân Đồn on the coast, General Trần Khánh Dư kept a close watch on Mongol supply convoys. He caught the enemy fleet unaware, destroyed it and seized the cargoes of food. The enemy was greatly demoralized on hearing the news. The Mongols pillaged the countryside, but the population put up a heroic resistance. Thoát Hoan was told by his generals: "We have no more citadels left, no more food; the strategic passes have been lost, and summer will soon come with its retinue of diseases. We'd better withdraw". The Mongols retreated by land, through Lạng Sơn, and by sea, the fleet sailing down the Bạch Đằng River.

Trần Hưng Đạo used Ngô Quyền's old stratagem, iron-tipped stakes planted at the mouth of the river. General Phạm Ngũ Lão was sent to Lạng Sơn to guard the mountain passes. Trần Hưng Đạo himself took the bulk of the troops across the Hóa River (Hải Phòng) and launched a big offensive. When crossing the river, Hưng Đạo publicly swore the following oath, "If the Mongols are not defeated, we will not cross this river again."

At high tide, the Mongol fleet sailing down the Bạch Đằng was engaged by a small Vietnamese fleet that retreated quickly. Ô Mã Nhi's forces were pursuing it when Trần Hưng Đạo's army turned up. The Mongol fleet beat a hasty retreat, but by this time the tide was ebbing and the Mongol junks broke up on the iron-tipped stakes. Ô Mã Nhi was taken prisoner, and 100 of his junks were destroyed and another 400 captured (April 3, 1288).

Thoát Hoan was terrified on learning the news, and hurriedly withdrew. His troops were decimated during their retreat, the third Mongol defeat. In late 1288, the Trần King wisely sent a mission to China to negotiate, offering tribute to the Mongol court. In 1289, he handed over the captured Mongol generals and officers. The Chinese court wanted more than this formal recognition of suzerainty but its demands were not accepted. In 1293, the Mongols began organizing

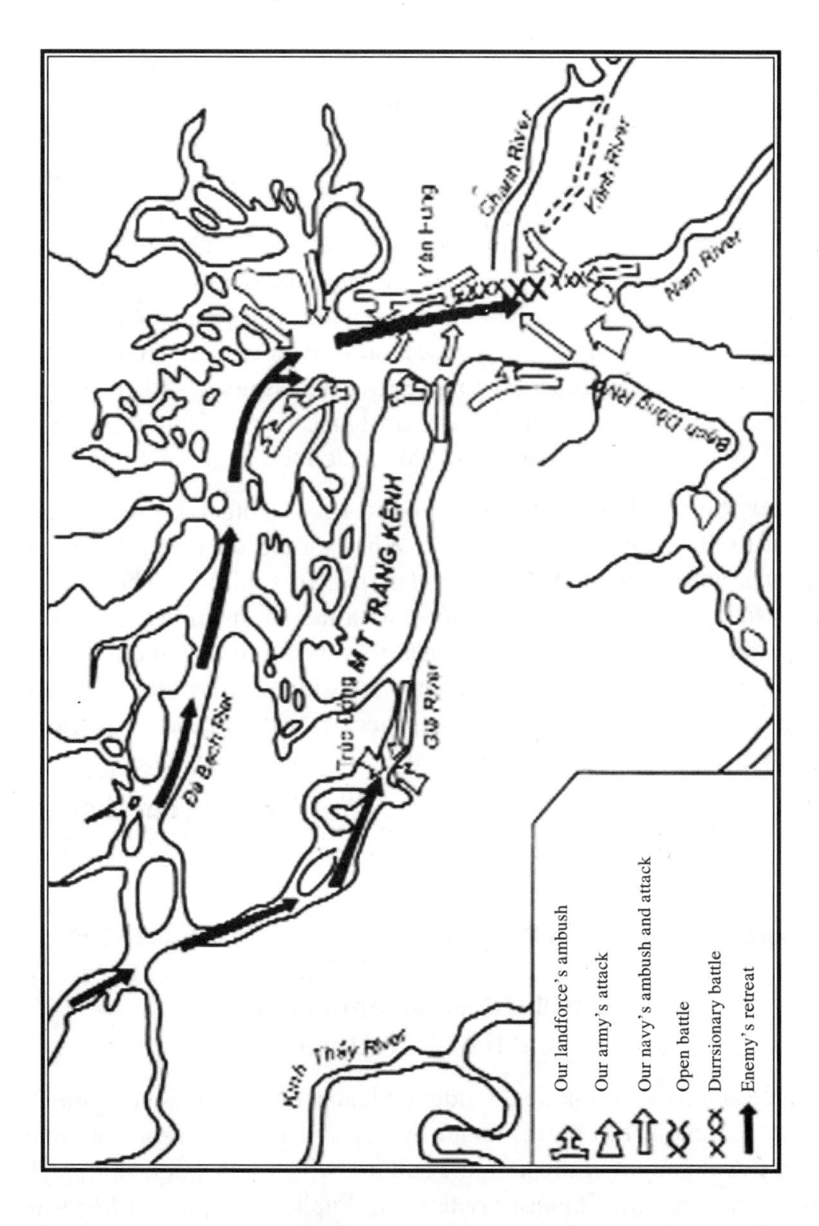
Chanh River
Nam River
MT TRANG KÊNH
Đá Bạch River
Giá River
Kinh Thầy River
Our landforce's ambush
Our army's attack
Our navy's ambush and attack
Open battle
Durrsionary battle
Enemy's retreat

Bạch Đằng Victory (1288)

another expedition but Kubilai died in 1294 and his son Timour abandoned the project. The new ruler established friendly relations with Đại Việt, which continued to pay tribute annually to the Mongol court.

The principal reason for the victory over the Mongols was the strength of the socio-economic system established under the Lý and Trần, and the successful military policy followed by the Trần command. The monarchy and nobles had promoted the development of agriculture and instituted a peasant -soldier system so that when a war occurred, the whole

nation united around its chiefs, each man becoming a combatant. Ethnic minority chieftains in mountainous regions also contributed to victory. National unity became a reality. National consciousness, molded over the course of centuries of struggle against foreign aggressors and consolidated by the establishment of stable centralized power, had been considerably strengthened. General Trần Hưng Đạo never failed to seek the support of the population in his fight against an enemy superior in numbers and armaments, and used appropriate strategy and tactics. He willingly left towns, and even the capital when necessary, avoided combat when the enemy was too strong, resorted to guerrilla harassment, and resolutely took the offensive whenever the circumstances were favourable. The fierce determination of his command galvanized the men.

Shortly before Trần Hưng Đạo died in 1300, King Trần Anh Tông, on a visit to the general, asked him, "What should we do in the event of a new invasion from the north?" Hưng Đạo replied: "The enemy relies on numbers. To oppose the long with the short - therein lies our skill. If the enemy makes a violent rush forward, like fire and tempest, it is easy to defeat him. But if he shows patience, like the silkworm nibbling at the mulberry leaf, if he proceeds without haste, refrains from pillaging, and does not seek a quick victory, then we must choose the best generals and effective tactics, as in a chess game. The army must be united and of one mind, like father and son. It is essential to treat the people with humanity, so as to strike deep roots and ensure a lasting base." Ever since then, the memory of Trần Hưng Đạo has been honoured at the Kiếp Bạc temple.

Cultural Development under the Lý and the Trần Dynasties

The consolidation of national independence, economic development, and of stable centralized power under the Lý and Trần dynasties brought about the development of the nation's culture, which was unique although strongly influenced by Chinese civilization. Public and spiritual life was inspired by two great doctrines: Buddhism and Confucianism. Integrating with the nation's traditions, these doctrines constituted a treasury of ideas and creeds running through all literature and art.

The Predominance of Buddhism

Buddhism was at its peak under the Lý, whose accession to the throne had been favoured by the Buddhist clergy. In return the latter received the highest privileges. The kings themselves were interested in the study of doctrine and often took bonzes as advisers. The pagodas owned large domains worked by serfs, and bonzes were exempt from taxes and military service. Kings and princes had large numbers of pagodas built and bells cast, and promoted the dissemination of sacred books. In 1018, King Thái Tổ sent a mission to China to gather texts of the Tam Tạng; in 1068, King Thánh Tông oversaw the creation of the Thảo Đường sect, and several kings became patriarchs of Buddhist sects. Princes and nobles followed their example. Beautiful pagodas were built under the Lý, some of them preserved up to this day, such as Quan Thánh (Great Buddha) in Hà Nội, built in 1102, Diên Hựu (1049), Báo Thiên (1056) and Keo pagoda in Thái Bình province. Queen ỷ Lan, accused of ordering the assassination of one of her rivals, spent the rest of her life building 100 pagodas to redeem herself.

Vietnamese Buddhist sects and schools were founded. After his victory over the Mongols, King Trần Nhân Tông gave up the throne in 1293, retired to a monastery and, together with two other bonzes, founded the Trúc Lâm (Bamboo Forest) sect. A doctrinal work from the Trần period, the *Khóa Hư Lục*, has been preserved, with the following famous lines:

Nothing is born,

Nothing dies,

When this has been understood,

The Buddha appears,

The round of incarnations ends.

King Trần Thái Tông, who reigned from 1225 to 1258, described in the foreword to a doctrinal work how he had sought the monastic life:

"Ever since the king, my father, handed over the kingdom to me, then only a child, I have never been free from care. I told myself: My parents are no longer here to give me advice; it will be very difficult for me to win the people's confidence. What should I do? After thinking deeply, I came to the conclusion that to retire into the mountains, to seek the Buddha's teachings in order to know the reasons for life and death and to pay homage to my parents would be the best way. I decided to leave. On the third day of the fourth month of the fifth year of Thiên ứng's reign, I dressed as a commoner and left the palace. To the guards I said I want to mix with the people, learn about their hardships, and know their thoughts. Seven or eight men followed me; when the hợi *hour had passed, I crossed the river then told the truth to the guards, who burst into tears. The next day, while passing the Phả Lại ferry, I hid my face in order not to be recognized. We spent the night at Gia Chánh pagoda. The next day, we*

went straight to the top of the mountain on which the Great Master Trúc Lâm resided. Overjoyed, the Great Master greeted me with these words:

"The old bonze that I am, who has retired into the midst of the forest, whose body is nothing but skin and bone, who lives on wild herbs and berries, drinks from the stream and wanders among the trees, has a heart as light as the clouds and unburdened like the wind. Your Majesty has left your sumptuous palace to come to this remote place. May I ask you what compelling need has prompted you to make this journey? With tears in my eyes, I replied:

"I am very young, my parents are no longer in this world and here I am, alone, reigning over the people without any support. I think that thrones have always been fragile and so I have come to these mountains with my only desire that of becoming a Buddha."

"The Great Master replied, "No, the Buddha is not to be found in these mountains, he is in our hearts. When the heart is at peace and lucid, the Buddha is there. If Your Majesty has an enlightened heart, you immediately become the Buddha; why then seek elsewhere?"

(The Court came to beseech the King to return and the Prime Minister threatened to commit suicide if the King refused).

"The Great Master took my hand and said, "Since you are King, the will of the kingdom must also be your will, the heart of the kingdom must also be your heart. The whole kingdom is now asking you to return, how can you refuse? There is, however, one important thing you should not forget when you are back in your palace: studying the sacred books."

"I returned to the palace, and against my will, remained on the throne for several decades. In my leisure time, I would gather together eminent old men for the study of the Thiền doctrine (Dhyana) and of the sacred books, none of which was omitted. When studying the Diamond Sutra, I often stopped at the sentence: Never let your heart cling to any fixed thing. I would then close the book, and remain a long time in meditation. Enlightenment came to me, and I composed this initiation to the Thiền..."

It would be naive to think that during this period, Buddhism confined itself to these purely spiritual exercises. It was the state religion with all its pomp and vigour; it provided people with spiritual consolation, the ruling class with divine prestige, and some minds with a means of escape; it was imbued with superstition in many of its manifestations and with Taoism in its doctrine. It left a lasting imprint on the Vietnamese soul. However, as the monarchical order was gradually

consolidated, the social hierarchy became increasingly complex, and the royal administration extended its power to the detriment of the aristocracy. Buddhism was no longer enough.

The Growth of Confucianism

In a society whose members had to unite in the face of great natural calamities and the permanent danger of foreign invasion, and who came under the absolute power of a monarch governing through a complex mandarin bureaucracy, a doctrine was needed to direct the mind of each individual towards his social obligations, obedience and loyalty to the monarch, and unconditional respect for the social hierarchy. Chinese imperial dynasties had, since the Han, made Confucianism the state doctrine; the Vietnamese monarchy was to gradually adopt it.

In 1070, Lý Thánh Tông had the Temple of Literature built, a school dedicated to Confucius and his disciples, where the sons of high-ranking dignitaries received moral education and training in administration. In 1075, the first mandarin competitions took place, through which Confucian scholars could accede to public office; but they were open only to the sons of aristocratic families. In 1086, competitions were held to recruit members of an Academy whose task was to preserve the archives and write royal edicts. In 1089, the mandarin hierarchy began to be strictly organized. The appearance of Confucianism on the scene was the consequence of a dual phenomenon: on the one hand, the necessity of creating a mandarin bureaucracy, on the other, the increasing accession of educated commoners to public office. At first, these men were given only subaltern positions, higher offices being reserved for members of the royal family and of the aristocracy.

Confucian culture grew in importance under the Trần; the competitions were better codified and held more regularly. The title of doctor was bestowed, enhancing the prestige of Confucian studies. Institutes were created in the capital for the study of Confucian literature; subjects in the competitions comprised in particular the composition of poems, royal ordinances and proclamations, and essays on classical literature. As well as public schools, private schools also appeared under the direction of famous people, the most prominent of these being Chu Văn An. In the field of culture, Buddhist bonzes were increasingly eclipsed by Confucian scholars; in 1243, the title of doctor was awarded to Lê Văn Hưu, who was to become Việt Nam's first great historian.

Confucian scholars monopolized more and more positions in public life, displacing nobles of military origin, often uneducated, and Buddhist bonzes. In the 13th century, the ideological struggle between Buddhism and Confucianism became increasingly acute, a struggle which reflected the antagonism facing the nobles, owners of great domains, from the fast-growing class of peasant-owners of lowly origin. The great domains were also shaken by revolts among serfs and domestic slaves at the close of the 13th century. Thus divisions appeared between the aristocracy and Buddhist clergy on one side, and on the other the class of peasant-owners allied with the serfs and slaves, having the Confucian scholars as their spokesmen in the field of ideology.

"In the face of Buddhism which affirmed the vanity, even the unreality of this world, preached renunciation, and directed men's minds towards other-worldly aspirations, Confucianism taught that man is essentially a social being bound by social obligations. To serve one's king, honour one's parents, remain loyal to one's spouse until death, manage one's family affairs, participate in the administration of one's country, contribute to safeguarding the peace of the world - such were the duties prescribed by Confucianism for all. To educate oneself, to improve oneself so as to be able to assume all these tasks, - this should be the fundamental preoccupation of all men, from the Emperor, Son of Heaven, down to the humblest commoner."[1]

The scholars directed their attacks not only against Buddhist beliefs, but also against the place granted to them by the state and society. The historian Lê Văn Hưu wrote:

"The first Lý king, hardly two years after his accession to the throne, at a time when the ancestral temples of the dynasty had not yet been consolidated, had already built eight pagodas in Thiên Đức district, and many others restored in different provinces. He kept more than a thousand bonzes in the capital; much wealth and labour had thus been wasted! These riches had not fallen from the sky, this labour had not been supplied by the gods; to do such things was to drain the blood and sweat of the people!"

The scholar Lê Quát lamented:

"To implore the Buddha's blessing, to dread his malediction - how had such beliefs become so deeply rooted in the hearts of men? Princes of the blood and common people alike squandered their possessions in venerating the Buddha, quite happy to give them away to pagodas, as if they had been given a guarantee for life in the other world. Wherever there was a house, one was sure to find a pagoda next to it; a crumbling

1. Nguyễn Khắc Viện. Marxism and Confucianism in Việt Nam, La Pense, October 1962.

pagoda was soon replaced by a new one; bells, pagodas, drums, towers - half the population were engaged in making these things."

Trương Hán Siêu also made a direct attack on the bonzes:

"Scoundrels, who had lost all notion of Buddhist asceticism, only thought of taking possession of beautiful monasteries and gardens, building for themselves luxurious residences, and surrounding themselves with a host of servants... People became monks by the thousand so as to get food without having to plough and clothes without having to weave. They deceived the people, undermined morality, squandered riches; they were found everywhere, followed by numerous believers, very few of them were not real bandits."

But several centuries were to pass before Buddhism was eliminated from the scene, at least from public office, and Confucianism could stand alone. Competitions in the three doctrines (Buddhism, Confucianism and Taoism) still took place under the Trần kings. No war of religion ever broke out in Việt Nam. By the 14th century, however, Confucianism had risen to pre-eminence.

The Birth of a National Literature

With the recovering of independence, a national literature took shape and gradually developed. Popular and oral literature in the national language became ever richer, but it is difficult to date most of the works, songs and stories handed down from generation to generation. In the 10th century, a scholarly literature appeared in classical Chinese, the common language of culture of the Far East, using Chinese characters. But more and more need was felt for the development of a script for the Vietnamese language; the *nôm* script, derived from Chinese, was thus created. The exact date of its creation is not known, but the first works in *nôm* appeared in the 14th century.

The first works in classical Chinese were mostly Buddhist texts expounding the doctrine or expressing the bonzes' reactions to certain events, for example, a poem by the bonze Vạn Hạnh, who died in 1018:

Man is a shadow, gone as soon as born,
The trees, so green in spring, are bare in autumn.
Greatness and decline, why should we care?
The destiny of men and empires is like a dewdrop on a grass leaf.

The bonze Viên Chiếu (998-1090) was also a poet who wrote:

Escorted by the wind, the sound of the horn slips through the bamboo grove,

With the moon rising behind, the shadows of mountains climb the ramparts.

With the consolidation of the kingdom, Buddhist inspiration on the evanescence of things gave way to the contemplation of nature; then with the struggle for national independence, patriotism prevailed in the writings. The same men, who in peacetime sang of the beauty of the land, took up their pens at critical moments to exalt the nation's struggle.

King Trần Nhân Tông, the victor over the Mongols, left this twilight landscape:

Villages grown dim in the mist,

They now vanish, now reappear in the sunset.

Buffalo-herds blowing their horns take their cattle home,

A flock of white egrets swoop down on the fields.

His general, Trần Hưng Đạo, when the country was invaded by the Mongols, wrote a proclamation to the army which is one of the jewels in the treasury of our national literature:

"I can neither eat nor sleep, my heart aches, and tears trickle down from my eyes; I am enraged at being unable yet to tear the enemy to pieces, pluck out his liver, taste his blood. But you are neither disturbed nor ashamed by the humiliation suffered by your King and your fatherland. You who are officers and generals of our royal army, how can you serve the enemy without feeling hatred? How can you listen to the music greeting enemy envoys without choking with anger? You spend your time watching cockfights, gambling, tending your gardens, and looking after your wives and children. You are busy making money and forget about state affairs. The pleasures of hunting prevail in your minds over your military preoccupations. You are absorbed in wine and song. If the country were invaded by the Mongols, your cock's spurs would not be able to pierce their armour, your gambling tricks could not replace military strategy. You may possess immense gardens and fields but even a thousand taels of gold could not redeem your lives. Your wives and children would only encumber you; all the gold in the world could not buy the enemy's head, your hunting dogs could not drive him away, your wine could not intoxicate him to death, sweet songs could not seduce him. Then both you and I would be in the enemy's clutches. Not only could I no longer enjoy my appanages, but you too would lose all your privileges; not only would my family be broken up, woe would also befall your wives and children; both royal ancestral temples and your own ancestors' graves would be trampled upon; dishonour would stain both my name and

yours, not only during our lifetime, but for centuries to come. Would you then persist in pleasure seeking?"

Among the author who left great literary works were Mạc Đĩnh Chi, Trương Hán Siêu, Chu Văn An, Nguyễn Trung Ngạn, Phạm Sư Mạnh, who in 1345 led a mission to China, and Lê Quát. Trương Hán Siêu, who glorified the two victories won in 939 and 1288 on the Bạch Đằng River, in a famous poem ending with these verses:

The enemy has fled, peace is restored for centuries to come,
Terrain played no role, noble virtues were decisive.

Of this period two works of religious tendency remain: *Việt Điện U Linh*, a collection of texts on genii, divinities, and deified famous men, which was attributed to Lý Tế Xuyên, and *Thiền Uyển Tập Anh*, a collection of texts and biographies of bonzes up to the Trần dynasty.

Literature in *nôm* appeared in the 14th century with Nguyễn Thuyên and Nguyễn Sĩ Cố whose works, though mentioned in the annals, have not survived. Tradition has it that when King Trần Nhân Tông married Princess Huyền Trân to the king of Champa in exchange for the Ô and Lý districts, this act was severely criticized in satirical poems in *nôm*. The appearance of poems in *nôm* was an important landmark in the development of a national literature. By the end of the 13th century, Hồ Quý Ly had translated the *Kinh Thi* (Book of Poems), a Confucian classic, into *nôm*.

The Lý -Trần period also saw the appearance of the first historical works. Under the Lý reign, Đỗ Thiện compiled a history of the country which, now lost, was mentioned in *Việt Điện U Linh* and *Lĩnh Nam Chích Quái*. An annals department was created under the Trần. Trần Tấn wrote *Việt Chí*, a monograph, to which the great historian Lê Văn Hưu often referred when he compiled, in 1272, the *Đại Việt Sử Ký* (History of Đại Việt) in 30 chapters, covering the period from Triệu Đà (Chao To) to the end of the Lý dynasty. Lê Văn Hưu's work was also lost, but it was the major inspiration for the complete history of Đại Việt written later by Ngô Sĩ Liên. At the close of the Trần dynasty, the *Đại Việt Sử Lược* (Short History) was written by an anonymous author. This book was to be reprinted in China in the 18th century. It is reported in the annals that Hồ Tông Thốc wrote two historical chronicles, the *Việt Sử Cương Mục* and *Nam Việt Thế Chí*. Both these works have been lost. Under the Trần, chronicles were also written describing military exploits in the wars against the Mongols and the kingdom of Ai Lao. Lê Tắc, who had taken refuge in China, wrote the *An Nam Chí Lược* at the beginning of the 14th century.

The Arts under the Lý and the Trần

Independence and stability led to the development of a national art, marked by Chinese, and to a lesser degree, Chàm influence. Under the Lý, Chàm influence was felt particularly in music. According to the *An Nam Chí Lược*, in Trần times people played a small cylindrical drum, introduced from Champa, which had a clear, pure sound. This drum was used in the great music played only for the king; even princes and dignitaries were not allowed to play great music, except at ceremonies. Guitars - *cầm, tranh, tì bà* with seven or two strings, and flutes of various kinds could be used by all, nobles or commoners. Countless pieces were played.

Chèo popular theatre, which first appeared in the 10th century, continued its development. A prisoner captured during the Mongol invasion, Lý Nguyên Cát, made a notable contribution to *tuồng* classical theatre.

It was architecture and ceramics that reached a level of excellence during the Lý period. With the spread of Buddhism, many pagodas were built. Some of the most famous have been preserved. Unfortunately, however, the ravages of war and climate have destroyed the majority of the works of art from this period. What remains can only give us an idea of what was being achieved at that time. Some works from the Lý period have been erroneously classified by French historians as being from an earlier period, that of Đại La (9th century).

On the stele of Linh Xứng, erected in 1126, an inscription records that "wherever there was beautiful scenery a pagoda was built." One of the essential characteristics of these pagodas was harmony with the surrounding landscapes, the building nestling amidst trees, gardens and ponds, an integral part of the construction. Most often, the background was a hill or winding stream, and the slow ringing of bells in the calm morning or evening seemed part of nature itself.[1]

Some pagodas had to be of significant size, since they would accommodate thousands of pilgrims coming to take part in great celebrations. The Diên Hựu pagoda, commonly known as the One-Pillar pagoda and built in 1049, is a graceful pavilion built on a stone pillar standing in the middle of a pond, the whole complex resembling a lotus flower in bloom.

1. This is in contrast to Catholic churches, which strike a discordant note in the middle of Vietnamese villages, seeking to dominate nature.

The lotus flower motif often appears on monuments. The flower symbolizes beauty and purity, for though springing from mud, it is free from the stench of mud. Stone pillars, some of significant size, often rest on lotus flowers; the remains of a pillar in Giám pagoda, built in 1086, has a base measuring 4.5 metres in diameter and is over 3.5 metres in circumference. At the foot of some of these pillars are carved stones representing waves, and the columns seem to emerge from a stormy sea. A couple of dragons climb the pillar, forming graceful but complex spirals.

The pagodas have curved roofs and often comprise a tower, with as many as 12 storeys. These pagodas are noted for their architecture, statues and sculptures.

At Phật Tích pagoda, the bases of pillars have stone sculptures representing the bodhi tree (of Buddhist enlightenment) in the centre with two worshippers presenting offerings and behind them, four musicians dancing and playing various instruments. The ground is littered with flowers. The atmosphere is gay, the gestures graceful, far from Buddhist meditation on the unreality of this world.

Relics found in the northwestern suburbs of Hà Nội, where the palace of the Lý was located, show a great variety of sculpture, statues and decorative motifs on ceramics. A frequent motif is that of the crocodile, with head raised, protruding eyes looking to right and left and quivering nostrils; the body is lithe, and the beast standing on its hind legs seems ready to spring. Stylized lions on ceramics have also been found.

Excavations in 1965 on the site of the Chương Sơn pagoda built in 1105 unearthed images of birds with human bodies among other motifs - chrysanthemums, phoenixes and dragons - all frequently found on works of the period. The dragon appears on almost all monuments, a mythical animal whose image is deeply engraved in the national tradition. According to legend, the Vietnamese are descendants of the dragon, and when the monarchy was established., it became the symbol of the king. The dragon made its appearance in China as early as the Han period, with a marked hieratic character, each detail - feet, claws, scales and mane - clearly outlined against a background of stylized clouds. The whole image appears majestic, even awe-inspiring. The dragon in works from the Lý period looks more natural, closer to the snake from which it springs, with a little, curving body, pointed tail and without complex details. Its feet recall the talons of birds and its mane that of a horse. The head is small, with wide nostrils and on top, an S-shaped double curve, a feature typical of bronze drums from the Đông Sơn period. With the Trần, as the monarchy consolidated its power, the dragon became stiffer and more hieratic looking. The conflict between two tendencies is clearly seen: the one, natural and popular, looked upon the dragon as a synthesis of ancient beliefs; the other, royal, even imperial, considered it the majestic, awesome symbol of the monarch.

Statuary art also developed in two directions. On the one hand, there were Buddhas sitting on lotus flowers, lost in meditation, the folds of their gowns and the relaxed features of their gentle faces giving an impression of peace and tranquillity. One can imagine behind their closed eyelids the inner glow of enlightenment. On the other hand, there were statues of guardian genii, with the martial bearing of energetic military men, ready for action.

While Buddhism was responsible for the building of countless pagodas, an example of Confucian art under the Lý was the Temple of Literature, with porticoes and pavilions arranged in a simple design amidst gardens. A kiosk with lattice woodwork and moon-shaped windows stands in the middle of the central alley, at the end of which is the temple, a long building with phoenixes and dragons on its roof.

Ceramics saw vigorous development under the Lý. Important production centres such as Bát Tràng and Thanh Hóa are still active today. There is a great variety of products: articles for both daily use and decoration, and pottery and porcelain ware with fine enamel. Among the most beautiful enamels are the opalescent-greens and brown-greys with a low shine and in various shades. The decoration is varied - flowers, dragons, lotuses, birds, and where the surface permits, frescoes and landscapes with human figures. The drawings and bas-reliefs always have a natural look with graceful lines and a gay environment: the movements of birds, elephants and dancers, harmonize with flowers in bloom or contrast with the antics of warriors. Particularly remarkable are the richly decorated porcelain items. Ceramics were sent as far as China to be sold, or presented to the imperial court. Under the Lý dynasty, this art reached its peak.

The art of the Trần period continued that of the Lý. Palaces and royal mausoleums continued to be built. The Phổ Minh tower, built in 1305, is 14 stories high, the two lowest made of stone and the rest brick. The base was shaped like a gigantic lotus flower emerging from the water. The Bình Sơn tower still stands to this day, leaning slightly with its remaining 12 stories totaling 15 metres in height. The whole construction is of terra cotta, and the surfaces are richly decorated with lotus and other flowers, dragons, lions and leaves of the *bồ đề* tree. The dragons have lost their natural look and the S-shaped decoration on their heads. Remarkable woodcarvings have survived from the Trần period. This art form appeared during a much earlier period, but the works have suffered badly from the ravages of climate and insects. Wood carvings also used all the above-mentioned motifs and themes.

Among the great monuments from the Trần period are the Tây Đô citadel, built by Hồ Quý Ly in Thanh Hóa province in 1397, which served as a capital for a short time. Rectangular in shape, 900 metres long and 700 metres wide, with 6 metre-high ramparts, it was built of large stone blocks, some of them 6 metres long, 1.7 metres wide and 1.2 metres high and weighing 16 tons. Of the ancient palaces, only a few traces have survived, such as stone dragons decorating flights of steps. The arched porticoes were built from huge stone blocks.

Architecture had thus reached a high level. Among other forms of technology was the casting of cannon. Hồ Nguyên Trừng, taken prisoner by the Ming, was entrusted by the Chinese emperor with making cannon for the Chinese army. Astronomy also developed to some extent. It is recorded in the annals that the mandarin Đặng Lộ, in charge of astrology under the Trần, invented an instrument used to observe celestial phenomena.

During the reign of Trần Duệ Tông (1341-1369), lived the famous physician Tuệ Tĩnh who made a special study of the healing properties of local plants and herbs. In 1352, he was invited to China to attend the Chinese empress. He left several medical treatises, the most famous of which is the *Nam Dược Thần Hiệu* (About the Marvelous Effects of Southern Medicines).

The Temple of Literature

Chapter IV

A NEW STAGE IN THE FEUDAL MONARCHY

The Lê Dynasty (15th to 16th centuries)

Towards the end of the 14th century, a great crisis shook the country. The Ming court, then reigning in China, took advantage of this to invade Đại Việt and impose on it a form of direct rule which was to last for twenty years (1407-1427). However, the invaders encountered stiff resistance right from the beginning and national independence was eventually wrested back in 1427 by Lê Lợi, the founder of the Lê dynasty.

The Ming Occupation

As early as July 1407, the Ming Emperor had incorporated Đại Việt into the Chinese empire under the title of Chiao Chih province, set up a central administration, and divided the country into *phủ* and *châu*, trying to reach down to village level by 1419. The high-ranking officials were all Chinese; only subaltern posts were given to natives. A general census revealed that there were 3,129,500 inhabitants and 2,087,500 men (barbarians) from mountain-dwelling tribes, i.e. a total of more than 5.2 million. But many doubtlessly evaded the census. Order was maintained throughout the country by large military garrisons, joined by a tight network of relays. All opposition was harshly suppressed.

There was a very heavy system of taxation, which included land tax on rice fields and mulberry fields, and a poll-tax. The occupiers held a monopoly over the salt trade. All able-bodied people, aged 16 to 60.

were subject to military service and multiple corvée: road-building, mining, pearl-oyster fishing, hunting, and so on. In 1419, family records were made obligatory for control over the population.

Thousands of skilled craftsmen and intellectuals were taken to China, among them Nguyễn An, who was to become the architect of the Imperial City in Beijing. The Ming also confiscated personal property, animals (elephants, buffaloes and horses) and other valuables.

The people were forced to adopt the Chinese style of dress and Chinese ways and customs. Ming troops sought to destroy all traces of the nation's culture; they burnt or took away books that were specifically Vietnamese. This was a true cultural disaster: almost all the literary works from before the 15th century were destroyed.

The oppressive occupation soon triggered fierce resistance. As early as the end of 1407, many uprisings began to occur. A descendant of the Trần dynasty proclaimed himself king in 1407, taking the name Giản Định and setting up his headquarters in Nghệ An province. In late 1408, his army marched on the capital, attracting along the way enthusiastic crowds of supporters. Giản Định defeated the Ming forces at Bô Cô in Nam Định province, but the resistance was weakened by internal dissension due to the murder of Giản Định by his able lieutenants Đặng Tất and Nguyễn Cảnh Chân. Their sons and followers rallied around another Trần prince, Quý Khoáng, in 1409. Starting from Hà Tĩnh, the movement spread to other provinces.

Meanwhile, 47,000 reinforcements allowed the Ming general Trương Phụ to launch an offensive and push the insurgents back to Nghệ An. In 1410, hostilities between the Ming court and Mongols made it possible for Quý Khoáng to reoccupy Thanh Hóa, but in 1411, having defeated the Mongols, the Ming counter-attacked and in 1413, the latter's leaders were captured. The Trần princes and aristocrats had proved themselves incapable of providing effective leadership for the resistance, which was to finally achieve victory under the leadership of a commoner, Lê Lợi.

The Lam Sơn Insurrection and the War of Independence

Lê Lợi, a landowner from Lam Sơn in Thanh Hóa province, was born in 1385. Before launching the insurrection against the Ming, he had gathered around him about 1, 000 followers. On 7 February 1418 in Lam Sơn, he proclaimed himself king under the name Bình Định Vương, and

began gathering under his banner anyone who opposed Ming domination. Nguyễn Trãi, a famous scholar, became his closest adviser on strategy and politics. The two men working together brought the insurrection to victory after years of struggle.

Lê Lợi at first launched guerrilla operations in the mountainous areas of Thanh Hóa. Although he inflicted losses on the Ming, he often found himself in a critical, even desperate, situation. However, his forces held out thanks to the courage of the men, the resolve of the leaders, and the dedication of the officers. Other popular uprisings in various provinces helped loosen Ming pressure on Lê Lợi. In 1420, his troops were able to camp on the banks of the Mã River and threaten the capital of Thanh Hóa province. A Ming counter -attack, however, drove them back to the mountains in 1423. But the Ming troops were also worn out, and their command agreed to a truce proposed by Lê Lợi, who resolutely resisted all attempts to buy him off with promises of riches and honours. In 1424, the Ming again attacked, but the insurgents had time to strengthen their positions.

On the advice of Nguyễn Chích, Lê Lợi took his troops to Nghệ An and turned it into a resistance base. The insurgents were enthusiastically welcomed by the local people. Fortified enemy positions fell one after another, and soon the whole province was in Lê Lợi's hands. Next came Thanh Hóa, and then provinces south of Nghệ An. By the end of 1425, the whole southern part of the country had been liberated, with the exception of the Nghệ An and Tây Đô (Thanh Hóa) citadels. A vast rear base had thus been created for the war of national liberation. In 1426, Lê Lợi was in a position to launch a counter -offensive.

The Ming sent from China 50,000 reinforcements under the command of Vương Thông. Even before they arrived, Lê Lợi had started his offensive to seize back the Red River delta. In September 1426, he dispatched three armies northward; one was to intercept Ming reinforcements coming from Yunnan, the second those coming through Lạng Sơn, and the last was to march on the capital. Everywhere the people rallied to his banner with enthusiasm, while panic-stricken Ming troops withdrew into their citadels and tried to hold out until the reinforcements arrived.

In November, Vương Thông's troops joined the Ming troops who had shut themselves up behind the walls of the capital, bringing their strength to 100,000. They thought they were now in a position to counter-attack, but instead suffered a crushing defeat at Tốt Động (west of the capital) and again had to withdraw into the citadel. The Vietnamese troops had gained control of the area. Lê Lợi left Thanh

Hóa and concentrated his forces around the capital. Vương Thông proposed a truce. In a letter to the Ming general, Nguyễn Trãi said that the Vietnamese command would agree to a truce if Vương Thông were to withdraw his troops from the country, thus sparing our people the ravages of war and the Chinese troops the sufferings of battle.

But for Vương Thông, the truce was just a stratagem to gain time and obtain more reinforcements. While maintaining the siege and eliminating isolated outposts, the Vietnamese command, on Nguyễn Trãi's recommendation, conducted a campaign of political persuasion directed at the Ming troops, driving home to them the inevitability of defeat, the strength of the Vietnamese national movement and the vulnerability of the Ming empire. This seriously demoralized them.

In October 1427, Ming reinforcements came in two prongs: one, 100, 000 strong and led by Liễu Thăng, through the Lạng Sơn pass; the other, 50, 000 strong and led by Mộc Thạnh, via the Red River valley. The Vietnamese command decided to destroy the more important army. Liễu Thăng's troops, overconfident about their strength, were ambushed and routed at the Chi Lăng pass. The commander was killed and several generals captured together with 30,000 men. The other Ming prong was filled with panic on hearing of this disaster and fled in disorder, pursued by Lê Lợi's troops.

After the destruction of these reinforcements, Vương Thông, besieged in the capital, was forced to sue for peace. His request was granted by Lê Lợi, who gave the Ming troops the necessary food supplies and means of transport to get home. It was 29 December 1427.

The war of independence led by Lê Lợi and Nguyễn Trãi had lasted ten years. Starting with few resources, the movement had expanded, gradually establishing powerful bases and forces, and eventually destroying huge enemy armies. The command had combined guerrilla warfare with mobile warfare and attacks on fortified positions, political struggle with military action, and had shown magnanimity toward the enemy and avoided pointless massacres. Lê Lợi, from the land-owning class rather than the landed aristocracy, and Nguyễn Trãi, a Confucian scholar with an encyclopedic knowledge, had succeeded in bringing about national unity and inspiring patriotism, and had shown resolve and wisdom at critical and decisive moments. The war was both national and popular in nature and conducted with appropriate strategy and tactics. Never again would the Ming try to reconquer Đại Việt. The following time of peace between China and Đại Việt was to last for over three centuries.

The Great Era of the Earlier Lê

The winning back of national independence and major changes in socio-economic structure, especially the disappearance of large aristocratic estates in favour of private land ownership which resulted in the emergence of a land-owning class, provided a strong base for the new regime set up by Lê Lợi. The country made further progress and the feudal monarchy reached its peak under King Lê Thánh Tông (1460-1497).

The Land System and Economic Development

After achieving victory, Lê Lợi ordered the confiscation of all property belonging to Ming functionaries, traitors and Trần princes, and dignitaries who had died or left. State land was utilized in part by the administration itself and partly distributed to dignitaries and mandarins. In contrast to the Trần estate owners, the benefiting mandarins could only collect land rent, but not do as they pleased with the peasants themselves, who were subject to the direct authority of the state. Administrative centralization was thus promoted and the status of the peasants improved.

Lê Lợi in 1429, then Lê Thánh Tông in 1477, regulated and improved the distribution of communal rice fields based on the following principles:

- All were entitled to distribution according to respective title and rank;

- Distribution was to take place every six years;

- Rent was paid to the state and was generally lower than that demanded by the landlords.

The distribution of communal lands had been a practice since ancient times, but it was the first time that the monarchical state had intervened so directly in communal affairs. Given that the area covered by such lands was significant, the regulations resulted in increased production.

The Lê kings paid great attention to the development of agricultural production. Lands left fallow during war time were quickly brought into cultivation, while the state set up state farms on uncultivated land so as to, in the words of King Lê Thánh Tông, "concentrate our strength in agriculture and increase our potential". Individuals were also encouraged to cultivate virgin lands. New areas were thus cleared both in the highlands and reclaimed coastal regions. Dykes were kept in good repair and in emergencies, students and soldiers were mobilized in order to repair them. Solders and palace staff were sent in turns to the fields to work. Harvests and cattle were given particular attention.

This policy greatly encouraged agricultural production, and no serious famines occurred during the 15th century.

Handicrafts were still a subsidiary activity. However, they were widely practised, and many villages came to specialize in certain occupations such as silk weaving, wine making, pottery or porcelain making, lime burning, and so on. Leather processing was introduced from China. In towns, particularly in the capital Thăng Long, craftsmen lived in certain quarters and were grouped in guilds with strict rules.

Silver, tin, iron, lead, gold and copper mines were opened.

Royal workshops were run by a special royal department and produced items needed at court and not to be sold on the market. They also minted coins. The personnel comprised craftsmen forced into service and slaves. This did not favour progress in handicrafts.

The development of trade was encouraged by the spread of regional markets. Lê Lợi abolished the paper currency issued by Hồ Quý Ly, ordered the use of copper coins and had units of measurement (length, weight, volume and area) and the sizes of certain goods (fabrics and paper) standardized. Foreign trade was strictly controlled by the state; transactions could be conducted only with government authorization and in specified places. Many foreign trading vessels were banned from entering port. This restriction on foreign trade remained one of the main characteristics of the feudal monarchy.

Administrative, Military and Judicial Organization

With the disappearance of large estates, administrative centralization reached a peak. The court was reorganized, with six ministries; the posts of prime minister and general were abolished, these functions being taken over by the king himself. Provincial and regional administration was handled by the mandarin bureaucracy. Functionaries were appointed to head villages in numbers that varied according to population. The establishment of new villages and election of notables became subject to detailed regulations. In 1467, Lê Thánh Tông ordered maps made of all villages and one of the whole country, the first ever to be drawn up. The country was divided into regions (*đạo*), provinces, districts and villages.

The army, 250,000 strong towards the end of the war of liberation, was reduced to 100,000 and divided into five sections that took turns in doing military service and agricultural work. The peasant-soldier system inaugurated under the Lý was thus maintained. Besides conscripts there were also reservists.

The mandarin bureaucracy enjoyed special privileges such as land, houses and special attire, but were no longer entitled to own large estates with serfs, or have their own armed forces as in the time of the Trần. Members of the royal family enjoyed even more privileges, but not to the extent of being allowed to participate in the nation's leadership or administer important provinces, as had occurred under the Trần.

The legislative apparatus was streamlined to serve the centralized administration and evolving society. In 1483, the Hồng Đức Code was promulgated, grouping in a systematic way the rules and regulations already in force. This was the most complete code to be drawn up in traditional Việt Nam and remained in force until the end of the 18th century. Completed under subsequent reigns, it comprised 721 articles and was divided into six books.

The Hồng Đức Code sought in particular to safeguard ownership of land by the state and landlords, and ensure the authority of the father, first wife, and eldest son. It also determined the rites of marriage and mourning. The ten capital crimes were severely punished, especially rebellion and neglect of filial duties. Feudal and Confucian in inspiration, the Hồng Đức Code was, however, progressive in several respects. The rights of the woman were protected; she could have her own property and share equally with men in inheritance. Where there was no male offspring, daughters could inherit the whole family fortune. A wife could repudiate her husband if the latter had abandoned her for a certain time. All these points were to be suppressed in its most reactionary form. The Hồng Đức Code was specific to the Vietnamese society of the time and showed no Chinese influence.

With the first Lê kings, Lê Thánh Tông in particular, the feudal monarchy in Việt Nam reached its peak; for some more time, the monarchical regime and mandarin bureaucracy were to play a positive role in Việt Nam's history.

Ethnic Minority Policy

Việt Nam comprises many ethnic groups; minority groups living in mountainous regions, while the majority group, the Kinh, are plain-dwellers.

During the insurrection against the Ming, ethnic minorities living in the highlands allied themselves with the Kinh to fight the occupiers. But after liberation, the feudalists in the delta resumed their policy of exploitation and oppression vis-a-vis the minorities. The Lê monarchy ruled over the highlands through tribal chieftains upon whom it bestowed mandarin titles. These chieftains collected taxes. Control over

mountainous regions was tighter than under the Trần. The Kinh mandarins ruling over the uplands also sought to exploit the ethnic minorities.

This policy provoked frequent revolts among the mountain-dwelling minorities, and this was for centuries one of the weak points of the feudal monarchy. The Thái of the northwest rose in revolt in Lai Châu in 1432, in Sơn La in 1439 and in Thuận Châu in 1440; the Tày of Lạng Sơn, Cao Bằng and Tuyên Quang also did so on many occasions. In the western part of Nghệ An, the head of the Cầm family succeeded in holding out from 1428 to 1437.

All these revolts were firmly suppressed by the Lê troops. The secession advocated by the rebel chiefs also ran counter to historical trends, the deltas and highlands being complementary economically. But antagonism among ethnic groups was to disappear only with the advent of socialism.

Cultural Development in the 15th-17th Centuries

While the plastic arts and architecture made little progress compared with the Lý -Trần period, literature flourished during this time. Buddhism was relegated to second place behind Confucianism, whose ideology inspired mandarin competitions and national literature.

Confucianism and the Scholar

Confucian works, as interpreted by Zhu Xi (of the Sung period in China), made up a body of doctrine that had to be digested by candidates entering mandarin competitions. In 1484, the names of laureates at the central competitions were inscribed on stone stele erected at the Temple of Literature in Hà Nội. The doctrine was carefully studied by the kings. Lê Thánh Tông was an outstanding scholar and wrote moral texts intended for the people.

Confucianism served the regime, which was based on the absolute authority of the king and a carefully graded hierarchy of mandarins. The people had been liberated from the bonds of serfdom but were still subject to corvée and many taxes. Setting aside all mysticism, Confucianism directed man towards the fulfillment of his social obligations, at the top of which were absolute fidelity to the king and respect for the social hierarchy. To serve one's husband and, after his death, to his memory, run one's household and participate in the administration of the country were the duties taught to all. Everyone was urged to improve himself through study and the performance of rituals so as to be able to fulfil every obligation.

There was a dual aspect to the adoption of Confucianism as the official doctrine in 15th-century Việt Nam. On the one hand, it served as an ideological tool in the hands of the monarchy and the mandarin bureaucracy. On the other hand, since that regime represented an advance on the aristocratic government of the Trần, Confucian rationalism was a step forward with regard to the Buddhism of past centuries. Two types of Confucian scholars thus emerged: those serving the king who were often against the interests of the people and bent on safeguarding their privileges, and those with ideals regarding social and individual morality, remaining faithful to their country, anxious to fulfil their obligations as human beings, dedicated to study and good manners, but often trapped in strict ritualism.

In the early stages of the Lê period, when the monarchy was still playing a positive role, and especially during the heroic struggle for independence, the two types merged into one, the scholar putting his ideals into action by serving the king. When the monarchy entered its decline, it became difficult for the scholar to serve his king without running counter to his ideals. Often the two types coexisted within one and the same person, protagonists in an agonizing battle of conscience. The more clear-sighted scholars were not blind to the faults of the monarchy. But for them, refusing to serve the king and withdrawing from public life would have meant shirking their duties. Yet, obeying the king often meant harming the people. It should be noted that one trend in Confucian ideology gave the people the right to rebel whenever the king showed himself to be unworthy. But for all Confucians, rebelling against a king remained the greatest of crime in the whole social, even cosmic, order.

NGUYỄN TRÃI

The first decades of the 15th century were dominated by the major figure Nguyễn Trãi, a Confucian-trained scholar whose spirit and works went far beyond the limits of that doctrine. Patriotism and love for the people instilled an exceptional vigour into his Confucianism.

Nguyễn Trãi was the strategist and political adviser for the national insurrection that drove the Ming out and won back the nation's independence. He was also a poet, and left behind a book on geography; in short, a humanist in the most complete sense of the term.

His military strategy was inspired by the great principle, *Better to conquer hearts than citadels*, laid down in his messages to Lê Lợi, offering his services. In a series of writings during and after the war of

liberation, he set forth his concept of a policy based on love of the people. The following are quotes from them:

To ensure peace for the people is the basis of humanity and justice.

Think of those who till the land when enjoying its stipends.

To hold in high esteem those with the virtue of humanity is to ensure the approval of the people, who carry the throne just as the ocean does the boat but can also overturn it.

The role of the people was thus clearly defined. It could be said that in Nguyễn Trãi the humanist tendency of Confucian doctrine reached its fullest development. It was on the people that he relied to fight the war of independence, and he also thought of the sufferings of enemy soldiers and of the Chinese people. He emphasized this in every message he sent to Ming generals. When victory came, the people and soldiers, burning with hatred for the aggressors, wanted to take revenge on the surrendering enemy garrisons. But on Nguyễn Trãi's advice, Lê Lợi allowed more than 100,000 men to return to China.

After the victory, in the name of the king, he composed several texts regarding political morality intended for the crown prince, including the following:

"Do not seek pleasure, strive to follow the rules that make it possible for you to safeguard the national heritage and give command to the army, and learn to discipline yourself and govern the country. Preserve harmony with your relatives, and show them cordial feelings. Be generous with the people. Let rewards not be prompted by personal sympathy nor punishments by fits of anger. Do not pursue wealth, do not indulge in wasteful extravagance, and abstain from beautiful women and debauchery."

"Whether to promote a man of talent, receive a criticism, work out a policy, or even pronounce a word or make a gesture, follow the rules of the golden mean and observe the classical principles; you will conform to the will of Heaven and to rites. To hold in high esteem those with the virtue of humanity is to ensure the approval of the people, who carry the throne just as the ocean does the boat but can overturn it. To help men of virtue is to earn the protection of Heaven, whose will is always so difficult to probe and predict."

But with his victory also began tragedy for Nguyễn Trãi. His integrity and righteousness prevented him from becoming a courtier. The king took offence at his prestige, while the other mandarins envied him because of his authority. For many years, he was kept out of public affairs and lived the life of a hermit. In 1442, Court dignitaries devised a plot to incriminate him, and he was executed. His works were scattered and only partly preserved.

Among his literary legacy are the *Dư Địa Chí* (Geography of the Country), the *Bình Ngô Đại Cáo* (Proclamation of Victory over the Wu), the *Quân Trung Từ Mệnh Tập* (Writings Composed While in the Army), the *Lam Sơn Thực Lục* (The Lam Sơn Insurrection), the *Quốc Âm Thi Tập* (a collection of 254 poems in the national language), and many poems in classical Chinese.

The Proclamation of Victory over the Wu (here the Ming), full of national pride, is one of the finest works of Vietnamese literature (translated in full on page 76). Nguyễn Trãi's poems in *nôm* were the first important works written in the national language and have survived. Besides being an indication of their author's talent for poetry, these poems provide an interesting insight into the Vietnamese people of the 15th century. The following verses were written either in *nôm* or classical Chinese:

Monkeys wail at the setting sun,

On the empty hillslopes the shadows of the bamboo lengthen.

Is a heart beating in all these things?

I could give an answer if I had not forgotten it.

*

Happiness and misfortune do not come in a single day,

All through the centuries great men have left us their tragedies.

Of the universe, of the past and present, where does the meaning lie?

In that mist yonder over the trees at the edge of the water?

* * *

On the plains, on the deserted paths, not a shadow,

All day long a lonely boat lies sleeping on the beach.

* * *

Literature and History under the Lê Dynasty

During the reign of Lê Thánh Tông, a Confucian inspired literature started to emerge. The king himself liked to write and gathered together 28 dignitaries who were great scholars to form a type of academy known as the Tao Đàn, over which he presided. The Tao Đàn left many poems written in a refined style and praising the regime and the nation. Many of its other writings were included in a collection called the *Thiên Nam Dư Hà Tập*. And Lê Thánh Tông himself left a collection of poems in *nôm*.

The period of the first Lê kings also produced many historical works, the most important of which was written in 1479 by Ngô Sĩ Liên. This was the *Đại Việt Sử Ký Toàn Thư*, dealing with Vietnamese history from its beginnings to the founding of the Lê dynasty in 1428. An unknown author left the *Lĩnh Nam Chích Quái*, a collection of popular legends indispensable for finding one's way through the beliefs and customs of ancient Việt Nam. Early in the 16th century, Nguyễn Dữ wrote the *Truyền Kỳ Mạn Lục*, a collection of stories which, disguised as legends, contained many criticisms by the author of the society and the rulers of his time.

The figure of Nguyễn Bỉnh Khiêm (1491-1585) towers over all others in the 16th century. This Confucian scholar, after being a mandarin for some time for the Mạc, retired to his hermitage, the Bạch Vân Am, founded a school and trained many disciples. Disgusted by the practices and morals of the court and among the mandarins, he professed his love of nature and his attachment to "*nhàn*," i.e. a life of seclusion without material or social preoccupations and inspired by the Taoist doctrine of "non-action." However, as a Confucian, he remained deeply interested in the country's political life. These were troubled times. The throne was usurped by the Mạc; when it was restored to the Lê, the rise to power of the Trịnh and Nguyễn families created a political imbroglio which perplexed even the best minds. Advice from the hermit of Bạch Vân Am was sought by all parties concerned.

Thus, in 1556 when the general Trịnh Kiểm wanted to seize the Lê throne, he sent an emissary to Nguyễn Bỉnh Khiêm to consult him. The scholar turned to one of his servants and said, "The harvest has been lost because of bad seeds; for the next, you must pick an old strain". Then he visited a pagoda, lighted a few joss sticks and told the bonze: "If one takes care of the pagoda and honours the Buddha, one may have rice cakes to eat". The emissary repeated these words to Trịnh Kiểm, who took the advice and contented himself with handing over the throne to a descendant of the Lê.

A century separated Nguyễn Trãi from Nguyễn Bỉnh Khiêm. The former had served the monarchy with dedication, but the latter could no longer do so. The feudal regime was going through a period of deep crisis. In the view of scholars, Nguyễn Trãi had "gone out" to serve the king and play his role in society; Nguyễn Bỉnh Khiêm was "staying on"

at his retreat, living close to nature and to the people for the sake of his conscience. To "go out" or "stay on" - this dilemma was to haunt talented scholars for many centuries with regard to the feudal monarchy. Nguyễn Bỉnh Khiêm left more than 1,000 poems in classical Chinese and in *nôm*, all influenced by ancient wisdom, extolling the quiet life of a hermit and the beauty of nature, or joking about the vicissitudes of life. The following are two of the better-known poems:

A hoe, a pick and a fishing rod,
I wander about, leaving people to their pleasure,
Foolish as I am, I seek solitude,
More clever, they join the crowds.
Bamboo shoots in autumn, soya sprouts in winter: such is my food,
In the spring I bathe in the lotus pond, in summer in the lake.
With my back against a tree, sipping a cup of wine,
I watch wealth and honours pass as in a dream.

*

Harrying others will bring you trouble,
Better abstain and sleep soundly
The harder you clench your fist, the less easily you will open it,
Whoever laughs too much, one day may choke.
As a rule, cats hunt mice,
Let some misfortune happen, and oxen are eaten by ants.
Win or lose: either will bring repentance,
Having nothing to worry about is best.

PROCLAMATION OF VICTORY OVER THE WU[1]

(BÌNH NGÔ ĐẠI CÁO, 1428)

NGUYỄN TRÃI

It was said:

To ensure peace for the people, such is the essence of humanity and justice,

To eliminate violence, such is the primary aim of our soldiers.

Our country Đại Việt has long since been

A land of ancient culture,

With its own rivers and mountains, ways and customs.

Different from those of the north.

The Triệu, Đinh, Lý, Trần[2] *built up our independence*

And stood as equals of the Han, Tang, Sung, Yuan.[3]

We had known both days of greatness and times of decline,

But never had we lacked heroes.

That was why we brought to naught Lưu Cung's ambitions

And Triệu Tiết's dreams of conquest,

Killed Toa Đô at Hàm Tử,

And captured Ô Mã on the Bạch Đằng River [4]

Proof remains of these exploits.

*

1. Written after the victory over the Ming. Wu is a generic term designating invaders. Proper nouns designate historical personalities and battlefields.
2. Vietnamese dynasties.
3. Chinese dynasties.
4. Past victories over invaders

In the recent past the troublesome policy of the Hồ
Provoked anger and resentment.
The truculent Ming took advantage of it to bring distress upon our land,
And the traitors sold the country for money and honours.
The people were burnt on the flames of barbarity,
Or buried in the tombs of disaster.
To deceive Heaven and men, the invaders resorted to a thousand machinations;
For twenty years they killed and oppressed.
Humanity and justice were condemned, the land trampled,
Rates and taxes drained forests and fields empty.
Men were sent to shark-infested seas to dive for pearls,
Others into fever-ridden forests to sift gold from sand.
Everywhere nets and traps were set for pheasant and deer,
Neither plants nor insects were spared,
Wretched was the fate of widows and orphans.
The people were lean and hungry, but the blood suckers were never satisfied;
Earth had to be moved, wood carved, houses and palaces built;
Endless corvée caused the looms to stay idle.
To record the oppressors' crimes all the bamboos of the Southern Mountain would not suffice;
All the water of the Eastern Sea could not clean away the filth.
How could Heaven condone such felonies!
The people's anger had reached its peak

*

In our retreat on Mount Lam,
We brooded over the wrongs done to our land,
Swearing not to live under the same vault of heaven as the oppressors.
For years we suffered in our heart and mind,
Tasting gall and lying on thorns.
We hardly touched our meals, devoting our time to studying strategies,
Pondering the past and present, weighing the chances of success.
Even in our dreams plans for insurrection were hatched,

Our only thought day and night was national restoration.
When the banner of revolt was raised, enemy strength was at its peak;
On our side, talent was rare as stars at dawn and leaves in autumn,
Officers and advisers were lacking.
Burning with impatience to save the people, we longed to march eastward;
In our chariot, the best seat was left empty, waiting for a talented general
Alas, friends were late to come: it was like watching the fog at sea!
We had to rely on our own forces: a drowning man waited to be rescued!
The enemy was on the rampage, the nation in distress.
In Linh Sơn, for weeks we ran short of supplies;
At Khôi Huyện, not a brigade was left intact.
But Heaven entrusted us with a great responsibility,
And we had to surmount all obstacles.
With the people united like one single family, we held high the standard of revolt;
With officers and men like father and son, we shared the last drop of wine.
Relying on surprise, we placed our weak forces before much stronger ones,
In skilful ambushes, our few troops destroyed large units.
Successfully we confronted barbarity with justice,
And fought truculence with humanity.
At Bồ Đằng, we struck them like lightning;
In Trà Lân, their troops were cut to pieces.
The higher our soldiers' spirit,
The farther their prestige spread.
Trần Trí, Sơn Thọ were frightened out of their wits,
Lý An, Phương Chính showed a clean pair of heels.
We pressed them hard, soon Tây Kinh was ours;
Advancing again, we recovered Đông Đô, the old capital.
The streams of blood shed by the enemy at Ninh Kiều stank for a thousand miles,
The piles of corpses left by them at Tốt Động for a thousand years would be reminders of their shame.
The traitors Trần Hiệp and Lý Lượng were beheaded.
Vương Thông tried to reverse the disaster: the flames only rose higher!
Mã Anh rushed to the rescue: our troops struck even harder.

Running out of breath, the enemy was at the end of their rope;
Relying on intelligence and skill, aiming at men's hearts we won without further fighting.
For a time we thought they would repent,
In fact they were only plotting more crimes.
One man's obduracy created miseries for thousands,
Thirsting for power and glory, he turned himself into a laughing stock
And so that little tyrant Tuyên Đức sent troops after troops,
And the cowards Mộc Thạnh and Liễu Thăng tried to put out the fire with oil.
In the ninth moon of the year of the Goat, Liễu Thăng moved his army from Khâu Ôn,
In the tenth moon, Mộc Thạnh came with his troops from Yunnan.
First we stopped them at key spots and crushed their vanguards,
Then we cut off their communications and supplies.
On the 18th, we defeated Liễu Thăng at Chi Lăng,
On the 20th, at Mã Yên, he lost his life.
On the 25th, Count Lương Minh died,
On the 28th, Minister Lý Khánh committed suicide.
Fired by our victories, we rushed forward,
Confused by their defeats, they turned on each other.
On all sides we besieged their citadels,
Bent on annihilating them by the middle of the tenth moon.
Crack troops and officers were selected for the task;
Drinking at rivers, our elephants dried the streams,
Whetted on rocks, our swords eroded mountains.
On our first onslaught, all the sharks were exterminated,
After the second assault, not a single vulture remained.
We were the hurricane that blew away the dry leaves,
And the stubborn ants that caused dykes to collapse.
On his knees, Thôi Tụ begged for mercy,
Tying his hands, Hoàng Phúc planted his flag
Enemy corpses piled high on the road to Lạng Giang and Lạng Sơn,
At Xương Giang and Bình Than, their blood tinged the river with red.
Winds and clouds changed colour,

Sun and moon waned.
Cornered at Lê Hoa, the Yunnan troops went mad with panic,
Defeated at Cần Trạm, Mộc Thạnh's soldiers trampled on each other in their flight.
The Lãnh Câu stream was clogged with blood, the air filled with moans;
Corpses formed knolls in Đan Xá, amidst clotted grass.
The two relief armies were shattered before they could escape,
All the garrisons took off their armour and surrendered.
Captured generals, tigers reduced to impotence, implored pardon;
Generous victors, sensitive to the will of Heaven, we granted them quarter.
For Mã Kỳ and Phương Chính we provided five hundred junks;
Out at sea their faces were still green with fear.
To Vương Thông and Mã Anh we gave several thousand horses;
Back in their country, their legs still shook with terror.
Fearing death, they asked for peace;
We preserved our forces and let our people have a rest:
Such was our wisdom
From now on our land is safe,
Rivers and mountains will see a new era.
Calm comes after the storm,
Light has driven away darkness.
For ever we have cleansed ourselves of shame,
For ever we shall have peace.
Both Heaven and our ancestors helped us in battle:
We took up arms, fought and won.
All the four seas are now serene, great changes are forthcoming
Let everybody everywhere be so informed.

Translated by Đ.T.B.

Chapter V

THE TÂY SƠN ERA

(18th century)

The feudal society built under the first Lê kings in the 15th century flourished for about a hundred years, but the structures set up had ceased to play a positive role as early as the 16th century. By the 17th century, decadence manifested itself more and more clearly, and finally culminated in a deep and irreversible crisis in the 18th century.

The feudal structure was built on an agrarian system based on private land ownership coexisting with the ancient institution of communal lands, which were subject to periodic distribution. While under the law everyone had access to ownership and enjoyed the same civil rights, in practice a minority of landowners had taken possession of most of the land and appropriated the best communal lands, reducing to misery the majority of working peasants. In the villages, landowners and notables would lay down the law, collect very high land rents, and exact exorbitant interest payments on debt.

The feudal state administered the country by means of a bureaucracy of mandarins recruited through competitive examinations. One of its main functions consisted of building and maintaining an important network of dykes and irrigation canals to protect agriculture against natural disasters. The diligence of state services or negligence in water conservation had far-reaching consequences.

The prestige of the monarchical state and the mandarin bureaucracy rested on the teaching of Confucianism, which was disseminated throughout the country and instilled in the people absolute respect for the king and strict observance of social hierarchy.

Handicrafts and trade were undervalued, as the mandarin bureaucracy tried to hinder its development. Techniques used did not improve, for the landowners, mandarins and notables obtained their incomes from the direct exploitation of peasants. Handicrafts and trade were only promoted so as to meet the needs of court pomp or of luxury consumption.

A new factor must have been of paramount importance - territorial expansion to the south. Starting from the plains of the Red, Mã and Cả Rivers, the country's territory was extended, with the coastal plains as far as the basin of the Đồng Nai and Mekong Rivers being brought under cultivation. From the capital to the southern provinces communication routes, stretching for over 1,000 kilometres, were particularly difficult to negotiate at the time. Orders issued by the central government did not reach the regions, just as taxes from remote provinces could not reach the royal court.

Under these circumstances, secession was inevitable. Under the nominal authority of the Lê kings who established themselves in Thăng Long, two administrations were set up - one in the north under an aristocratic family, that of the Trịnh, and the other in the south under the sway of the Nguyễn lords. Throughout the 17th century, without the ability to put an end to secession, the country was de facto divided at the Gianh River, which did not, however, prevent continuous expansion to the south.

In the 18th century, elements of crisis and change began to accumulate: an agrarian crisis, the development of handicrafts and trade, a political and administrative crisis, ideological crisis, contact with the outside world, and corruption among ruling circles. The country was shaken by great peasant uprisings, which culminated in the Tây Sơn movement. A century of upheaval, it was also one of renewal, or at least of great hope. With the Tây Sơn, Việt Nam experienced one of the shortest but most brilliant periods in its history. The nation's culture, inspired by the great peasant insurrections and more or less liberated from feudal bonds, began to flourish.

The Crisis of the Trịnh regime in the North

The Agrarian Crisis

The appropriation of land by landowners, notables and mandarins had greatly increased, especially in the north, the domain of the Trịnh, where uncultivated land was scarce. With population growth, the problem took on potentially disastrous dimensions. In 1711, the Trịnh

issued an edict that forbade "great families, functionaries and notables taking advantage of ruined peasants to enlarge their estates under cover of buying". Indeed, sale and purchase contracts were used only to legalize appropriations effected to the detriment of small farmers. Nor did communal lands escape the landowners' greed. In 1739, the aristocratic court had to admit that "there remains nothing for the peasants to live on."

The situation became so disturbing that in 1740, a Trịnh lord planned the nationalization of all lands for redistribution to peasants who would pay land rents to the State. But the entire mandarin bureaucracy and landowning class opposed the project, which was quickly buried.

One of the clearest indications of this agrarian crisis was the increasing number of lawsuits involving the appropriation of land, but the peasants who appeared before mandarin courts were mistreated, had to pay bribes, and usually lost the case. Complaints reached the court in such great numbers that in 1723 the Trịnh were compelled to set up a real supreme court of appeal at the gates of the palace. A report dated 1718 said:

"In the villages, the notables, using thousands of tricks, ruling arbitrarily, grabbing other people's property to enrich themselves, oppressing the poor, despising the illiterate, avail themselves of the least opportunity to indict people and bring suits against them. If the judgement, though a just one, does not satisfy them, they appeal against it once, twice, even three times. The poor are not able to carry on the suit and even well-off people are ruined."

The same report described the multitude of ways used by notables to extort property from the poor, seize communal lands and create divisions. Village administrations were, therefore, thoroughly corrupt, but the State remained powerless, and was no longer able to take proper care of the irrigation works. As a result, even minor natural disasters sometimes led to disastrous famines. Peasants were forced to leave their villages, wandering in search of food and dying by the thousands on the roads. The State was able to do little more than dole out inadequate supplies of food. The *Cương Mục* annals describe the 1735 famine in this way:

"Thieves and bandits multiplied in number, especially in Hải Dương. Peasants gave up all cultivation. All food reserves were exhausted in the villages, except in Sơn Nam. People roamed about carrying their children in search of rice. The price of rice soared; 100 coins were no longer enough to pay for a meal. People lived on vegetables and herbs, and ate rats and snakes. Dead bodies lay about on the roads."

The number of ruined peasants wandering about the country increased so dramatically that in 1730 the Trịnh had to appoint 12 high - ranking court dignitaries to try to return them to their homes, but in vain. A census showed that 1,730 villages were particularly affected. This ruined and wandering peasantry was to make up the bulk of insurgent groups in the 18th century revolts.

The Political and Administrative Crisis

While the village administration showed itself to be rapacious and cruel, the mandarin bureaucracy and court sank into corruption and debauchery. The building of palaces and pagodas drained the budget, as did the lavish court celebrations. In 1718, a censor submitted a report stressing the people's misery and proposing to forbid all squandering of funds, stop all building and repairs to palaces, cut down the number of pleasure trips undertaken by the court and reduce the number of administrative inspection tours.

The censor was congratulated, but his advice remained unheeded. The Trịnh lords ordered the building of many recreation facilities, pagodas and mansions, requiring excessive contributions and labour from the population. Ceremonies were held amidst great pomp. To meet all these expenses, in the 18th century the Trịnh instituted, with the help of a loyal mandarin, Nguyễn Công Hãng, a new system of taxes and duties which encompassed all areas of production, leaving nothing outside state control. The principle of this financial reform was stated in 1721 as follows:

"Formerly, expenditure was set on the basis of receipts; now we are going to set receipts to be collected on the basis of expenditure".

A fatal blow was dealt to the institution of the mandarin bureaucracy by the putting on sale of offices. Money thus began to eat away the feudal structure; anyone could buy mandarin titles, and the promotion of mandarins was facilitated by money. Bribery became de facto legal, as the mandarin squeezed the common people to get back what he had had to pay for his office and enrich himself. Edicts were promulgated to fight this evil, but were ineffective.

While the Trịnh lords sank into debauchery and extravagance, factionalism grew at the court. Palace intrigues in which eunuchs and favourites played an important part, helped foster greater and greater instability. Honest, upright mandarins were eliminated, and special units of the army often made and broke laws, deposing mandarins and lords at will in a capital city beset by anarchy.

Peasant Revolts under the Trịnh

Occurring sporadically in the 17th century, peasant revolts spread during the 18th century. In mountainous regions, ethnic minority groups rebelled under the leadership of local chiefs. The annals indicate that as early as 1715, the delta provinces were infested with bandits. In 1737, the Trịnh had to set up watch -towers nearly everywhere so as to indicate by means of signal fires, the movements of insurgents who were becoming increasingly active in many regions. This agitation took on a political character with clandestine writings, slogans, and false rumours designed to discredit the regime. Writings were disseminated in which the authors launched attacks on the administration in the guise of stories and fables. In 1718, the Trịnh court banned the printing and circulation of such writings and had them seized and burnt. Various security measures were implemented, particularly the establishment of village guards made up of notables, and of military commands in the provinces. In 1721 and again in 1727, the army was reinforced. None of these measures, however, were able to stop successive peasant revolts. The following were the most important.

In 1737, under the leadership of the bonze Nguyễn Dương Hưng, thousands of peasants occupied the Tam Đảo Mountains northwest of the capital, with news of the move causing panic. The revolt was harshly suppressed but shortly afterwards, in the mountainous region of Thanh Hóa province, a descendant of the Lê, Lê Duy Mật, led an uprising which involved both peasants from the delta and highlanders.

In 1739, centres of insurgency were developing in every province, particularly in the Red River delta. The *Cương Mục* annals relate that poor people gathered there "by the hundreds, thousands, even tens of thousands, and besieged the towns in an irresistible upsurge." Contacts were established between insurgent organizations in various provinces in order to coordinate actions, but the uprisings remained in most cases local in character.

The Trịnh then created village guards, choosing two out of every ten young men and arming them for the defence of rural communes. But the village guards often crossed over to the insurgents and the measure was soon abandoned. In 1740, the Trịnh reinforced the army's special units. The Trịnh army had to carry out continuous mopping -up operations, for hardly had one uprising been quelled when another broke out. In Hải Dương province, even after the death of rebel chiefs Nguyễn Tuyển and Nguyễn Cừ in 1741, their partisans again rallied, appearing and disappearing among the villages and reed-covered swamps.

In the uplands and highlands, in Lạng Sơn, Bắc Giang, in the provinces of Tuyên Quang, Thái Nguyên and Cao Bằng, and in the mountainous areas of Thanh Hóa, the ethnic minorities, sometimes allied with rebel groups in the delta, rose in revolt against the Trịnh. However, the main centre of insurgency remained the delta. Four of these peasant revolts achieved particular strength and lasted for years.

Starting in Sơn Tây province in 1740, the movement led by Nguyễn Danh Phương stretched until 1751. The insurgents succeeded in gaining control of the provinces of Vĩnh Yên, Phú Thọ, Tuyên Quang and part of Sơn Tây, collected taxes on forest produce from the highlands, and for eleven years "maintained a real state in defiance of the Thăng Long court". After successive failures by the Trịnh troops, Lord Trịnh Doanh himself took command of a strong army in 1751, and the insurrection was put down only after several hard-fought battles.

In Hải Dương province, after the defeat of the peasant leader Nguyễn Cừ in 1741, his deputy Nguyễn Hữu Cầu succeeded him and incited one of the greatest peasant revolts of the century. A talented scholar, disgusted with the system of mandarin competitions, Nguyễn Hữu Cầu attacked the rich and handed out their property to the poor, calling himself the "Great General Protector of the People". He settled in the coastal region of Đồ Sơn, Vân Đồn, occupied Kiến An province, and built a flotilla of combat junks. He was a supreme strategist and his troops, highly mobile and capable of fighting on both land and water, inflicted a major defeat on the Trịnh troops in 1744, which caused panic even in the capital. His influence spread to Kinh Bắc province, and his name inspired the peasant masses, while causing terror among the mandarins and soldiers. The Trịnh had to mobilize strong armies commanded by their best generals to fight him. Whenever he was beaten, he quickly reorganized his forces, rallying thousands of peasants under his banner using the slogan, "Take from the rich to give to the poor"; hence the legend of his invincibility. Finally overcome only by sheer force of numbers, Nguyễn Hữu Cầu was captured in 1751 and executed. During his captivity, he wrote a poem, *The Bird in the Cage*, in which he expressed his aspiration for freedom.

The movement led by Hoàng Công Chất, which arose in Sơn Nam in the lower regions of the delta, lasted from 1739 to 1769. Mainly practising guerrilla warfare, establishing no permanent bases, and concentrating and scattering his forces with rapidity, Hoàng Công Chất succeeded in keeping the Trịnh armies at bay for years. In 1751, when a Trịnh offensive was imminent, he went to the mountainous region of Thanh Hóa, then to

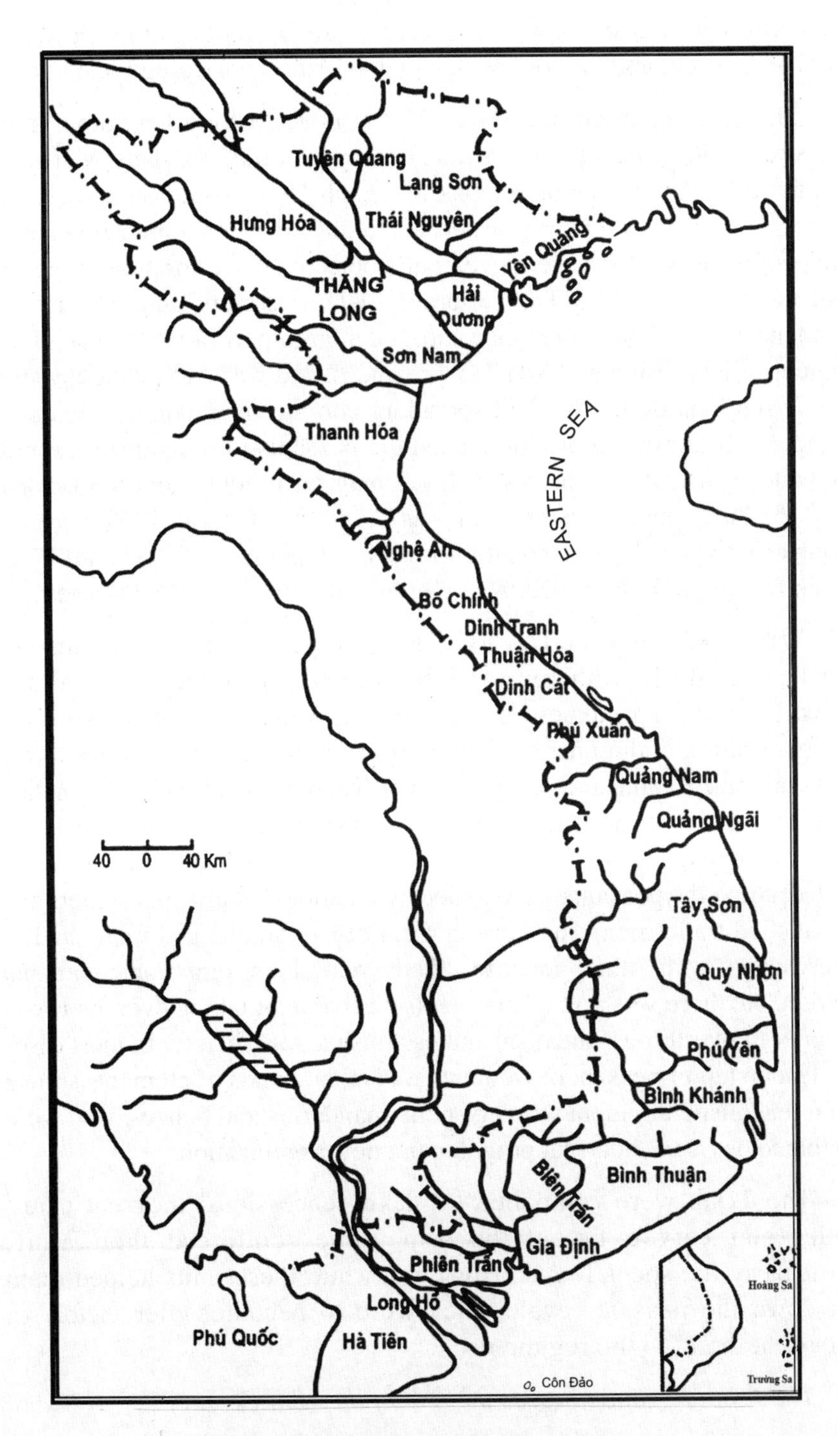
Tuyên Quang
Lạng Sơn
Hưng Hóa
Thái Nguyên
Yên Quảng
THĂNG LONG
Hải Dương
Sơn Nam
Thanh Hóa
EASTERN SEA
Nghệ An
Bố Chính
Dinh Tranh
Thuận Hóa
Dinh Cát
Phú Xuân
Quảng Nam
Quảng Ngãi
40 0 40 Km
Tây Sơn
Quy Nhơn
Phú Yên
Bình Khánh
Bình Thuận
Biên Trấn
Gia Định
Phiên Trấn
Long Hồ
Phú Quốc
Hà Tiên
Côn Đảo
Hoàng Sa
Trường Sa

Việt Nam in the 18th Century

the northwest of Bắc Bộ, where in 1761 he set up posts on the Đà River. In 1768 he died, and his son, beaten by the Trịnh, took refuge in Yunnan.

The movement led by Lê Duy Mật also lasted for a long time, from 1738 to 1779. A descendant of the Lê royal family, Lê Duy Mật took refuge in the mountainous regions of Thanh Hóa, where he created an initial base relying on poor peasants and highlanders. In a proclamation to the people, he set forth the movement's objectives - restoration of the Lê and the ousting of the Trịnh usurpers, whose cruelty and rapacity he denounced. By 1740 his forces controlled a large part of the mountainous regions of Ninh Bình and Sơn Tây provinces, and was expanding towards the Thanh Hóa delta, by 1752 spreading into the mountainous region of Nghệ An. In these regions, he helped the peasants to reorganize farming by building irrigation works and developing farm equipment workshops. By 1763 his domain extended as far as Trấn Ninh. Only in 1769 were the Trịnh able to launch a real counter -offensive. Operations lasted until 1770, when Lê Duy Mật, betrayed by one of his subordinates, killed himself.

With the death of Lê Duy Mật, the great peasant movements against the Trịnh gradually withered away, but they had dealt the regime a fatal blow. Their major weakness lay mainly in their dispersed nature and lack of organization in the face of a centralized state with a professional army and seasoned administrative organization. There was at times coordination between different movements, but never organization at national level. Revolts broke out spontaneously, and were always local in character. In the 18th century, the peasants were joined by unemployed artisans, miners and dissatisfied tradesmen. The development of handicrafts and trade, and of interchange with other countries, had created an embryonic national market, but there was no real bourgeoisie capable of taking over the revolt in order to overthrow feudalism and establish a new society. In most cases the leadership of peasant movements was in the hands of elements sprung from feudalism: dissident scholars, petty mandarins and bonzes, who were unable to devise a clear-cut program and new organization.

The Trịnh were compelled to make concessions; they cut taxes, duties and corvée but at the same time reinforced their army, particularly the special units. However, while these units helped them put down the peasant revolts, they were to become, after victory, a persistent threat to the regime itself.

The Trịnh Regime towards the End of the 18th Century

Although the Trịnh succeeded in putting down the revolts, they were unable to stop land seizure or prevent their own decline. Edicts

from the court, petitions from censors, and reform projects proposed by mandarins concerned about public welfare were all without result. In the 1770s and 1780s, famines repeatedly occurred.

With the advent in 1767 of Trịnh Sâm, a debauched and corrupt lord, power came into the hands of his favourite, Đặng Thị Huệ, and her family. The court was split into two rival factions, the followers of the heir apparent and those of the favourite. It was the latter's son who came to power on the death of Trịnh Sâm in 1782. The newly -enthroned lord was only six years old, and it was Hoàng Đình Bảo, Đặng Thị Huệ's paramour, who wielded real power. Late in 1782, troops rose in revolt, killed Hoàng Đình Bảo, and restored the heir-apparent to the throne. From that date on however, the special units imposed their will on the court, stealing from the people, deposing princes and dignitaries, and assassinating those who opposed their actions.

Peasant revolts broke out again, without, however, reaching the scale of the previous movements. By the end of the 18th century, the Trịnh regime was on the point of collapse.

The Tây Sơn: Reunification and Renewal

As had happened with the Trịnh, the Nguyễn regime in the south was affected by the same deep and irreversible crisis. Towards the end of the 18th century, an insurgency movement, that of the Tây Sơn, was to emerge from the Nguyễn domain and sweep away both the Trịnh and Nguyễn, reunifying the country and laying the foundations for national renewal. Unfortunately, for various reasons, the Tây Sơn did not stay in power for long, and early in the 19th century, conservatives gained the upper hand, restoring feudalism in its most reactionary forms.

The Crisis in the Nguyễn Regime

As in the north, land seizure in the Nguyễn domain by landowners, mandarins and notables forced peasants into misery and ruin. For a time, the effects were less serious due to the colonization of new lands in the Mekong delta; the lands reclaimed by peasants, although seized by landowners later on, were extensive and fertile enough to make the crisis less serious. But in the provinces of Trung Bộ, the shortage of arable land meant that any seizures condemned poor peasants to an impossible life. As early as 1613, the Nguyễn court had to intervene by establishing a cadastral register so as to limit the extent of landed property. This administrative intervention had only a temporary effect; in the villages, landowners and notables, with the complicity of mandarins, ignored it. In 1669, faced with a serious crisis, the court again ordered that communal estates should not be appropriated. Despite this, by the 18th century, according to the historian Lê Quý Đôn, many villages no longer had any communal lands left for periodic distribution to the peasants. Rice production in these provinces suffered and as early as the 18th century, central regions were forced to buy rice from Gia Định (Saigon).

The poverty-stricken peasantry toiled under heavy and multiple burdens imposed by a court which, on the one hand, carried out a policy of nearly continuous warfare - war against the Trịnh, and territorial expansion at the expense of Cambodia - and on the other indulged more and more in pleasure and luxury. The Nguyễn levied taxes on all agricultural, handicraft and trading activities, extracting from the population contributions in cash and kind such as valuable timber, rattan, cloth and so on. The records of Cao Xá village, Thuận Hóa province (near Huế), for example, showed that of 53 registered adults, nine were exempt, while the other 44 paid taxes every year, and duties totaling 138 strings of coins (the price of a large buffalo was 40 strings in difficult times). Not counting contributions in kind, the Nguyễn court collected every year between 338,000 and 423,000 strings of coins, between 840 and 890 ounces of gold, and many thousands of ounces of silver.

The historian noted that *"for every amount the state collected, the mandarin-collectors took twice as much for themselves"*.

As early as the 17th century, with their power consolidated the Nguyễn lords and their mandarins were indulging in a life of extravagant luxury. The harems were full; the lord Nguyễn Phúc Chu had as many as 146 children. Lords and mandarins built palaces and pagodas using rare timbers, richly decorated. They dressed in silk and brocade and the capital Phú Xuân (Huế) grew into a large metropolis. Lê Quý Đôn noted that:

"Since the reign of Võ Vương (1738) luxury had prevailed, and petty mandarins were imitating higher officials. Houses were sculptured, walls built of stone, hangings and curtains made of silk, plates and dishes of bronze or porcelain, the furniture of valuable timbers, and harnesses were decorated with gold and silver. They regarded gold and silver as sand, rice as dirt."

Around 1765 real power fell into the hands of the regent Trương Phúc Loan, who amassed a colossal fortune for himself by every possible means. Oppression and injustice prevailed, and the feudal class became predatory and corrupt. The bureaucracy of mandarins and petty officials was expanding beyond measure at all levels.

Famines occurred repeatedly in the provinces of Trung Bộ; in 1751 a report by the mandarin Nguyễn Cư Trinh noted that many inhabitants had failed to register, either to escape taxes or because they had been reduced to misery and vagrancy. Foreign trade was dwindling, one of the major causes being bribes extorted from foreign merchants by the mandarins in positions of responsibility.

Another factor in the upheaval was monetary depreciation. Unlike the Trịnh domain, the south under the Nguyễn did not have any copper mines, and the court was compelled to mint zinc coins (in reality an alloy of zinc and tin), much less durable than copper coins. Even private citizens were allowed to make zinc coins. This resulted in rapid depreciation of the currency, soaring prices and speculation by merchants.

The above-mentioned report by Nguyễn Cư Trinh included the following warning to the Nguyễn lords:

"I beg to observe most humbly that the people's misery has reached an extreme level; if you continue to rule with indifference, without thinking of taking appropriate measures, even the administration of a village will become impossible, let alone that of a province, or the whole country... The people no longer have anything to live on; how can their hearts be at peace?"

In the late 17th century, uprisings occurred in various provinces, involving tradesmen and highlanders together with peasants.

The End of the Nguyễn Lords

In 1771, in Tây Sơn village, Bình Định province, three brothers named Nguyễn Nhạc, Nguyễn Huệ and Nguyễn Lữ launched an insurgency movement that swiftly spread to neighbouring localities. Nhạc was a petty functionary who had worked as a tax-collector; his brother Huệ was soon to reveal himself as one of the most brilliant figures in Việt Nam's history.

The Tây Sơn brothers managed to give the movement an effective political orientation right from the beginning. On the one hand, they presented themselves as defenders of poor peasants, thus rallying the peasant masses; on the other, they claimed that they only opposed the regent Trương Phúc Loan in order to restore the authority of the Nguyễn lords. This sowed division among the followers of the regime. They also knew how to rally various ethnic minorities, especially the Bahnar.

"They began moving through villages," reported a Spanish missionary, *"announcing to the inhabitants that they were not bandits, but envoys from Heaven, that they wanted to see justice prevail and liberate*

the people from the tyranny of the king and his mandarins. They preached equality in everything. And faithful to their doctrine, these forerunners of modern socialism robbed mandarins and the rich of their property, which they distributed to the poor. The villagers, labouring under exorbitant tributes, were willing to swear allegiance."

(Quoted by Chesneaux in *Contributions to the History of the Vietnamese Nation*)

The rallying of the people and especially of the peasants gave great strength to the movement, which also had the support of highlanders. In 1773, the Tây Sơn seized the city of Quy Nhơn; rich merchants, oppressed by the mandarin bureaucracy of the Nguyễn, gave them support. They then took the provinces of Quảng Ngãi and Quảng Nam.

The Trịnh lords took advantage of the Nguyễn's difficulties in order to invade their territory. Late in 1774, a Trịnh army seized the capital, Phú Xuân, and the Nguyễn, caught in the crossfire, had to flee. The Trịnh and Tây Sơn troops found themselves facing each other in Quảng Nam in 1775, and joined forces so as to concentrate their efforst against the remainder of the Nguyễn army.

After the conquest of the provinces of Trung Bộ, the Tây Sơn entered Gia Định in 1776. The Gia Định landlords organized themselves to resist, but failed in their attempt, and the last bulwark of the Nguyễn lords thus crumbled. Only one prince, Nguyễn Ánh, managed to escape. He dug in with his partisans in the western area of the Mekong delta. In 1778, Nguyễn Nhạc proclaimed himself king, establishment his capital at Đồ Bàn in Bình Định province.

After reorganizing his forces, Nguyễn Ánh counter-attacked, for a time with success, reconquering Gia Định and the province of Bình Thuận; but in 1783, a counter-offensive led by Nguyễn Huệ routed his forces, forcing him to take refuge on Phú Quốc Island. Nguyễn Ánh then resorted to the classic tactic of feudal lords in distress - calling in foreigners. He asked for help from the Siamese monarchy which sent to rescue him an army of 20,000 men (some documents say 50,000) with 300 vessels. In 1784, the Siamese army invaded the western part of the Mekong delta. Nguyễn Huệ set out to meet them, and lured the Siamese fleet into an ambush on the Mỹ Tho River in the district of Rạch Gầm -Xoài Mút. Only 2,000 of the Siamese army survived, fleeing overland to the west (25 January 1785). It was one of the finest victories in Việt Nam's history, remarkable for the speed with which it was won. It cut short Siamese attempts at expansion into Nam Bộ.

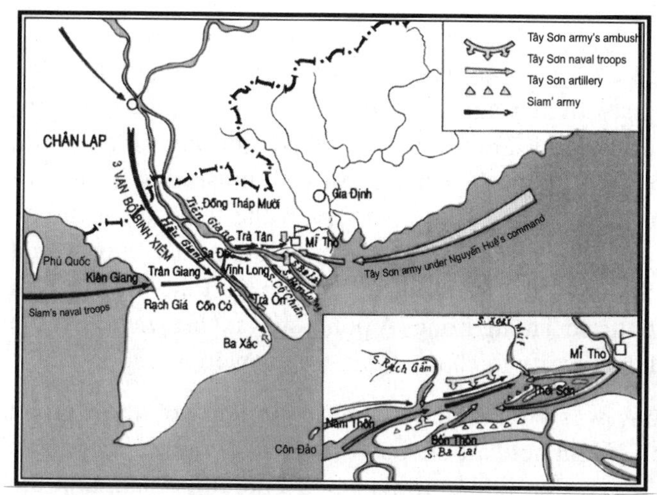
Tây Sơn army's ambus
Tây Sơn naval troops
Tây Sơn artillery
Siam' army
CHÂN LẠP
3 VẠN BỘ BINH XIÊM
Đồng Tháp Mười
Gia Định
Tiền Giang
Hậu Giang
Trà Tân
Mĩ Tho
Sa Đéc
Phú Quốc
Kiên Giang
Trần Giang
Vĩnh Long
Tây Sơn army under Nguyễn Huệ's command
Siam's naval troops
Rạch Giá
Cồn Cỏ
Trà Ôn
Ba Xắc
Côn Đảo
Mĩ Tho
S. Rạch Gầm
Thới Sơn
Nam Thôn
S. Ba Lai

RẠCH GẦM - XOÀI MÚT BATTLE (19.1 - 1785)

Nguyễn Huệ emerged as a brilliant strategist and national hero in contrast to Nguyễn Ánh, who had tried to win back his throne by relying on foreign troops.

The End of the Trịnh and National Reunification

Having removed the Nguyễn, the Tây Sơn turned against the Trịnh, whose army had occupied Phú Xuân. In June 1786, Nguyễn Huệ led his troops across the Pass of Clouds, capturing Phú Xuân then Quảng Trị and Quảng Bình provinces. The general public assisted the Tây Sơn troops everywhere. The Trịnh court was then in crisis, with different factions competing for power. The Tây Sơn swiftly advanced northwards and reached the Red River delta as early as July 1786. Nguyễn Huệ shrewdly represented himself as a defender of the Lê royal dynasty whose authority had been usurped by the Trịnh. Support from the population, the Tây Sơn troops' enthusiasm and excellent command by Nguyễn Huệ rapidly got the better of the Trịnh army. The Trịnh-Nguyễn secession was brought to an end and the country reunified. This was one of the great achievements of the Tây Sơn.

Nguyễn Huệ paid homage to King Lê who gave him his daughter Ngọc Hân in marriage. The Lê monarchy was thus restored. Shortly afterwards, King Lê Hiển Tông died, leaving the throne to Lê Chiêu Thống. Nguyễn Huệ returned to the South.

The new king, who understood nothing about these past events, thought he could outwit the Tây Sơn with the help of adventurers, but the latter were soon executed by Nguyễn Huệ, and King Chiêu Thống had to flee the capital.

Victory over the Qing

Defeated, King Chiêu Thống resorted to treason, appealing to the Manchu Qing dynasty then reigning over China. The Qing Emperor Kien-lung, who harboured ambitions of re-conquering Việt Nam, charged Governor Tôn Sĩ Nghị (Soun Che-y) with mustering a force of 200,000 men for an invasion. On the 20th day of the tenth lunar month of the year 1788, the Qing troops set out, proclaiming that they would "destroy the Tây Sơn and restore the Lê." On the 21st day of the 11th lunar month, they entered Thăng Long. A pontoon was thrown across the Red River, on both banks of which the Qing troops were camped.

Lê Chiêu Thống was proclaimed "King of Annam" by the Beijing Court; in fact, Tôn Sĩ Nghị held all the power, and every morning people in the capital could see the king and his small entourage summon the Qing governor for an audience. The actions of the Qing troops managed to open the eyes of those who had been mistaken about the real intentions of the invaders. Only Chiêu Thống and the reactionary feudal lords who wanted to defend their privileges at any cost still clung to the coattails of the occupiers. Feelings ran high among the population; the prestige of the Lê dynasty was destroyed.

At this time Nguyễn Huệ was in Phú Xuân. The Tây Sơn brothers had divided the country among themselves; the eldest, Nguyễn Nhạc, reigned over the central region from Quy Nhơn, Lữ was charged with governing Gia Định and the Mekong delta, and Huệ took charge of the area north of the Hải Vân (Pass of Clouds).

To deal with the Qing invasion, Nguyễn Huệ acted in the name of the whole nation betrayed by the Lê. In a solemn ceremony, he proclaimed himself king, taking the royal name of Quang Trung, and immediately ordered his troops to march on Thăng Long. It was 21 December 1788. By December 26, the Tây Sơn army was in Nghệ An; 100, 000 men were reviewed by Nguyễn Hueệ, who addressed them in the following words:

"The Qing have invaded our country and occupied the capital city, Thăng Long. In our history, the Trưng sisters fought against the Han, Đinh Tiên Hoàng against the Sung, Trần Hưng Đạo against the Mongols, and Lê Lợi against the Ming. These heroes did not resign themselves to standing by and seeing the invaders plunder our country; they inspired the people to fight for a just cause and drive out the aggressors... The Qing, forgetting what happened to the Sung, Mongols and Ming, have invaded our country. We are going to drive them out of our territory."

The year was drawing to a close. It was the 20th day of the 12th lunar month. Arriving at Ninh Bình, Nguyễn Huệ ordered his troops to celebrate New Year's Day in advance and told them:

"On the seventh day of the first month of the New Year, we shall enter Thăng Long and celebrate the spring festival there. Mark my words. That is what will happen."

The Tây Sơn army took ten days' rest to recruit new troops, then on the 30th day of the 12th month began marching on Thăng Long in three

RESISTANCE AGAINST THE QING INVADERS
(1788 - 1789)

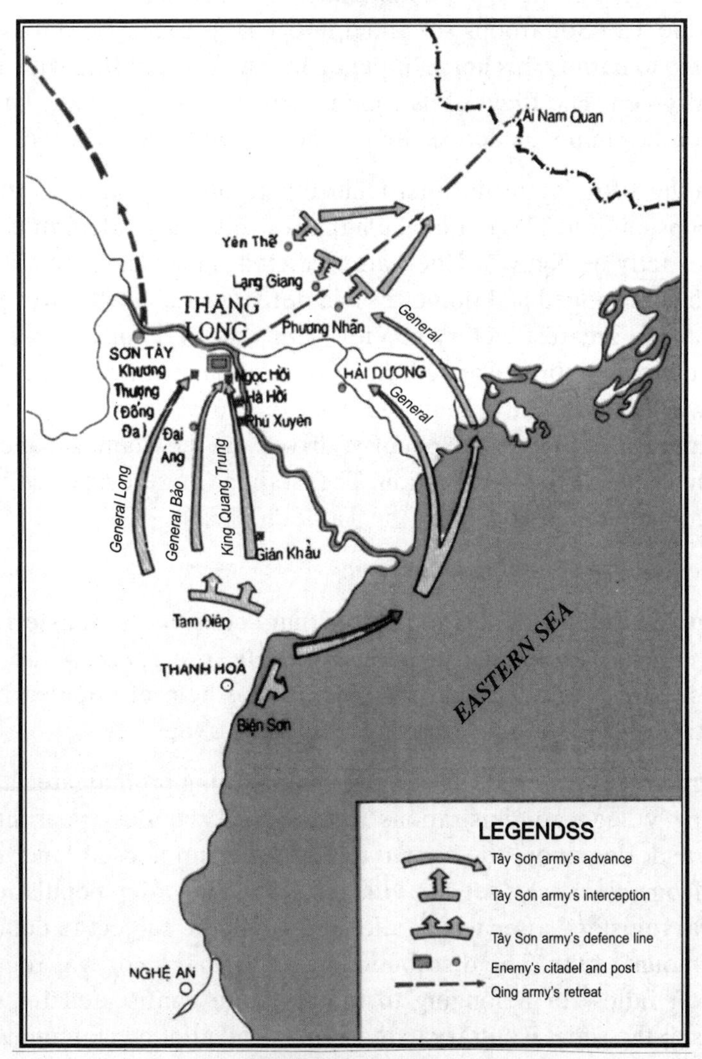
Ải Nam Quan
Yên Thế
Lạng Giang
THĂNG LONG
Phượng Nhãn
SƠN TÂY
Khương Thượng (Đống Đa)
Ngọc Hồi
Hà Hồi
Phú Xuyên
HẢI DƯƠNG
General
General
Đại Áng
General Long
General Bảo
King Quang Trung
Gián Khẩu
Tam Điệp
THANH HOÁ
Biện Sơn
EASTERN SEA
NGHỆ AN
LEGENDSS
Tây Sơn army's advance
Tây Sơn army's interception
Tây Sơn army's defence line
Enemy's citadel and post
Qing army's retreat

different columns. The one commanded by Nguyễn Huệ rushed towards Thăng Long, overran Qing outposts and on the third day of the first month of the New Year encircled the post of Hạ Hồi, 20 kilometres south of the capital. The Hạ Hồi garrison surrendered on 28 January 1789. On January 30, the Tây Sơn, with troops riding elephants forming the spearhead, attacked the post of Ngọc Hồi, 15 kilometres south of Thăng Long, and swiftly captured it. The road to Thăng Long was open.

The two other Tây Sơn columns rapidly overran the posts that defended the capital to the west; the Đống Đa post (now in Hà Nội itself) was taken after a day of fierce fighting. The post's commander hanged himself on a tree. The Tây Sơn victories were so quickly won that Tôn Sĩ Nghị, the Qing commander-in-chief, had no time to react before the Tây Sơn troops streamed into Thăng Long. He did not even have time to harness his horse or put on his cuirass, and fled with a group of cavalrymen. The flight of its commander-in-chief threw the Qing into panic. In the stampede across the pontoon many were drowned.

On the fifth day of the first lunar month of the year 1789, the Tây Sơn troops entered Thăng Long. On the seventh, they celebrated victory there, exactly as Nguyễn Huệ had predicted. In six days, the Tây Sơn troops had advanced 80 kilometres and defeated a 200, 000 strong army. This was the greatest victory in Việt Nam's history, and was won in an extremely short time. Carried along by a popular movement, Nguyễn Huệ, who had already achieved the defeat of the Trịnh -Nguyễn secession, had reunified the country, driven out the Siamese, and saved the country from Qing domination. The Beijing Court reconciled itself to making peace and recognizing the Tây Sơn.

The Achievement of Quang Trung

Nguyễn Huệ, now King Quang Trung, considered transferring his capital to the province of Nghệ An. He reorganized the army, administration and education system with the help of talented people. Lê partisans tried to incite uprisings, but to no avail.

Immediately after his accession, Quang Trung promulgated an edict enjoining village administrations to take back landless peasants who were wandering about the country, and to reclaim unused land. A time limit of one year was set for villages to put in order population and cadastral registers, after which idle land would be subject to double the usual amount of tax. The distribution of communal lands was regulated; lands left fallow or belonging to traitors were confiscated for use by villages or the state. Contrary to the Trịnh, who allotted communal lands

chiefly to officials and soldiers, Quang Trung gave them mainly to peasant. "The important task of a king," proclaimed the edict on agriculture, "is to attend to the roots and lop off the top, so that the people enjoy peace and have land to till, that nobody is jobless and the fields do not lie unused."

As early as 1791, agricultural production had returned to normal. Quang Trung also strove to develop handicrafts and trade. In 1788, he said to his adviser Nguyễn Thiếp: "I wish we did not buy so many articles from abroad". He abolished restrictions imposed on trade by the Trịnh. Nguyễn Huy Lượng, a poet of the time, celebrated the rebirth of trade in Thăng Long as follows:

Wreaths of smoke crown the kilns of Thạch Khối
Shuttles sing in the hands of brocade-weavers
From Yên Thái comes the sound of pestles pounding paper pulp
In Nghi Tàm fishing nets fence in the waters
Markets are crowded with traders from east and west
Like butterflies, junk sails are pressed together.

King Quang Trung also sought to develop exchanges with China. Accounts by European merchants and missionaries tend to confirm that the Tây Sơn practised an open -door policy. Fiscal laws were simplified as compared with those of the Trịnh.

The major reform carried out by Quang Trung in the field of culture was the adoption of *nôm*, the national script, for official texts and in education, instead of classical Chinese, which had been in use for centuries. In 1791, Nguyễn Thiếp was charged with directing the translation of Confucian classics intended for use in education. This was opposed by reactionary and backward -thinking scholars. Quang Trung also sought to reform the content of education, which had degenerated into repetition of empty formulas. Each village was required to choose a scholar capable of founding a school; scholars from the old regime had to undertake new examinations. Adventurers and exploiters, who had taken refuge in pagodas and monasteries, had to return to secular life, and only genuinely religious people were allowed to stay. Catholic missionaries were not persecuted.

The reign of Quang Trung was a significant one on account of its military achievements and its economic and educational reforms. Unfortunately, in 1792, Quang Trung died suddenly and neither his brothers nor his son Quang Toản proved capable of carrying on the work he had begun.

End of the Tây Sơn and the Nguyễn Restoration

The most vulnerable part of the Tây Sơn kingdom was Gia Định in the south, where landlords were able to organize themselves, and where administration was entrusted to the youngest Tây Sơn brother, Nguyễn Lữ. In 1784 a Nguyễn prince, Nguyễn Ánh, had tried to restore the influence of his family with the help of the Siamese, but Nguyễn Huệ drove out the invaders.

Sticking to his policy of treason, Nguyễn Ánh did not content himself with asking for help from the Siamese; he also contacted a French missionary, Pigneau de Béhaine, Bishop of Adran, who advised him to appeal to France. The French missionary took one of Nguyễn Ánh's sons to France where, with the help of the Foreign Missions, he managed to obtain an audience with Louis XVI. On 28 November 1787, a treaty was signed between a representative of France and Pigneau de Béhaine representing Nguyễn Ánh. France promised military aid in exchange for the ceding of the port of Tourane and the Poulo-Condore Islands, and the right to free trade inside Việt Nam to the exclusion of other European nations. Thus Nguyễn Ánh, by opening the way to French imperialism, "introduced a snake into the family henhouse." The French monarchy, soon to be overthrown by the 1789 Revolution, was unable to keep its promise of military aid to Nguyễn Ánh, although Pigneau de Béhaine, with the help of French merchants and adventurers, supplied him with some equipment and military instructors. However, it was not this assistance but the internal difficulties of the Tây Sơn regime that enabled Nguyễn Ánh to set foot again on Việt Nam territory.

Nguyễn Huệ's brothers had neither his military nor political abilities. Dissension arose between the three brothers, and Nguyễn Huệ being fully occupied in the North, Nguyễn Ánh took advantage of this to seize Gia Định (1788). After strengthening his forces, he pushed his offensive northward. The deaths of Nguyễn Huệ in 1792 and Nguyễn Nhạc in 1793, and the accession to the throne of Nguyễn Huệ's son, Quang Toản at only ten, brought about a series of internal squabbles which weakened the Tây Sơn considerably. In the meantime, Nguyễn Ánh implemented a skilful policy that gradually strengthened his position. From 1790 to 1800, the two adversaries conducted an indecisive war, the prize being the city of Quy Nhơn, which changed hands several times.

After 1800, Nguyễn Ánh gained the upper hand and increased his attacks northward. In 1801, while the Tây Sơn forces were pinned down around Quy Nhơn, those of the Nguyễn captured Phú Xuân, where

Nguyễn Ánh established his headquarters. In 1802, his forces were ready to march northward to conquer the Red River delta. On 1 June 1802, before undertaking this expedition, he proclaimed himself king under the name Gia Long. The Tây Sơn offered only sporadic resistance. On July 20, Nguyễn Ánh entered Thăng Long, inaugurating a new dynasty, the Nguyễn.

The Tây Sơn had been brought to power by the great peasant insurrections of the 18th century. Commercial elements had joined in, without however playing a prominent role. Nguyễn Huệ's military and political genius, relying on this vast strength of the peasants in revolt, had enabled the insurrection to achieve rapid, sometimes lightning, success. It is impossible to overestimate the importance of the Tây Sơn who achieved the reunification of the country, long divided by the Trịnh -Nguyễn secession, and the glory of having twice saved the fatherland, first from the Siamese then from the Qing invasions. The Tây Sơn must also be credited with economic and cultural reforms, which brought peace and prosperity for a short period of time.

The Tây Sơn movement, however, had inherent weaknesses. The peasantry in revolt, though constituting a major force, could not assume the task of renewing a feudal society torn apart by insurmountable contradictions. The distribution of property on a more equal basis could not constitute a basis for a revolutionary program or new system. In the 18th century, Vietnamese society still had no social class associated with a new mode of production and a new ideology. The merchant class, certainly progressing in comparison with previous centuries, remained however in an embryonic state incapable of providing the movement with leadership. Neither the development of handicrafts, nor the beginning of exchange with Europe in the 17th century, was able to promote the development of a sufficiently strong bourgeoisie.

The result was that the leadership of the movement, after a period of intense activity, could only turn back to feudal structures. The "rebels" established a new monarchy and promulgated various reforms, but did not touch the underlying basis of the feudal system, the system of land ownership. Feudal ideas continued to prevail in all spheres, both socially and ideological. The division of power among the three Tây Sơn brothers, and the internal dissension that followed, also sprang from feudalism. The administrative apparatus of the Tây Sơn simply carried on the work of former dynasties using the same methods of government. Following Nguyễn Huệ's death, the first reforms soon tapered off and the new dynasty quickly lost its authority. The large landowners of Gia Định, then those of other provinces, supported Nguyễn ánh and eventually succeeded in overthrowing the Tây Sơn and restoring feudalism.

It was thanks to the great victories won by Nguyễn Huệ that the southern secession came to an end and the Siamese and Chinese invasions were repelled. His legacy, a unified and sovereign country, lapsed however, after the death of the hero and the enthronement of his adversary.

Gia Long established his capital in Huế, set up an absolute monarchy with a mandarin bureaucracy recruited through competitive examinations, and adopted Confucianism as the official doctrine in its most conservative and ritualistic form. The Nguyễn kings built a royal citadel and magnificent tombs in Huế and its vicinity. The exploitation of the Mekong delta began, with the digging of large canals.

However, the regime was unable to solve all the major problems of Vietnamese society, which was in crisis at the time. The peasants and ethnic minorities in mountainous regions rebelled time and again. The mandarin bureaucracy stifled all signs of the growth of a merchant class. Foreign trade was monopolized by the state, which was content to place orders with Chinese and other foreign traders. In foreign relations, the Nguyễn kings recognized the symbolic authority of Beijing, but pursued a policy of influencing Laos and Cambodia. It was from this position of weakness that in the middle of the 19th century the regime was to face French colonial aggression.

Chapter VI

HISTORICAL OVERVIEW OF THE STATES ON THE INDOCHINESE PENINSULA

It is impossible to understand the historical development of the Vietnamese nation without seeing it within the framework of the Indochinese peninsula, where over the centuries various states were created and maintained amongst themselves sometimes friendly and sometimes hostile relation. All of these states saw various ups and downs before the emergence in the 19th century of Việt Nam. Cambodia, Laos, Siam (Thailand) and Burma. One of the early states - Champa - after many centuries of struggle marked by victories and defeats, was annexed by its neighbours - Việt Nam and Cambodia.

The State of Champa

In the 1st century B.C. when imperial troops imposed Chinese domination on Vietnam, various Malayo-Polynesian ethnic groups living south of the 18th parallel, together with proto-Vietnamese elements, gathered together to form autonomous principalities. Those living on the territory of present-day Quảng Nam, Quảng Ngãi and Bình ằịnh provinces - called the Coconut-palm group, or Narikelavamsa in Sanskrit - also had to accept Chinese domination, their territory becoming the commandery of Jenan integrated into the Chinese Han empire.

Further to the south the Areca-palm group - or Kramukavamsa in Sanskrit - founded in the 1st century an autonomous kingdom which would later adopt the name Panduranga, the territory of which extended from the Cù Mẳng Pass to the Đồng Nai River basin. Confronted with Chinese imperial domination and threats, the Malayo-Polynesian groups

coordinated efforts with those of the Vietnamese against the common enemy. Many insurrections broke out, often in coordination with those of proto-Vietnamese groups, especially in the southernmost regions. By the end of the 2nd century, China was being shaken by serous disturbances; the population in the territories south of the Hải Vân Pass and belonging to the Coconut-palm group rose in revolt, declared their autonomy and created a kingdom extending from the Hải Vân Pass to the Cù Mông Pass (present-day Quảng Nam, Quảng Ngãi and Bình Định provinces) which Chinese historians called Lin Yi (or Lâm Ấp in Vietnamese). In the 4th century, troops advancing northwards killed the Chinese governor of Jenan and extended their territory to the Ngang Pass on the 18th parallel. It was only in the 6th century that the name Champa would appear on the stone stelae of the kingdom. There were in that era, therefore, two kingdoms, Champa-North and Champa-South (formerly Panduranga), probably allies and both with mainly Malayo-Polynesian populatons.

The unification of the kingdom may have been achieved during the reign of Bhadravarman I, the territory of Champa then extending up to the Ngang Pass. However, the northern part of Champa was frequently invaded by Chinese troops each time an imperial dynasty managed to ensure a long period of stability, and each time there were disturbances in China. Champa reconquered its lost territories. Chinese troops attacked the capital of Champa several times, destroying palaces and monuments, and carrying off large quantities of booty. But the Cham put up stubborn resistance each time, compelling the Chinese troops to withdraw.

Under the Gangaraja dynasty (6th to 8th century), which comprised nine successive kings, the capital was transferred to Sinhapura (or City of Lions) on the present-day site of Trà Kiệu, on the southern bank of the Thu Bồn River, southwest of Đà Nẵng. About 20 kilometres from Sinhapura was the temple complex of Mỹ Sơn, intended for the veneration of Hindu gods, the construction of which lasted for several centuries.

It was an era of predominance for the Coconut-palm group of Champa-North, which drew its power from the resources of the vast region covered by present-day Quảng Nam, more populous than the plains situated further south. The dissensions and conflicts between the two parts of Champa without a doubt constituted an element of weakness for the kingdom, together with the threat from Chinese expansion on to the territory of ancient Việt Nam.

However, it is difficult to know exactly why in the 8th and 9th centuries Champa was compelled to transfer its capital southwards to Po

Nagar on the site of present-day Nha Trang. Although firmly established in the south, the royal dynasty kept enforcing its rule over the northern part of the country.

From the middle of the 9th century to the end of the 10th century, the groups ruling the north re-established their supremacy and the capital was transferred to Indrapura (or City of the God Indra), 15 kilometres from the former capital, Sinhapura.

In the 7th century, Champa adopted Buddhism without giving up Hinduism, and royal palaces were situated next to Buddhist pagodas. Champa entered a period of prosperity and conducted three offensives against territories under Chinese domination in A.D. 851, 862 and 865, according to Chinese annals. In the south, Champa not only repelled a Khmer invasion from the kingdom of Chen La in A.D. 889-890, but also pursued the enemy on to their own territory, inflicting serious losses.

*

*　　*

The territory of Champa comprised a chain of small coastal plains hemmed in by the East Sea, Trường Sơn range and the Central Highlands. The country was divided by transverse mountain ranges, making communication between provinces quite difficult. However, although the plains were small, the territory had a coastal area and mountainous region rich in plant and mineral resources. In particular, gold from various deposits was used to make many statues of Hindu gods or the Buddha, which impressed foreign visitors while arousing the jealousy of sovereigns of neighbouring countries and of the Chinese governors of Chiao Chih. Moreover, to the south of the 16th parallel, below the Hải Vân Pass, warm temperatures all year round favoured the development of agriculture, and particularly rice cultivation. Thus, mineral exploitation, ocean fishing, forest exploitation and especially agriculture constituted a solid base for the kingdom, provided political stability could be ensured.

The Cham already knew how to obtain two rice crops a year and built a system of hydraulic works, the remains of which suggest greater sophistication than those built by the Vietnamese at that time. They managed to obtain a rice strain with a short three-month ripening period, introduced to China in the 11th century by an imperial decree ordering its cultivation in all southern Chinese provinces.

Coconut and areca-palms constituted two essential resources in both the economic and religious life of the country, having given their names

to the kingdom's two most important clans. Further south, near the Đồng Nai River basin, the climate was drier and vegetation more abundant, while the coast was favourable for the development of ocean fishing and salt production.

It was on the basis of a relatively developed economy that the Cham were able to build their unique monuments, temples in the form of towers on hills, still seen along the coast of central Việt Nam. Dedicated to Hindu gods or the Buddha, they are quadrangular in shape and made entirely of baked bricks put together using an unidentified mortar. The towers were topped with conical turrets. The insides and outsides of the walls were decorated with lively sculptures showing sophisticated artistic techniques. The characters and subjects were drawn from Indian myths but portrayed in Cham style. This art form, together with Cham music, had a marked influence upon that of Việt Nam.

Surviving documents and relics suggest that Cham society was governed by an absolute monarch, royal power relying on ownership of all the land in the country. Royal functionaries did not have salaries but were allotted land and the right to collect rent from the peasants who lived on it. Lands were also allotted to temples, so that peasants who had to deliver part of their crop for religious purposes were exempt from taxes and corvée. The ruling aristocracy comprised the members of the royal family, high-ranking dignitaries and high priests.

The peasants led a communal life style in rural communes, making up the main workforce. There were also domestic slaves in the great families, and slave-musicians, dancers and builders of palaces and temples. It is difficult to know exactly what role slaves played in the economy, but they were probably quite numerous, judging by the number of royal and religious edifices.

We do not know how the apparatus of power comprising the aristocracy and royal functionaries worked. However, given the Indian structure on which it was modeled, we can surmise that it was fairly loose and that the principle of absolute royal authority did not preclude clan rivalries in the race for supreme power, particularly as centralized power could not be easily imposed on a geographically divided territory with difficult communications. The northern and southern clans continued to clash with each other. When Việt Nam in the 15th century adopted a system of centralized monarchy with a body of mandarins trained in the Confucian school and recruited through examinations, Champa with its strict administrative apparatus and without appanage and serfdom faced its northern neighbour from a position of weakness.

It was also caught at this time in a pincer movement, as it was being simultaneously pressured by the Khmer kingdom, which had been expanding since the 9th century, from the south.

The monarch - the supreme civil authority - was also the incarnation of the divine, of Shiva when Hinduism was predominant, and later on of the Buddha. Indian Brahmans lived at court as advisers to the king. After the 7th century, the adoption of Buddhism did not entail the exclusion of Hinduism and the two religions coexisted. Judging by the land devoted to religion and the number of religious edifices built, considerable work was required of the population; religious practices literally exhausting the country's material and human resources, constituting another factor in its weakness.

The Khmer kingdom and the glory of Angkor

In the 10th century, when ancient Việt Nam had gained its independence under the name Đại Việt, there was already a developed kingdom in the Mekong delta, Kambuja, which Chinese historians called Chen La. The Mekong delta, one of the largest river deltas in Asia, extended from the Tonle Sap to the sea. Chen La consisted of a 'Land' Chen La, covering the present-day territory of Cambodia, particularly the region around the Great Lake, and of a 'Water' Chen La, around the estuary of the Mekong. In fact, until the 17th century, the lower part of the delta, still in the course of formation, comprised virtually uninhabited vast swamps and forest. This region came under Javanese influence until the Khmer King Jayavarman II managed to drive out the Javanese and reunify the country in the 9th century, founding the kingdom of Angkor. As in Champa, the influence of Indian civilization was predominant.

From the 10th to 13th centuries, the Angkor-based Khmer kings succeeded in establishing a stable regime, particularly significant for the construction of major hydraulic works and palaces, sanctuaries and temples, the best known being Angkor Wat and Angkor Thom. The magnificence of the Angkor monarchy, which the Angkor monuments give us a fairly good idea of, was described by Chou Ta Kuan, a member of a Chinese mission visiting Angkor in 1296, as follows:

"When the king goes out, his troops lead the vanguard, then come flags, pennons and musical troupes. From three to five hundred girls of the palace clad in floral fabrics, with flowers in their hair, bring lighted candles in their hands - even in full daylight. Then come girls of the palace

carrying gold and silver royal utensils and a host of the ornaments with unique patterns and of unknown use. After them, other girls of the palace carry spears and shields - the private guard of the prince. In their footsteps follow she-goat and horse-drawn carts decorated with gold. Courtiers and princes ride elephants, preceded by countless red parasols. Behind them come the king's wives and concubines in palankeens, carts, on horses or elephants, with more than a hundred parasols dotted with gold. At the end, the king stands on an elephant with a precious sword in his hand. The elephant's tusks have golden sheaths. There are more than twenty white parasols dotted with gold and whose handles are made of gold. Many elephants crowd around the king and his escort".

The might of the Angkor royal house reached its peak under Suryavarman II in the 11th century, the builder of Angkor Wat, and Jayavarman VII in the 12th century, also a great builder of palaces and temples. This development was interspersed with tragic episodes. While conflicts with neighbouring states sometimes led to territorial expansion, even as far as the Menam delta in the west, at the expense of Champa in the east, and northwards up to the present-day territory of Laos, they sometimes led also to disaster. This policy of grandeur, marked by the construction of gigantic complexes of monuments within the country and by continual wars against neighbouring states, was to bring the Angkor royalty into decline.

Conflicts: Đại Việt - Champa - Chen La - Siam

The territory situated between the Ngang and Hải Vân passes (present-day Quảng Bình, Quảng Trị and Thừa Thiên Huế provinces), inhabited by a population comprising proto-Vietnamese and Malayo-Polynesians, was a frequent bone of contention between Champa and the Chinese occupiers of ancient Việt Nam. When the latter achieved its independence, the Đại Việt and Champa kingdoms contended with each other for the same region.

It could be said that until the 14th century the balance of forces was not absolutely in favour of one or the other, each of them experiencing periodic internal crises which gave the enemy the opportunity for attack. Thus in 981, when the Đại Việt King Lê Hoàn was forced to deal with Chinese troops, Champa sent an expedition against the Vietnamese capital, then located at Hoa Lư, but to no avail. Having repelled the Chinese aggressors, Lê Hoàn led his troops on to the capital of Champa.

This victory was by no means decisive, as Đại Việt was to sustain many more large -scale Chinese invasions and was also rocked by periodic crises. The transfer of the Chàm capital in the year 1000 southwards to Vijaya (near present-day Quy Nhơn) did not perhaps mean a change in the balance of forces in favour of Đại Việt. In 1371, the Chàm king Chế Bồng Nga, with a powerful army, entered the capital of Đại Việt to plunder it. The Trần dynasty was then in complete crisis, and it was only when Chế Bồng Nga died on the battlefield that Đại Việt was saved from disaster. After a period of peace, hostilities resumed early in the 15th century when Champa took advantage of an invasion of Đại Việt by the Ming army to attack it from the south. Once the Ming aggressors were driven out, the Lê kings were able to rapidly eliminate the Chàm threat.

From the 11th to 15th centuries, however, Việt Nam's might kept increasing, while Champa also had to confront the challenge of the Khmer kingdom to the south, gradually losing its offensive capability. In the 6th century, before the Khmer kingdom was firmly established, Champa was making incursions into the Mekong delta. With the consolidation of the Khmer kingdom, the conflict then went through alternate victories and defeats for one or the other party. In 1100, the Khmers incited a revolt in Champa and occupied part of the country for a time. A few years later, the Chàm took their revenge, to again be attacked by the Khmers who drove the Chàm troops up the border with Đại Việt, occupied the capital Vijaya in 1145 and imposed Khmer rule for four years. Then in 1147, Champa took its revenge, occupying the Khmer capital and imposing its rule also for four years. However, early in the 13th century, the Khmer King Jayavarman VII built a powerful army, invaded Champa and annexed one of its provinces, merging it with the Khmer kingdom.

Caught in a pincer movement between its two neighbours, and suffering from many internal dissensions as aristocratic clans continually clashed, Champa finally had to yield. In 1471, an expeditionary force from Đại Việt conquered Vijaya, beginning the dismembering of the Chàm kingdom, and while their country was being systematically annexed by Đại Việt, the Chàm kings only held symbolic religious power.

In the 17th century, Đại Việt saw its frontiers reach the basins of the Đồng Nai and Mekong rivers, thus confronting the Khmer kingdom. The first clashes had in fact taken place in the 12th century when the territory of the kingdom of Angkor included part of present-day Laos and shared borders with Đại Việt. In 1128, the Khmer King Suryavarman II sent an expedition against Đại Việt, and the next year a fleet to plunder the

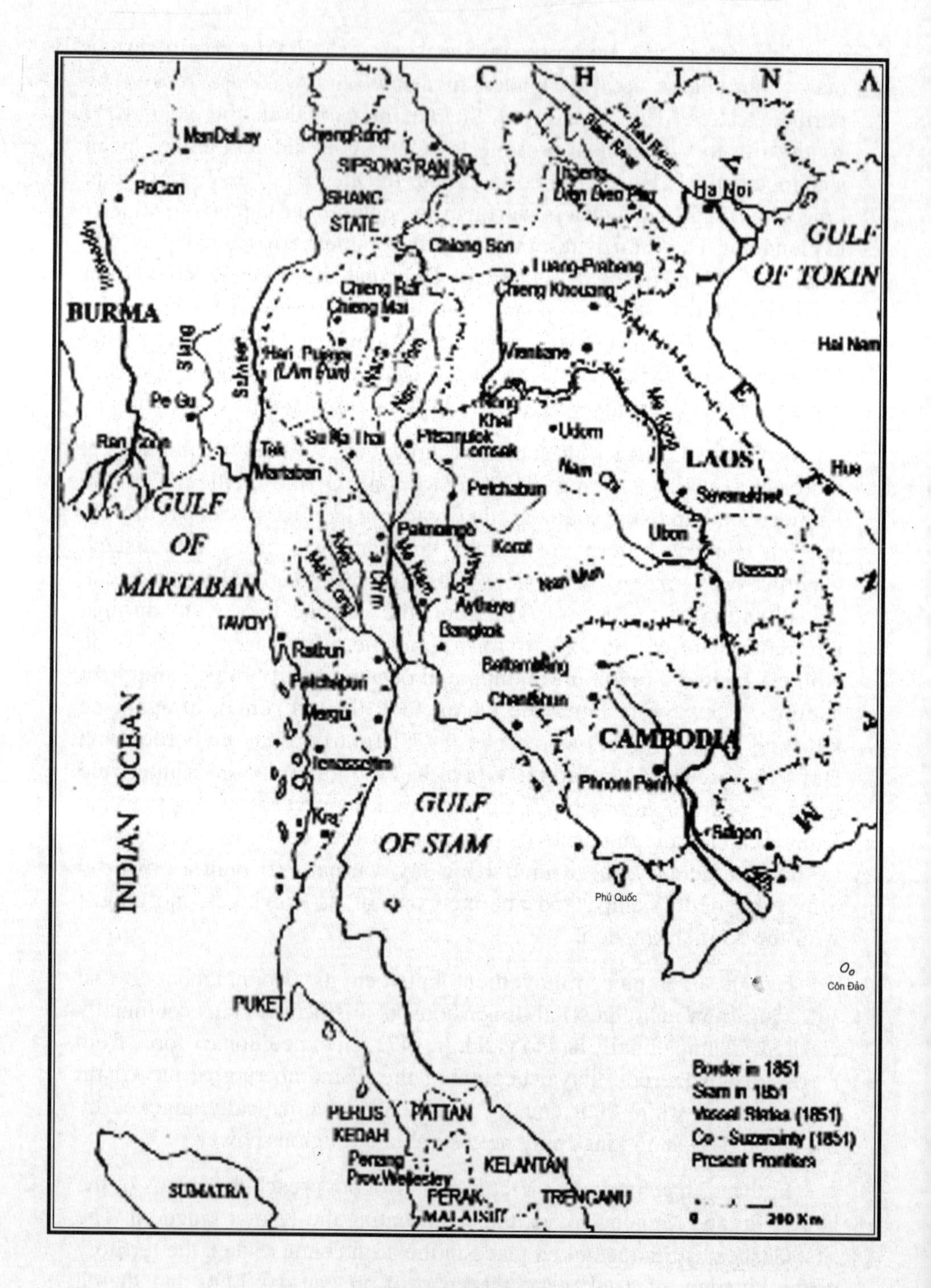
C H I N A
ManDaLay
PaCan
BURMA
Pe Gu
SHANG STATE
SIPSONG RAN NA
Chiang Son
Luang-Prabang
Cheng Khouang
Chiang Mai
Vientiane
Nong Khai
Ha Noi
GULF OF TOKIN
Hai Nam
Udom
LAOS
Hue
Savanakhet
Ubon
Bassac
Pitsanulok
Lomsak
Petchabun
Paknampo
Korat
Aythaya
Bangkok
Martaban
GULF OF MARTABAN
TAVOY
Ratburi
Petchaburi
Mergui
Kra
INDIAN OCEAN
GULF OF SIAM
Battambang
CAMBODIA
Phnom Penh
Saigon
Phú Quốc
Côn Đảo
PUKET
PERLIS
KEDAH
PATTAN
Penang
Prov.Wellesley
KELANTAN
PERAK
TRENGANU
SUMATRA
Border in 1851
Siam in 1851
Vassal States (1851)
Co - Suzerainty (1851)
Present Frontiers
0
200 Km

Siam in 1851

Vietnamese coast. After being repulsed, the Khmers returned to the charge, this time together with Champa. As Đại Việt proceeded to defeat the aggressors, Champa dropped its Khmer ally. The Khmer king then turned his thirst for conquest against Champa, conquering Vijaya in 1145. In 1150, another Khmer expedition against Đại Việt again ended in failure.

The Khmer kingdom did not only have to contend with its eastern neighbours, but also with the Thai threat from the west.

Migrating from southern China, the Thai travelled down the basin of the Menam Chao Phraya River and set up small kingdoms including that of Sukhotai, which recognized the suzerainty of the Khmer kingdom. Following the 13th century Mongol invasions, which began the destruction of the Đại Lý kingdom (present-day Yunnan) in southern China and the conquest of the Pagan kingdom in Burma, the Thai wave of migration reached such a strength that it threatened local Mon kingdoms and Malayan principalities. Confronted with the Mongol threat, the Thai groups and kingdoms united, and gained control of the Menam Chao Phya basin during the reign of Rama Phamheng. Their might constituted a threat to neighbouring countries, the Khmer kingdom in particular.

In the mid-14th century, the Thai settled further south, establishing their capital at Ayutthaya and calling their kingdom Siam. Many conflicts divided the two kingdoms of the Thai and Khmer. Angkor was occupied but the Khmers were able to repel the aggressors thanks to disturbances in Siam. The Thai also had to cope with the Lao kingdoms of Luang Prabang and Vientiane to the northeast, and with the Burmese to the west. Conflicts and alliances, more or less stable, between the various Khmer, Thai, Lao and Burmese kingdoms marked the history of these countries for centuries. Finally, the pre-eminence of Siam began to make itself felt. In the 15th century, the Khmer kings transferred their capital to the present site of Phnom Penh, leaving Angkor, which was too near the Siamese border. In 1473, the Siamese invaded the provinces of Korat and Chantaboun, and occupied Angkor. In the 16th century, the Khmer King Ang Chan restored his country's power, established a capital at Lovek and defeated several Siamese offensives; his successor even invaded Siam, then at war with the Pegwans in Burma. Siam soon took its revenge, again conquering several Khmer provinces and Lovek. The fall of Lovek, after the abandonment of Angkor, marked the irreversible decline of the Khmer kingdom, henceforth to be sandwiched between two more powerful neighbours - Siam to the west and Đại Việt to the east. The ruling oligarchy of the country was then divided into two clans, each dependent on Siam or Đại Việt.

In the 17th century, as Champa disappeared under the twin pressure of Đại Việt and Chen La, the Vietnamese began reclaiming the Đồng Nai basin and later the Mekong basin; these territories were then virtually uninhabited, and the few Khmer colonies living there coexisted peacefully with the newcomers. By the end of the 17th century, a large group of supporters of China's Ming imperial dynasty, overthrown by the Manchu, arrived to seek refuge in Đại Việt, and were allowed by the Nguyễn lords to settle partly in the Đồng Nai basin and partly in the Mekong. The present -day population of Nam Bộ, therefore, has a triple origin: Vietnamese, Khmer and Chinese, with the Vietnamese predominating. In the 18th century, the exploitation of the Mekong delta began; starting from the junction of the two branches of the Mekong, the Vietnamese colonizers dug canals, moved into the interior and reclaimed the immense delta swamps.

For its part, after setting up its capital in Bangkok, consolidating its territory and repelling Burmese attacks, Siam again laid claim to the Khmer kingdom, coming up against Đại Việt ambitions. The Siamese, availing themselves of internal disturbances in Đại Việt, moved their troops up to the present-day town of Mỹ Tho where they were defeated by Nguyễn Huệ.

From the late 18th to mid-19th century, the rivalry in Cambodia between Đại Việt and Siam was intense. The Khmer monarches were supported at times by Đại Việt, then by Siam, these neighbouring countries being ready to send troops to Cambodia to impose their will.

It was the European colonial intervention - the British in Burma and French in Việt Nam - that gave the peoples of Indochina a common enemy, which ended conflicts that had lasted for centuries and ended in the 19th century with the formation of states with roughly their present frontiers. Of these, only Siam escaped direct colonization; a buffer state between the British colony of Burma and the three Indochinese states conquered by the French, Siam retained nominal independence but remained under the thumb of European imperialism. For all the peoples of the region, a new stage of history had begun - the colonial era.

Chapter VII

CULTURAL DEVELOPMENT

(From the 7th c. to the beginning of the 19th c.)

The decline of the feudal system, which began in the 17th century and resulted in a profound and irreversible crisis in the 18th century, had profound repercussions in the area of culture. While Confucianism, the official ideology, began to experience unprecedented upheaval, popular enthusiasm and certain elements of renewal instilled a new spirit into the nation's culture. Literature in *nôm* (national and popular language) saw considerable development, taking a significant lead over that written in classical Chinese. After the Tây Sơn dynasty was overthrown in 1802, a period of feudal restoration began. However, it could be said that in the area of culture, many works, which came into being at the beginning of the 19th century, had in fact been conceived in the 18th century. The works of Nguyễn Du, including *The Tale of Kiều*, is an example of this type of time lag between political and cultural history, which was a frequentl occurrence.

The Crisis in Confucian Ideology

Since the 15th century, Confucianism had been the only doctrine on the map, having become the official one of the monarchical state and mandarin bureaucracy. While putting aside all mysticism and containing positive elements inspired by practical humanism, it relied on extreme social conservatism and strict ritualism - two factors which kept people imprisoned by an immutable social hierarchy, stereotypical attitude, and rigid morality. As the feudal regime underwent a process of decline, the negative aspects of Confucianism finally prevailed. Confucianism taught absolute loyalty to the king, the cornerstone of the whole system. The king reigned by virtue of a mandate from Heaven; his great virtue not only held sway over the social order but was also part of the unfolding of the cosmic order. The whole social hierarchy rested upon this absolute loyalty to the monarch, and rebellion was held to be not only a political crime, but a religious one as well. So long as the monarchy played its central role and remained the symbol of national unity, its prestige was maintained. But with the decline of the Lê dynasty prior to the period of the Trịnh and Nguyễn families over two centuries, and a succession of debauched and incompetent kings, the concept of absolute respect for the monarch collapsed, and with it, the whole system of moral and spiritual values inherent in the regime. The Confucian scholar could no longer believe in the values he had to teach. After his capture, the scholar Phạm Công Thế, a participant in the Lê Duy Mật revolt, was asked reproachfully by the authorities, "How can a scholar have become a rebel, and lost all sense of hierarchy and social values?" He replied, "For a long time now, all concepts of hierarchy and values have disappeared. How can one distinguish between the rebel and those who are supposed to be on the right path?"

The mandarin regime, the mainstay of the feudal monarchy, drew its prestige from the competitions held amid great pomp. Those who ruled in the name of the king were supposed to have been recruited from among the most virtuous and best educated. Candidates went through regional, then central competitions before being awarded the much-coveted title of *tiến sĩ* (doctor). The examination paper included commentaries on classical texts, the writing of an administrative document (an edict or proclamation by the king), the composition of a poem or piece of rhyming prose, and a moral or philosophical dissertation. Of several thousand candidates, only about a hundred passed the regional competitions and even fewer the central ones. The latter received the greatest honours and enjoyed very great prestige. Between 1529 and 1787, 102 competitions were held, with 1,136 candidates becoming *tiến sĩ*.

With the decline of the regime, the system of competitions also degenerated. The examination papers became exercises in pure rhetoric on worn-out scholastic themes. The candidates contented themselves with reproducing models and clichés, and indulged in pointless stylistic exercises. The 18th century historian Lê Quý Đôn wrote: "Our elders had composed texts which read well; their successors simply copied them after trimming them of long drawn-out parts". Fraud was common, lowering the value of the competitions, and when mandarin offices were put up for sale, the prestige of the system suffered a severe blow. The result was the emergence of an incompetent, unscrupulous and greedy mandarin bureaucracy, whose members no longer possessed either the cultural or moral values of past centuries.

The decline of Confucianism allowed something of a renaissance for Buddhism. Kings and lords set about building pagodas, and frustrated scholars entered the monastic life, while the people sought solace in the religion. These conditions turned a few minds towards Taoism, which also experienced something of a renewal. Many people adopted a syncretic attitude, combining all three doctrines - Confucianism, Buddhism and Taoism in a reasonably successful synthesis.

The regime's moral and ideological crisis also allowed Catholic missionaries to win converts, particularly in the 17th century. The beginnings of Vietnamese Catholicism date back to this period. With Catholicism, the *quốc ngữ* script was created, in which the Vietnamese language was transcribed in Latin characters.

The Development of Literature in *Nôm*

The crisis in Confucianism had one positive aspect; it freed many minds from a somewhat sterile ideology. Liberated from dogma and carried along by a popular movement whose clearest manifestation was the great peasant insurrections, many people, especially poets and writers, cast a critical glance at traditional society and sought to express new aspirations. Fresh themes appeared, while the language became richer, more concise and more flexible. Many historical works were also written, and there were advances in medical knowledge.

While historical and medical studies continued to be written in classical Chinese, *nôm* prevailed in the area of literature. It was the turning point leading to the pre-eminence of *nôm*, although classical Chinese remained in use until the early 20th century.

Stories and Fables of the 17th Century

A particular feature of this period was the appearance of stories and fables written in *Nôm*, a new literary genre for Việt Nam. Criticisms of feudal society, the theme of love, and humanistic ideas began to emerge in these works.

The Story of Vương Thông reflects the existence of a corrupt court, a parasitic mandarin bureaucracy, and an unjust society, which trampled on the lives of women. *The Story of the Toad and the Catfish* is a fable with animal characters that denounces the notables' and mandarins' habit of taking advantage of even the smallest lawsuit to extort money from the people.

In another fable, The *Virtuous Mouse,* the author castigates the debauchery of important people and praises the morality of ordinary women.

Written in the form of a fairy tale, *The Story of Bạch Viên and Tôn Các* tells of the love between two young people freed from feudal shackles. Also noteworthy among works from the 17th century is the *Thiên Nam Ngữ Lục*, a historical story in verse (8,136 lines) which recounts the history of the country from its origins to the fall of the Mạc in 1592.

Literary Development in the 18th Century

The stories and fables of the 17th century heralded the full flowering of the 18th century. Literature in *nôm* was to achieve prominence, particularly due to the quality of the works. The influence of popular oral literature grew in terms of both the language and content of written works. The simple and flexible colloquial language, colourful expressions in proverbs and songs, and the satirical content of popular stories were used in literary works. Prominent authors created a successful synthesis of popular speech and the classical literary language, and of popular wisdom and classical Chinese culture, in unique works written in a lively and expressive language. It constituted a real turning point in the development of the Vietnamese language. Poetry flourished.

The greatest development came in stories and novels in verse, most of them written anonymously. Stories of the 17th century had fairly simple plots. Those of the 18th were to become more complex, with greater scope, multiple episodes, and vividly depicted characters.

Also worthy of note was the appearance of satire in the form of poems and stories in which officials of the feudal society, even the king himself, were ridiculed. This criticism was also found in novels in verse, depicting corrupt and cruel mandarins and tyrannical and debauched kings. Historical chronicles revealed life at the royal court to have been rotten with debauchery, intrigues and plots hatched by various factions.

The more important authors and works are described hereunder.

The Great Poets of the 18th Century

Two great works of poetry from the 18th century stand out, the *Chinh Phụ* (Laments of a Soldier's Wife) and *Cung Oán* (Laments of an Odalisque), as well as the satirical poems of Hồ Xuân Hương.

Chinh Phụ, written in classical Chinese by Đặng Trần Côn, is better known in the translation in *nôm* by Đoàn Thị Điểm. It is a long poem (408 lines) that depicts the sorrow and anguish, and also the hopes, of a woman

whose husband has gone to war. In feudal classics, war is often represented as an opportunity for subjects to prove their loyalty to the king and achieve glory, but here, it only brings suffering, separation and misery. The endless wars waged by kings and feudal lords in order to entrench their system of privileges or eliminate rivals no longer inspired enthusiasm. *Chinh Phụ* echoed popular anti-war songs. The *nôm* translation was written in delicate but simple language, a very musical one which subtly describes the feelings of a warrior's wife. For the first time a literary work focused on a woman's inner feelings; it was a truly romantic work.

Cung Oán was written by Nguyễn Gia Thiều. It portrays a beautiful and talented woman who is forced to lead a solitary life in the royal palace, forsaken by the king. The author was a descendant of a great mandarin family allied with the Trịnh and a close observer of the decadence of the feudal monarchy; his work denounced one of the most retrograde aspects of system.

The destiny of women, depicted in *Cung Oán* and *Chinh Phụ*, was to become one the main themes of Hồ Xuân Hương, who was no longer content to lament but resolutely attacked male supremacy; it was society, not nature, which relegated women to inferior status.

If only I could change my destiny and be a man,

I wouldn't content myself with such feats of valour.

Though a learned scholar, she was not afraid to use popular and colourful language, rich in bold expressions, and handled risque words and phrases skillfully without ever sliding into vulgarity. She mercilessly chastised hypocritical sycophants, unmasked social conventions, and vehemently protested against polygamy. In her own inimitable style, dotted with allusions and *double entendre*, she castigated the most respected people in feudal society. Thus her poem *The Fan*, after suggestive allusions, ends with the following line:

Kings and lords only love that little thing.

This was a direct attack on the debauchery of the Lê kings and the Trịnh lords. Buddhist bonzes were not spared either:

Before the reverends are big trays of delicacies,

Behind them lurk graceful nuns.

The poet reserved her greatest affection for unhappy women, and did not hesitate to defend unmarried mothers in a strait-laced society. A very popular author, Hồ Xuân Hương occupies a special place in Vietnamese literature.

Satirical Stories

Satire against feudal society took on systematic form in the popular stories *Trạng Quỳnh* (Doctor Quỳnh) and *Trạng Lợn* (Doctor Pig). *Trạng Quỳnh* attacked the Trịnh lords directly and by name. One of the characters is a Trịnh lord, corrupt, mean and debauched, who is hoodwinked at every turn by "Doctor" Quỳnh, despite all the power at his disposal.

Trạng Lợn tells the story of a poor down -and-out who, through a series of lucky happenstances, reaches the top of the mandarin hierarchy, is appointed ambassador to China where he greatly impresses the emperor. He eventually seizes complete power, and his "genius" is recognized by all in the court. The incompetence of kings and mandarins is exposed in a series of comical adventures.

Novels in Verse by Anonymous Writers

The flowering of stories and novels in verse marked a new stage in literary development, with new themes. For the first time, in a feudal society whose ideology left no room for individual aspirations, new sentiments emerged. In particular was the individual's right to freedom in love and the free development of all his abilities, and the aspiration for a more just society in which he could find happiness. Women in particular courageously defended love based on free choice and opposed marriages imposed on them by their families. Previously, woman had been virtually absent from literature; a few verses and songs likened her to "a drop of rain, which cannot know where it will fall" or "a silk scarf destined for unknown hands". Now, the heroines in 18th-century novels married the men of their choice in the face of opposition from their families, and fought hard whenever their happiness was threatened. Their love was extolled in romantic tones.

In many respects, the works were realistic in their critical portrayal of feudal society; some positive characters were drawn in a vivid manner. Humanistic tendencies thus appeared in opposition to the sterile morality of Confucianism. It was not yet a complete, coherent humanism, as in the European Renaissance, but the new ideas nonetheless instilled a breath of fresh air into the Vietnamese literature of the 18th century and the beginning of the 19th century. The great peasant insurrections and the emergence of a mercantile economy gave literature a new impetus.

It should be noted that many novels borrowed themes from Chinese stories, just as French classical works of the 17th century adopted Greek or Roman themes.

The main works of this type were *Phan Trần, Tống Trân Cúc Hoa, Phạm Công Cúc Hoa, Hoàng Trừu and Lý Công*. A special place must be reserved for the story of *Thạch Sanh*, the wood-cutter who gets the better of monsters and foreign invaders, a hero sprung from the toiling people, the saviour of the country, a man who is courageous, valiant and humane. *Thạch Sanh's* only possessions are a loincloth and an axe, but he defeats all enemies and overcomes all difficulties.

Nguyễn Du and Kiều [1]

Although the works of Nguyễn Du (pronounced Zu) appeared only in the early years of the 19th century, they belong incontestably to the 18th century in content and style. They depict social upheaval in the 18th century, expressed humanistic aspirations and criticized feudal society. A member of a great mandarin family serving the Lê, Nguyễn Du was forced to retire to his native village when the Lê was overthrown by the Tây Sơn. Later he served under Gia Long. The upheavals he witnessed left a great impression on him, as did the years he spent in the countryside close to the people. This was shown in his great compassion for the latter's misery, his occasional outbursts of anger against kings and mandarins, and his profound sympathy for those living unhappy lives. It appeared also in his incurable pessimism.

Nguyễn Du left behind many poems in classical Chinese, a famous one in *Nôm - Calling the Wandering Souls* - and a masterpiece, *The Tale of Kiều*. In his poems in classical Chinese, he describes the fate of the poor in poignant words. In *Calling the Wandering Souls*, he gives a sombre picture of society where people from all walks of life suffer unhappiness and misery. In contrast, he depicts greedy mandarins who throw away food after gorging themselves rather than give it to the poor, and who "eat human flesh like barleysugar".

With *Kiều*, Nguyễn Du reached the peak of his creative talent. This 3,254-line poem relates the story of a beautiful and talented young woman, doomed to 15 years of tribulation by the machinations of a mandarin. It achieved great popularity as soon as it was published. Illiterate peasants knew long passages from it by heart, while scholars considered it a masterpiece. This extraordinary success was due as much to the beauty of the language as to the content of the poem.

---

1. For a more detailed study of Nguyễn Du and his works. See *Vietnamese Studies No 4*: "Nguyễn Du and Kiều".

Nguyễn Du achieved a remarkable synthesis between popular speech and classical literary language. *Kiều* marked an important stage in the history of the Vietnamese language, which it helped enrich and make more flexible by giving it unequalled precision and conciseness. A romantic, Nguyễn Du knew how to extol the beauty of a landscape as well as express the feelings in a lover's heart, sorrow, melancholy, despair, or triumphant joy. A realist, in just a few works he was able to fully portray a character or describe a scene. The novel is written with remarkable concision, without any long drawn-out passages. At no time does the reader's interest wane.

Kiều's great fame is due not only to its beauty of form but also its content. In this great work of realism, Nguyễn Du denounces oppressive and corrupt feudalism; not a single mandarin in *Kiều* is portrayed in sympathetic terms. Beautiful *Kiều's* misfortunes sprang from the greed of a mandarin who, for the sake of a bribe, does not hesitate to destroy the happiness of a whole family. A shiver runs down the reader's spine when he penetrates the prime minister's palace; at the same time he finds the atmosphere stifling, for the First Marshall at the court, in order to gain the upper hand over his enemy, does not hesitate to engage in trickery. On the other hand, with regard to the monarchy, the "rebel" Từ Hải cuts a fine figure, "moving heaven and earth, deporting himself proudly, recognizing only the star-dotted sky to be above his head". This glorification of a rebel in Confucian society identifies the author as having a truly bold spirit. Từ Hải is reminiscent of those great leaders of peasant insurrections, Nguyễn Hữu Cầu and Nguyễn Huệ in particular, who left their own indelible mark on history.

It was no less courageous of the author to extol the love of two young people who meet of their own free choice. What is more, it is the girl who, in the absence of her parents, decides to go and see her beloved. What a scandal for a society in which the woman must show complete feminine submission! The most passionate lines are devoted to describing effusively the tender feelings of the lovers. Love based on free choice, so frowned upon by feudal society, found in Nguyễn Du its advocate, putting aside the sacrosanct concept of faithfulness which obliged the woman to devote her life to only one man and to remain "loyal" to her husband even after his death. In her tribulations, *Kiều* is forced to sell herself several times; she knows her second passionate love when she meets a hero worthy of her. This second love, which a Confucian scholar would have criticised vehemently, is ardently defended by Nguyễn Du. Confucian Puritanism prohibited all allusion to physical love, yet Nguyễn Du dared to write about it, without ever sliding into vulgarity. *Kiều*, compelled by a ferocious society to prostitute herself, is able to say to her loyal sweetheart that she has remained pure despite all her difficulties and that faithfulness in love must be seen from a much more human viewpoint than that held by conservatives. Amidst the convulsions and upheavals of the 18th century, love was part of the new aspirations and was extolled by Nguyễn Du.

However, Nguyễn Du's work bears the imprint of his century. The defeat of the Tây Sơn sounded the death -knell for the hopes raised by the peasant insurrections. With the coming to power of Gia Long, Việt Nam fell back into the shadows of feudalism. No prospects remained for those who struggled and those who meditated on man's fate. Nguyễn Du deeply sympathized with the sufferings of the people, felt the aspirations in their hearts, but was lost in a blind alley of reflections on human bondage. Confucianism no longer offered sufficient explanation for so much misery and injustice. He had to fall back on Buddhist ideas, yet had little faith in them. But these ideological conflicts did not prevent Nguyễn Du from being a very great poet, whose work is still deeply loved by all Vietnamese, and through many translations, is now known throughout the world.

Historical Works

Parallel to this literary flowering, many historical works were written including official annals, monographs and chronicles.

The *Đại Việt Sử Ký Toàn Thư* (Complete History of Đại Việt), published in 1697, comprised 24 volumes and was compiled under the direction of Ngô Sĩ Liên. It relates the history of the country from its beginnings to the 17th century. Among other major works are the *Lê Triều Thông Sử* (History of the Lê Dynasty) by Lê Quý Đôn, with a preface dated 1789, and the *Phủ Biên Tạp Lục* by the same author, which is in six volumes and provides information on geography, economics, the administration, lifestyles and customs in the days of the Nguyễn. Also by Lê Quý Đôn is the *Kiến Văn Tiểu Lục*, a collection of notes and documents on institutions, outstanding men, rules and regulations, scenic locations, mines and Buddhist sects, from the time of the Trần to the Lê.

Lê Quý Đôn (1726-1783) was both a historian and true encyclopaedist. While carrying out his civilian and military responsibilities at the Trịnh court, he collected documents and studied

current issues for use in his works. His intellectual curiosity led him to study, among other things, rice strains, and Chinese translations of European works on the belief that the earth is round - a view he adopted. Besides books on history, he left a kind of encyclopaedia, the *Vân Đài Loại Ngữ*, one chapter of which dealt with his concept of the universe. Contemporary philosophical debates were about the primacy of either *Lý* (logos) or *Khí* (breath, substance); of either *Vô Cực* (nothingness) or *Thái Cực* (the prime being). Lê Quý Đôn wrote:

"Thái Cực *is one. It is a prime, undifferentiated substance that undergoes ceaseless transformation while existing eternally. One cannot say that Being comes out of nothingness, Prime and undifferentiated* Khí *is the substance of all Being and exists before all beings.* Lý *has no form; it exists only thanks to* Khí *and is included in* khí *itself.*"

He insisted on the constant nature of natural phenomena: *"Heaven is tens of thousands of leagues from earth. Yet, with the help of a few figures, one may determine the positions and trajectories of celestial bodies. So while the Being is immense and its manifestations limitless and marvelous, it nonetheless follows a constant rule"*.

Lê Quý Đôn's inquisitive mind explored many areas; his was a pre-scientific intellect born in the upheavals of the 18th century.

Among important historical chronicles is the *Hoàng Lê Nhất Thống Chí* (Chronicles of the Lê Dynasty), which gives a vivid description of the plots and intrigues which plagued the Lê and Trịnh courts. *Vũ Trung Tùy Bút* (Essays Written in the Rain) by Phạm Đình Hổ (1768-1839) is a collection of notes and observation on the institutions, customs and practices at the time of the last Lê kings. The same author also wrote, in collaboration with Nguyễn Án, the *Tang Thương Ngẫu Lục*, a collection of stories mostly about the 18th century. *Thượng Kinh Ký Sự* (Journey to the Capital), by the physician Lê Hữu Trác, also gives valuable information about life at the Trịnh court.

Upholding the tradition of works from the previous century, the historical school at the beginning of the 19th century also produced some important works. The historians of the Nguyễn court brought out two great works, one dealing with the nation's history from its origins - the *Cương Mục* (Historical Records) in 52 volumes - and the other on the history of the Nguyễn lords from the war of secession to the advent of the Nguyễn dynasty - the *Đại Nam Thực Lục* in 453 volumes. The most striking work was the *Lịch Triều Hiến Chương* (Chronology of the Dynasties), a true encyclopaedia on the political, social, economic and

cultural institutions of Việt Nam over many centuries. This is now the most valuable source used in the study of traditional Việt Nam.

Lê Hữu Trác and the Development of Medicine

With Lê Hữu Trác, better known under the pseudonym Hải Thượng Lãn Ông, major advances occurred in medical science. A learned scholar, he shunned the career of mandarin, retired to his village, and devoted his life to the study of medicine. Following decades of observation and study, he wrote a medical treatise in 28 volumes in 66 parts, which includes a theoretical section, a section on pathology, with special studies on small-pox, measles, infant diseases and women's disorders, sections on drugs and pharmacology, a collection of clinical observations and a section on hygiene.

Lãn Ông's great achievement is the laying of the foundations for a medical science based on observations of clinical work, climatic conditions, and the properties of local plants and other products. His observations and formulas remain of great value even up to the present day. He had a thorough grasp of classical Chinese medical theory, but relied mostly on observation. His medical data was collected with great care, forming mental documents that were added to the experience of others. Another of his great principles was the importance of hygiene in disease prevention, hygiene in its widest sense as organization of daily life. Lãn Ông did not hesitate to give advice to mothers on questions of food and clothing.

He also laid down the principles of a humanistic medical deontology. He wrote:

"Medicine is a humane art, which must seek to preserve life, attend to man's illnesses and sorrows, and help him, without caring about wealth or honours."

"Rich men do not lack physicians, but the poor can rarely afford good ones. One must pay special attention to them."

"Medicine is a noble art. We must strive to preserve our moral purity".

Both scientist and humanist, Lê Hữu Trác was a key precursor to the great figures of the 18th century.

PART TWO

CONTEMPORARY VIỆT NAM

(1858 - 1990s)

Chapter I

VIỆT NAM LOSES ITS INDEPENDENCE

On 31 August 1858, a French naval squadron attacked Đà Nẵng, launching a war of colonial conquest waged by French imperialism, in several episodes between 1858 and 1884, and resulting in the total annexation of Việt Nam.

French imperialism, then in full expansion, was attacking a decaying feudal monarchy. The Nguyễn dynasty, which had ascended the throne after repressing a large-scale uprising, had restored the feudal system with all of its repressive institutions. Peasant revolts however, continued unabated, driving into a tight corner an administrative apparatus made up essentially of a body of mandarins trained in a very conservative and ritualistic Confucian ideology, and duplicated in the villages by a body of notables born into the landlord class. With a rudimentary infrastructure, the Royal Court was unable to rule effectively over a territory stretching for more than 2,000 kilometres from North to South. It was in the most vulnerable part — the South — that the French colonialists started their aggression.

Faced with French invasion, the Vietnamese side split into two opposing parties, one arguing for compromise and the other for resistance. The king and high-ranking Court dignitaries were afraid of the modern weapons used by the French. They were also misled as to the latter's objectives, believing that the French, having come from so far away, were thinking less about conquering the country than of obtaining trade concessions. Moreover, the Nguyễn monarchy, constantly suppressing internal revolts, neither wanted to, nor was able to, mobilize all the nation's energies to oppose aggression. All this prompted the king and Court dignitaries to implement a policy of appeasement, termed *hòa nghị* (peace and negotiation), trying to limit the aggression by granting more and more important concessions. By contrast, a number of mandarins, the great majority of scholars and the people as a whole, who had inherited a long tradition of struggle for national independence, put up tough resistance. While the armed struggle waged by the royal troops was feeble, that of the people's forces was protracted, compelling the French to fight a long and costly war. But the defection by the monarchy, the sole force that could have assumed a leading role nationally, undermined the efforts of the Vietnamese patriots.

The tactics of the French colonialists were particularly clever. They began by securing a foothold over part of the nation's territory, then forced the Huế Court to make concessions in the form of a treaty. The aggressors thus had at their disposal a starting base for preparations for further annexations, and had gained a respite during which to eliminate the popular resistance that was growing in enemy-held areas. But before long, the French violated the treaty and continued their conquest. New concessions were made by the Huế Court, and a new treaty was signed. Further violations occurred and more conquests followed. The scenario was repeated in this way until the total annexation of the country had been achieved. The monarchy, making one concession after another, finished up with capitulation and treason. The king and high-ranking dignitaries chose to barter the nation's independence for the preservation of a few privileges granted by the conquerors. From defenders of the nation's independence and honour, they gradually became agents of a foreign power, helping it by suppressing the popular patriotic movement. Assistance sought by the Huế Court from the Chinese Empire, itself in decline and a victim of European aggression, was unable to change the course of events.

The Fall of Sài Gòn and the Three Eastern Provinces of Nam Bộ[1]

After taking Đà Nẵng, French troops set fire to and destroyed the town, but were not strong enough to threaten the capital city or force the Huế Court to make further concessions. Bishop Pellerin proposed that the French command attack the Red River delta in the North where 400,000 Vietnamese Catholics would be prepared to rise up in support

1. Nam Bộ was at that time known as Cochinchina and Sài Gòn - Gia Định province

of the operation. But the French command preferred to head for the South, where the rice trade was already flourishing.

The siege of Sài Gòn (Saigon) began on the morning of 17 February 1859. By the end of that day, the royal troops had left the city, while reinforcements had arrived from neighbouring provinces, among them 5, 800 volunteers recruited by dignitaries from the region. The Sài Gòn garrison, thus reinforced, encircled the French troops that had penetrated the city, putting them in a difficult position. The Huế Court, however, did not order a counter-attack, as it was seeking a compromise through negotiation. The French took advantage of this indecision to buy time. In 1860, after a new victorious offensive by European powers against China, France was able to muster all its naval forces operating in the Far East to send them to Sài Gòn to break the siege. In 1861, they conquered the three eastern provinces of Cochinchina, which then comprised six provinces — three in the east, and three in the west.

The defeat of the royal troops, however, did not put an end to the Vietnamese resistance. The people, under the leadership of patriots, rose in revolt everywhere to fight the French troops. The French officers who wrote the book, "Military History of Indochina", had to admit that "the defeat of the Annamite army had no effect whatsoever on the state of insurrection in the occupied territories."

Resistance was widespread. An eyewitness, the French historian Pallu de la Barrière, wrote:

"The fact is that the centre of the resistance was everywhere, endlessly sub-dividing into nearly as many units as there were Annamites. It would have been more accurate to consider each peasant tying a rice stack as a centre of resistance."[1]

The popular nature of the resistance was also apparent in the difference in tactics used. Royal troops operated in close-knit formation, and were scared by the long-range weapons of the French. The people's forces pursued either guerrilla warfare or mounted surprise attacks, and engaged in close combat. Troops commanded by the patriot Nguyễn Trung Trực, using hand-to-hand fighting, managed to set fire to a French warship, the Espérance, and to inflict a stinging defeat on the French at Nhật Tảo. The people's forces succeeded in retaking many localities, and the French command had to hastily call for reinforcements.

1. History of the Cochinchina Expedition, 1861.

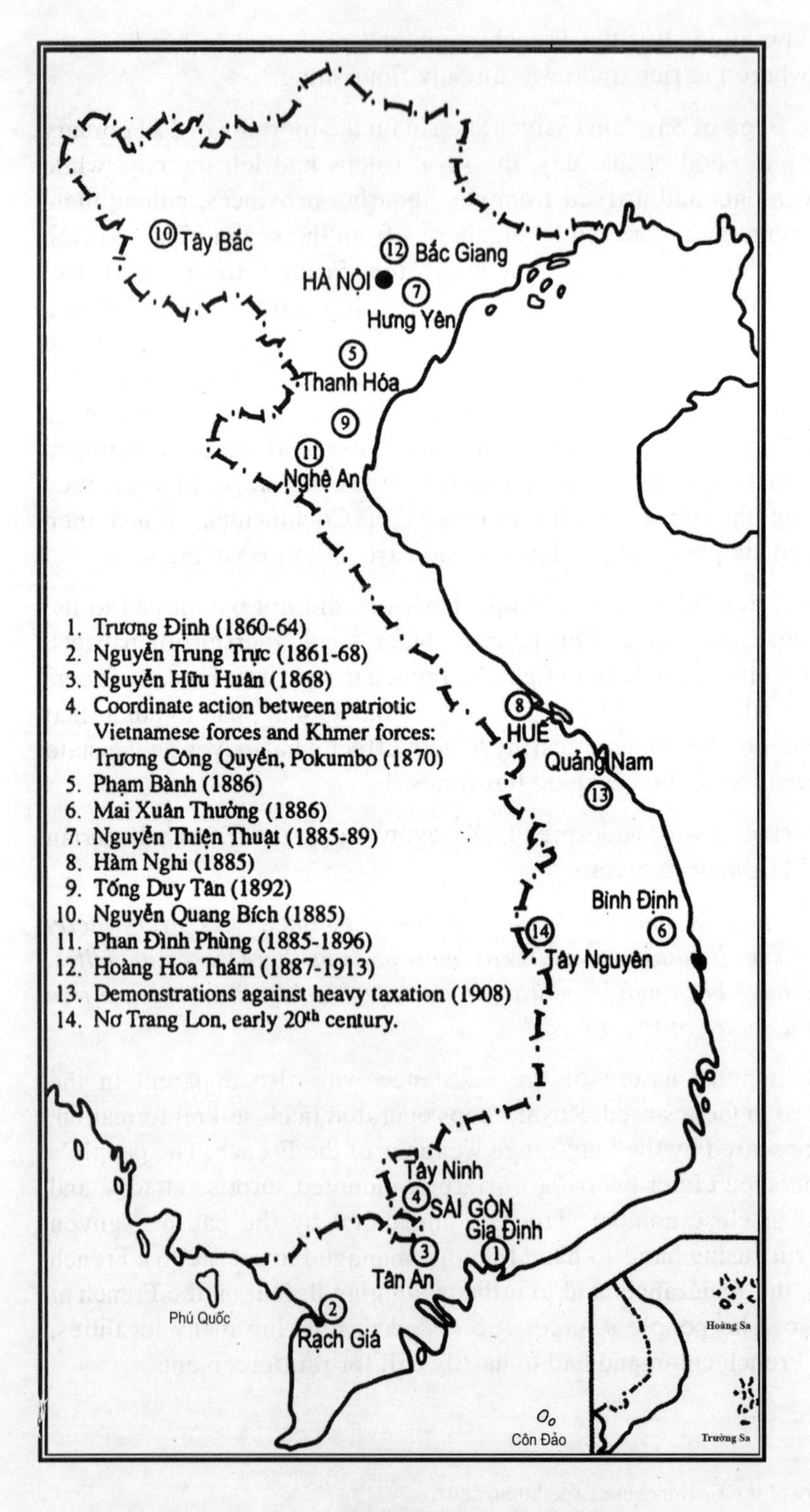
10 Tây Bắc
12 Bắc Giang
HÀ NỘI
7
Hưng Yên
5
Thanh Hóa
9
11
Nghệ An
8
HUẾ
Quảng Nam
13
Bình Định
6
14
Tây Nguyên
Tây Ninh
4
SÀI GÒN
Gia Định
3
1
Tân An
2
Phú Quốc
Rạch Giá
Côn Đảo
Hoàng Sa
Trường Sa
1. Trương Định (1860-64)
2. Nguyễn Trung Trực (1861-68)
3. Nguyễn Hữu Huân (1868)
4. Coordinate action between patriotic Vietnamese forces and Khmer forces: Trương Công Quyền, Pokumbo (1870)
5. Phạm Bành (1886)
6. Mai Xuân Thưởng (1886)
7. Nguyễn Thiện Thuật (1885-89)
8. Hàm Nghi (1885)
9. Tống Duy Tân (1892)
10. Nguyễn Quang Bích (1885)
11. Phan Đình Phùng (1885-1896)
12. Hoàng Hoa Thám (1887-1913)
13. Demonstrations against heavy taxation (1908)
14. Nơ Trang Lon, early 20th century.

Main pockets of resistance between 1860 and 1913 together with the names of their leaders

It was the Huế Court that helped the French troops out of this tight corner by proposing negotiations. On 5 June 1862, Phan Thanh Giản negotiated with France's Admiral Bonard a treaty involving the three eastern provinces of Cochinchina, agreed to pay a 20 million franc indemnity and to open up to French commerce three ports in Annam and Tonkin. The court soon ordered the people's forces to withdraw from the provinces conceded.

The order, however, was not obeyed. The French historian F. Vial wrote:

"*While the Admiral thought he had happily ended the war, he came across one perhaps more active, more redoubtable than a serious war against the king's regular troops.*"[1]

It was Trương Định who led the insurrection. He was managing an agricultural estate when the French attacked Sài Gòn. Trương Định, with his party of volunteers, came to the rescue of the city. When Sài Gòn fell into French hands, he withdrew to Gò Công province where he recruited an army of 6,000 volunteers and received from the court the title of deputy commander. Following the signing of the Treaty of 1862, the king ordered him to pull back towards An Giang province and give up all resistance (by naming him commander). Trương Định hesitated for some time; a genuine patriot, he did not want to give up the struggle. Stronger still however, was his Confucian training, which would not permit him to disobey an order from the king. He was about to carry out the king's order when delegates from the people's forces and the people streamed into his camp, asking him to remain at his post as commander of the patriotic movement and hailing him as "Commander, Conqueror of the French!" Trương Định bowed to the people's will and took command of the uprising.

The patriots of the resistance fought with heroism:

"*The Annamites, with powerless weapons against our rifles, threw themselves upon our men with a blind energy which demonstrated extraordinary courage and self-sacrifice.*"[2]

Their guerrilla tactics placed the French troops in a predicament. Pallu de la Barrière wrote:

"*No sight is more miserable, more monotonous, more tiring than that of the French on land and on water. One enemy is constantly in sight, but*

1. The First Years of French Cochinchina
2. F. Vial, ibid.

the other is hiding. From the way the enemy continually gets away, it seems that we are beating at the air."[1]

Civilian resistance was also organized, and took many forms. The majority of dignitaries and mandarins refused to collaborate with the occupiers. The poet Nguyễn Đình Chiểu, though blind, left an enemy-held area to live elsewhere, and together with many other scholars wrote volumes of patriotic literature.

In a funeral oration, Nguyễn Đình Chiểu painted the following portrait of the peasant -patriot:

Worries, poverty and wretchedness are your lot.
You aren't used yet to the bow and the horse
Never have you trod a drilling ground.
Handling a hoe, a plough, a harrow, transplanting rice
Are nothing new to your hands.
Yet never before had your eyes witnessed
But the art of handling a shield, a spear, a gun, or a flag
A ragged shirt girding your loins
You didn't wait for a sheath
None of you ever had a sword by your side...
Those Europeans fired
Small bullets, and large shells
But you smashed doors and rushed forward
Ignoring all obstacles
You thrust and slashed with your clubs
Throwing the mercenaries into a panic...
You fell
But you paid your debt to our mountains and rivers
Your renown sweeps down to the provinces
And thousands of voices sing your praises
You fell
But the temples celebrated you honour
Your renown through thousands and thousands of generations will live...
Never will the tears shed for heroes dry
They loved those we call our people
How nice it is, the perfume of joss-sticks

---

1. Pallu de la Barrière, ibid.

Which burn for the partisans
So strongly attached to our royal land.

However, the Court's order to cease all resistance had planted doubt in the people's minds. Huế sent a mission led by Phan Thanh Giản to France to negotiate the return of the lost provinces. France, in difficulties over its war in Mexico, made a number of promises. On 20 August 1864, Trương Định, wounded during a battle, took his own life so as not to fall into enemy hands. His son, Trương Quyền, carried on the resistance. Meanwhile, in 1863, France had forced on the king of Cambodia a treaty proclaiming a protectorate. Cambodian patriots, led by the bronze Pokumbo, joined forces with Vietnamese insurgents to oppose the French conquest. It was the first step in an alliance that brought the two peoples of Cambodia and Việt Nam together in their struggle against European imperialism.

In 1867, France, having resolved the Mexican problem, launched a new offensive in Việt Nam. French troops marched into the three western provinces of Cochinchina. Finding all resistance useless, Phan Thanh Giản, then the governor of these provinces, ceded them to the French before committing suicide. The people's resistance in the western provinces brought Vietnamese and Khmer together with other ethnic groups - Chàm, Mường and Stiêng - and covered a vast territory extending from the huge lakes of Cambodia to the gates of Sài Gòn. From 1866 to 1868, fighting raged in Tây Ninh province, while Khmer insurgents reached the vicinity of the capital, Udong. Pokumbo, however, was killed, and the resistance in northwestern Cochinchina and Cambodia's border areas was scaled down. In the western area of the Mekong River delta, two of Phan Thanh Giản's sons took over the leadership of the people's movement, while the patriot Nguyễn Trung Trực, who in 1861 had set the French frigate *Espérance* ablaze, was in command of operations. On 16 June 1868, he captured the post of Kiên Giang in Rạch Giá province. Captured shortly afterwards, Nguyễn Trung Trực refused to submit and, before falling under a hail of bullets from a firing squad, shouted:

"So long as grass still grows on the soil of this land, people will continue to resist the invaders."

The French, now occupying the whole of Cochinchina, hastened to explore the entire length of the Mekong River to see whether it was possible to divert towards Sài Gòn all trade with southern China. It was soon recognized, however, that this waterway was unusable.

The Huế Court in Disarray and the Fall of Hà Nội

The loss of Cochinchina was deeply resented in Việt Nam. Patriots submitted many petitions to King Tự Đức, advocating reforms which would strengthen the country's defence capability. A plan submitted by Nguyễn Trường Tộ in particular, proposed reforms in all areas: political, administrative, agricultural, commercial, industrial, educational, financial, diplomatic and military. Reforms advocated by many people aimed to achieve the opening up of the country to international commerce, renew handicrafts, develop industry and trade, change the educational system, send students abroad, and reorganize the army along European lines.

The Court, floundering in conservatism, refused to consider any of these petitions. Unaware of international developments, they were incapable of taking advantage of the difficulties confronting France to regain the initiative. They believed that with a policy of "peace and negotiation," they could reach a settlement with the aggressors. They also banked on the support of the Qing dynasty in Manchuria, which was then ruling China.

This conservatism and weakness stemmed from the fact that the reactionary feudal regime of the Nguyễn dynasty was facing numerous popular uprisings. In 1862 near Hà Nội, the movement led by Cai Vàng protested against wasteful practices by the State. In 1866, workers and prisoners building the tomb of King Tự Đức rose in revolt. French missionaries took advantage of this instability to foment agitation among the Catholic communities of the Red River delta, this eventually flaring up into open rebellion led by Lê Bảo Phụng.

Another difficulty arose with the influx from China of Taiping troops driven back by Ching forces. Taking refuge in northern Tonkin, these bands, known as White, Yellow and Black Flags, carved out territories for themselves, which they then plundered. Only the Black Flags, led by Liu Wing-fu, submitted to the authority of the Huế Court.

Thanks to Catholic missionaries, the French command was kept well informed about this situation. Finding it impossible to reach southwestern China via the Mekong, the French attempted to seize the mouth of the Red River and the ports in Tonkin, using force when necessary. In 1872, without seeking permission from the Vietnamese authorities, the French adventurer Jean Dupuis, leading some one hundred mercenaries, sailed up the Red River into Yunnan province with a cargo of arms for the Chinese general Ma. On his first journey the mandarins were conciliatory, but when Dupuis tried to pass a second time, he was stopped.

The pretext used by the French command was immediately exploited. The French lieutenant Francis Garnier was sent to Hà Nội with an armed escort. Garnier made contact with Bishop Puginier, who gathered together the defeated followers of the rebel Lê Bảo Phụng. Francis Garnier, on his own initiative, ruled that from then on shipping would be free on the Red River and customs duties abolished.

The Vietnamese authorities refused to agree to this edict. On 19 November 1873, the French opened fire on and seized Hà Nội. The old general Nguyễn Tri Phương, charged with defending Hà Nội but wounded and taken prisoner, refused all advances by the French, and chose to starve to death. With the complicity of certain Catholic communities, French troops swept into Nam Định, Hải Dương and other localities in the Red River delta. But Vietnamese forces counter - attacked, encircled Hà Nội, and killed Garnier on 21 December 1875, in an ambush at the entrance to the city.

France, not yet recovered from its defeat at the hands of Prussia in 1871, did not want to become too deeply involved in Việt Nam. King Tự Đức, sticking to his policy of compromise, failed to exploit the favourable military situation. He negotiated the Treaty of 1874 under which France handed back the towns it had seized, but obtained permission to establish garrisons in Hà Nội and Hải Phòng and open up the Red River to commerce.

Capitulation of the Monarchy and Establishment of the Colonial Regime

During the last two decades of the 19th century, the capitalist economies of Europe experienced boom conditions. European powers rushed to other continents, proceeding to divide the world up between them. France's colonial policy, until then somewhat low-key, became tougher and more systematic. Britain's conquest of Burma helped speed up the implementation of French plans for Việt Nam.

In 1882, violating the 1874 Treaty, France sent new military units to Tonkin, commanded by Henry Rivière. Declaring themselves to be threatened by the "war -seeking" preparations of the Vietnamese, Rivière sent an ultimatum to the governor of Hà Nội, demanding the demolition of defensive works and evacuation of Vietnamese forces from the city. On 25 April 1882, French troops attacked and seized Hà Nội. Its governor, Hoàng Diệu, committed suicide. The mandarins of Tonkin wanted to counter-attack, but King Tự Đức still believed in negotiations, thinking he could win back Hà Nội as in 1874. But in the meantime, the French had occupied the coal mining areas of Hồng Gai and Cẩm Phả, then Nam Định province. Tự Đức, who had little confidence in his troops, appealed to the court in Beijing. The latter sent 10, 000 men who took up positions to the northwest of Hà Nội but did not go into action.

As in 1873, the Vietnamese forces encircled Hà Nội, and defeated French troops in a battle at the gates of the capital, killing Henri Rivière at the very place where Francis Garnier had fallen. Paris sent 4, 000 reinforcements. Tự Đức continued to sound France out about negotiations, and dismissed mandarins who advocated armed struggle.

In 1883, Tự Đức died without leaving an heir. In Huế, clans and different factions were at one another's throats. Within only a few months, three kings were enthroned, while high-ranking dignitaries were split over which policy to follow regarding France. Some of them called for armed resistance, others for negotiations, while others openly planned treason and collaboration with the invader. The Court did not even know of the military successes of Vietnamese forces in Tonkin.

Taking advantage of this confusion, the French command mustered its troops to take Đà Nẵng and advance on Huế. On hearing French cannons tender at the mouth of the Thuận An River, which formed a defensive bulwark at the entrance to the royal capital, the mandarins hastened to sign a treaty with France, agreeing to every condition. Việt Nam, having lost its sovereignty, became a French protectorate on 25 August 1883. The mandarins split into two camps. Many, disobeying the Court, tendered their resignation in order to carry on the resistance, while others put themselves at the service of the French.

There remained just the Qing troops sent by the Beijing Court that wanted to avoid a head-on clash with France. Paris and Beijing agreed to sign the Treaty of Tientsin on 11 May 1884. The regents Tôn Thất Thuyết and Nguyễn Văn Tường, hostile to the Protectorate Treaty of 1883, had to resign themselves to endorsing it in June 1884. However, while the Qing troops were pulling out through Lạng Sơn Pass, a local incident pitted them at Bắc Lệ against French troops, and they were subsequently defeated. The French command launched a large-scale attack on China, landing troops on Taiwan (then known as Formosa), and shelled the port of Fuchow. Vietnamese forces, cooperating with Qing troops, inflicted a new defeat on the French at Lạng Sơn in February 1885.

The Beijing Court, however, did not want to prolong hostilities, and signed a new treaty on 9 June 1885 under which it renounced all claims to.Việt Nam.

The Cần Vương Movement and the People's Struggle

Even after the capitulation of 1885, members of the resistance, led by Regent Tôn Thất Thuyết, continued their activities while elsewhere, the people as a whole organized themselves to carry on the struggle. Thuyết ordered the construction of Fort Tân Sở, in Quảng Trị province, and transferred the royal treasury there. In July 1884, King Hàm Nghi, then only 12-year-old, was enthroned. France sought to impose a new treaty under which Việt Nam would be divided into three zones: Cochinchina, administered as a French colony, Tonkin, as a semi-colony and semi-protectorate, and Annam as a protectorate. The unity of the country was significantly undermined.

Meanwhile, popular resistance in Tonkin remained strong. The French command wanted to strike at Huế in an attempt to destroy the movement from the top, and demanded the dismissal of dignitaries supporting the resistance, Thuyết in particular. They demanded that the Court hand over its artillery and reduce its armed forces, and urged the Royal Council to resign, to be replaced by a new body of pro-French mandarins.

In June 1885, France's General De Courcy arrived in Huế to demand the disbanding of the Vietnamese army. Thuyết and the mandarin Trần Xuân Soạn reacted by ordering an attack on French positions on the night of July 4. A bloody battle ensued, following which French troops occupied the royal capital.

But King Hàm Nghi and the Court had left Huế for the mountains, from where the king issued a proclamation calling on the whole country to support the monarchy through struggle *(Cần Vương)*. Mandarins sacked for advocating resistance were reinstated, and throughout the country the people and scholars responded with enthusiasm to the appeal. However, the defeatist faction returned to Huế where, in connivance with the French, it enthroned another king, Đồng Khánh, on 19 September 1885.

Hàm Nghi's main base was in the mountainous region of Quảng Trị and Quảng Bình provinces, linked to the north by a road that also led to Laos. Early in 1886, as the people's resistance in Tonkin grew in strength, the French command was forced to station troops there. The Vietnamese resistance in Quảng Bình was thus able to extend its base towards the sea, along the rivers that flowed down from the Trường Sơn Range. However, the Vietnamese patriots were short of arms. French troops were gradually able to drive them back towards the thinly inhabited and infertile mountainous area of Quảng Bình. Thuyết had left for China to request assistance. Hàm Nghi was unable to move his headquarters to the north, where the resistance base was large and more populous. The French proceeded methodically to encircle Hàm Nghi's retreat, and the king, betrayed by a military chief from the Mường ethnic group, was captured on 1 November 1888, and exiled to Algeria.

Hàm Nghi's call had made it possible to mobilize significant forces in many regions from north to south. In the southern province of Annam, the patriot Mai Xuân Thưởng led the movement until his capture and execution by the French in 1888. In Hà Tĩnh, Nghệ An and Thanh Hóa provinces, the resistance was particularly strong. Generally speaking, it was renowned scholars who called for struggle, recruited volunteers, and organized armed forces made up of courageous and committed ordinary people.

In Thanh Hóa province, patriots led by Đinh Công Tráng had built the Ba Đình fortress, an islet in the middle of a swamp. Cleverly camouflaged, Ba Đình looked from afar like an ordinary village. In fact, the fortress was surrounded by high ramparts and a deep moat. On the ramparts were thousands of baskets filled with earth, with gaps between them through which the defenders could watch the assailants and fire on them. A thick belt of bamboo protected the fortress, the approaches to which bristled with sharp-pointed stakes. Numerous trenches and underground tunnels were dug inside the fortress. Masson, a French officer who took part in an attack later wrote:

"*Our reconnaissance inside Ba Đình fortress really surprised us, as it showed us with what art the fortifications had been built. Food supplies were plentiful, and discipline rigorous. Two theatrical troupes gave performances to the combatants. In the mountainous part of Thanh Hóa province, a fall-back position, Mã Cao, had been built in case Ba Đình fell.*"

Between September 1886 and January 1887, several attacks by French troops were repelled. The French command had to send 2, 500 men with four pieces of artillery. French missionaries mobilized Catholics in Phát Diệm to help supply the French troops. While the citadel in Hà Nội, defended by royal troops, only held out against smaller French forces for one day, the Ba Đình garrison resisted for 35 days despite shelling by French artillery. French officers paid tribute to the bravery of the defenders. Masson wrote:

"*Another prisoner whom we interrogated coldly said to us: "You are wasting your time asking us things we don't want to tell you, since we consider it harmful to the interests of our country. So do whatever you please with us.*"

"We have mentioned among a hundred others, a few of the facts of this nature which we have witnessed, so as to give an idea of the character of the Annamite race. If we have only spoken of facts relating to the courage of the mandarins, we may add that the people and ordinary soldiers also deserve praise for their bravery and their scorn for death."

In the Red River delta, the French had to carry out endless operations against numerous pockets of resistance. One such pocket was the resistance base of Bãi Sậy, led by Nguyễn Thiện Thuật. Here the patriots, supported by the people, did not build fortresses, but waged an active guerrilla war and occasionally engaged in larger battles. The same situation prevailed in every province. Peasants who rose in revolt against the occupiers were labelled "pirates." A letter written in 1886 by the French Governor of Bắc Ninh province states:

"A strong gang of pirates, with the complicity of people in Yên Sơn village, has just attacked the post of Yên Sơn. Nobody had signalled the arrival of the pirates who left without stealing anything from the inhabitants."

The same courage and ingenuity could be seen everywhere. The French and their collaborators had to set up a complex network of posts and carry out endless swoops. In 1889, the Bãi Sậy area was temporarily pacified.

In the mountainous regions of Tonkin, the French only succeeded in holding a few main communication routes and strategic points. The country was entirely under the control of local chiefs who, keeping in close contact with insurgents in the Red River delta, made life difficult for French troops. In the northwest, Hàm Nghi's delegate, Nguyễn Quang Bích, led operations along with the chiefs of ethnic groups. To force him to surrender, the French and their collaborators arrested Bích's old mother, but neither he nor she gave in to the enemy. Not until the end of 1888 were the French troops able to reach Lào Cai, Nghĩa Lộ and Điện Biên Phủ.

In the northwest, the French maintained loose control over the Hà Nội -Lạng Sơn road. On the coast, the border town of Móng Cái, retaken in 1885 by the patriots, was not finally occupied by the French until 1886. In the Việt Bắc, the French rarely ventured out of the towns of Thái Nguyên and Tuyên Quang, which they had taken in 1884.

Unlike the resistance by royal troops, this patriotic people's struggle, inspired by Hàm Nghi's appeal, had caused enormous difficulties for the French troops, inflicted severe losses on them, and sparked a strong reaction among the public in France and in the French National Assembly. At times, under pressure from public opinion, the parliament had to reduce budget allocations for the conquest of Việt Nam. However, the colonialists would have the last say.

The Second Phase of the Resistance

The capture of King Hàm Nghi did not put an end to the people's patriotic movement. Loyalty to the king was really just one manifestation of the patriotism deeply rooted in the minds of the people and scholars. Many new uprisings occurred in various provinces up until 1897.

In Thanh Hóa province, the scholar Tống Duy Tân, with the support of the Mường ethnic minority, carried on the struggle until the fall of the Ba Đình fortress in 1892. Imprisoned by the enemy, he took his own life by ripping his belly open with the handle of a writing brush. His Mường aide, Cầm Bá Thước, carried on the fight until 1895.

In Hà Tĩnh province, the scholar Phan Đình Phùng and his principal aide Cao Thắng had organized a strong resistance base in the area of Hương Khê, and the insurgents' field of activity covered the four provinces of Quảng Bình, Hà Tĩnh, Nghệ An, and Thanh Hóa. Cao Thắng, a commoner, was a great military leader who knew how to organize his forces effectively, issuing them with a standard rifle copied from the French rifle of 1874. The movement was launched in 1885. In 1893, Cao Thắng and his men marched on the provincial capital of Nghệ An and began to seize a large number of outposts. His death in battle at the age of 29 put a halt to the uprising. The French and their agents, however, had to muster as many as 5,000 men to clear the region of guerrillas. In 1896, Phan Đình Phùng died of dysentery, and the movement gradually dwindled.

From 1889 to 1893, in the valley of the Đà (Black) River and the upper valley of the Red River, following the death of Nguyễn Quang Bích and the defection of the Thái chief Đèo Văn Trì to the French, leadership of the movement was held by Đề Kiều and Đốc Ngữ.

Of all the movements that continued the struggle after the capture of Hàm Nghi, the most remarkable was that of Yên Thế, which began in 1885. In this mountainous area situated on the fringes of the Red River delta, peasants revolted against French colonizers who had usurped their land. Insurgents from the delta joined the peasants, and the leader of the movement, Hoàng Hoa Thám (Đề Thám) gave it strong impetus by waging a brilliant and protracted guerrilla war. The regular forces comprised hundreds of combatants only, the main force consisting of peasants who continued to farm the land, but took part in the fighting when necessary.

From its Yên Thế base, the movement spread to the provinces of Bắc Giang, Bắc Ninh, Thái Nguyên and Lạng Sơn. Several operations conducted by the French against Yên Thế were defeated. Frey, a French officer, wrote:

"One cannot explain why these men, gathered in a narrow area, and pinned down by four artillery pieces fired from 300 metes, were able to hold out for so long. While the enemy our troops are fighting against do not have the fanaticism of the Kabyles or the guerrilla fighters of Sudan, they have a keener intelligence, and a remarkable knack for assimilating our means of action and tactics. They demonstrate superior skill in their choice of positions, in knowing how to reinforce them, and show the same indifference, the same cool as the former in the face of death. The rebels are commanded by genuine leaders. They wait until the gun barrels are nearly touching, until they can feel their opponents' breath before cutting them down in large numbers."

In 1894, the French proposed a truce, and granted Đề Thám the right to administer four cantons. In 1895, breaking the truce, they made a surprise attack on Yên Thế. But Đề Thám was on his guard, and his scattered forces kept harassing French troops with guerrilla actions. In 1897, the French negotiated a second truce. By this time, Yên Thế was the only base left, the other resistance movements having been crushed one after another.

In mountainous regions inhabited by ethnic minorities, the people had resisted for a long time, but the French were able to manipulate them, sow dissension in their ranks, and win over local chiefs. The French command, after seizing several major vantage points, sought to carry through these attempts at division before launching new military operations. The resistance movements were defeated one after another and the regions came under French control.

Between 1861 and 1867, unlike the royal troops which had literally crumbled in the face of French attacks, the people's resistance, conducted with popular support, organized by various leaders and using various forms of combat, waged a widespread and protracted armed struggle throughout the country. The defection of a monarchy crippled by a mandarin bureaucracy and Confucian ideology, however, robbed it of any possibility of unified action on a nationwide scale. A monarchy with faith in the people would probably have been able to wage a victorious resistance against foreign aggression.

Chapter II

ESTABLISHMENT OF THE COLONIAL REGIME

(1897 - 1918)

Owing to popular resistance, the war of conquest conducted by the French colonialists dragged on until 1896. Not until that date was the colonial regime really able to establish its authority, the people's armed struggle having been temporarily quelled and the sole important pocket of insurrection remaining being that led by Đề Thám in Yên Thế. The appointment of Paul Doumer as Governor -General of Indochina marked the decision of the French to establish a classic colonial regime with all the elements — economic, political, administrative, military and cultural.

Political and Administrative Organization

The prime concern of the conquerors was to set up a stable and efficient political and administrative system. In Cochinchina, annexed in 1862, the French encountered systematic non-cooperation by mandarins and scholars. The French historian Cultru wrote:

"If by some miracle the scholars had come over to the French and betrayed their sovereign, the administration of Cochinchina would have been perfectly straightforward. But the learned Annamites, the élite faithful to the laws of their country, could not but consider us as enemies. The peasants, tied to their fields and their cattle, remained in the countryside in a state of an outward obedience which in no way implied moral submission."

The French thus had to resort to direct administration by recruiting subaltern agents — uneducated elements without any standing — to serve as intermediaries. Moreover, the continuing rebelliousness of the population foiled all attempts at inducement by the colonial administration which, to maintain its rule, shamelessly used the most violent and cruel means of repression. Until its end, the colonial administration was characterised by its dual shortcomings: on the one hand cruelty, on the other collusion with the most regressive and corrupt elements in the Vietnamese nation. Later, US neo-colonialism in Việt Nam further refined these tactics, inherent in all colonialist undertakings.

As far back as 1886, in a report addressed to the Governor of Tonkin, the provincial governor Muslier wrote:

"...*Native mandarins hesitated to rally to our side or at least to serve us without having after-thoughts, and abandoned their posts, preferring to retire, while others, fewer in number and more energetic, became effective political chiefs of the rebellion. In administrative posts there were only a few ambitious mandarins who had more awareness of the future. The rest were made up of plotters, rascals, or people who only events have brought to our side and on whom we have sometimes conferred a high rank, which they use to hold to ransom the country without any scruples and make our presence hated. Worming their way up without merit and outside all the rules of hierarchy, they had no prestige whatsoever.*"

France's Rear-Admiral Rieunier complained: "*We only have ruffians on our side.*"

To create a support base, the colonial administration worked hand-in-hand with the feudalists, or at least with the most reactionary elements of this social class. The feudal regime was not abolished, but instead reinforced, the king, mandarins and notables becoming auxiliary members of the French administration, while landowners were able to continue to exploit the peasants as much as they wished.

Việt Nam was divided into three different "countries," different administrative regions — Tonkin, Annam and Cochinchina — each country separately integrated into so-called "French Indochina", which also included Cambodia and Laos and was ruled by a French Governor-General. France's intention was clearly aimed at destroying the unity of the Vietnamese nation so as to more easily enslave it.

Each of the five "countries" of Indochina (Tonkin, Annam, Cochinchina, Cambodia and Laos) had at its head a French Governor or "résident-supérieur." All important services — security, finance, public works, posts, agriculture, health, trade and so on — were in the hands of the French. The Governor-General ruled all of Indochina, assisted by

the High Council of Indochina, made up of the governor and the French directors of the most important services.

Vietnamese administrations were preserved intact or assigned only minor tasks. The Vietnamese Council of Ministers was presided over by the French Governor, and each minister was flanked by a French counsellor. The governor also presided over the Council of the Royal Family.

In 1899, the French administration denied the royal administration the right to levy taxes and pay its own functionaries. In Tonkin and Annam, at the provincial level, besides the French provincial governor, there was a Vietnamese administration whose members were mere puppets. The governors were assisted by "elected councils" whose members were carefully selected from among a small group of landowners, rich merchants or industrialists and high functionaries to serve as ornamentation for the colonial administration.

The administration set up by Doumer existed without major changes until the end of French colonial domination.

This administration was really only able to exist thanks to continued military protection. After 1896, sporadic uprisings occurred, showing that the national movement remained alive and vigourous. Around a nucleus of French and African troops and Foreign Legionnaires, the French set up a "native militia" at provincial level. The Vietnamese royal guard was essentially assigned the task of "pacification." None of these measures, however, prevented members of the militia from turning their guns time and again on their French officers and defecting to the national movement.

Organization of Education and Culture

The colonial administration was less concerned with improving standards of education among the people than with training subaltern agents for the administrative apparatus. They also nurtured a "denationalised" intelligentsia that had lost all contact with the nation's culture and spirit of independence.

Before Doumer, the first Governor-General had thought of using traditional education as a means of domination. Doumer maintained the system of mandarin competitions until 1915 in Tonkin, and 1916 in Annam. From 1861 onwards *quốc ngữ*, the Vietnamese language transcribed into the Latin alphabet, was used in Cochinchina. Its use gradually spread throughout the country. In 1896, the colonial administration ordered that *quốc ngữ* be used in some subjects in the mandarin competitions, which after 1903 included a compulsory French-language essay.

The traditional education system was gradually replaced by a so-called "Franco-Vietnamese" system specially designed for the recruitment of workers and lower-level functionaries for the colonial regime. A number of professional schools were opened. In 1901, the Medical College was inaugurated in order to train auxiliary physicians (health officers). At all levels it was education "on the cheap." Even the University of Indochina, opened in 1908, provided only a lopsided, poor quality education. French became the medium of instruction, and the study of the national language and history of Việt Nam was downgraded accordingly. Students recited by heart: "Our ancestors were the Gauls," and talked endlessly of Racine and Chateaubriand without ever properly studying Vietnamese culture. Some 18th century French writers such as Montesquieu and Rouseau were even banned from the curriculum. There was neither a faculty of sciences nor an engineering school at the University of Indochina.

The most obvious feature of the colonial culture was its Malthusianism. The regime limited the spread of education as much as possible. In traditional Việt Nam, despite the obstacles created by the feudal regime, the people in their thirst for knowledge had managed to organize classes for infants in almost every village. The substituting of traditional eduction with colonial education resulted in a drastic reduction in the number of schools and students, and in growing illiteracy.

One of the major demands made by the Vietnamese people throughout the colonial era was the spread and Vietnamization of education. Given this constant pressure, the colonial administration was forced to open a number of schools. The university had the basic aim of training young people wanting to go and study in Japan. But education was never widespread: 90 percent of children were unable to attend school. At the best of times there were only three high schools for the whole of Việt Nam (plus three high schools for the children of French colonists, totaling a few thousand students). Thirty years after its founding, the university had only 600 students.

In order to better assess the nation's resources, towards the end of the 19th century the colonial administration set up a number of research institutes, including the Ecole de L'Extrème Orient, Pasteur Institute, Meteorological Service, Geological and Geographical Services,

Forestry School and others. In some areas French researchers produced interesting work, but generally speaking, the activities of these institutes were designed to serve colonial exploitation. Vietnamese were systematically excluded from research work.

One of the most important cultural factors was the substitution of *quốc ngữ* for the old (Chinese) ideographic script. The printing of newspaper and books in *quốc ngữ* proceeded rapidly. The colonizers wanted to use it as a propaganda tool, but *quốc ngữ* rapidly became for the Vietnamese national movement a means of disseminating ideas about independence and development.

Taxes, Duties, and Excise

The establishment of a cumbersome and oppressive colonial administration created a huge burden for the country. The cost of French officials and the military was very high, the more so as the colonial administration was overstaffed, French politicians and political parties readily planting their agents there. By 1910, the number of French officials in Indochina was about 5,000, almost equaling that of British functionaries in India.

Taxes were substantially increased. In 1897, the poll-tax went up from 0.50 piasters to 2.50 piastres and land tax from 1 to 1.50 piastres. The overall budget increased, mainly as a result of the levying of customs excise on alcohol, salt and opium.

The monopoly on the making and selling of alcohol was conceded to a French company (Fontaine) in 1902, and the drinking of alcohol became compulsory, each village having to consume a set quantity each year in proportion to its population. All private distilling of alcohol was banned and severely punished by means of prison terms, confiscation of property, and even deportation. The Fontaine company, with a capital investment of 3.5 million francs, earned 2 to 3 million francs in profits each year. Alcohol, which cost 5 to 6 cents a litre in 1902, was being sold at 29 cents per litre in 1906.

The administration bought salt from small producers and resold it at greater and greater profits every year — 0.05 piastres for every 100 kilogram in 1897, and 2.50 piastres by 1907. Thus over ten years the price of salt increased fivefold.

The colonial administration reserved for itself a monopoly on the purchase and sale of opium, the consumption of which was encouraged.

Between 1896 and 1899, the price of one kilogram of opium shot up from 45 to 77 piastres. By the time Doumer left the income from opium had reached 15 million gold francs, double the 1897 figure. According to official data, there were 210,000 opium-smokers in Việt Nam in 1907; several times the number from before colonization.

The income from these three sources went up from 8 million piastres in 1899, to 10.4 million in 1903, and to 12 million in 1911, making up an important part of the overall colonial budget which soared from 20 million piastres in 1899, to 32 million in 1903, and 42 million in 1911. Taking into account the various taxes and duties, we can estimate that by Doumer's departure, the Vietnamese people were having to pay more than 90 million gold francs, about three times as much as before. In October 1908 Colonel Bernard wrote in *Revue de Paris* that:

"*This drastic increase in taxes and duties has been dominating Indochina's financial policy for eight or nine years now.*"

The introduction of customs excise, moreover, was accompanied by a costly system of repression. On the slightest denunciation, customs officers would search and arrest anyone, without even so much as a warrant. The increasing financial charges weighed ever more heavily on the already needy peasants, and many families had to do without salt. All spices in fact, became extremely valued.

Colonial Economic Exploitation

This entire administrative, military, financial and cultural apparatus, in the end served to establish a colonial economic structure that was exploitative to the benefit of French companies investing in Indochinese enterprises. The colony became an outlet for French industrial products and a supplier of cheap raw materials and labour. Priority was thus given to the import of French industrial goods, which then competed with traditional handicraft industries and eventually ruined them. The French refused to develop the local industry and concentrated French capital on the production of immediately exportable goods, such as coal, minerals and rubber, and used every means to prevent the emergence of a capitalist industry in Việt Nam. Heavy customs duties were levied on products form countries other than France, which virtually ensured a French monopoly over the Indochinese market. Moreover, in contrast to the heavy burden on Vietnamese taxpayers, French companies were subject to only the most nominal taxation, benefiting from exemptions, subsidies, and advantageous contracts signed with the administration. The whole system was, naturally, being financed by taxes paid by the Vietnamese.

An 1897 decree granted mining concessions to French companies on particularly favourable terms. By the beginning of the 20th century, as well as the Quảng Yên collieries, the French were already exploiting tin, gold, wolfram and antimony mines. Almost all these products were exported; processing industries only saw limited development, as the colonial administration took care not to create a Vietnamese industry that could compete with French production. In the early years of the 20th century, mills first appeared in Cochinchina to husk rice for export, and were later expanded in order to produce hundreds of thousands of tonnes of rice a year. In Tonkin, various companies were set up: the Textile Mill (spinning and weaving) in 1900, the Water and Power Company in 1900, French Distilleries in 1901, the Forestry and Match Company in 1909, and several brick-making factories. Then came the Hải Phòng Cement Works, the Đáp Cầu Paper Mill, and the Hà Nội Match Factory. In Annam, French companies invested much less, with only a few sawmills and match factories at Vinh and Thanh Hóa, a lime kiln in Huế, and a silk-weaving factory in Phú Yên.

Put together, these industries had only minimal production levels, but the profits were significant thanks to low wages, rather than to output. As the profits were taken back to France, the result for Việt Nam was a net financial deficit, constantly exacerbated by the repatriation by French officials of their savings.

In agriculture, the French administration facilitated the seizure of fertile and sparsely inhabited areas by French colonizers or companies. Whole villages were evacuated in the uplands of Tonkin during military operations, while in the Tây Nguyên (the Central Highlands), land was distributed to French settlers or companies. In Cochinchina, drainage works in the Mekong River delta made it possible to allocate vast estates to French settlers or Vietnamese agents of the colonial administration. As a result, between 1897 and 1913, settlers and companies seized 470,000 hectares (306,000 of these in Cochinchina), not counting the 90,000 hectares conceded to the Forestry Company. Before 1918, almost all the estates allocated to French settlers were put under rice. Indochina, and Cochinchina in particular, had to supply a rapidly increasing quantity of rice for export — 800,000 tonnes in 1900, 1.2 million tonnes by 1920.

No technical innovations, however, were made in traditional rice farming. The yield remained one of the lowest in the world at an average of 1.2 tonnes per hectare. French settlers were keen to exploit the labour of Vietnamese peasants, and rice exports continued at a high level, even when the country was in the grip of famine.

In the field of commerce, French goods flooded the market, and were exempt from all custom duties beginning in 1892. They were expensive while Vietnamese products were exported at low prices. Between 1892 and 1913 the value of exports skyrocketed from 26 million piastres to 102 million, and imports from 19 million piastres to 110 million. The profits from foreign trade went almost entirely to a few large companies such as UCIA and Denis Frères.

For economic and strategic purposes, the colonial administration, under Doumer in particular, had given fairly high priority to the development of transportation routes. Narrow-gauge single-track railways were built: Hà Nội - Lạng Sơn in 1902, Hà Nội -Vinh in 1905, Huế-Đà Nẵng in 1906, Sài Gòn - Nha Trang and Hà Nội -Yunnan Phu in 1919. In Cochinchina, many canals were dug to expand the area under rice and facilitate rice exports. It was during the early years of the 20th century that the largest number of transportation routes were built under the colonial regime.

Chapter III

TRANSFORMATION OF THE STRUCTURE OF VIETNAMESE SOCIETY AND NEW FORMS OF THE NATIONAL MOVEMENT

The establishing of the colonial regime saw profound changes in the traditional structure of society. New social classes appeared and new ideas entered the people's consciousness, while poverty was exacerbated as a result of colonial exploitation and the multiple burdens imposed by the occupiers.

Impoverishment of the Peasantry

Long drawn-out military operations had caused serious damage to villages, some of which had been razed to the ground. The seizure of land by the colonizers, mandarins and dignitaries who placed themselves at the service of the French, the increase in financial charges, the duties on alcohol and salt, with all the harassment and exactions they entailed, and the ruin of handicrafts considerably worsened the peasants' plight. The colonial administration was more concerned with building railways and roads of strategic importance or serving colonial enterprises than with building the hydraulic works essential for protecting the crops from natural calamities. Drought, floods and constant food shortages, punctuated by recurrent famine, afflicted the peasantry. Dykes became the object of attention only after many catastrophic floods.

While they carried on their shoulders all the burdens of colonialism, the peasants enjoyed no advantages whatsoever. They were too poor to buy French imported goods and no one was concerned with providing them with new farming techniques to improve production. They were treated by the agents of the administration with extraordinary brutality.

Feudal exploitation and oppression, far from being eliminated by the colonial regime, was reinforced. Land owners and dignitaries gradually became the willing agents of the colonial administration in maintaining order and levying taxes in the countryside. Interpreters, "boys" (servants of the French), and security agents on the French payroll were allotted land, and formed a new class of land owners. Land became concentrated in fewer and fewer hands.

After just a few years of colonial domination, rice consumption per capita had dropped noticeably, from 262 kilograms in 1900 to 226 in 1913. Sometime in the first years of the 20th century a Frenchman made the following observation:

"*Those who have traveled through Indochina are struck by the dire wretchedness of its inhabitants. Almost all the dwellings are just wooden or mud huts covered with straw. Yellow or red strips of paper with inscriptions in Chinese characters hang on the wall; a few wooden implements, occasionally one of bronze, decorate the ancestral altar, as reminders of past prosperity.*"[1]

The conditions of the peasantry, already poor under the feudal regime, worsened under the colonial administration.

Working Class, Bourgeoisie, New Intelligentsia

The establishment of colonial industrial and commercial enterprises and the construction of railways and other means of communications gave rise to a new social class — the working class. Lacking the numerical strength of its European counterpart, the Vietnamese working class nevertheless played a crucial role as it emerged before the national bourgeoisie and was closely related to the colonial rule. Soon after it emerged in the mines, on construction sites, and in factories it came in direct contact with the harsh realities of colonialism. They experienced starvation wages and backbreaking labour with neither restrictions nor safety from brutality, but also the conditions of modern industry.

1. Colonel Bernard. *Indochina, Mistakes and Dangers.*

With regard to public works, the construction of roads and railways in particular, the colonial administration conscripted peasants from every village. On the construction sites where they had become "coolies" they worked in appalling conditions. A French author, Jean Ajalbert, reported:

"Requisitioning became an ill-disguised form of deportation...the public works drained whole communities in favour of construction sites from which only a small number returned...In 1901, I travelled in Lang Biang region where I lived for several weeks. The Public Works were run by a captain of the Cuirassiers. The mortality rate was frightful. Rice arrived there irregularly...There was only one physician for an area covering 120 kilometres."

The construction of the Hà Nội-Yunnan Phu railway, which involved 80,000 men, cost 25,000 lives. Of course there was no real class-consciousness, but right from the beginning struggles, opposition movements, and workers' demands started to emerge on these sites.

The Vietnamese bourgeoisie appeared later. In the early years of the century, its size and significance were negligible. Traditional Vietnamese society hindered on the development of a sizeable class of traders. In commercial operations, the French preferred to deal with Chinese merchants. A number of agents for French companies, however, succeeded in making large fortunes, forming the first nucleus of the Vietnamese comprador bourgeoisie. Some Vietnamese bourgeois elements that tried to set up enterprises were discouraged or driven to bankruptcy by the administration. The nascent Vietnamese bourgeoisie was thus thrown back into land ownership and usury and remained on the sidelines.

New towns began to rise on the foundations of former administrative centres such as Hà Nội and Nam Định, and ports such as Sài Gòn, Hải Phòng and Đà Nẵng. In these towns, elements of new lifestyle began to emerge. Trade became more energetic, factories began to operate, newspapers were published, and electricity appeared. However, working people lived in dire poverty, as these towns accommodated only a fraction of the population.

The first intellectuals trained in French schools were not yet playing any significant role. In Tonkin and Annam, scholars still make up the bulk of the intelligentsia, but their prestige had decline significantly. It was becoming evident that Confucian doctrine could no longer serve as a springboard for the restoration of national independence and social progress. Modernist scholars appeared who sought other paths for the national movement than those advocated by their predecessors.

Modernist Scholars and the National Movement

Towards 1900, the armed struggle which had lasted for four decades (from 1858 to 1898) had virtually ceased. One pocket of armed resistance remained at Yên Thế led by Hoàng Hoa Thám. The resistance, however, continued in new forms and was inspired by modern ideas related to colonial exploitation and oppression. Political struggle appeared in the towns, while demonstrations and strikes by peasants and workers reflected clear-cut economic and social grievances.

The new social strata — the working class and bourgeoisie — were not yet able to assume leadership of the national movement, and it was still the scholars who inspired it. Under the impact of events, new ideas had penetrated intellectual circles. Neither the missionaries nor the conquerors from Europe had brought with them modern scientific or democratic ideas, and the colonial administration banned the teachings of all literary and philosophical works, particularly those of Rousseau and Montesquieu, which only reached Vietnamese scholars through Chinese translation. China, brutally awakened by European aggression, witnessed the rise of a modernist movement towards the end of the 19th century. Renowned scholars such as Kang Yew-wei and Liang Ki-chao inspired a reformist movement aimed at renovating traditional Chinese society. In the first decade of the 20th century, the revolutionary ideas of Sun Yat-sen dominated the Chinese political stage.

Patriotic Vietnamese scholars, coming into contact with new ideas, were no longer content just to protest against aggression and in support of national independence after the re-establishment of the former monarchical regime and Confucian ideology. They began to make proposals for programs for social and ideological change. The scholar split into traditionalist and modernist factions, the former proposing reforms to the colonial regime, the latter advocating armed struggle to topple it.

In 1905, Japan's victory over Tsarist Russia resounded throughout Asia. It proved that through renovation, an Asian state was capable of defeating a European power. Despite the fact that Japan, having turned capitalist, had conquered Taiwan and Korea, Vietnamese patriots showed great admiration for the country, nurturing the hope that Japan, as an Asian power, would offer aid and possibly support even in their struggle against French colonialism.

Many scholars and students left to study in Japan as part of what became known as the *Đông Du* (Go East) movement.

It was Phan Bội Châu who dominated the patriotic movement in the first two decades of the 20th century. A renowned scholar, he had, after 1900, brought together members of the defeated Cần Vương movement to form a new organization, the *Duy Tân* (Renovation) movement. The Duy Tân advocated the reorganization of internal forces, sending people to other countries to study new military and political techniques, and preparations for armed struggle. Phan Bội Châu planned to solicit Japanese aid. A member of the royal family, Prince Cường Để, who had been nominated in case of the movement's success, to head a progressive monarchy, was sent to Japan to establish contact with the Japanese authorities. Towards 1908, about 200 young students, mostly the sons of scholar who had taken part in the national resistance, were sent to Japan. Money was collected throughout the country to pay for their studies.

But Phan Bội Châu had not reckoned with the duplicity of the Japanese. In 1909, capitalist Japan, in exchange for financial concessions offered by France, recognized French conquests in Asia and expelled Vietnamese patriots. One Vietnamese student committed suicide in protest against this policy. Phan Bội Châu and Cường Để had to take refuge in China and Siam, while other members of the Duy Tân movement fell into the hands of the French police.

Within the country, the activities of modernist scholars were marked by great effort towards intellectual renovation. Thanks to financial collections the scholars, under the leadership of Lương Văn Can and Nguyễn Quyền, founded in March 1907 in Hà Nội an association for free mass education called the *Đông Kinh Nghĩa Thục* (the Tonkin Study Institute). Many intellectuals gave it their support and many people joined it, the students soon being numbered in the thousands.

Besides regular courses where new subjects were taught, public lectures attracted large and enthusiastic audiences keen to discuss economic and social problems. A group of scholars published a journal, the *Đăng Cổ Tùng Báo*, which criticized outdated ways and customs, and advocated reforms and the development of industry and trade. Books in the same vein were published. Alarmed by the movement's success, the colonial administration ordered the closure of the Institute and the arrest and exile of its leaders. Although in existence for just one year, the *Đông Kinh Nghĩa Thục* marked an important turning point in the nation's intellectual development and laid firm foundations for the future.

Unlike Phan Bội Châu, an advocate of armed struggle, another patriotic scholar, Phan Chu Trinh, advocated a movement aimed at encouraging the colonial administration to introduce reforms, particularly the abolition of the monarchy and mandarin system and the adoption of republican institutions. His reformist ideals proved to be no protection for him, as he was arrested in 1909 by the colonial authorities and his life saved only through the intervention of members of the French Assembly. Phan Chu Trinh, however, had the sense to be wary of Japanese intensions right from the start.

Peasant Demonstrations, Armed Resistance

Advocates of progressive reforms and those in favour of armed struggle did agree nevertheless to conduct joint activities particularly against old customs and extortion by dignitaries and the colonial authorities. The masses reacted promptly to the appeals from the scholars. The peasants, living in misery and weighed down by taxes, soon added their demands to those of this movement, including reductions in taxes and the abolition of corvée. Confrontation between the masses and the colonial authorities became inevitable.

The campaign slogan "No Taxes for the French" was launched in February 1908 and rapidly spread. The colonial administration and Huế court (which had become its agent and accomplice) soon cracked down on the movement, which nevertheless continued to gather strength. The first peasant demonstrations were staged in Đại Lộc district, Quảng Nam province. Thousands of peasants arriving from different villages gathered in front of the French administrator's residence, demanding a reduction in taxes. For weeks, thousands of ragged peasants replacing the previous group picketed the building. In passionate speeches, the population was urged to oppose the levying of taxes and duties. On some days, over 8, 000 people took park in the demonstration. In Đại Lộc, the colonial authorities had to promise not to raise taxes any further.

From Đại Lộc, the movement spread to other districts of Quảng Nam, then to the neighbouring province of Quảng Ngãi, and finally to Bình Định, Phú Yên, and Thừa Thiên. Reactionary dignitaries as well as guards from the local militia were taken prisoner or executed. The residence of the puppet mandarin Nguyễn Thân, who had helped the French suppress Phan Đình Phùng's uprising, was ransacked. In Huế, demonstrators gathered in impressive numbers for two days in front of the governor's office. The movement later spread to Hà Tĩnh province, where it continued on for months. For the first time, the masses were waging an unarmed political struggle in the form of large demonstrations, a show of strength to back up concrete demands.

The response of the colonial authorities was one of ferocity. Demonstrators were fired upon. Patriotic scholars, among them Trần Quý Cáp, were executed. Others such as Phan Chu Trinh and Huỳnh Thúc Kháng (who in 1945 became Minister for the Interior of the Democratic Republic of Việt Nam), Ngô Đức Kế, Lê Văn Huân and others were deported to Poulo Condor Island. Thousands of people arrested by the colonialists were kept for days in the burning sun. Whole villages were razed to the ground. While the peasant masses had shown their vigour, the colonial regime had given proof of its cruelty.

During this period, Hoàng Hoa Thám was still holding on at Yên Thế, keeping in touch with Phan Bội Châu's Duy Tân movement and insurgent groups organized within the puppet Vietnamese armed forces. In 1909, breaking a truce signed in 1897, the French threw 15, 000 men and powerful artillery into battle against the Yên Thế base. Hoàng Hoa Thám, combining guerrilla with regular attacks, held out for ten months, but the absence of armed uprisings elsewhere made it possible for the colonial administration to concentrate its forces in Yên Thế and overrun it. Hoàng Hoa Thám resisted for another three years before being assassinated by a traitor on 10 February 1913. The Yên Thế base had resisted for twenty years from 1889 to 1909 thanks to the use of guerrilla tactics supported by the peasant masses.

The first two decades of the 20th century were also marked by numerous uprisings by mountain dwellers, which unfortunately were not coordinated with the patriotic movement of the deltas, and were therefore doomed to failure. They included uprisings by the Mường of Hòa Bình (1909-10) and Mông (H'mông) in Hà Giang (1911-12) and numerous uprisings of ethnic groups in Tây Nguyên: the Xơ -đăng, Hrê, Bana, Giarai, and others.

Neither the failure of the Duy Tân movement nor that of Hoàng Hoa Thám affected the enthusiasm of Phan Bội Châu, who in 1912 founded a new league, the *Việt Nam Quang Phục*, whose program was aimed at toppling the colonial regime and establishing a Vietnamese republic. Following the success of the Chinese Revolution in 1911, Phan Bội Châu sought asylum in China and his ideas evolved in the direction of republican ideology. After various uprisings and demonstrations had been savagely put down, the Quang Phục also advocated spectacular assassination bids aimed at arousing public enthusiasm, proclaiming sentences of death on Governor-General Albert Sarraut and the puppet mandarins Hoàng Trọng Phu and Nguyễn Duy Hàn. The latter was killed by a bomb in 1913. In the same year a patriot hurled a bomb into a Hà Nội hotel, killing two French officers. Many people were arrested following these attacks and Phan Bội Châu was sentenced to death *in absentia.* When the First World War broke out, Quang Phục broke up after the failure of several armed attacks near the Sino -Vietnamese border.

Việt Nam During the First World War (1914-1918)

While seeking to make maximum the use of Indochina's natural resources and manpower to fight the war, France cracked down on all patriotic mass movements in Việt Nam. Indochina, and mainly Việt Nam, had to provide France with 50,000 soldiers and 49,000 workers, forcibly drafted from villages to serve on the French battlefront. Indochina also contributed 184 million piastres in the form of loans, and 336,000 tonnes of food. These burdens proved all the heavier as agriculture was hard hit by natural disasters in the years 1914 -1917.

Lacking a unified, nationwide organization, the Vietnamese national movement, though still vigourous, failed to take advantage of the difficulties France was experiencing as a result of war to stage any significant uprisings. The scholars' movement had declined while new social forces were not yet strong enough to promote large-scale campaigns.

The Quang Phục movement had planned to seize Hà Nội through the combined action of patriots within the country and revolutionary army trained abroad. The secret operation was betrayed however, and many members of the movement were arrested. Other members joined different organizations, armed themselves with rudimentary weapons, and sought to bring soldiers from the local militia over to their side. On 6 January 1919, 150 armed patriots attacked the garrison at Phú Thọ. Meanwhile, enemy posts in other provinces such as Nho Quan in Ninh Bình and Móng Cái near the Chinese border were besieged, but the attacks failed. The Quang Phục had the ambition of launching a series of attacks against many military and administrative centres in Tonkin, but plan was not implemented.

Again in Tonkin, on 31 August 1917, soldiers of the Thái Nguyên garrison mutinied under the leadership of Sergeant Trịnh Văn Cấn, a former partisan of Hoàng Hoa Thám, and of Lương Ngọc Quyến, a member of the Quang Phục movement. Joined by many soldiers, the insurgents killed the post's French commander, seized a large haul of arms and munitions, and liberated many political prisoners who then joined the ranks of the combatants; the town of Thái Nguyên was liberated. The insurgents, after a series of discussions, gave up their plans for extending their activities to other provinces. They dug in at Thái Nguyên instead, in the hope of consolidating their strength. On September 4, the French retook the town, forcing the insurgents to leave. Scattered in the mountainous region around Thái Nguyên, the insurgents continued their struggle against 2,000 French troops for another six months.

In Annam, the most important event was the call for an uprising made by King Duy Tân, enthroned in 1907 at the age of seven at the instigation of patriotic mandarins and scholars, particularly Thái Phiên and Trần Cao Vân. The principal forces on which he relied were soldiers gathered in their thousands in Huế and about to leave for France. The signal for the start of the revolt should have been given on 3 May 1916. Unfortunately, the secret was leaked and the French disarmed the soldiers before the day of their departure. Duy Tân attempted to flee the capital but was captured and exiled to the island of Réunion. Scattered armed groups were rapidly eliminated by the French, and the patriots Thái Phiên and Trần Cao Vân were executed.

In Cochinchina, patriotic activity manifested itself in the early years of the century by the creation of underground societies, the most important of which was the *Thiên Địa Hội* (Heaven and Earth Association) whose branches covered many provinces around Sài Gòn. These associations often took the form of politico -religious organizations, and one of their main activities was to punish traitors in the pay of the French.

Connected to these clandestine societies, a movement led by a former bonze, Phan Xích Long, came into being in 1913. Its members, wearing white clothes and turbans, attacked the cities with primitive weapons. Phan Xích Long was eventually captured and executed by the French. In 1916, underground societies in Cochinchina tried to attack several administrative centres, including the central prison in Sài Gòn and the residence of the local French governor. On the night of 14 February 1916, thousands of people armed with knives and wearing amulets infiltrated Sài Gòn and fought French police and troops who succeeded in routing them.

The colonial administration, while harshly suppressing the national movement, sought to appease the élite by introducing a few paltry reforms, with promises of important postwar reforms from the more generous "liberal" governors. These promises were never fulfilled. The fact that France succeeded in holding on to Việt Nam during the war years was mainly due to the weakness of the national movement. There were of course patriots to still carry on the fight for national independence, but the new and still embryonic social forces failed to give the movement the necessary vigour and direction. Not until these forces had developed further over subsequent decades was the national movement able to be revitalized on a new basis.

Chapter IV

ECONOMIC TRANSFORMATION AND THE BEGINNINGS OF THE NATIONAL DEMOCRATIC REVOLUTION

(1919 - 1929)

The decade following the First World War was marked by intensified economic exploitation of Việt Nam by the French colonialists, entailing important modifications to the structures of Vietnamese society. On the other hand, with the emergence of new social forces, the national movement took on new forms, laying the first foundations of the national and democratic revolution to come.

Intensification of Colonial Economic Exploitation

After the First World War, French imperialism sped up the development of its colonies for its own economic rehabilitation. The devaluation of the franc and speculation in rubber on the world market boosted French investment in Indochina.

The Bank of Indochina increased its assets from 48 million to 72 million piastres. The bank, a lending institution established by several leading French financial and industrial groups, controlled the main economic and financial activity in Indochina. In effect, it ruled the country. The Land Credit Office saw its assets rise from 6 million piastres in 1923 to 50 million in 1925, and those of the Financial and Colonial Company from 5 million in 1920 to 50 million by 1926.

Between 1888 and 1918, the French invested 490 million francs in Indochina and between 1919 and 1929, 8,000 million. These investments, however, in no way benefited the country's economy. The influx of capital responded not to the needs of the country but to the interests of French creditors who, above all else, were concerned with seeing a high return on their investments. More than half of this capital was retained in France for market and financial operations. Investment was directed in particular into mining and rubber plantations, operations aimed at exporting large quantities of raw materials from the country. The repatriation to France of profits and savings by French officials, and the payment of interest on credits, caused a continuing financial deficit. In reality, the situation was such that the French investment, far from injecting new life into the country, functioned like a suction pump plugged into the Vietnamese economy.

By ignoring the industrial sector and focusing economic activity on the production and export of coal, rubber, and minerals, these investments, instead of developing the national economy, made it completely dependent on fluctuations in the world market. There was a rush on rubber. On the red soils covering the basaltic plateau of Cochinchina and Cambodia, huge estates were granted to French companies including Michelin. The area given over to rubber grew from 15,000 hectares in 1924 to 120,000 hectares in 1930, and the number of employees from 3,000 to 80,000. From 298 tonnes in 1915, rubber output increased to 10,309 in 1929. Coffee and tea plantations were also set up.

Indochina also experienced a "mining boom." The number of mining permits rose from 496 in 1923 to 1,347 in 1924, 8,185 in 1928, and 17, 685 in 1929. Most of the mines were in Bắc Bộ. One of them produced 501,000 tonnes of coal in 1913 and 1,972,000 in 1929. Tin, wolfram and lead mines were established (but not iron), and all minerals were exported.

On the other hand, processing industries hardly existed. Only the sectors not competing with French industry were able to survive, and really only benefitted. French companies in particular, the national bourgeoisie having practically no share in them. This included the expansion of the rice husking mills, the Nam Định Textile Mill, Hải Phòng Cement Works, and brick and tile factories. All told, they amounted to only a few enterprises concentrated mainly in the area of Sài Gòn -Chợ Lớn and Hải Phòng, and employed a total of 86,000 workers by 1929.

It was low labour costs that, above all, brought in such sizeable profits. In 1925 the Bank of Indochina declared a profit of 36 million

piastres on a capital investment of 72 million piastres, and the Rubber Financial Company a profit of 31 million piastres on an investment of 100 million piastres. These profits were repatriated to France instead of being used to improve the local economy.

The budget continued to be boosted by poll and land taxes and the duties on alcohol, salt and opium; heavy taxes levied on a poor population to maintain a cumbersome administrative, military and police machine. Seventy per cent of the budget was spent on paying officials and the police. The French door-keeper at the University of Indochina earned three times as much as a Vietnamese professor. Customs barriers made imported goods exceedingly expensive. French consumers had to pay high prices for Vietnamese rice and rubber. The only beneficiaries of this "development" of Indochina remained the big colonial companies.

The colonial administration practically gave away vast estates to the French colonialists; 10,000 hectares in 1930 alone.

In the political sphere, the promises loudly proclaimed during the war were forgotten, and the regime remained as oppressive as ever. However, through "liberal," glib and demagogic Governor-Generals, the colonial administration attempted to win over a small élite through empty speeches and cosmetic reforms. An example of this can be seen through the founding of the Economic and Financial High Council of Indochina, and the Chamber of Agriculture, which in principle was supposed to advise the colonial government. In Cochinchina, representatives of Vietnamese land-owners and the bourgeoisie were allowed to participate in the Colonial Council, which was the consultative body for the French Governor-General, in numbers equal to the French. In Annam and Tonkin, Chambers of Representatives were set up and elected by a minority as consultative bodies for French governors.

These carefully-selected delegates or representatives only had cosmetic purposes and the people nicknamed them *nghị gật* (yes-men). The colonial administration did not want to give the Vietnamese bourgeoisie and feudalists any real power. The king himself retained no privileges other than the authority to confer honorific titles and ranks on village deities.

Việt Nam continued to be divided into three "countries" with different regimes, but in none of these "countries" was the most minimal democratic freedom tolerated. There was no freedom of association, of the press, of opinion, or movement, even within the country. The sole religion encouraged was Catholicism.

Feudalists and Peasants

The process of social restructuring which had begun early in the century gathered speed in the postwar years.

The feudalists included land-owners on the one hand, and on the other hand, the former state apparatus, comprising the king, mandarins and dignitaries. In order to retain their privileges, they all placed themselves totally at the service of the colonial administration which sought to maintain the feudal apparatus as an instrument of repression and tax collection. Mandarins and dignitaries, using their power, little by little seized communal land and land belonging to peasants. Despite the dividing up of estates between the sons of land-owners, the concentration of estate ownership continued unabated, due to the rapid impoverishment of a peasantry who, due to the financial charges and other burdens, had to sell the little land they had left. The clearing of new land, as well as the soaring price of rice resulting from the rapidly growing export trade, brought huge profits to the land-owners.

The landlord class, comprising some 3-5 percent of the population, owned about half of the land. In Tonkin, the land had been divided up many times, and each landlord owned many scattered plots. In Annam, there was plenty of communal land, which in principle was subject to periodic redistribution, but the village dignitaries always reserved the bulk for themselves. It was in Cochinchina, especially in the southern and western areas of the Mekong River delta, that large-scale land-ownership emerged under the colonial regime. Land reclaimed thanks to the building of canals and other public works by the population was allotted to faithful servants of the colonial administration. Estates of more than 50 hectares accounted for almost half the total land area, and by around 1930 were owned by 6,500 landlords, representing 2.5 percent of the population. Some of these landlords owned up to several thousand hectares. French colonists in Cochinchina also owned over 200,000 hectares of rice fields. Despite the vast size of the estates, owners there also rented their lands to *tá điền*[1], who had to pay rent equivalent to half their crop yields. In Cochinchina, the rent could be paid in cash, while in Tonkin and Annam it was paid in kind. In

1. Tenants

Cochinchina, Vietnamese land-owners joined with French colonists to found the "Rice Growers' Society."

The appearance of large estates and the moving in of French colonists, did not in any way alter the backwardness of farming techniques. Land-owners and colonists thrived thanks to their ruthless exploitation of the peasants' labour and made no attempt to improve farming techniques. The cultivation of a single crop, rice, still prevailed, and while production increased as the area under cultivation expanded, the yield was for export, while the peasant's food rations rapidly decreased. The few rice-husking mills and mechanized means of transport functioned solely for purposes of export. By contrast, as the French geographer Gourou put it, one could travel the length and breadth of the Tonkin delta without seeing a single motor or mechanized vehicle.

The peasantry accounted for over 90 percent of the population.

With the development of the cash economy, a class of rich peasants who both tilled their own land and employed paid labour gradually emerged, not as capitalists but as land-owners. At the same time, the rapidly increasing concentration of land-ownership led to the decline of the middle strata of peasants, those who owned just enough land to meet their needs.

Poor farmers who owned either no land at all or only tine plots made up the bulk of the peasantry. In Cochinchina, the *tá điền* were all landless peasants. In Tonkin and Annam, many peasants owned a few tiny plots but one after the other they were robbed of their land, buffaloes and farm equipment. Since they were unable to sell their labour in the cities, as there was so little industry, they found themselves among the thousands begging for a piece of land from land-owners and colonists. As a result, land rents skyrocketed and rural overpopulation took on dramatic proportions, recruiters of "coolie" for the mines and plantations imposed harsh conditions, and famines caused by natural disasters occurred periodically. At harvest-time, thousands of landless peasants gathered in marketplaces, waiting for employment. In the off season, thousands crowded into the cities looking for work, which was becoming harder and harder to find, and then returned to their villages for the harvest.

The difficulties caused by high land rents were compounded by the exorbitant interest rates peasants had to pay on their debts to land-owners and other creditors, rates reaching an average of 10 percent per

month. Even a mild illness or accident meant the poor peasant had to obtain a new loan; he was often bound for life by such loans, unable ever to pay them back due to the accumulated interest. Quite often, he had to sell his children and his plots of land to pay off his debts. Land-owners demanded gifts in kind from poor peasants at each anniversary, wedding, or other festive occasions.

Poor peasants also had to undertake all the corvée imposed by the communal, mandarin, and colonial administration. The payment of a poll-tax, which on average represented the fruits of a month's labour, was a heavy burden. Each year, when the colonial administration ordered the collection of taxes by mandarins and notables, villagers wept and cried with despair, and hundreds of thousands of peasants were arrested and whipped until their wives and children could find a few piastres with which to pay.

The colonial administration thus reinforced feudal structures with the rapid impoverishment of the peasantry and the disappearance of traditional ways and customs, and life in the villages lost all its best aspects. No innovations and no new ideas penetrated villages weighed down by misery, and where almost all the inhabitants were illiterate. The leaden cloak of feudal and colonial society had descended over millions of landless peasants. These millions of peasants, deprived of their livelihood and terribly oppressed, were to become, once a visionary leader arose, the main driving force behind the national and democratic revolution in Việt Nam.

The Proletariat, Force of the Future

The Vietnamese working class was also growing in numbers. In 1929 there were almost 220, 000 workers throughout Việt Nam, with 53,000 in the mines and 86,000 in the rubber plantations. Most of the French enterprises in Cambodia, Laos and even New Caledonia employed tens of thousands of Vietnamese workers.

Numerically, the working class represented only a tiny proportion of the population, but it was concentrated in regions of vital importance for the colonial economy such as the mines, rubber plantations, and major cities. It was the only social class to directly and continuously face colonial economic exploitation and to come into direct and daily contact with modern production techniques. It therefore occupied a strategic position of prime importance in Vietnamese society.

Few skilled workers, or even nominally qualified workers, had a stable factory job. Many were employed on an irregular basis, and returned to their villages when unemployed, or when their contracts ended. The result was close mixing of workers and peasants, and the numbers of those who had experienced life as workers in colonial enterprises were much higher than official figures suggested.

Workers were subject to naked exploitation. Many women and children were employed in heavy work. Recruiting agents traveled throughout the countryside, getting illiterate peasants to sign "contracts" which they were supposed to have read and under whose terms they were obliged to work in mines or plantations for three to five years. These agents were paid according to how many workers they recruited. The labourers thus hired were sent to rubber plantations in Cochinchina, or nickel mines in New Caledonia, where they lived and worked in appalling conditions.

There was virtually no limit on working hours, and workers were ill-fed and at risk from malaria. The *cai* (foremen) subjected them to constant surveillance and often used corporal punishment. Fines and partial withholding of wages further reduced workers' paltry incomes. Mines and plantations had their own prisons where workers could be held without trial. The French directors had the right of life and death over their workers. The meagre wages earned by workers were spent on food and other necessities at canteens run by the companies. The money paid out by the latter in the form of salaries thus returned to them in a closed circuit system. Many workers died of disease and ill-treatment, and those who escaped were caught by the police. There was no legislation protecting workers and no trade union freedoms. All strikes were crimes punishable by imprisonment, torture or exile. It was virtual slavery which a number of French journalists passionately denounced in their reports, including Louis Roubaud in *Les Jauniers*.

An important aspect was the absence of a "working class aristocracy," which stopped any reformist or chauvinist tendencies from developing within the Vietnamese working class movement. The Vietnamese working class under the colonial regime suffered across the board in extreme poverty as a result of appalling living and working conditions. Besides workers employed in sizable enterprises, there were many in the cities and ports and domestic servants with insecure employment, living a precarious existence and suffering from chronic unemployment.

The Vietnamese bourgeoisie grew to some extent in the years 1919-1929 but remained weak, restricted by the monopoly practices of

French companies and strong competition from Chinese merchants. Between 1924 and 1929 a number of privately-owned Vietnamese companies emerged but never compared in scale with Chinese or Indian capitalist enterprises. The Vietnamese bourgeoisie with great difficulty managed to secure a foothold in domestic trade, small industry and the transport and building sectors. Foreign trade, heavy industry and mining were practically closed to them, and they rarely employed more than a few dozen workers.

Those who sought to develop the nation's resources met with strong opposition from the colonial administration, which saw them as interests which nurtured aspitarions for independence. The others usually became agents distributing French goods or obtained contracts from the administration. This sector formed the comprador bourgeoisie. The dividing line between these two groups remained imprecise. The comprador bourgeoisie, especially in the south, essentially comprised merchants of Chinese origin, the Hoa, who were closely associated with colonial companies in Indochina and the rest of Southeast Asia. Bullied and strangled in its development, the Vietnamese bourgeoisie often invested its profits in the purchase of land which it exploited according to feudal patterns. The Vietnamese bourgeoisie never developed as did its counterparts in other countries.

The petit bourgeoisie in the cities was numerically more significant. In consisted of small traders, artisans, and a body of students and intellectuals trained in the new schools. High school students often took part in political and social movements. Neither the high schools nor university had many students, but these elements were active, and like small traders in the cities reacted strongly to events. Many intellectuals including professors, lawyers, physicians and journalists were strongly influenced by progressive ideas from France.

Artisans, 200,000 to 250,000 in number, lived in both the cities and countryside. Many town quarters, and some villages in Tonkin, devoted themselves exclusively to handicrafts. Handicraft production faced strong competition from French industrial products, was heavily taxed, and only survived because the craftsmen accepted very low prices for their work. Many worked for private companies which retained most of the profits.

The petit bourgeoisie, particularly its lower stratum, deeply resented the suffering and humiliation caused by the colonial regime, and its national aspirations soon turned towards revolutionary ideas.

New Upsurge in the National Movement

In a changing Vietnamese society, internal pressures were soon compounded by significant external influences, some of which became decisive in the postwar years.

The 1917 October Revolution had ushered in a new historical era by announcing an irreversible crisis in imperialism, and created new opportunities and hopes for the liberation of colonies around the world. In India, Indonesia and Egypt, the national movement was given a new impetus. In China events unfolded with greater urgency, while in France, the founding of the French Communist Party (1920) marked a new stage in the workers' movement.

In the years 1918-1921, armed uprisings were again launched in Việt Nam, but were limited to a few mountainous areas in Tonkin - revolts by Nùng and Dao soldiers in the northeast, and by the H'mong (Mèo) in the northwest.

The bourgeoisie began to flex its political muscle in 1919 by launching a boycott, not of French goods (it was too weak to directly oppose the occupiers) but of these enterprises. Meetings were held and acts of violence occurred against these enterprises, but the movement never really took off. The colonial administration did not view this movement unfavorably as it had a diversionary effect, and the people did not respond en masse to its calls. In 1923, the Sài Gòn bourgeoisie openly voiced its opposition to a plan to concede Sài Gòn harbour's import -export monopoly to a French company. The movement was supported by Chinese merchants and one section of public opinion as well as left-wing members of parliament in France. The plan failed as a result. It was from among this Sài Gòn bourgeoisie, made up mostly of former employees of the colonial administration made rich by rice farming, that members of the "Constitutionalist" party, founded in 1923, were recruited. This party simply demanded a better deal for the bourgeoisie under the colonial regime.

Much more important was the general ferment spreading among the working class and the petit bourgeoisie, in the cities in particular. New newspapers in Vietnamese and French appeared. In Cochinchina there was *La Cloche fêlée* (The Cracked Bell), edited by Nguyễn An Ninh, an intellectual back from France who drew his inspiration from the theoreticians of the French Revolution, and *L'Annam*, also published in French and edited by Phan Văn Trường, a progressive intellectual. In Sài Gòn, Trần Huy Liệu founded the *Đông Pháp Thời Báo* (Times of

Indochina). In Hà Nội, Ngô Đức Kế founded the *Hữu Thanh*. In Huế, Huỳnh Thúc Kháng published the *Tiếng Dân* (The Voice of People). All three were in Vietnamese. Publishing houses were established, producing books which advocated patriotic struggle or spread modern political and scientific knowledge. New political organizations, groups and parties were set up to wage constant political agitation in the form of meetings, demonstrations, petitions, strikes, and so on.

Thus, political activity gradually took on modern forms of expression, despite the fact that increasing repression by the colonial administration meant the organizations remained clandestine, and that the press was subject to constant restriction and hindrance such as censorship, seizure, banning and often the imprisonment or deportation of journalists.

Following the failure or armed uprisings launched during the war years, the organizations which had taken refuge in China broke up. Their leader, Phan Bội Châu, stayed in China until 1925 when he was arrested and sent back to Việt Nam. Meanwhile he had studied Marxism -Leninism, and made contact with communists and planned a rapprochement with them. The younger and more active members of these organizations had regrouped to form the *Tâm Tâm Xã*, which took drastic action in 1924 - a bomb attack by the young Phạm Hồng Thái against French Governor -General Merlin in Canton on his way to Japan. Merlin was unhurt, and Phạm Hồng Thái drowned himself in the Canton River, but the event had profound consequences.

Among the Vietnamese who had gone to study in France or who had been mobilized — the colonial administration had forced 100,000 Vietnamese to go and fight in France — many were inspired by bourgeois democratic ideas and influenced by French political currents. Some moved in non-revolutionary left-wing circles, the most prominent being Phan Chu Trinh, a former patriotic scholar deported to Poulo Condor and then sent to France by the colonial administration. He advocated progressive struggle for the abolition of feudal institutions and establishment of democratic freedoms under the colonial regime so as to move gradually towards autonomy, but discarded the idea of armed struggle. He did not found any political party.

The second tendency came under the direct influence of the October Revolution through the French workers' movement. Its most celebrated representative was Nguyễn ái Quốc (who later took the name of Hồ Chí Minh). He had arrived in France, taken on many different jobs, and made contact with many French left-wing parties, groups and personalities and many militants from Africa and Asia. He had also travelled to the United

States and Britain. The October Revolution and the works of Lenin had taught him that only Marxism-Leninism could be the key to the liberation struggle of colonized peoples. A member of the French Socialist Party, he opted at the Tours Congress in December 1920 to joint the Third International and set up the French newspapers *L' Humanité* and *La Vie Ouvrière*, founded the newspapers *La Paria*, organized the *Fédération des Peuples Coloniaux*, and wrote the pamphlet *Le Procès de la Colonization Franơaise* (French Colonization on Trial). His militant activity and writings had a profound impact on the Vietnamese and nationals from other colonies living in France, and on public opinion in Việt Nam. In 1923, he left France for the Soviet Union and in 1924, as a delegate to the Third International, went to Canton where he laid the foundations for a new type of revolutionary organization.

While political ideas and organizations were experiencing a renewal, the Vietnamese working class were beginning to engage in an increasingly wider struggle. Strikes became more frequent. In 1919 and 1920, officers and sailors on French ships went on strike. Vietnamese sailors on their trips to France and China could make contact with the world revolutionary movement. The years 1924-25 were marked by major strikes in Chợ Lớn, Nam Định, Hải Dương and Hà Nội. In August 1925, a political strike occurred at the Sài Gòn arsenal; when two French warships en route to China docked for repairs, their crews launched a strike and go-slow in support of the Chinese revolution. The workers also demanded a 20 percent pay increase and the reinstatement of workers sacked for demanding a 30-minute break in their work-day. This eight-day strike was supported by several thousand workers and was an outstanding success. The two warships only left Sài Gòn after having remained at anchor for four months. One of the leaders of the strike—Tôn Đức Thắng, who had taken part in many political campaigns in France —together with French sailors was sent to the Black Sea to fight for the Russian revolution. He later became President of the Democratic Republic of Việt Nam.

On the national level, the years 1925-1926 were marked by three important campaigns demanding the release of Phan Bội Châu, then Nguyễn An Ninh, and a nationwide demonstration on the day of Phan Chu Trinh's funeral. The colonial administration was forced to grant an amnesty to Phan Bội Châu who had been sentenced to death. Tens of thousands demonstrated on these occasions, especially in Sài Gòn and other major cities.

One should bear in mind the savage nature of colonial repression in order to gain an appreciation of the courage and political maturity of the masses and the leaders who organized these strikes and demonstrations.

Regrouping of Patriotic and Revolutionary Forces

Faced with a patriotic movement that was gaining in strength, the colonial administration reluctantly implemented some minor reforms aimed at appeasing popular anger and exploiting opportunistic elements. The French socialist Varenne was instrumental in this respect. Only the Constitutionalist party made up of Sài Gòn's prominent rice growers was satisfied with such crumbs. Patriots and revolutionaries knew they had to organize the masses who were beginning to engage in political action so as to throw them into the struggle, a necessary condition for any progress and liberation struggle.

Starting in 1925, new patriotic and revolutionary organizations began to emerge: In Canton, with the *Tâm Tâm Xã* as its nucleus, Nguyễn ái Quốc founded the *Thanh Niên Cách mạng Đồng Chí Hội* (Revolutionary Youth Association, referred to in this text *Thanh Niên* for short). Young people from Việt Nam or the Vietnamese community in Siam were sent to China to attend a revolutionary training course organized by Nguyễn ái Quốc. They were later sent back to Việt Nam to lay the foundations of the revolutionary movement. In comparison with other organizations, the *Thanh Niên* had the advantage of having clear theoretical and organizational principles, which enabled it to train cadres to rapidly win over the masses and prominent organizations. The activists acquired a basic grounding in Marxism-Leninism, summarized and adapted to Vietnamese conditions by Nguyễn ái Quốc in his booklet, *Đường Kách Mệnh* (The Revolutionary Path), which emphasized three principles totally new to the Vietnamese patriotic and revolutionary movement:

1. Revolution is the duty of the worker and peasant masses and not of just a few heroes, hence the necessity to organize these masses and draw them into the struggle.

2. To achieve success, revolution must be led by a Marxist-Leninist party, hence the need to create a new type of party.

3. The national revolution must integrate with the world revolution, and the Vietnamese people must act together with the worldwide proletariat, hence the necessity to act in accordance with the policy of the Third International.

The *Thanh Niên* published an underground newspaper and was the only organization which was able to do so regularly.

Its members were encouraged to get jobs in factories, plantations and mines, and promote awareness among peasants, students, small traders, and

intellectuals. Their theoretical concept of Marxism, like their practical experience, was still limited. But they offered enlightened criticism of the reformist or chauvinistic views of the bourgeoisie and the petit bourgeoisie.

The first important challenge for *Thanh Niên* was the failure of the Canton commune in December 1927. Several of its members were arrested, and the Kuomintang put pressure on the organization for it to adopt a nationalistic line. *Thanh Niên* accepted the challenge and continued to develop its mass organization networks in Việt Nam, China, and among the Vietnamese community in Siam. By 1928, it had became the most powerful underground organization in the country.

At the same time as *Thanh Niên*, a Marxism-oriented party was established, the *Tân Việt* (New Việt Nam), bringing together young students and former political prisoners from Poulo Condor. It sent several of its members to Canton, among them Trần Phú, for revolutionary training under Nguyễn ái Quốc's leadership, and to negotiate a merger between the two parties. *Tân Việt* later had to work out a programme and regulations similar to those of *Thanh Niên*.

In Cochinchina, Nguyễn An Ninh founded an underground party whose members were recruited mainly from among Sài Gòn's intellectuals. However, its vague structure and program did not survive the arrest of its leader first in 1925, and again in 1928.

The trend towards nationalism was not clearly expressed in the founding of the *Việt Nam Quốc Dân Đảng* (National Party of Việt Nam), with the *Nam Đồng Thư Xã* as its nucleus, whose main activity until then had been to publish patriotic literature. The publishing house was banned by the colonial administration. Support for the armed struggle was predominant within the organization, and under Nguyễn Thái Học's leadership, the *Quốc Dân Đảng* was founded on 25 December 1927. It recruited its members mainly from among intellectuals, students, rural officials, and patriotic dignitaries. It did not concern itself with creating mass organizations, but sought to recruit members among soldiers with a view to armed action. The *Quốc Dân Đảng* worked out a program aimed at gaining national independence and establishing a democratic government, but its social program remained very vague. Strongly influenced by China's Kuomintang, it showed anti-communists tendencies. It was based mainly in Tonkin, and was practically non-existent in central and southern Việt Nam.

In the south, the movement which soon gained predominance was a unique politico-religious organization, the Cao Đài, which brought together in a broad synthesis elements from several regions —

Christianity, Buddhism, Islam —and various other doctrines as well as cults surrounding deities and historical figures ranging from Jesus Christ to Nguyễn Bỉnh Khiêm a (the Vietnamese poet) and Victor Hugo. In Cao Đài, rites inspired by spiritualism developed alongside liturgical forms drawn from Catholicism. But the most prominent feature of the Cao Đài was its close -knit hierarchy organized on the model of the Catholic Church, with a "pope" and well-organized clergy. It had its "Holy See" at Tây Ninh in Cochinchina, and recruited its many faithful from among the peasantry and petit bourgeoisie.

It owed its widespread appeal as much to religious customs persisting among a peasantry which had not yet felt the influence of the revolutionary movement, as to the need of certain politicians to find a smoke screen for their activities. The colonial administration planted its agents in the movement to direct and observe it. The Cao Đài faithful numbered over a million and hundreds of churches were built; the top hierarchy was most of the time in the pay of landlords or high-ranking functionaries and often easily manipulated by the colonial administration.

The emergence of all these parties, organizations and newspapers gave the national movement an ever more solid basis. The years 1927-1929 in particular were marked by a series of strikes in Hải Phòng, Nam Định, Sài Gòn and the rubber plantations. Even in Huế which until then had been in the iron grip of the royal and colonial administrations, students and high school pupils began to involve themselves. The colonial administration rapidly gave up its pretence of liberalization as argued for by Varenne, and swung back into blatant repression. Varenne was replaced in 1928 by a colonial official, Pasquier. A head-on collision between the colonial administration and the Vietnamese patriotic and revolutionary forces was soon to occur.

Yên Bái: Failure of the *Quốc Dân Đảng*

In February 1929, the *Quốc Dân Đảng*, faithful to its strategy of using terrorist attacks, assassinated Bazin, a French recruiter of coolies for the plantations and mines. The colonial police tightened their noose around the Nationalist Party, threatening it with disbandment. It reacted by closing ranks, trying to expel the traitors who had infiltrated it, recruiting more members from the military, and speeding up preparations for armed struggle. But it still failed to organize mass actions. Arms caches were discovered by the colonial police, branches organized in a number of barracks were betrayed, and party leaders came to the conclusion that it was necessary to expedite the armed rising. They were aware that conditions were not yet ripe, but believed that "if the revolution failed, at least honour would be saved." They decided to launch into action, taking an oath to "die to show the whole world that the spirit of the Vietnamese people is still alive."

On the night of 9 February 1930, soldiers at Yên Bái garrison, in the northwest of the Red River delta, rose in revolt, killed their French officers, and seized the arms store. Similar action was taken in the neighbouring provinces of Phú Thọ and Sơn Tây, while a number of bombs were thrown in Hà Nội. Uprisings occurred in several localities in the provinces of Hải Dương and Kiến An. The rest of the country did not respond however, and neither did the people in the cities and provinces where the uprisings had taken place. The insurgents failed to take control of the town of Yên Bái. The uprising was doomed and party leaders were arrested and executed. They died with great courage. The Yên Bái incident had profound repercussions for Vietnamese and French public opinion. The newly - founded Communist Party of Indochina supported the uprising, which was also backed by the French Communist Party in the National Assembly.

The repression was bloody. The *Quốc Dân Đảng* was now leaderless and its grassroots organizations destroyed. Yên Bái was its first and last action. Without deep roots among the masses, the party was unable to survive the repression and rebuild. The younger and more dynamic members of the party rapidly turned to other revolutionary paths. The leaders and militants took refuge in China where, under the protection of Chiang Kai-shek, they sought to rebuild their party. But the *Quốc Dân Đảng* disappeared from the political stage, and those who were to return to Việt Nam in 1945 in the wake of Chiang Kai -shek troops had nothing in common with the Yên Bái patriots.

Founding of the Communist Party

The development of national and socio-economic struggles among workers, peasants and intellectuals, and the failure and disappearance of the *Quốc Dân Đảng* required more than ever the creation of a party capable of leading the movement and co-ordinating the struggle. Members of *Thanh Niên* who participated in all these struggles understood the pressing need to create a Marxist-Leninist party. In March 1929, the first Communist Party cell was set up in Hà Nội. In May 1929, at the National Congress of *Thanh Niên,* delegates proposed the founding of a communist party. The congress did not oppose this, but the majority postponed the decision so as to have time to make the necessary preparations. The Tonkin delegation, which had made the proposal, found on its own the *Đông Dương Cộng Sản Đảng* (Communist Party of Indochina), issued a manifesto, recruited members from *Thanh Niên*, and published the newspaper *Búa Liềm* (Hammer and Sickle). It set up a trade union federation with a press office which had great influence, especially in Tonkin and Annam.

The Central Committee of *Thanh Niên* in its turn decided to create the *An Nam Cộng Sản Đảng* (Communist Party of Annam). The Tân Việt also transformed itself into a new party, the *Đông Dương Cộng Sản Liên Đoàn* (Communist League of Indochina). Thus, urged on by the grassroots and historical circumstances, three communists parties one after another came into being. *Thanh Niên* and *Tân Việt*, having fulfilled their historic mission, made room for the new parties. The urgent necessity for a merger became obvious immediately.

In February 1930, Nguyễn Ái Quốc presided over a conference bringing together delegates from the three parties in Kowloon, China. On February 3, a merger was agreed on and the constitutions of the united party and of mass organizations such as trade unions, the communists youth union, peasants' and women's organizations, and a people's aid society, adopted.

It was a turning-point not only in the history of the working class, but also in the Vietnamese national movement, which now had a leading party armed with a scientific theory, clear-cut principles for action and organization, and close ties with the world revolutionary movement. It possessed the capability of drawing the masses into a wide-ranking struggle and working out for the nation and various social classes a concrete program and vision of the future. All these were sadly lacking in the organizations and parties which preceded it in the struggle against imperialism. As the three countries of Việt Nam, Laos and Cambodia were directly under the control of the one French colonial administration, it was necessary to rally their revolutionary fighters into a communist party.

At the first plenum of its Central Committee in October 1930, the party took the name *Đảng Cộng Sản Đông Dương* (Communist Party of Indochina) and adopted the political program presented by Trần Phú, its first General Secretary.

Proceeding from a detailed analysis of colonial and semi-feudal society in Việt Nam, the Party's political program considered that the Vietnamese revolution was essentially a bourgeois democratic revolution, but led by the working class and having to evolve directly toward socialist revolution, bypassing the stage of capitalist development. It had to assume two essential tasks during the first stage:

- To struggle against French imperialism, and regain national independence;

- To struggle against feudalism, and give the land to the tillers.

These two tasks — anti-imperialist and anti-feudal — were closely connected. For the first time, a party clearly linked issues of nationalism to the issue of land, whereas the bourgeois and petit bourgeois parties, incapable of clearly formulating an agrarian program, also proved incapable of leading the struggle for national liberation to victory.

The political program made it clear that the essential driving force behind the revolution was the workers and peasants. The leading principles of action were encouraging the masses to struggle for their rights and interests, so as to heighten their political awareness and capacity for organization in order to make it possible, when conditions were ripe, to launch an armed uprising, seize power and establish a worker-peasant state. The essential condition for success was the existence of a leading Marxist-Leninist party capable of charting the right political direction, of maintaining within its ranks tight discipline and unity, maintaining close ties with the masses, and totally loyal to the revolution.

On this basis, the Party soon engaged in a complex and difficult struggle which led it to seize power fifteen years later. The following is an extract from the Political Program put forward by the Communist Party at the time of its founding.

NATURE AND TASKS OF THE INDOCHINESE REVOLUTION

At the beginning, this is a bourgeois democratic revolution as the revolution cannot directly resolve the organizational problems of socialism, the national economy is still very weak, the vestiges of feudalism numerous, the balance of forces between the classes has not yet tilted in favour of the proletariat, and moreover, imperialist oppression remains. In view of these conditions, the revolution at the present stage can only be an agrarian and anti-imperialist one.

The bourgeois democratic revolution will be a time of preparation for the socialist revolution. With the success of this revolution, and a worker-peasant government having been established, the nation's industry will be able to develop, proletarian organizations will gain in strength, the leadership of the proletariat will be strengthened, and the balance of forces between the classes will tip in favour of the proletariat. The struggle will then grow in depth and scope, taking the bourgeois democratic revolution forward along the path of socialist revolution. This period will be that of proletarian revolution on a worldwide scale and of socialist construction in the Soviet Union. Thanks to the dictatorship of the proletariat in other countries, Indochina will develop and directly embark on the socialist path without going through the stage of capitalist development.

The proletariat and the peasants are the two main driving forces in the bourgeois democratic revolution, but the latter will only achieve success if it is led by the proletariat.

The bourgeois democratic revolution essentially consists, on the one hand, of doing away with the vestiges of feudalism, eliminating the means of pre-capitalist exploitation and carrying through land reform, and on the other, of overthrowing French imperialism and making Indochina fully independent. These two aspects of the struggle are closely interlinked, for only when imperialism is toppled can the landlord class be abolished and the agrarian revolution successfully carried out; and only when the feudal regime is eliminated can imperialism be overthrown.

To fulfill these essential tasks, it is vital to establish worker-peasant soviet power which alone can serve as a powerful tool for overthrowing imperialism, feudalism and the landlords, giving land to the tillers and enacting legislation protecting the interests of the proletariat.

The essential tasks of the bourgeois democratic revolution are:

1. To overthrow French imperialism, feudalism and the landlords.

2. To establish a worker-peasant government

3. To confiscate all land belonging to foreign and native land-owners and the churches and share it out among middle-level and poor peasants, the right of ownership belonging to the worker-peasant government.

4. To nationalize all large foreign capitalist enterprises.

5. To abolish current taxes and duties, and levy a progressive tax.

6. To decree an eight-hour workday, and improve the living conditions of workers and working masses.

7. To regain complete independence for Indochina, and gain recognition of the right of its peoples to self-determination.

8. To set up a worker-peasant army

9. To promote equality of the sexes

10. To support the Soviet Union, and become allied with the world proletariat and the revolutionary movement in colonized and semi-colonized countries.

Chapter V

FROM ECONOMIC CRISIS TO THE SECOND WORLD WAR

Regrouping of the National and Democratic Forces (1930-1939)

The economic crisis of 1930 revealed the fragility of the colonial economy and exacerbated the people's plight, thus creating the conditions for major upheavals. In the following years, the rise of fascism throughout the world, particularly Hitler's rise to power in Germany and Japan's aggression against China, with the ensuing development of the anti-fascist struggle and the emergence of the Popular Front in France, had a profound impact on Indochina, especially on Việt Nam. The decisive domestic factor was the birth of the Communist Party of Indochina which soon revealed itself as the leading organization in the national and democratic movement. The colonial administration, in the face of opposition from this national and popular movement, reacted with brutal and large-scale repression, but proved incapable of putting it down. The Vietnamese national movement was moving forward with the new momentum when the Second World War broke out.

Economic Crisis

The economic crisis of 1930 had a particularly serious impact on Indochina due to the innate weakness of the colonial economy which, moreover, had to suffer many of the consequences of the French crisis, the metropolitan capitalists seeking to make up for their losses through increased exploitation of the colonies.

Falling prices for raw materials on the world market, especially rice, rubber, and coal, had a serious effect on the economy of Indochina, whose "prosperity" depended on its exports. These dropped in value from 228 million piastres in 1929 to 102 million in 1932, and imports from 227 million piastres to 94 million. The prices of rice and rubber were as follows:

	1928-1930	1930	1932
Rice (100 kg in piastres)	10.80	6.72	4.52
Rubber (kg in francs)	22	5	3

Rice exports dropped from 1.9 million tonnes in 1928 to 960,000 tonnes in 1931, and the cultivated land area in Cochinchina from 2.2 million hectares to 1,850,000 hectares. Hundreds of rice-husking mills were closed down and thousands of junks scrapped. Only one-third of the 126,000 hectares under rubber produced any profit.

The work force in the mines dropped from 46,000 in 1930 to 33,700 in 1932. Most of the workers became unemployed. Coal production dropped from 1,972,000 tonnes in 1929 to 1,592,000 in 1933, and the Cổ Định chromium mine in Thanh Hóa was closed down. All new building projects were stopped.

In Sài Gòn, the number of construction projects decreased as follows:

1922	1929	1930	1931
100	214	90	39

Apart from a few sectors which continued to develop (electricity, cement and alcohol), the whole economy was in a disastrous mess. The above-mentioned figures are concerned only with the commercial and industrial activities of colonial capitalism, and it is difficult to quantify the dire situation faced by the Vietnamese small traders and land-owners. More visible was the massive unemployment which hit workers and petty functionaries whose incomes dropped significantly.

Even some lower-ranking French officials lost their jobs and some went as far as pulling rickshaws in the streets of Sài Gòn in order to press home their demands. One -third of the workforce was unemployed. No relief or benefit was granted, and the large majority of the unemployed had to return to their families and villages which were already hard hit by worsening poverty. Wages dropped significantly, as shown in the following table:

Daily payment (in piastres)	1931	1934	1936
Coal miner	0.70	0.40	0.36
Skilled labourer in Sài Gòn	1.50	1.22	1.13
Unskilled female labourer in Hải Phòng	0.31	0.21	0.17

According to the French economist Paul Bernard, in the 1930s a Vietnamese worker earned 49 piastres a year on average, i.e. 490 francs compared to 6,200 francs for a French worker and 123,000 francs for an American worker at the time.

Officials found themselves in a very difficult situation. Their workday was extended, and many jobs were eliminated, resulting in the dismissal of many officials and employees, while the salaries of newcomers dropped by half. In 1931, the administration let go one-seventh of its officials, reduced salaries by 25 percent, and compelled many officials to retire early. Many college, high school and even university graduates were unable to find jobs. Many revolutionaries were recruited from among this population.

To deal with the crisis, the colonial administration took a series of measures aimed specifically at making up the budget deficit resulting from financial losses (a consequence of widespread impoverishment among the population) and saving the threatened large colonial companies. These new burdens fell on a population already hard hit by taxes and duties and vulnerable to unemployment. Custom duties levied on imported goods were raised.

Large loans were granted to rubber plantations — 100 million francs a year to 14 companies covering 1,005 planters, mainly French, who received a subsidy of 2 to 3 francs for each kilogram of rubber they produced. Indebted rice-growers also benefited from loans. But as no loan was less than 5,000 piastres, and none could be granted without offering land as a guarantee, the money went mainly to land-owners. The *tá điền* (landless peasant) who was hardest hit by the effects of the crisis, received neither relief nor subsidies. In the end, the administration took money from the most dispossessed strata of the population to help companies and big land-owners. Never before had colonial exploitation been so blatantly oppressive or obvious.

The Indochinese economy was tied more closely to that of France. The exchange rate for the piastre, which was tied to the franc and gold, was set at 10 francs. Giving play to the notion of "imperial preference", France significantly increased its share of trade with the colonies. The Vietnamese economy was thus further cut off from its geographical environment and oriented towards France. Government loans approved in Paris placed new credits at the disposal of the colonial administration, but the population had to pay the interest on them, and France-based industrial enterprises then became more vigilant in their efforts to hinder the industrialization of Indochina. Big colonial companies thus weathered the crisis without suffering major damage, while small companies, mostly set up by Vietnamese, disappeared. The slightest demand for autonomous economic development was throttled.

It might seem at first glance that the fall in rice exports would have eased food shortages in Việt Nam's countryside. But this did not occur. To pay their taxes, poor peasants had to sell three to four times as much rice to earn the money needed. While 15 days' work on average produced enough to pay the poll-tax before 1930, two to three months was not even enough during the years of crisis. Food shortages affected even the wealthiest provinces of Cochinchina, for example Bạc Liêu, while famine hit the northern province of Annam. The price of land dropped dramatically; in Cochinchina, a hectare of rice land which cost 1,000 piastres before the crisis could now only be sold at 150 or 200 piastres. Indebted peasants had to sell their plots to wealthy landlords while other land-owners mortgaged their estates to the Land Credit bank. Further concentration of land ownership and impoverishment of the peasantry was the result.

Another indication of the slowing down in economic activity was, according to Paul Bernard, the quantity of money in circulation which by 1935 had dropped 35 percent compared to the 1920s.

The economic crisis thus fully revealed the shortcomings of the colonial economy.

The Great Struggle of 1930-1931

The failure of the *Quốc Dân Đảng* at Yên Bái had in no way hindered the development of the national and popular struggle, as the newly-founded Communist Party was acting as a catalyst among the masses whose living conditions had been so badly affected by the economic crisis. It assumed leadership of the mass struggle, driving it in a new direction.

In 1930, the underground trade union formed by the Party had about 10,000 members; Party policy was to organize the working class to help it lead the people's revolutionary movement. The goal was to turn factories into revolutionary strongholds. Major strikes occurred between April 1929 and April 1930, 32 of them starting on 1 May 1931.

The strikes were less important in terms of number than in strength, level of organization and the political awareness of their participants. Strikes were legal actions in Europe. In Việt Nam, strikers risked five years behind bars, and were often exiled for being "communists". The police and soldiers had no hesitation in firing on strikers and demonstrators. Strikers often reacted strongly against police brutality. In March 1930, strikers at the Phú Riềng rubber plantation in southern Việt Nam disarmed soldiers at the local post, felled trees to bar the way to police cars, and women raped by Foreign Legionaries daubed their eyes with a mixture of ash and lime.

For the first time, Vietnamese workers celebrated May Day at Bến Thủy in Nghệ An province. Their French employer and the police opened fire, killing seven and injuring 13 others.

Going on strike meant major sacrifices from workers who were already leading a life of misery. This, however, did not prevent the 4, 000 workers of the Nam Định Textile Mill from striking repeatedly in 1930, one of the stoppages lasting 40 days. Not just workers from other factories, but also peasants from the villages came to support the strikers, cementing the alliance between workers and peasants thanks to local Party organizations which led both the workers' and peasants' struggles. The responsibility for all the strikes was accepted solely by underground trade unions and Communist Party organizations. No nationalist party or employers' union succeeded in establishing bases in the factories. All these strikes were watched with sympathy by the rest of the population who saw in them both a struggle for workers' interests, and a patriotic anti-colonialist movement. The strikes of 1930-1931 were nationwide, reaching almost all major enterprises — rubber plantations, Hải Phòng Cement Works, Nam Định Textile Mill, the railway stores at Vinh and Dĩ An, Sài Gòn power station, the Shell and Standard Oil depots, coal mines, and so on.

Alongside the strikes by workers, mammoth peasants' demonstrations were held, attracting about half a million participants in 25 provinces, especially in Tonkin and Annam. Here too the leadership was provided by grassroots cells of the Communist Party which had set up peasant unions with a total membership of 70,000 by 1930. The close unity between the workers' and peasants' struggles under the Communist Party leadership became the new and vital factor in the national movement. No other political party had before then succeeded in establishing a worker-peasant alliance, which would play a decisive role in the national struggle.

Both the workers' strikes and peasants' demonstrations were prompted by economic and political demands including pay rises, shorter working hours, abolition of corporal punishment, trade union rights and the freedom to strike for workers, a fair share of communal land, and reduced taxes, land rent and loan interest rates, postponement of debt repayments, and the granting of subsidies to protect the peasants against famine. The slogan "land to the tillers" was promoted in a number of places. Peasants burned debt contracts and property deeds and attacked local administration offices. The struggle came to a head in the two provinces of Nghệ An and Hà Tĩnh. The twin cities of Vinh - Bến Thủy constituted a substantial working class agglomeration, with a large peasant population living in misery on infertile lands. The tradition of national struggle there was particularly strong, for this was the birthplace of many patriotic scholars.

On 1 May 1930, workers and peasants demonstrated together to celebrated Labour Day, and the movement continued to grow over the following months. On September 12 near the town of Vinh, 20,000 peasants gathered in a demonstration. The colonial administration ordered troops to fire on an aircraft to strafe the crowd, killing 217 and injuring 126. These reprisals did not, however, prevent the movement from growing. In nine districts of Nghệ An and Hà Tĩnh, local officials fled to the city, while the village authorities handed power over the peasants. Peasant unions assumed local administrative functions, creating a nucleus of revolutionary power in an area of territory with 100,000 inhabitants.

The revolutionary power proceeded to share out communal land, gave land previously owned by reactionaries to the peasants, and ordered reductions in land rents and loan interest rates, postponement of debts, and the abolition of the poll-tax. It also set about reorganizing production and working for the abolition of outdated customs and practices, and for the elimination of illiteracy. People's self-defence militia units were set up and traitors were punished. The liberated areas were alive with enthusiasm. Many songs and poems were written to express the people's joy. It was a truly democratic and people's power which the people named the *Nghệ Tĩnh Soviet*.

For several months, the Nghệ Tĩnh Soviets valiantly resisted troops and aircraft sent by the colonial administration to suppress the revolt. However, conditions were not yet ripe for a victorious uprising.

The movement declined towards the middle of 1931. The Nghệ Tĩnh Soviets, however, were an important landmark, a true prelude to the coming revolution. A peasant uprising also took place in Quảng Ngãi province, while in Cochinchina many peasant demonstrations took place in Sa Đéc, Vĩnh Long, Sóc Trăng and other provinces.

Colonial Repression and Terror

The colonial administration, deeply concerned at the growth of the movement, and compelled to deal with it on many different fronts, sought to redress the situation by using increasingly brutal repression. Police, regular troops and the air force were mobilized against large gatherings. Torture was widespread and imprisonment, exile and the death penalty were used on the patriots; in the worst moments, troops, particularly the Foreign Legion, carried out summary executions, spreading terror in many localities.

The following compiled by the colonial administration — although drastically underestimating the reality - give an idea of the scale of the repression:

1929: 1,490 people arrested, 3 sentenced to death, and 300 imprisoned.

1930: 689 people killed during strikes and demonstrations, 2,963 people detained, 83 sentenced to death, 543 sentenced to a total of 3,648 years' imprisonment, and 780 deported.

1931 (first four months alone): 1,419 people arrested, 1,023 sentenced to life imprisonment, 604 sentenced to hard labour.

1932: the number of political detained at various prisons, including Poulo Condor and in Guyana, reached almost 10,000.

The repression brought some results, most notably in temporally depriving the movement of its leadership. The General Secretary of the Communist Party, Trần Phú, was arrested and tortured to death. The magnitude of the upheaval and repression even turned the climate of public opinion in France in favour of the convicts, a movement supported by the French Communist Party and the United General Confederation of Labour (CGTU).

To cover up the repression, the colonial administration implemented a number of sham reforms aimed at misleading the masses and seducing the "élite." They created "conciliation committees" in factories, and initiated a program creating small peasant ownership of five to ten hectares in the western part of Cochinchina, the Central Highlands and the uplands of Tonkin. Some modifications were made to school curricula while the Huế court created a "Ministry of Education". Supplementary seats were allocated to Vietnamese in the colonial councils. King Bảo Đại, who was living in France, was brought back to Huế, purportedly to reform the monarchy. Phạm Quỳnh, a docile servant of the colonial administration, was appointed to lead the Cabinet, along with the Catholic mandarin Ngô Đình Diệm who had distinguished himself in the repression of 1930-31. Fierce rivalry soon erupted between these two men, each supported by a different colonialist faction. Out of spite, Diệm tendered his resignation and turned to Japan.

The colonial administration also made use of Catholic missions to regain control of troubled regions, and instigated the setting up of Buddhist groups and organizations working for the revival of Confucianism. It prompted a movement to organize balls, fairs, beauty contests, and so on, with the aim of attracting young people into amusements and pleasure-seeking.

A New Start for the National and Popular Movement

The repression had removed nationalist parties and groups from the political arena but could only temporarily hinder the activities of the Communist Party, which had deep roots among the masses. Many militants, particularly in the villages, had evaded the police thanks to protection from the population. Others who had sought refuge abroad returned to the country, and those released after short terms of imprisonment immediately resumed their activities. In the prisons, political and theoretical courses gave the detained militant a sound training. A committee of leading militants headed by Lê Hồng Phong was set up. In 1932, a program of action set down general policy directions, and the mass organizations gradually resumed their activities.

Strikes resumed at rubber plantations, printing houses, and rice-husking mills. The year 1935, one of economic booms, also witnessed major strikes in Sài Gòn. Vietnamese landlords and bourgeois elements along with a number of Frenchmen worked to oppose the tying of the

piastre to the franc and domination by the Bank of Indochina. Divisions thus began to appear even among the colonialists.

New forms of action were adopted. Nguyễn Văn Tạo and Nguyễn An Ninh founded the newspaper *Trung Lập* (Neutrality). In 1933, during the municipal elections in Sài Gòn, a "workers' state" headed by Nguyễn Văn Tạo saw several of its members elected despite the limited franchise. Large meetings, often attracting thousands of people, were held where speakers defended the interests of working people and demanded democratic freedoms. A French-language newspaper, *La Lutte* (Struggle), was set up, and soon enjoyed great influence in intellectual circles. The rostrum of the Sài Gòn Municipal Council became a platform for airing various demands. Thus, echoing the actions of the masses which remained central to the battle, legal forms of action appeared for the first time in the history of the national movement.

In 1936, new municipal elections were held in Sài Gòn; Nguyễn Văn Tạo's group had four members elected out of six seats reserved for Vietnamese, against 12 for the French. Successes were also recorded in elections to the Colonial Council. For the Party, these electoral successes in no way constituted the main objective of the struggle, but provided opportunities for publicizing demands and spurring the political consciousness of the masses, so as to prepare them for more important action.

First Congress

The international political situation was rapidly developing. The fascist powers had reinforced their alliance, forming the Berlin-Rome-Tokyo Axis, while the Soviet Union and Western European powers moved closer in order to deal with the threat of fascism. In China, the Japanese aggressors pushed southwards, and the war moved closer to the Indochinese border. The Chinese Communist Party and Kuomintang had become allies in the fight against the Japanese. Japanese fascism aimed not only for the conquest of China but also at extending its domination over the whole of Southeast Asia.

In France, in the light of the fascist threat, a merger had brought together with the Popular Front the three major leftist parties — Communist, Socialist and Radical. The success of the Popular Front in the 1936 elections led to the formation of a government headed by the Socialist Party and supported by the Communist Party. Fascism was defeated in France, the French working class gained important political and social advantages, an amnesty law for political prisoners in the colonies was passed, and a commission of enquiry was set up to study possible reforms. The formation of the Popular Front government in France without a doubt created a favorable opportunity for the rapid advance of the Vietnamese national movement.

It was obvious, however, that the decisive factor remained action by the Vietnamese masses who had resumed the struggle, and that the crucial condition for success was the adoption of correct policy directions to be laid down by the Communist Party of Indochina, the sole political organization to have bases throughout the country and in all social strata.

The Central Committee of the Party, meeting in the summer of 1938, made a series of important decisions. In the circumstances prevailing at the time, it was decided that the Indochinese revolution had to take its place as part of the international anti-fascist front fighting for democracy and peace. The slogans "Overthrow French imperialism" and "Confiscate land belonging to landlords and give it to the peasants" were withdrawn, and the formation of a broad anti-imperialist popular front bringing together all social strata was advocated. Political parties and religious and ethnic groups in Indochina were to fight for basic democratic freedoms — freedom of assembly, association, speech, publication, circulation, travel abroad, amnesty for political prisoners, an eight-hour workday, labour legislation, and the broadening of the elected economic and social councils. These demands, however, did not succeed in creating divisions within the ranks of the colonialists, so at its plenary session in March 1938, the Party Central Committee advocated the founding of a United Democratic Front of Indochina to bring together democratic and progressive forces in the struggle against the most dangerous enemies of the moment — the French fascists and reactionary colonialists.

The Central Committee advocated a move towards legal and semi-legal forms of action, with strong participation from the masses to struggle tenaciously for democratic freedoms. The Party nonetheless kept its underground bases and objectives with regard to the national and democratic revolution.

The colonial policy of the French Popular Front provided an opportunity for the Party to launch a major campaign to convene an "Indochinese Congress," a kind of forum where the various social strata and other groups would present their demands, while the working classes in the cities and countryside would continue to work for improvements in

living conditions. Action committees were set up throughout the country to involve large sections of the population. Under dual pressure from the popular movement in Indochina and progressive opinion in France, the colonial administration had to free many political prisoners who had made valuable contributions to the movement. A wave of militant activity, starting from Sài Gòn where a provisional National Committee was elected, reached Annam and Tonkin. Here, under the auspices of the "Democratic Front of Indochina," large meetings were held and patriots elected to the Hà Nội Municipal Council and the Chambers of People's Representatives, in Hà Nội and Huế.

Meetings, political demonstrations, and strikes took place without let-up. The colonial administration implemented a series of measures aimed at closing the floodgates on political activity. It outlawed gatherings such as the provisional National Committee of the Indochina Congess, then ordered its disbanding. The Committee refused to do so. The administration put pressure on the leaders of the Constitutionalist Party, calling on it to leave the Congress and hold a conference to present the "people's aspirations." The administration soon ordered the arrest of the main leaders of the Congress, which it then broke up.

The disbandment of the Indochinese Congress did not prevent the movement from continuing to grow, nor the population from scoring important successes. The greatest victory was a call for an amnesty for political prisoners. The watchword rapidly became popular, and diverse groups including newspapers representing all shades of political opinion rallied behind it. Several thousand detainees were thus freed and subsequently made important contributions to the movement. However, several thousand prisoners were still detained by the colonial administration.

Another success was the passing of a number of social regulations. The workday was reduced to 10 hours in November 1936, to 9 hours on 1 January 1937, and to 8 hours on 1 January 1938. It was forbidden to employ women and children on night shifts. Workers gained the right to a day's rest each week and five to 10 days' paid leave annually. Wages had to be paid in cash, and the deducting of fines from wages was forbidden. Women workers had the right to eight weeks' maternity leave. Employers did not have to pay their wages but could no longer fire women who had given birth. The social legislation did not include trade union freedoms, the freedom to strike or social benefits, i.e. workers' basic rights. It nonetheless constituted an important advance on the past. Moreover, the application of these new laws soon met with stiff resistance from the colonial administration as well as employers, and a long struggle was necessary before they were finally implemented.

In this political atmosphere, Việt Nam's working class encouraged by their successes, underwent a period of great activity. During the second half of 1936, 36 strikes were held, some of them overtly political, such as the strike by Sài Gòn workers protesting against the arrest of leaders of the Indochinese Congress. The most important strike involved 25, 000 workers at the Quảng Yên coal mine. Pay rises, reductions in working hours, and trade union and democratic freedoms were the workers' main demands. In 1937, a total of 400 strikes occurred. In 1938, the political leadership of the movement advocated concerted action against the large colonial companies, while with smaller Vietnamese capitalists they sought agreements with reciprocal concessions so as to broaden the democratic front.

The trade unions remained illegal, but workers and public employees founded "friendship societies," sports associations and reading clubs. A newspaper, *Lao Động* (Labour), served as a mouthpiece for the movement.

It should be noted that during this period a Trotskyist group emerged, based out of Cochinchina, and had some influence on politically inexperienced elements of the petit bourgeoisie attracted by ultra-leftist or extremist slogans. However, the anti-communist philosophy of the Trotskyist leaders was repudiated by the grassroots. Hostile to a policy of broad national union, the Trotskyists opposed the creation of friendship societies by workers, and irresponsibly urged the people to go on strike. Trotskyism in effect, introduced a divisive element into the national and popular movement. It would not survive the coming confrontations.

In the villages, political activity was also on the increase. Countless meetings and strikes were held. On big occasions, peasants from villages near the cities marched on provincial capitals to present their demands or support demonstrations by city-dwellers. The underground peasant unions of the previous era were replaced by friendship societies and associations for transplanting rice, harvesting, building houses, arranging funerals, fishing and so on. These associations drew broad sections of the peasantry into a range of political and social activities.

The Communist Pasty launched a program of action for the peasantry which included:

- reduction of land rent, which should not be more than the equivalent of one-third of the harvest;
- exemption from land rent in the case of bad harvests;

- a fair share of communal land, and the prohibition of its sale by auction;
- freedom to reclaim land, which should be allotted to the peasants who clear it; and the handing over to peasants of land left idle by its owners;
- creation of land credit agencies in villages for the granting of low-interest loans to peasants, and prohibition of usury;
- abolition of the poll-tax; and
- implementation of basic democratic freedoms.

Numerous associations and friendship societies were set up everywhere to rally to the cause women, young people, and professionals. An association for the teaching of *quốc ngữ*, which mainly campaigned against illiteracy, played an important role in the field of education.

It was thus a period of political fervor in which political parties themselves played a far less important role than the various mass organizations; the various political parties of the bourgeoisie and petit bourgeoisie had no real power, while the Communist Party, practically clandestine, put forward only a few of its militants so as to invigorate the mass organizations. The Democratic Front, subsequently launched to replace the Anti-Imperialist Front, was thus not a grouping of parties like the French Popular Front, but a gathering of various social strata and political, religious and cultural groups, aimed at organizing specific joint activities. Participating in this front were the Hà Nội and Sài Gòn branches of the French Socialist Party which had begun to recruit Vietnamese members.

Situation in Việt Nam shortly before the Second World War

From 1938, the world situation was evolving very rapidly; fascist powers both in Europe and Asia, encouraged by the appeasement of the European and US governments, moved on to the offensive. War was imminent. Early in 1939, the Japanese occupied Hainan Island, less than 300km from Hải Phòng, while in China, Japanese troops pushed southwards down to the borders of Indochina. What was be done in the face of Japan's impending invasion?

In France, the Popular Front government was replaced by a rightist cabinet which, while preparing for war, sought to repeal the reforms put in place in Indochina. Early in 1939, repression began again in Indochina

and the colonialists sought to abolish all democratic freedoms. In 1938, the colonial administration issued a 40 million piastre government loan purportedly to buy war material in France. Early in 1939, new taxes amounting to 10 million piastres were levied in order to build airfields and finance other war preparations. The French government decided that Indochina would supply France with a contingent of 1.5 million soldiers and workers, 15 times as many as during the First World War.

In October 1938, the Communist Party of Indochina, in a manifesto addressed to all, denounced France and Britain's policy of compromise with the fascists, drew attention to the threat of Japanese aggression, and called on all parties, groups and social strata, including French democrats, to unite within the Democratic Front of Indochina and to struggle in defence of the country.

The campaign to defend Indochina against Japanese invasion went alongside the struggle against the large colonial companies and diversionary tactics of the colonial administration. The administration had in effect decided to tie Tonkin to Annam under the aegis of the Huế court, which was a step towards the reconstituting of a reunified Việt Nam. The proclaimed aim of this operation was to draw the people into the struggle against the Japanese. But this maneuvre deceived no -one. A campaign was launched to show that the operation would only place further limitations on the few democratic freedoms left in Tonkin, by handing it over to a monarchy entirely controlled by the colonialists. The newspaper *Dân Chúng* (The Masses), the mouthpiece of the Communist Party and published in Sài Gòn, wrote that the path to reunification in no way included the merging of Tonkin and Annam under the aegis of the monarchy, but would involve a long and difficult struggle for democratic freedoms, against the reactionary colonialists and Japanese aggression. Faced with tough opposition, the colonial administration was forced to abandon the plan.

Thus, on the threshold of the Second World War, the masses in Việt Nam were involved in intense political activity, and were led by a close-knit and experienced political party. These factors would later play a decisive role in the course of events. As a result, the situation was much more favourable than on the threshold of the First World War.

The Literary Movement from 1930 to 1945

A quick overview of the development of Vietnamese literature after 1930 will complete the historical and social picture of Việt Nam

at the beginning of the Second World War, followed by the August 1945 Revolution.

The profound changes in Việt Nam society, especially after the First World War and the political turmoil of the years 1930-1945, had a considerable influence on the development of Vietnamese literature. A modern literature was born, clearly distinguishing itself from traditional forms, responding to the needs of a new audience, and written by learned men different from the earlier scholars.

Mandarin competitions were abolished in 1918 (in 1915 in Tonkin), and *quốc ngữ* finally replaced the ideographic script. The new generation of intellectuals no longer knew the Chinese classics, but were influenced instead by European authors, French in particular. Modern printing techniques facilitated a wider dissemination of literary works than xylography had. The publication of newspapers and periodicals gave rise to new genres of expression. New forces and aspirations sought novel forms of expression. The public had also changed. Scholars had previously written either for a minority of connoisseurs, or for peasant communities. Modern writers wrote for an urban audience — university and high school students, officials, workers and intellectuals.

Traditional literature, with its preponderance of poetry, had conformed to strict literary and stylistic rules. Thoughts were often expressed in an elliptical, suggestive way, often concealing the real meaning. Modern authors had to break away from these rules and habits. The breach which occurred in poetry caused quite a stir; in the 1930s violent clashes took place between the devotees of traditional and modern poetry. The "old school" was defeated, although Vietnamese poetry did not lose all its rhythm, and the combinations of tones were able to associate more freely with one another to express more intimate and personal thoughts or feelings.

Prose took pride of place in reflecting the many faces of a changing society. New literary genres, novels in prose, short stories, reports, and modern plays appeared. History, philosophy, moral fables, and essays, formerly written in literary Chinese, were now written in the national language. Prose had lost its rhyming character, its clauses were no longer opposed to each other in perfect symmetry, and the logic of its thought became more explicit.

All these changes, first appearing in the 1920s, became more firmly established by 1930. The authors of the 1920s remained imbued with traditional culture, but the following generation was essentially modern. Political events had a profound effect on them all.

For many writers from the intellectual petit bourgeoisie, the defeat of the *Quốc Dân Đảng* (at Yên Bái), the economic crisis and the administration's bloody repression dashed all hopes of renewal. They withdrew into a melancholy romanticism, born directly out of the revolt of the urban petit bourgeoisie against the colonial regime and outdated feudal structures, a powerless revolt which was mercilessly crushed. At the start, literature still found ideal material in the struggle of the individual against the feudal rules governing life. Freedom in love, protests against forced marriage, and the dream of a free life had inspired copious writings by poets animated by an overwhelming enthusiasm and lively novels. But these dreams of liberty and change had quickly vanished in the face of colonial and feudal reality. Within a few years, romanticism had turned into darkness. A veil of sadness "coming from the depth of centuries" descended on poems and novels. The Japanese occupation on top of the colonial regime had ended by blocking all prospects for liberation and driving the romantic school into mysticism and asceticism.

After 1930, a group of romantic poets emerged, including Thế Lữ, Lưu Trọng Lư, Xuân Diệu, Phạm Huy Thông, and Huy Cận, welcomed with enthusiasm by a new generation. Ego won pride of place in poetry which sounded new notes. Novels and short stories, particularly those of Khái Hưng and Nhất Linh, essentially told of family dramas about conflicts between young people of the new generation and parents clinging to traditional concepts. The feudal family was the target of bitter criticism. Love became the central theme of these works, love hindered by outdated social taboos, and forced to fight to free itself, but often in vain.

After flourishing for a short period, the romantic school went into rapid decline, and was gradually replaced by other, stronger currents. The economic crisis had inspired the masses to action and spurred the consciousness of many intellectuals. The founding of the Communist Party introduced a new catalyst into culture and ideology. In the press, its militants raised issues of art and literature — art for art's sake, or art for life sake — which the public followed with passionate interest. The actions of the Party and the participation of educated people in the broad national and democratic movement in the years 1938-39 steered the writers towards social realities. A strong realist movement emerged, gradually eclipsing the romantic current. Novels by Ngô Tất Tố, Vũ Trọng Phụng, Nguyễn Công Hoan, Nguyên Hồng, and others, as well as Nam Cao's short stories often reflected in a poignant manner the misery and the struggles of the peasants, and the oppression by mandarins and village dignitaries. The workers' struggles, and more, the disenfranchised elements in cities, inspired many novels. Poet Tú Mỡ attacked the officials of the day using biting satire.

However, the drastic censorship considerably limited the field of action of realist writers. They could criticize the mandarin class, but not touch the colonial regime. This is, why besides the published literature, there existed a clandestine literature, mostly by revolutionaries directly engaged in action. Anonymous works were also circulated. A flowering of songs and poems followed the uprising of the Nghệ Tĩnh Soviets; the militants imprisoned after 1930 composed numerous poems exalting patriotism and revolutionary heroism, and expressing their faith in final victory. The optimism of the militants echoed through the world of literature.

In 1930, a young poet, born in 1920, a communist activist imprisoned from 1939 to 1942 when he escaped from prison, edited a collection of poems entitled *Từ ấy* (Since Then) headed by two lines of verse which quickly became imprinted on young people's minds:

Since then summer has been glowing in me

My heart is enlightened by the sun truth

Revolutionary romanticism was born, taking the place of pessimistic romanticism. Patriotic and revolutionary themes were to become predominate in underground literature and that of liberated zones during the Japanese occupation, while the literature authorized by the French and Japanese became bogged down in asceticism.

An important event soon gave a new impulse to the revolutionary current. In 1943, the Communist Party made public its theses on cultural issues, advocating the promotion of a "national, popular and scientific" culture. In 1944, renowned writers and people of culture founded the *Cultural Association for National Salvation,* which soon joined the Việt Minh. A new era began for Vietnamese literature which soon joined the revolutionary path, closely bound to the national and people's struggle.

Special note should be taken of a work written in 1942-1943 by Nguyễn Ái Quốc (later President Hồ Chí Minh) during his detention by Chiang Kai-shek's men in southern China — his Prison Diary, a collection of poems written in literary Chinese, brimming with revolution optimism, poetic sentiment and a sense of humour.

Hồ Chí Minh's political writings, like those of other Party and government leaders of the Democratic Republic of Việt Nam, may be regarded as examples of the new Vietnamese prose style.

Chapter VI

VIỆT NAM DURING THE SECOND WORLD WAR AND THE 1945 AUGUST REVOLUTION

(1939 - 1945)

First Battles

Right from the early days of the war, the colonial administration endeavored to reinforce Indochina's defensive potential while mobilizing as much manpower and as many material resources for France's benefit as possible. Indochina's armed forces were increased to 100,000 men, and the police and security forces were doubled. By the end of 1939, tens of thousands of Vietnamese soldiers and workers had been sent to France.

A Higher Economic Council was set up to manage the country's economy, and Paris assigned Indochina the task of providing France with 3.5 million tonnes of food, 800,000 tonnes of tea, coffee and sugar, 300,000 tonnes of rope, and 600,000 tonnes of rubber. The working week was extended from 48 hours to 60 for men and 54 for women. All taxes and duties were increased.

On the political plane, all activities allegedly fomented by communists were forbidden, all organizations allegedly run by communists were dissolved and all communist propaganda documents seized. Even many Cao Đài sanctuaries were closed. Several thousand political detainees and suspects were jailed, and many prisons were built for this purpose, the most notorious being those of Lao Bảo, Nghĩa Lộ and Poulo Condor. Some convicts were exiled to Madagascar. Governor -General Catroux declared that communism had to be eliminated so as to pre-empt any unrest in Indochina and guarantee its loyalty.

The colonial administration had ample grounds for fearing the Communist Party, the sole party to have maintained and increased its support and have a comprehensive progam. The Party had been prepared to go underground once more, and as a result its losses were insignificant. It was active mainly in the countryside where the repressive colonial machine was more thinly spread than in the cities, but its militants remained active in the towns.

In November 1939, the Party Central Committee outlined the situation and the tasks to be carried out as follows:

- The war in 1939 was a war between the imperialist powers aimed at a new dividing up of the world.

- The main task of the Vietnamese revolution was to overthrow imperialism, whatever the skin color of those who led it. National liberation was the prime objective; all other objectives, including the agrarian question, were secondary.

The crucial task was setting up a united anti-imperialist front. Calls for land reform were temporarily suspended and replaced by calls to confiscate the property of land-owners who had betrayed the country. Calls for the establishment of a democratic republican government replaced those arguing for the establishment of a worker-peasant government.

The plenary session of the Party Central Committee laid down a new political policy of prime importance for the following years.

The French defeat in June 1940 threw the colonialists in Indochina into confusion. All desire to resist Japanese aggression had vanished, and faced with Japanese demands, the colonial administration surrendered all the way down the line. The Japanese obtained without much effort control of the Sino-Vietnamese border as well as the right to land in Tonkin to strike at China's armies from the rear. Japanese troops coming from China's Guangxi province routed France's Lạng Sơn garrison, which fled to Hà Nội along the Bắc Sơn road.

Seizing upon this incident, the people of Bắc Sơn rose in revolt, disarmed the fleeing French troops, and used their weapons to capture the post of Võ Nhai, some of whose defenders then crossed over to the insurgents.

Colonial circles violently opposed to the Vietnamese people's national movement chose to side with Japanese fascism, which was

hostile to the revolutionary movement, anxious to exploit Indochina's resources to the utmost, and sought to make the best possible use of the French administrative apparatus. This collusion between French colonial circles and Japanese fascism aimed at holding back the Vietnamese national movement lasted until 1945.

The Lạng Sơn incident was quickly suppressed and the colonial administration was able to concentrate its forces on putting down the Bắc Sơn uprising. The insurgents withdrew into the mountains and formed the first guerrilla groups led by the Communist Party.

In Southern Indochina, the French had to deal with claims from Thailand which, backed by the Japanese, demanded territories situated to the northwest of Cambodia's Tonle Sap and on the right bank of the Mekong River in Laos. Units of Vietnamese troops were sent to the front to fight the Thais. Some of these units stationed in Sài Gòn decided to rebel against being sent to the front. This plan was part of the program of the Party Committee for Cochinchina, which from June 1940 on had actively prepared for an uprising. A plan of action was worked out with the aim of combining the actions of military units with those of worker and peasant organizations throughout Cochinchina.

The insurrection was launched on the night of 23 November 1940. Unfortunately the colonial administration, which had been warned of the plan, had disarmed the mutinous units and the Sài Gòn revolt failed to take place. Despite this setback, uprisings took place in eight of Cochinchina's 20 provinces. In Mỹ Tho province in particular, 54 of its 100 villages took part. It was there that the red flag emblazoned with a gold star, now the national flag of Việt Nam, was raised for the first time. With the tacit consent of the Japanese, the colonial administration savagely suppressed the insurrection. Many villages were destroyed, and over 20,000 people were killed or arrested.

Another uprising took place on January 13, 1941 at Đô Lương in Nghệ An province. A garrison had mutinied and marched on Vinh, the provincial capital, but it was rapidly dispersed by the French.

In just the first year of the Second World War, the Vietnamese people under the leadership of the Communist Party had clearly shown their desire to regain their independence through revolutionary violence. The first battles were lost, but they constituted valuable experience. It became clear that the assistance of soldiers from the colonial army could not be relied on, and that it was necessary to

prepare the people politically and militarily to seize power at the most favourable moment.

Under the Dual Franco-Japanese Yoke

From 1941 to 1945, Việt Nam thus lived under a French colonial regime intensified by Japanese occupation. The French and Japanese agreed between them on the tapping of the country's resources to the maximum, and on maintaining order and concentrating their efforts against the revolutionary movement. This collusion, however, did not prevent them from applying their own separate policies aimed at consolidating their positions with a view to later confrontation. Economic exploitation was intensified to meet both the interests of France and the demands of Japan's wartime economy. Repression was intensified and political maneuvering increased with the aim of misleading public opinion and rallying reactionary or politically naive Vietnamese citizens.

Admiral Decoux, sent as French governor-general of Indochina by the Vichy government, carried out a dual policy of dictatorship and demagogy. At the end of 1940, the handful of elected councils which gave the colonial regime a facade of democracy were abolished, and all power was concentrated in the hands of the governor-general and the all-powerful security services in particular. The Decoux administration also sought to promote the cultural movement aimed at inspiring loyalty to France and reviving reactionary concepts drawn from Petainism and Confucianism. New schools were opened and enrolments rose from 450,000 to 700, 000 by 1943. A fund was instituted for the setting up of Hà Nội University, while Vietnamese mandarins, landowners and the bourgeoisie were encouraged to create funds to assist poor students. The colonial administration sought to take over the leadership of the anti-illiteracy movement, which had been headed by patriots to that point. It organized literary competitions and painting exhibitions, awarded prizes and utilized every opportunity to promote French cultural values.

A special effort was made with regard to young people whom the administration sought to educate politically through sporting organizations and paramilitary or scout groups. State employees were authorized to practice sports on Saturday afternoons. Some advantages were granted to them including increases in salaries and benefits, transfer of certain echelons of state employees to metropolitan status, and promotion to certain positions of leadership.

Young people and state employees were authorized to speak of patriotism on condition that it was a local patriotism integrated with loyalty to France.

None of these measures changed in any way the essence of France's policy, which was aimed at the total elimination of the national movement.

The French were forced to let Japanese troops enter Tonkin and later to cede 70,000 square kilometers of Cambodian territory to Thailand, then allied with Japan. The so-called Joint Defence Treaty signed on 9 December 1941 in effect sanctioned the occupation of all of Indochina by Japan. Indochina then became a Japanese base and a supplier of raw materials to the Japanese economy.

At first, the French colonial administration sought to supply rice to Japan: 585,000 tonnes in 1941, 973,000 in 1942, 1,023,000 in 1943, and 900,000 in 1944. Japan first paid in gold or industrial products, but Japanese reserves soon ran out and from December 1942 on, Japan paid in special yen, a kind of valueless military bond.

In fact, to cover the cost of occupation by Japanese troops, it was the colonial administration which supplied the necessary funds by issuing vast quantities of banknotes: 723 million piastres, which was seven times the 1939 budget for Indochina. In 1944, 1,052 million piastres were issued (as against 216 million in 1939). Prices soared as a consequence.

To meet Japan's needs, the colonial administration took control of a group of products including cement, jute, sugar, oil and coal, and for this purpose set up monopolies on the sale and purchase of many types of goods. Meanwhile, there was a shortage of raw materials, equipment, and means of transport. The large colonial companies made huge profits from this new commercial exchange with Japan. The French colonialists' submission to the Japanese proved rewarding, for some at least.

The heaviest burden for the Vietnamese people was the compulsory delivery of rice. Even Tonkin, disastrously short of food, had to deliver 130,205 tonnes in 1943 and 186,130 tonnes in 1944. Whether the harvest was good or bad, each region had to deliver a quantity of rice in proportion to its cultivated area at the ridiculous price of 19 piastres for 100 kilogrammes of unhusked paddy. After bad harvests the people had to buy rice on the market at a price of 54 piastres for 100 kilogrammes.

To provide sacks for the Japanese, peasants were forced to clear rice and plant jute over large areas. In 1944, when American bombing disrupted the transport of coal to Sài Gòn, the French and Japanese used rice and maize as fuel for the power stations. They hoarded rice for their own use. Meanwhile, no improvements were made in agriculture, and the hydraulic networks were not properly looked after. A single natural disaster was enough to cause food shortages followed by terrible famine. Beginning in 1943, a major famine escalated from 1944 onwards.

While in full agreement with the French administration over exploiting the nation's resources to the utmost and putting down all revolutionary activities, the Japanese continued their demagogic maneuvers. They held out the lure of national independence which Vietnam would achieve with their help, and the solidarity of the Asian peoples rising in revolt against whites, and of a mutually beneficial and prosperous Greater East Asia. They worked to recruit supporters, individuals such as Trần Trọng Kim, Ngô Đình Diệm and Nguyễn Văn Sâm, or small organized groups such as the *Đại Việt* (Greater Việt Nam) Party in Tonkin.

Right up till the end of the war, however, Japan found it was more important to maintain order in Indochina with the help of the French than to support any group of puppets. When French pressure became too strong, the Japanese chose to send their agents out of the country so as not to spark conflict with the French. Even in 1944, after the fall of the Vichy government in France, the Japanese continued this policy.

Birth of the Việt Minh

Under the dual yoke of both France and Japan, the entire Vietnamese people experienced increasing poverty. Between 1940 and 1944 prices soared 400 percent while salaries rose only 20 percent. In Tonkin and Annam, peasants suffered from famine, while in Cochinchina there was an acute shortage of consume goods. Millions of people went about clad in rags and even in leaves. Discontent spread among the richer peasants and landowners who had to sell their produce at cheap prices, as well as among merchants and industrialists who ran short of raw materials and equipment and were hit by monopolies set up by the administration. Only large colonial companies, black-market merchants and professional speculators profited from the situation.

While some patriots at first harboured illusions about potential Japanese support, the Communist Party immediately identified the

Japanese threat and continued to steer the struggle along the right path. In May 1941, Hồ Chí Minh convened at Pắc Bó (in Cao Bằng province) the eighth plenum of the Party Central Committee, which decided that the Vietnamese revolution had to stand without hesitation in the international anti-fascist camp of which the Soviet Union remained the nucleus. The Central Committee believed that Hitler would inevitably attack the USSR, bringing about the collapse of fascism, and that the world war would end with the emergence of new socialist countries. It was in the light of these expectations that the strategy of the Vietnamese revolutionary movement had to be decided.

The main task then was to liberate the country from Franco-Japanese domination. National liberation came first and the interests of all social classes had to be subordinate to this prime objective. A broad national union had to be created in order to fight French colonialism and Japanese fascism, a national front bringing together all social classes and strata, political parties and religious groupings. The following steps were advocated: a confiscation of land belonging to imperialists and traitors and its allocation to poor peasants, reduction of land rents and loan interest, and a fair share of communal lands. All these measures would be gradually applied in order to finally achieve the ideal of land to the tillers. Thus national union could be secured without neglecting the basic interests of poor peasants.

The Party Central Committee decided to speed up preparations for armed uprisings, reinforcing guerrilla and self-defence units and setting up guerrilla bases.

"The Pacific War and the Chinese people's resistance against Japanese aggression," the Central Committee resolution declared, "will be a favorable development for the Indochinese revolution. At this moment, by keeping our forces ready, we will be able to launch partial insurrections, and win victory in various areas to clear the way for a general insurrection."

Trường Chinh was elected General Secretary of the Party.

The Việt Minh Front was founded, which involved many workers, peasants, youth and women's organizations, and guerrilla units operating in the highlands. These organizations working for national salvation brought together all social strata including the bourgeoisie and land-owners, provided they agreed to struggle against the French and Japanese imperialists. The Việt Minh adopted as its emblem the red flag emblazoned with a gold star.

The Việt Minh rapidly gained support among the working class whose situation was rapidly deteriorating under the French and Japanese yoke. As this burden grew ever more oppressive, deep divisions arose among the bourgeoisie and intellectual and student circles, which little by little dissociated themselves from pro-Japanese and pro-French groups and turned to the Việt Minh. In 1943, a group of intellectuals and people from the middle-class founded the Democratic Party to rally together part of the nation's bourgeoisie. This party soon joined the Việt Minh. That same year, the Communist Party launched a program of action in the educational field, which aroused great interest in intellectual circles. A Cultural Association for National Salvation was founded. This was followed by the founding of the Military Association for National Salvation involving patriots who had enlisted in the colonial army. As the war progressed and conflicts flared between the French and Japanese, Việt Minh activity among the masses grew in scope. It even sought to rally to its cause French democrats who opposed Japanese occupation and the Vichy government.

The Việt Minh did not simply formulate a program. It tried above all to draw the masses into action on two levels, military and political.

With regard to the armed struggle, the guerrilla units involved in the Bắc Sơn uprising in 1940 had been compelled to scatter and take refuge among the population. Their political activities continued however, while simultaneously trying to set up armed contingents. A new type of action appeared - "armed propaganda". In 1943, the patriotic forces had become strong enough to re-establish the Bắc Sơn - Võ Nhai base and to fan out from there towards the provinces of Thái Nguyên and Bắc Cạn, even pushing southwards towards Vĩnh Yên in the upland region. By the end of 1943, Việt Minh armed propaganda units operated throughout a vast region covering several provinces in the mountainous regions north of the Red River.

In 1944, a genuine liberated area took shape in these provinces. Networks of partisans were set up in central Annam and Cochinchina. In the border provinces of Cao Bằng and Lạng Sơn, people's organizations made preparations for armed uprisings. Nguyễn ái Quốc, who had returned from China, was convinced that an uprising would then be premature and postponed it to intensify political activity. In December 1944, the Party set up the *Propagation and Liberation Army* (a name chosen to emphasize the political nature of its activity). Võ Nguyên Giáp was appointed commander. Shortly after its formation, this new armed force took the posts of Phay Khắt and Nà Ngần on December 24-25, 1944, firing the first shots in a glorious campaign.

Alongside the armed struggle which developed in the highlands, plains and cities, the mass struggle was constantly expanding. The Việt Minh drew the peasant masses into a campaign opposing the order to abandon rice and other food crops and plant jute instead. In many villages from 1943 onwards, men, women and children, armed with sticks and pitchforks, gathered to oppose the order to clear the fields of rice.

Another call was for resistance against the forcible delivery of paddy. The peasant masses also rose in revolt under Việt Minh leadership, putting up stiff resistance to the French and Japanese. In the villages, tomtoms called on the people to oppose by every means possible the seizure of rice and, armed only with sticks and hoes, faced the guns of the French and Japanese troops.

In the cities, workers intensified the struggle. *The Workers' Association for National Salvation* was founded, urging strikes and demonstrations in support of pay rises and opposing brutality. These struggle provided a major stimulus for the activities of intellectual and student circles.

In the midst of these struggles, Charles De Gaulle's declaration on 8 December 1943 promising to liberate Indochina was hardly noticed.

The 1945 Turning Point

By 1945, it had become obvious that the Axis powers were going to be defeated. In France, the Vichy government had fallen. The Japanese had sustained defeat after defeat in China as well as in the Pacific. In Indochina, the Gaullists, particularly the military, began to prepare for the restoration of colonial rule. On 8 February 1945 in Brazzaville, De Gaulle proclaimed a new manifesto promising Indochina a degree of autonomy. The aim of the new French government was to deploy French troops to safeguard the French presence in the Far East. The Japanese found themselves in a difficult situation, faced with a revolutionary movement daily growing in strength and the possibility of an about-face by the French.

They decided to leave the French with no room to maneuver. On 9 March 1945, Japanese troops disarmed the French without meeting any real resistance. The whole colonial structure collapsed overnight. Meanwhile a major famine began to take hold, the seizure and hoarding of rice and speculation considerably worsening an already precarious situation. The masses were ready to move. The Việt Minh called on the people's forces to intensify guerrilla activity and the peasant masses to seize rice stores held by the Japanese.

Pro-Japanese parties, the *Đại Việt* in particular, attempting to convince people of Japan's generosity and the myth of independence regained with Japanese help, carried out an active propaganda campaign using slogans put forward by the Japanese: economic cooperation, national independence, and a military alliance to form a Greater East Asia. This had little impact on a population largely won over already by the Việt Minh. King Bảo Đại's proclamation of independence, abrogating all treaties signed with France and sealing the country's alliance with Japan, did not change the situation in the slightest. The Japanese and Bảo Đại finally and after much searching chose a prime minister, Trần Trọng Kim, whose cabinet made up essentially of intellectuals, was not appointed until April 17. The Trần Trọng Kim government proved totally incapable of solving the problems of the day. Famine continued to tighten its grip, no new institutions were established, and political amnesty was denied to the communists, who made up nine-tenths of all prisoners. A decree dated July 15 prohibited all trade union activities. The Trần Trọng Kim government had appeared from behind its mask as a mere agent of the Japanese.

The Việt Minh for its part warned the population, petit bourgeois circles in particular, against any illusions regarding the recovery of independence through negotiations with the Japanese and the Bảo Đại - Trần Trọng Kim puppet government. On the night of March 9, while Japanese troops were disarming the French, a Communist Party Central Committee meeting at Đình Bảng, 30 kilometers from Hà Nội, analyzed the situation and adopted a series of crucial resolutions.

Without discounting the possibility of return in force by the French, the party pointed out that the main enemy now was Japanese fascism, but that while the French administration had been dismantled, the pro-Japanese government was not yet functioning effectively. The world war had entered a decisive phase. Japan's defeat was in sight. In Việt Nam the masses, threatened by famine, nursed a bitter hatred for the occupiers and were ready to move into action. Việt Nam was in a truly pre -revolutionary situation. The problem now was for the Party and the Việt Minh Front to draw the masses into preparations for a general insurrection to seize power.

The pre-insurrection mobilization had three essential elements:

- Development of guerrilla activities in the highlands and uplands;
- Action by the peasant masses in seizing rice stores; and
- Political agitation in the major cities.

Liberation committees were formed at various levels in villages, districts and provinces. Forerunners of the revolutionary power, they functioned under the leadership of the national Committee for Liberation. In April, the revolutionary armed forces were merged to form the Liberation Army commanded by a Military Committee comprising Võ Nguyên Giáp, Chu Văn Tấn, and Văn Tiến Dũng. A military school was set up.

After March 9, guerrilla units took important posts in the provinces of Thái Nguyên, Bắc Cạn and Tuyên Quang. In the north, centre and south, escaped political prisoners organized the people in surrounding areas and prepared them for action. Traitors were punished, and revolutionary power was established in many localities and regions. By June 1945, almost all the six provinces north of the Red River delta (Lạng Sơn, Cao Bằng, Bắc Cạn, Hà Giang, Tuyên Quang, and Thái Nguyên) had been liberated, forming the nation's main revolutionary base. Many ambushes of Japanese troops took place, inflicting serious losses on them. In the provinces of Hải Dương and Quảng Yên, uprisings took place in a number of localities and revolutionary power was established.

In central Việt Nam, an armed uprising took place at Ba Tơ in Quảng Ngãi province.

While guerrilla warfare developed in Tonkin and the northern provinces of Annam, famine cut a swathe of destruction across the region and within a few months, two million people had died of starvation. Many villages lost a third or half of their population. In the cities, the bodies of famine victims lay in the streets. The Việt Minh called on the population not to rely either on the Japanese or on the puppet government, but to organize themselves and seize rice stocks and food convoys supplying Japanese troops. Large-scale mobilization by the masses ensued, which had become aware of their strength. Many self-defence units and liberation committees were born out of this struggle. Rice that had been hoarded was distributed to the population, ameliorating the effects of famine, a genuinely pro-revolutionary action.

In the cities, Hà Nội, Sài Gòn, and Huế in particular, political agitation continued to grow. In Hà Nội, although the city's Party Committee had been disbanded five times by the police between 1941 and 1945, each enterprise in 1945 had its own Workers' Section for National Salvation. Self-defence groups were set up. Strikes took place at key factories. Demonstrations and meetings with armed support were held in the streets, schools, factories and at the gates of the city. Pro-Japanese meetings were turned into revolutionary gatherings. Isolated groups of Japanese soldiers were disarmed in the streets and traitors punished. Peasants from the villages surrounding Hà Nội joined workers in attacking rice stores.

In Sài Gòn, the Workers' Sections for National Salvation had grown from 3,000 to 120, 000 members by March 9. The *Youth Vanguard* led by prominent intellectuals such as Dr. Phạm Ngọc Thạch and Thái Văn Lung, a lawyer, had 200, 000 members in Sài Gòn and one million in Cochinchina as a whole.

The August Revolution

In summer of 1945, popular discontent reached a climax and revolutionary action involving both political and armed struggle proliferated throughout the country, from north to south, in villages and cities, and among ethnic minorities in mountainous regions.

The decisive factor was the Việt Minh Front which led and coordinated all these actions nationwide.

On August 13, Japan surrendered following the defeat of the Japanese Kwantung Army by the Soviet Army and the atomic bombing of Hiroshima and Nagasaki by the US. The same day, the Communist Party of Indochina, meeting at a national congress, decided to adopt the following slogans:

- End foreign aggression;
- Seize back national independence; and
- Found the people's power.

Orders were given to combine political and military action in order to agitate and to demoralize the enemy, try to force them to surrender before attack, and focus on the most important targets.

On August 16, the Việt Minh convened a National Congress bringing together delegates from many parties, organizations, and ethnic and religious groups. The Congress decided on the following resolution:

"*To seize power from the hands of the Japanese and puppet government before the arrival of Allied troops in Indochina and receive in*

our capacity as masters of the country the troops which come to disarm the Japanese."

The problem was pre-emptying the Allies (Chiang Kai-shek, British, French and American) who all wanted to occupy Indochina in their own interests.

The Congress adopted a 10-point program:

1. Seize power and found the Democratic Republic of Việt Nam on the basis of total independence;
2. Arm the people. Strengthen the Liberation Army;
3. Confiscate the property of the imperialists and traitors, and depending on circumstances, nationalize it or share it out among the poor;
4. Abolish the taxes imposed by the French and Japanese, and replace them with a just and non-punitive budget system;
5. Guarantee the fundamental rights of the people:
   - Human rights,
   - Right to private ownership,
   - Civil rights: universal suffrage, democratic freedoms, equality among ethnic groups, and between men and women.
6. Share out communal land fairly, reduce land rent and loan interest rates, postpone repayment of debts, and provide relief to victims of natural disasters;
7. Introduce labour legislation: an eight-hour workday, minimum salary, national insurance;
8. Build an independent national economy, develop agriculture, and set up a national bank;
9. Develop a national education system: fight illiteracy, and introduce compulsory elementary education. Build a new culture;
10. Establish friendly relations with the Allies and countries struggling for independence.

A National Committee for Liberation was elected, with the functions of a provisional government and headed by Hồ Chí Minh. He soon made a moving appeal to the nation:

"*This hour is a decisive one for our nation's destiny. Let us all stand up and fight tenaciously for our own liberation. Many peoples of the world are rising up to regain their independence. We cannot lag behind. Forward! Under the Việt Minh banner, let us march courageously forward!*"

The Liberation Army promptly liberated the town of Thái Nguyên. Everywhere mass organizations and guerrilla and self -defence units swung into action. A tidal wave swept the country; between August 14 and 25, in every village and every town, large crowds backed up by armed groups laid siege to administrative offices. The local authorities fled or handed power over to the revolutionaries. Most of the garrisons of demoralized Japanese or puppet troops allowed themselves to be disarmed. Only a few cities remained under occupation: Lai Châu, then occupied by a large French column returning from China where it had taken refuge during the Japanese putsch of 9 March 1945, and Móng Cái, Hà Giang and Lào Cai on the Sino -Vietnamese border, then occupied by Chiang Kai-shek's troops.

In the three major cities of Hà Nội, Huế and Sài Gòn, the swift victory won by the uprising was of paramount importance. In Hà Nội, pro-Japanese agents trying to stem the revolutionary tide, set up a National Salvation Committee which failed to rally the masses. On August 17, a rally called by the Federation of Functionaries in support of the puppet government was turned by an enthusiastic crowd into a huge demonstration in favour of the Việt Minh. A general strike was launched. On August 19, more than 100,000 people demonstrated in the streets, and the puppet government was forced to resign and hand over power to the revolutionaries.

Huế was the royal capital and seat of the pro -Japanese puppet government. The Việt Minh, to avoid bloodshed, tried to persuade Bảo Đại to abdicate and his prime minister Trần Trọng Kim to resign. The reactionaries, wanting to hang on to power, were planning to ask the Japanese command for a 5,000 strong guard, but in order to prevent this, the people of Huế and surrounding villages, accompanied by armed groups, took to the streets to demonstrate and occupy various ministries. On August 23, Bảo Đại agreed to abdicate, and the Trần Trọng Kim government collapsed. On the 25th, a delegation from the people's government in Hà Nội led by Trần Huy Liệu received from Bảo Đại the dynastic seal and sword, the symbols of royal power. Bảo Đại became citizen Vĩnh Thụy.

In Cochinchina, pro-Japanese elements formed a united National Front on August 14. The king's envoy from Huế, Nguyễn Văn Sâm, asked the Japanese to arm the members of this front. But he was unable to withstand popular pressure. On August 25, one million people from Sài Gòn and neighbouring areas, protected by armed groups, marched through the city and established the revolutionary power.

The insurrection had won complete victory throughout the country.

The August Revolution of 1945 put an end to 80 years of French colonial domination, abolished the monarchy and re-established Việt Nam as an independent nation.

It dealt a severe blow at the colonial system, and along with other movements throughout the world, ushered in the era of the dismantling of colonial empires.

The August Revolution was characterized by a sound combination of political and armed struggle, one supporting the other, each playing its own unique role in the process. It showed the political maturity as well as the capacity for action of the masses and the leadership ability of the Việt Minh Front and Communist Party. Victory was achieved thanks to a leadership which had called for the right action at the right moment, and identified forms of action appropriate to each movement and each locality. It was also the product of long political and military preparations, begun at the start of the Second World War, which ended in creating a strong national union on the basis of a close alliance between the workers and peasants. It was able to succeed in inspiring the masses with a courage that held up against all challenges.

Chapter VII

THE FOUNDING OF THE DEMOCRATIC REPUBLIC OF VIỆT NAM

(1945 - 1946)

Following the triumph of the August Revolution, and brought to power by an irresistible revolutionary tide, the Provisional Government appeared before the people of Hà Nội on September 2, 1945 at Ba Đình Square, where President Hồ Chí Minh, before a vast and enthusiastic crowd, proclaimed the nation's independence:

"The French have fled, the Japanese have capitulated, Emperor Bảo Đại has abdicated. Our people have broken the chains which fettered them for nearly a century, and have won independence for Việt Nam...

"Việt Nam has the right to enjoy freedom and independence and has really become a free and independent country. The Vietnamese people are determined to mobilize their entire physical and intellectual strength, and sacrifice their lives and property in order to safeguard their freedom and independence."

Independence and freedom! After eighty years of colonial domination, these words sparked great fervor in millions of Vietnamese. After eighty years of uninterrupted struggle, the homeland was reconstituted as an independent state. Each Vietnamese felt that a new era was about to begin and that everyone, rich and poor, Communists, Confucians, Buddhists and Christians, peasants and workers, mountain people and inhabitants of the plains, manual workers and intellectuals, were prepared to shed their blood to defend that independence, which they knew was threatened from all sides. The situation was extremely precarious; famine was everywhere, the State treasury was empty, in the north Chiang Kai-sheck's troops were ready to occupy the country, and in

the south, the British and French were about to land. Việt Nam stood alone; no allied or friendly country could give it any help whatsoever. The Government of the Democratic Republic had no economic, administrative, military or diplomatic experience. It had nothing but the close union which cemented all strata of the people, the entire people's will to fight, and the clear sighted leadership of a Marxist-Leninist revolutionary party.

As early as 2 September 1945, the Central Committee of the Việt Minh underlined this fact:

"*Our independence is still fragile. To seize power is difficult, but to preserve it is still more difficult.*"

The Provisional Government made this appeal:

"*At this moment, let all thoughts be turned to the struggle for independence, and each person's concern be the struggle against foreign aggression. Only at this price can we avoid annihilation and smash the yoke of slavery.*"

Establishment of a National and Democratic People's State

People's power soon became the crucial factor in safeguarding independence and taking the national revolution forward. While the anti-imperialist task - the defence of the nation's independence - took first priority, the democratic task remained no less important. It was necessary to consolidate national unity while mobilizing the immense energy of the labouring masses, and weave ever closer ties between the revolutionary power and the masses. Against the imperialists who were attacking the country, we had to present a solidly united front, a determined people, and an unwavering ideal, while using flexible tactics. Domestically, urgent tasks had to be carried out: the fight against famine, broadening the national front, pressing democratic reforms, strengthening the people's state, and an immediate literacy campaign.

The famine of 1944 had still not been brought under control when the biggest flood in decades occurred in 1945, submerging the most populous provinces of the Red River delta. Serious shortages of manpower, cattle and seeds ensued, and the flood was closely followed by a prolonged spell of drought. About 250,000 hectares of land could not be sown, and one-third of the November rice crop, which is the most important of the year, was lost. The three provinces of Thanh Hóa, Nghệ An and Hà Tĩnh lost as much as half their crop. It was not possible to rely

any more on the rice which had once come from the south, because on September 23 the French had reoccupied Sài Gòn.

Famine was the major challenge of the moment for the popular government. On September 3, President Hồ Chí Minh launched a dual campaign against famine - for mutual aid and solidarity and for increased production.

In excitement at their newly-regained independence, and inspired by patriotism, millions of Vietnamese, following President Hồ Chí Minh's example, saved the tiniest morsels of food and shared their food with the most needy. All set about cultivating the smallest plots of land. Short-term food crops such as sweet potatoes, cabbages and marrows were grown on all available ground, even in public parks, while each family put aside a relief rice pot and groups of volunteers traveled throughout the country collecting food. The harvest of dry food crops at the end of 1945 and in early 1946 showed a dramatic increase:

- 230,000 tonnes of sweet potatoes as against 65,000 tonnes in 1938-1943;
- 220,000 tonnes of maize as against 56,000 tonnes in 1938-1943;
- 60,000 tonnes of soya beans as against 28,000 tonnes in 1938-1943 (figures for Tonkin).

At the same time, the river dykes were repaired for over 1,200 kilometres, involving 11 million workdays and the moving of 2 million cubic metres of earth.

For the first time in the history of Việt Nam, a government had overcome famine by taking active measures. Mobilizing the masses made it possible, in the summer of 1946, to obtain a good harvest, which continued the success of the previous winter and spring. The famine was contained and then brought under control. Following this ordeal, the entire people felt a close bond to the revolutionary power which had proved its organizational ability and dedication.

The fight against famine did not prevent the government from engaging in another nationwide campaign; one against illiteracy. On 8 September 1945, the Mass Education Department was set up. Almost 100,000 people came forward to volunteer as teachers and over 70,000 classes were organized in pagodas, communal houses, temples, factories, and hospitals, beneath shady banyan trees, in marketplaces, and next to rice fields.

The elderly sat alongside young people, learning to read and write. Children became teachers of their own parents and grandparents. From September 1945 to September 1946, while foreign troops still swarmed across the nation's territory and the fight against famine required enormous efforts, 2.5 million Vietnamese learned to read and write. Meanwhile, the basis of a national education system was being set up; the Vietnamese language, treated as a poor cousin throughout the colonial period, became the medium of instruction at all levels including higher education.

In its first years alone, the new administration won two major battles and proved its worth, carrying out to the letter the revolutionary program patriots had always dreamed of: giving rice and education to the people.

This mobilization of the nation's energies could only be done on the basis of broad national unity. Following the triumph of the revolution, the Việt Minh Front was expanded and strengthened, embracing new mass organizations and personalities, including patriotic associations of traders and industrialists, Buddhists, students and officials. Prime importance was attached to the question of uniting the various ethnic minorities and religions. On 8 December 1945, delegates from twenty ethnic minorities in all parts of the country met in Hà Nội to affirm the principles of unity, equality and mutual assistance among all ethnic communities. Representatives of the various religions - Buddhism, Cao Đài, Hòa Hảo, and Christianity - joined up, showing the will of the entire nation to defend its independence and build a new Việt Nam.

On September 8, President Hồ Chí Minh signed a decree calling for the election of a national assembly. The election campaign became a vast movement to strengthen revolutionary power in the face of the machinations of the imperialists, particularly the French colonialists, whose armed forces had landed in Sài Gòn on September 23. These were the first general elections in the nation's history; every citizen aged 18 or over had the right to vote, and given the grave situation the nation found itself in, each Vietnamese considered the act of voting as a personal contribution to safeguarding the nation's threatened independence. This sentiment prevailed throughout the country, especially in the south where French troops had begun their operation to reconquer Việt Nam. On 6 January 1946 all electors went to the polls in the south, where, despite repression by the French colonialists, over 90 percent of electors voted for candidates presented by the Việt Minh, the main architect of the regaining of independence. The Vietnamese thus confirmed their support for Việt Minh policy and their confidence in the government headed by Hồ Chí Minh, to whom Hà Nội's electors had given 98 percent of their votes.

More than 300 deputies from all social strata, political parties, and ethnic and religious groups were elected. The National Assembly gave its full backing to the Hồ Chí Minh government. All counter -revolutionary tactics intended to undermine the authority of the revolutionary government failed. The Hồ Chí Minh government remained the sole authentic representative of the Vietnamese nation, invested with the people's confidence, legitimately holding power, and having already proved its abilities in the fight against famine and illiteracy. Against it, the imperialists could only muster small groups of unknown puppets with no support among the population, and many of whom had a past history of blatant treason.

At the local level, the former mandarins and village notables in almost every province, district and village had already handed over power to the insurgents at the time of the August Revolution. A new document, Decree No. 63, set up people's committees elected at all levels, which then elected an administrative committee for each locality. From the capital city down to every village throughout the country, people's power was established, taking the nation's affairs into its own hands, working effectively, enjoying the people's trust, and supported by the efforts of the entire nation.

The new government immediately set to work, working in particular to promote a series of democratic reforms, to strengthen the people's armed forces and ensure healthy and independent finances.

On the social plane, the problem was to meet the legitimate demands of the peasants and workers without undermining the nation's unity. On the strategic plane, the two tasks — anti-imperialist and anti-feudal — were inextricably entwined, but on the tactical plane, could be carried out at different tempos. For the time being, the safeguarding of national independence was the major task, while democratic reforms, though substantial, would not be radical in nature.

In agriculture, the government proceeded to a more equitable sharing out of communal land which made up almost 12 percent of the nation's cultivated area. Land rents were reduced by 25 percent and debt repayments postponed. Land belonging to colonialists and traitors was confiscated and temporarily allocated to poorer peasants. Peasants obtained the right to clear waste or virgin land and to own the land they cleared.

Social legislation was introduced to provide for an eight-hour workday, trade union freedoms and the right to strike. Enterprises of national significance and with absentee owners were nationalized or

appropriated, and the workers had the right to participate in the management of them. Many enterprises and publicly-run workshops were set up to provide jobs for the unemployed.

The poll-tax custom duties on opium, alcohol and salt imposed by the colonial administration were abolished.

The new state at first had only 1,250,720 piasters in its coffers. The Bank of Indochina, an issuing bank, had evaded revolutionary control during the August Revolution, but nonetheless had to carry out Vietnamese government orders on payment. On 23 October 1945, however, the bank ceased all payments, hoping to trigger a financial crisis which could prove catastrophic for the government. Right from the beginning, the government issued to the population a vast collection of valuables, gold and silver to pay the most urgent expenses. All social strata responded with enthusiasm and officials worked without pay for several months. But an independent currency had to be issued at all costs.

On 31 January 1946, a decree brought into being the first Vietnamese *đồng* which were put into circulation first in central Việt Nam, then throughout the country towards the end of 1946. But what standard should this currency be based upon? The government had neither gold reserves nor foreign exchange. The Vietnamese state had not yet been recognized by, nor did it have any commercial relations with other countries. The currency was based on the patriotism of the masses, their trust in the government, and their will to safeguard the nation's independence. The *đồng* was exchanged on a par with the Indochinese piastre. The first step in building an independent national economy had been taken.

None of these urgent political, social, and financial issues prevented the new state from thinking of the central task of the moment, that of defending independence at any cost. Priority attention was given to strengthening the armed forces, regular units as well as regional and local self-defence forces.

Though only just born, the people's democratic state was sufficiently prepared in all respects to confront the challenges to come.

Opposition to Chiang Kai-shek

Threats to the new state came mainly from external forces. By virtue of the surrender agreements, Indochina was occupied north of the 16th parallel by Chiang Kai-shek's troops and in the south by British troops which were smoothing the way for the return of the French.

Behind the 200,000 Chinese troops commanded by General Li Han loomed US imperialism and in their wake small groups of politicians and adventurers, the remnants of former nationalist parties which Chiang Kai-shek wanted to impose as puppet rulers on the Vietnamese people. In the provincial capitals of border provinces such as Lào Cai and Lạng Sơn, Chiang Kai-shek's troops and men from the nationalist groups *Việt Cách* and *Việt Quốc* had expelled the revolutionary power and installed puppet authorities. It was not easy for these troops to topple a revolutionary government supported by the entire people, but they nonetheless demanded a cabinet reshuffle, and the resignation even of President *Hồ Chí Minh* and his replacement by Bảo Đại.

At the end of December 1945, Li Han sent an ultimatum to the Vietnamese government demanding the sacking of communist ministers, the handing over leadership of the government to nationalist reactionaries, the granting to the latter of 80 seats in the National Assembly (before the elections), and the replacing of the national flag. Meanwhile, the *Việt Quốc* and *Việt Cách* parties sought to win over bourgeois and feudal landlords and the regrouping of French and Japanese agents, with the aim of causing division inside the united national front. They kidnapped and murdered government officials and a number of Frenchmen, then accused the Việt Minh of these crimes. They demanded seven ministries after their national system: home affairs, national defence, finance, the economy, youth, education, overseas Vietnamese and foreign residents, and the posts of Chairman of the Council of Ministers and Chief of the General Staff. The *Việt Cách* and *Việt Quốc* exploited the crisis and put their demands at the precise moment that French troops were beginning their reconquest of the south.

Countering these small groups was easy since they had no popular support. It was against their masters, Chiang Kai-shek's men, that the government had to apply a policy of intransigence on questions of principle but one of great flexibility and pragmatism. Of the two imperialist forces, France was the more dangerous than Chiang Kai-shek, who was under threat in his own country from a tidal wave of revolution, and had little chance of launching a direct attack against Việt Nam. Li Han's 200,000 men, however, constituted a permanent threat to the new Vietnamese state.

It was vital to avoid direct conflict with these troops while frustrating their attempts to interfere in the country's internal policy, by mobilizing the masses into a political struggle each time the invaders tried to encroach upon the nation's sovereignty. Acts of sabotage and other crimes by *Việt Cách* and *Việt Quốc* agents were publicly denounced and punished when necessary, although the government also made political concessions to them. They were invited to propose candidates for the general elections. Knowing in advance they would be beaten, they refused, but nonetheless sent 70 of their men to the National Assembly as General Li Han had demanded.

Under pressure from the Chinese troops, in January 1946 the government was forced to accept Nguyễn Hải Thần of the *Việt Cách* as vice-president of the Republic, and Nguyễn Tường Tam of the *Việt Quốc* as foreign minister. The counter-revolutionary activities of these small groups remained limited, however, as the people repudiated them everywhere and power at all levels was firmly in the hands of the revolutionaries.

French Aggression in Nam Bộ

In the summer of 1945, the French government took a series of urgent measures aimed at re-establishing French sovereignty in Indochina following Japan's defeat. On August 16, it dispatched the Massu Unit and 9th Colonial Infantry Division with General Leclerc as commander-in-chief of the Expeditionary Corps and Admiral Theirry d'Argenlieu, a Catholic, as High Commissioner for France in Indochina. The commander-in-chief of British troops in Southeast Asia, Admiral Mountbatten, did all he could to speed up the dispatch of French troops to Indochina. British imperialism, anxious about the future of its own colonies in Asia, was anxious to see France restore its domination in Indochina.

On August 23, French troops, among them Cédile, a delegate from the High Commissioner, were parachuted into Nam Bộ (southern Việt Nam). Cédile was authorized by the Japanese to contact the French in Sài Gòn (the insurrection had not yet started in this city). On August 29, Cédile made contact with members of the Nam Bộ Revolutionary Committee and told them France recognized neither Việt Nam's independence nor its unity. The committee told him that independence and unity had already been achieved, and that the Vietnamese people would not recognize any form of colonial administration. On September 2, during a huge demonstration in favour of independence, French colonialists and their agents, hiding in a church, opened fire on the crowd, leaving 47 people dead or wounded.

In early September, British troops landed in Sài Gòn, freed thousands of French detained after the Japanese putsch (March 1945 -

Ed.), and supplied them with arms. The French indulged in numerous provocations, assured of protection by British troops. On September 13, British troops occupied the Palace of the Nam Bộ Committee, allowed the French to raise their *tricoleur*, and authorized French troops to replace the Japanese in several parts of the city. Faced with these provocations, the Nam Bộ Administrative Commitee called on the population on September 19 to prepare for armed resistance to any attempt at reconquest. On the same day, Cédile declared that order first had to be re-established and a government set up in keeping with De Gaulle's declaration of 23 March 1945.

On September 20, Britain's General Gracey banned all Vietnamese newspapers. On the following day, he imposed a curfew and ordered the disbanding and disarming of Vietnamese security forces. The latter of course did not obey the order. Gracey freed and re-armed 1,400 French prisoners-of-war, who, on September 22, carried out numerous provocations and occupied several police stations. On the night of September 22, French troops attacked Sài Gòn. The war for reconquest had begun. The Nam Bộ Administrative Committee immediately called on the people to fight back. The slogan "independence or death" appeared everywhere. On September 26, President Hồ Chí Minh made the following proclamation:

"*Let the Government and our people throughout the country do all they can for the combatants and people of the south who are valiantly fighting and sacrificing their lives to safeguard the independence of the homeland.*"

Units of the People's Army immediately began the march southwards.

Between August 25 (seizure of power in the south) and September 23, the revolutionary government in Sài Gòn had not yet had time to strengthen its armed forces. However, patriotism and the enthusiastic atmosphere created by the victorious insurrection had inspired an extraordinary fighting spirit among all Vietnamese. Armed with bamboo spears, the people of Nam Bộ rose in revolt against the enemy.

In Sài Gòn, where the enemy had occupied the main administrative offices, the people promptly began to wage both armed and political struggle. In many quarters, French troops backed up by British and Japanese were brought to a halt by barricades; fierce battles took in the streets and factories, where Vietnamese patriots made up for lack of weapons with extraordinary heroism. A general strike was declared and the people refused to cooperate with the French who were encircled in the European quarter lacking electricity and water. Workers set fire to numerous French enterprises or moved the machinery to the countryside. The French proved helpless, unable to extend their occupation outside Sài Gòn, and every night suffered harassment by guerrillas.

The French then sought negotiations, making contact on October 2. The Nam Bộ Administrative Committee demanded recognition of Việt Nam's independence, which the French refused to concede and hostilities resumed after a week's truce. Meanwhile, the first units of the French Expeditionary Corps had landed; and General Gracey was threatening to use force. The Nam Bộ Committee sent a note to Gracey with the following affirmation:

We respect the Anglo-Indian troops who are fulfilling their duties, but if they try to re-establish French sovereignty, they will see an entire people rise in defence of its independence.

People in urban areas, on orders from the committee, began to leave the cities to prepare for resistance. Anglo-Indian troops were greeted calmly by the population, but activity against the French was intensified and the blockade of Sài Gòn tightened. However, the arrival of the Expeditionary Corps provided the French with new strength. The British, in the name of the Allies, opened the way for them by occupying more and more urban centres and localities outside Sài Gòn. On October 21, the French and British launched a drive towards the Mekong River delta, the south's rice bowl, and the rubber plantations. They subsequently advanced towards the Central Highlands and landed troops in the southern towns of Trung Bộ (central Việt Nam). These operations lasted throughout November and December 1945. At the end of January 1946, deploying their armoured vehicles and navy, the French occupied Nam Bộ's main cities and communication routes and those of the southern part of Trung Bộ and the Central Highlands. After an unequal fight, the Vietnamese forces pulled out of the cities to begin organizing the resistance in rural areas. An economic blockade and acts of sabotage remained the main patriotic tactics employed in urban areas. The main resistance bases were situated in the Plain of Reeds, the Thạnh Phú region, Bến Tre province, the swampy region of U Minh and the western provinces of Nam Bộ. Việt Nam's central government considered that their main task at the time was to strengthen the resistance in the south as much as possible.

In December 1946 the leadership of the resistance was unified. Nam Bộ was divided into three military zones and the political, administrative and military structure of the resistance reorganized. The French had to disperse their forces and encountered great difficulties in setting up councils of reactionary dignitaries. They intensified their terrorist operations against the population, conducted summary executions, and subjected patriots to tortures but remained powerless to break the people's will. On November 5, President Hồ Chí Minh made the following declaration:

"The French colonialists must know that the Vietnamese people do not want bloodshed, that they love peace. But should they have to sacrifice millions of combatants, and fight for many years to defend the independence of their country and keep their children free, then they will do it. The resistance is sure to win."

On November 25, the Central Committee of the Communist Party set down the following for the resistance:

"...Cut all communications between enemy-held cities, blockade them economically, encircle them politically and harass them militarily...and carry out constant guerrilla operations, persuade the people in enemy-occupied cities to adopt non-cooperation, and those in the countryside to carry out scorched-earth tactics before the enemy's arrival. Maintain links between the different military zones to ensure a united command...the plans for offensives as well as withdrawals must be carefully worked out..."

Despite enormous economic and financial difficulties, reinforcements in the form of men and supplies from the north were constantly reaching the south. Many volunteers enlisted to go and fight in the south while the people gave all they could contribute to its defence. On 17 January 1946, Võ Nguyên Giáp, in the name of the armed forces, made the following declaration:

"Preparation for a long resistance and the dispatch of reinforcements to the south are for the time being the central concerns of our government and the entire people. We must contribute to them by all means available, and make every sacrifice for the resistance, for the southern front."

The reorganization of the resistance rapidly bore fruit, as France's general Pellet admitted:

"The enemy is everywhere. No continuous front, no well dug-in defence where our powerful and modern weapons of war can be used to effect. Each bamboo grove, each hut may conceal an adversary. What a burden on the minds of our soldiers who have to face an elusive enemy in all places, and at all hours of the day and night."

A French sailor, the son of a worker who, when leaving for Indochina, thought he was going to fight the Japanese, wrote the following:

"In Indochina, French troops have acted as the German fascists did in France. I am disgusted by their actions. Why do our planes daily strafe defenceless fishermen? Why do our soldiers plunder, burn, kill? Is it to civilize the country? It is not a handful of rebels we are facing, but a people resolved to defend their freedom. Here everybody is Việt Minh. Whatever happens, you cannot destroy a whole people."

The man who wrote these lines to his family in 1946 was Henri Martin, later to become a member of the Central Committee of the French Communist Party.

The situation in the early months of 1946 was thus as delicate for the French as for the Vietnamese government. The French had of course occupied the main towns of Nam Bộ and southern Trung Bộ, but found themselves unable to defeat the guerrillas, and as long as a revolutionary government was in power in Hà Nội, the hold of the occupiers on the south remained precarious. While continuing their military operations and the dispatch of reinforcements from France, the colonialists began to implement a plan for the secession of Cochinchina, with a puppet "autonomous government". On the Vietnamese side, while the will to defend independence remained unshakeable and mass support was guaranteed, the military forces and equipment remained limited. Time was needed above all in order to build them up. The presence of Chiang Kai-shek's troops in the north, with their reactionary hangers-on, posed a continuing threat.

The French colonialists began to negotiate with Chiang Kai-shek "about permitting French troops to take over from them in northen Indochina, while abandoning France's extra-territorial rights in China, a section of the Hà Nội -Yunnan railway, a "special zone" Hải Phòng, and a special statute for Chinese residents in Indochina." The agreement was signed on February 28, without consulting the Vietnamese government whose sovereignty was at stake.

Four thousand French soldiers who until then had been taking refuge in China entered Lai Châu, while reinforcements from France prepared to land in the north.

The Vietnamese government, to avoid having to fight both armies at the same time, sought a compromise with the French so as to put an end to the country's occupation by Chiang Kai-shek's forces and to buy time. The French, who were preparing for all-out reconquest, were not yet in a position to wage a large-scale war throughout the country. It was sufficient for them as a first step to just gain a foothold in the north and later extend the occupation as reinforcements arrived.

On 6 March 1946, President Hồ Chí Minh and Jean Sainteny, representing the French government, signed an agreement setting out the following main provisions:

1. The French government recognizes the Democratic Republic of Việt Nam as a free state with its own government, parliament, army and finances, and as part of the Indochinese Federation and the French Commonwealth. With regard to the reunification of the three *Kỳ*[1], the French government pledges to accept the decisions made by the population through a referendum.

2. The government of Việt Nam declares itself ready to offer a friendly welcome to the French army when it relieves the Chinese troops, in accordance with international agreements.

3. Immediately after signing, each of the contracting parties shall take all necessary measures to cease hostilities on the spot, maintain troops in their respective positions and create a favourable climate vital for the immediate opening of frank and friendly negotiations. These negotiations will concern Việt Nam's diplomatic relations with foreign states, the future status of Indochina, and France's economic and cultural interests in Việt Nam.

Following the signing of the agreement, a complex military, political and diplomatic struggle began over its implementation. Fifteen thousand French troops entered Hà Nội while Chiang Kai-shek's 200,000 men pulled out, taking with them the *Việt Quốc* and *Việt Cách* adventurers. The struggle was now concentrated against the French colonialists' military and political machinations.

In Nam Bộ, the French continued their bombardment as well as their repression against Vietnamese patriots. The French High Commissioner Thierry d'Argenlieu, a few weeks after the conclusion of the March 6 Agreement, set up, with a handful of puppets, the government of the Autonomous Republic of Nam Kỳ, so as to split the south off for good from the rest of the country. In Hà Nội, General Leclerc provocatively declared upon his arrival that Hà Nội is the last stage of liberation. French troops, shortly after their arrival in the north,

1. The three "Kỳ" were the three regions of Việt Nam, northern, central and southern Việt Nam, designated under the colonial regime as Tonkin, Annam, and Cochinchina, and since 1945 under their Vietnamese names: Bắc Bộ, Trung Bộ and Nam Bộ.

caused numerous provocations, murdered Vietnamese patriots, and encroached on Việt Nam's sovereignty. The French colonialists and the reactionary rulers in Paris firmly believed that the military reconquest of Indochina would be easy, and that the Vietnamese people had no way of resisting France's military might.

Under these conditions, the negotiations taking place between the French and Vietnamese simply led to endless wrangling. The preliminary talks at Đà Lạt, begun in April and still continuing in May of 1946, only revealed the fundamental points of deference between the two sides. The Vietnamese side defended its national sovereignty with regard to its internal and external policies, and the unity of the country from north to south, while the French put forward a plan for an Indochinese Federation headed by a French governor, and claimed to still represent Việt Nam in all its international relations. The French also wanted to integrate Việt Nam into the Franc zone. Thier aim was to camouflage the former colonial structure using new names. The main conflict centred on the status of Nam Bộ, which the French wanted to split off from the rest of the country. The Vietnamese delegation refused to give way on the principle of the country's unity. Võ Nguyên Giáp, headed of the Vietnamese delegation at Đà Lạt, declared:

"*If ever Nam Bộ should be split from the country, the Vietnamese people would struggle with all their might for its return to a unified Việt Nam.*"

For his part, President Hồ Chí Minh proclaimed:

"*Our brothers and sisters in Nam Bộ are citizens of Việt Nam. Rivers may dry up and mountains wear away, but this truth will always remain.*"

On 6 July 1946, negotiations opened at Fontainebleau near Paris. The French stuck to their guns, and the conference stalled. On August 18, the French socialist minister Marius Moutet declared that Cochinchina is "a French colony". While the French representatives were negotiating at Fontanebleau, the French High Commissioner in Indochina on August 1 convened a conference of puppets at Đà Lạt, setting up the Indochinese Federation. In Việt Nam, provocations by French troops multiplied. There was no point in the Fontianebleau conference continuing. President Hồ Chí Minh, then in France, made last-ditch effort at reconciliation by signing a modus vivendi with Marius Moutet. However, French reinforcements kept pouring into Việt Nam. The French government was feverishly preparing for a war of reconquest.

In October, Việt Nam's National Assembly entrusted President Hồ Chí Minh with setting up a new government on a basis of a broad national unity. At the same session, the assembly adopted a constitution which declared the fundamental principle that all power belongs to the people, and recognized people's democratic freedoms, and equality between men and women and among ethnic groups. The constitution declared that Việt Nam is a country united from north to south.

However, provocations by French troops continued, and the maneuvers by the colonialists were so cynical that their puppet President Nguyễn Văn Thinh of the autonomous government of Cochinchina committed suicide. French troops sought to provoke incidents everywhere as a cover for their violation of Việt Nam's sovereignty. In Hải Phòng, the only port through which northern Việt Nam communicated with the outside world, and whose customs duties provided a major source of income for the Vietnamese budget, the French attempted to set up their own customs service. On 20 November 1946, French troops opened fire on Vietnamese forces simulatenously in Hải Phòng and Lạng Sơn. In Hải Phòng, French naval artillery also shelled residential quarters, killing and wounding thousands of people. By occupying Hải Phòng and Lạng Sơn, the two main points of access to the north, the French command had revealed their true intentions. The Vietnamese government, while preparing the people to resist new attacks, make a last-ditch effort to secure peace, but the few agreements reached between the Vietnamese and the French civilian authorities were soon torpedoed by French troops.

The latter provoked incidents in Việt Nam's capital city. On December 17, an attack by French troops in Hà Nội's Hàng Bún killed a hundred people. On December 18, they occupied the Ministries of Finance and Communications, and increased their provocations in the streets. The people and self-defence militia in Hà Nội set up barricades, and made holes in the walls between houses, ready to resist French attacks. President Hồ Chí Minh cabled Leon Blum, who had just been appointed chairman of the French Council of Ministers, asking him to order that the signed accords be respected. He did not even receive a reply. On December 19, the French command sent an ultimatum to the Vietnamese government demanding the demolition of barricades, the disarming of self-defence forces, and the handing over to French troops of the right to keep order in the Vietnamese capital.

On the evening of 19 December 1946, President Hồ Chí Minh made an appeal to the nation:

"Compatriots,

"We want peace, and we have made concessions. But the more concessions we make, the more the French colonialists use them to encroach open our rights. They are determined to reconquer our country.

"No. We would rather sacrifice all than lose our independence and be enslaved. All of you, men and women, young and old, whatever your religion, ethnic origin, or political opinion, arise to struggle against French colonialism and save the homeland. Let those who have guns use their guns, those who have swords use their swords, those who have neither guns nor swords use hoes, pick-axes, and sticks. Let all arise to oppose colonialism and defend our homeland...

"The time has come to rise in revolt. We must sacrifice even our last drop of blood to defend the country. Even if we have to endure the greatest privations and hardships, we are prepared to make every sacrifice. Our people will win."

The war of resistance, until then limited to the south, spread across the country.

The new-born Democratic Republic of Việt Nam was confronted with a decisive challenge, a war against a heavily armed imperialist power far superior in strength in the technical and economic fields.

Chapter VIII

THE FIRST WAR OF RESISTANCE[1]

(1945 - 1954)

The war of resistance against French colonialist aggression which broke out on 23 September 1945 in Nam Bộ, and spread throughout the country after 19 December 1946, marked a decisive stage in an almost century-long struggle to regain the nation's independence and democratize the country. While armed struggle came ahead of all other concerns, economic reconstruction, educational advancement, and the establishing of new administrative structures also constituted major tasks. While national liberation was the prime objective, the democratic objectives were no less important, all the more so since the struggle was led by a party of the working class, and the fact that the worker-peasant alliance constituted the very foundations of the united national front.

Following the 1917 October Revolution and the Soviet Union's great victory over fascism, Việt Nam's democratic revolution of 1945, though not yet socialist, could no longer unfold within the framework of a bourgeois democratic revolution. As resistance grew, the political and ideological consciousness of the masses grew, their class consciousness developing along with their patriotism. The need for material resources and manpower also increased with the war effort, and an all-out effort was necessary to mobilize all the nation's energies. Internally the democratic and popular nature of the revolution increasingly came to the forefront, the people's democratic state was strengthened, and leadership by the working class became more and more concrete. On the international level the Vietnamese war of resistance, by attacking French

1. As distinct from the Second War of Resistance (against US aggression)

colonialism, dealt a severe blow to the imperialist system. It was not surprising that right from the start British and French imperialists joined forces while US imperialism also worked to undermine the resistance.

The national struggle of the Vietnamese people — like that of all colonial people — was an integral part of the world revolution, closely bound to the struggle being waged in the national and international spheres by the forces of peace, national independence, democracy and socialism. However, in 1946 Việt Nam was still geographically isolated and US imperialism, still preoccupied elsewhere, was not yet interfering to any great extent in the affairs of Indochina. The fight essentially pitted the Vietnamese people alone against French colonialism. The victory of the Chinese revolution and founding of the People's Republic of China in October 1949 profoundly altered the world's balance of forces. The resistance was then able to rely upon the socialist camp and break the colonialist encirclement. To make up for its failure in China, in 1950 US imperialism triggered a war of aggression in Korea and began to openly intervene in Indochina. The war became a Franco-American war against the Vietnamese people, and through it, against the national liberation movement in Asia.

Both internally and externally the year 1950 was, therefore, a major turning-point. There were two main parts to this long resistance, the first from 1946 to the end of 1950 during which the Vietnamese side gradually strengthened its military, political, economic, administrative and cultural bases, and the second from 1951 to 1954, a stage of important and decisive military victories and radical economic and social reforms. The Điện Biên Phủ victory and the Geneva Conference in 1954 ended this war of resistance against French colonialism, which was forced to recognize the independence, sovereignty, unity and territorial integrity of Việt Nam.

From the Battle of Hà Nội to the Battle of the Lô River

In launching its war of aggression, the French command wanted to take advantage of its clear superiority in armaments and the capacity of its regular troops to swiftly destroy the poorly armed, and still inexperienced, Vietnamese forces and capture resistance group leaders.

By contrast, the Vietnamese resistance was based on political superiority, the patriotism of the masses, the national alliance, the heroism of the combatants and the people, and the people's confidence in their government to wage a drawn-out war, a people's war, with the

participation of the entire nation, a total war covering all domains. Right from the first days, the doctrine of the resistance was clearly defined by Trường Chinh in his article, *The Resistance Is Bound to Win.*[1]

The problem was to develop, during the struggle, armed forces particularly suited to people's war, local self-defence forces made up of guerrillas operating in their villages while continuing farm work, regional forces which covered a relatively large area of territory, and well-trained regular forces capable of conducting important operations and dealing the enemy devastating blows. Thus while guerrillas harassed enemy troops, compelling them to disperse in order to defend captured localities, the regular army could go wherever deemed necessary, and concentrate its units on large-scale operations. These armed forces gained in strength and experience the more they fought, while the enemy soon tired of pursuing an adversary they could not lay hands on. On the strategic level, the resistance was mainly defensive depending on the time and circumstance. On the operational and tactical levels, offensive was the rule, the prime aim being to destroy as many enemy forces as possible rather than hold territory.

In 1946, vast liberated areas formed powerful rearguard bases. The Việt Bắc, a mountainous region running between the Chinese border and the Red River, constituted the very cradle of the resistance. But even in enemy-held areas guerrilla existed; people sheltered partisans and dedicated activists. These bases were constantly developing and threatened the enemy from the rear.

Political and ideological education of the armed forces and people was at the heart of the resistance. Only strong political awareness could help the people endure terrible hardship and suffering, and utilize to the maximum their initiative so as to face a powerful, battle-hardened enemy. All resistance would have been futile otherwise. All these elements demonstrated their effectiveness right from the first major battle, the battle of Hà Nội. The French command boasted that it could wipe out the resistance forces within 24 hours. But for two months the "regiment of the capital", supported by the population, dug in behind houses and operated in the maze of streets, proving their courage and resourcefulness by tying down a well-trained 6,500-strong enemy army with 40 tanks, armoured vehicles and 30 planes and inflicting severe losses on it, with 500 killed and 1,500 wounded. This two-month delay considerably slowed down the implementation of the French strategy while giving the resistance time to organize.

1. This text was published in full as a paperback by the Foreign Languages Publishing House (presently Thế Giới Publishers)

With the arrival of further reinforcements, the French Expeditionary Corps gradually extended its control, especially in the major cities which the Vietnamese resistance did not try to hold. Certain towns were destroyed by the people to prevent enemy troops from occupying them. In the south as well as the north, guerrillas harassed the French troops who were dispersed throughout the country.

The enemy did not remain idle. Politically, they sought to rally to their cause reactionary forces - former agents of the colonial administration - to sow division and spread rumours. In the south, they

VIỆT BẮC CAMPAIGN

(7.10 - 22.12-1947)

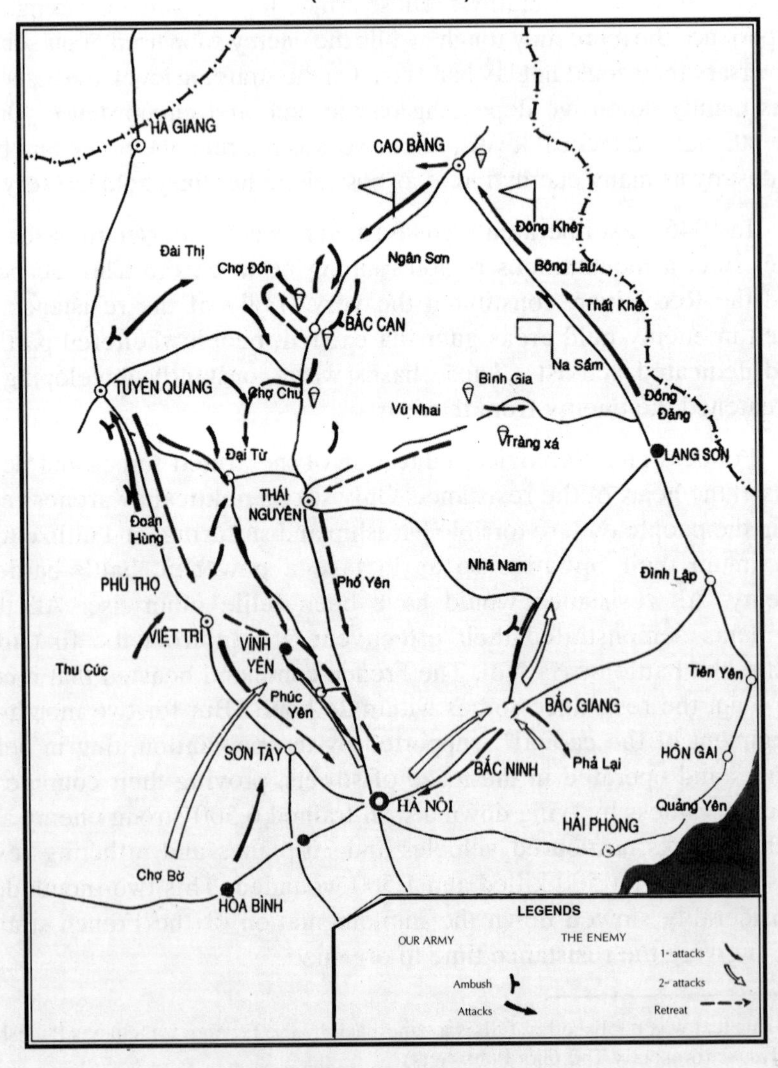
HÀ GIANG
CAO BẰNG
Đông Khê
Đài Thị
Chợ Đồn
Ngân Sơn
Bông Lau
Thất Khê
BẮC CẠN
Na Sầm
Bình Gia
TUYÊN QUANG
Chợ Chu
Vũ Nhai
Đồng Đăng
Tràng xá
LẠNG SƠN
Đại Từ
THÁI NGUYÊN
Đoan Hùng
Nhã Nam
Đình Lập
PHÚ THỌ
Phổ Yên
VIỆT TRÌ
VĨNH YÊN
Thu Cúc
Tiên Yên
Phúc Yên
BẮC GIANG
SƠN TÂY
Phả Lại
BẮC NINH
HỒN GAI
HÀ NỘI
Quảng Yên
HẢI PHÒNG
Chợ Bờ
HÒA BÌNH
LEGENDS
OUR ARMY
THE ENEMY
1st attacks
2nd attacks
Ambush
Attacks
Retreat

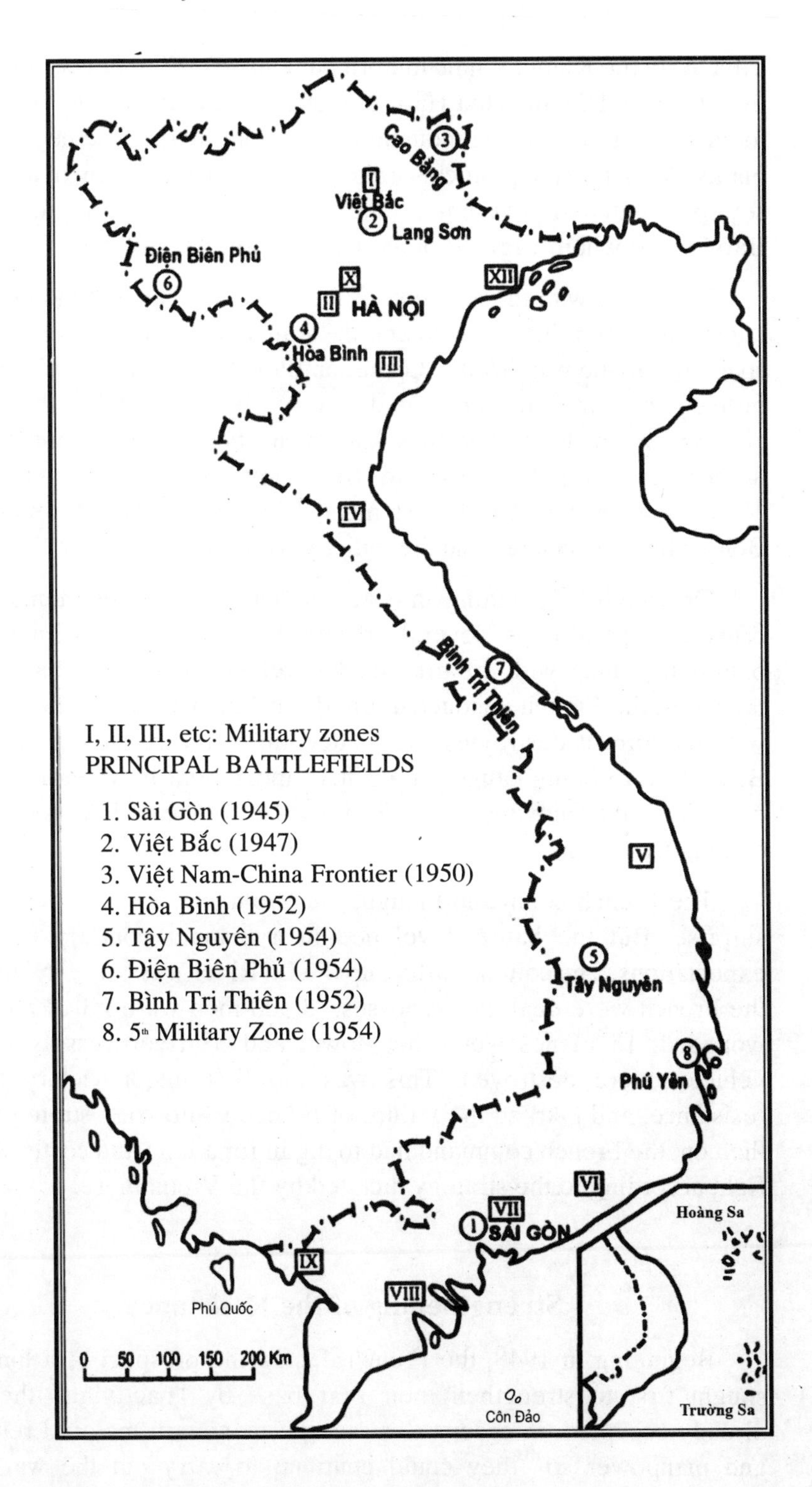
Cao Bằng
3
I
Việt Bắc
2
Lạng Sơn
Điện Biên Phủ
6
X
II
HÀ NỘI
XII
4
Hòa Bình
III
IV
Bình Trị Thiên
7
I, II, III, etc: Military zones
PRINCIPAL BATTLEFIELDS
1. Sài Gòn (1945)
2. Việt Bắc (1947)
3. Việt Nam-China Frontier (1950)
4. Hòa Bình (1952)
5. Tây Nguyên (1954)
6. Điện Biên Phủ (1954)
7. Bình Trị Thiên (1952)
8. 5th Military Zone (1954)
V
5
Tây Nguyên
8
Phú Yên
VI
VII
1
SÀI GÒN
IX
VIII
Phú Quốc
Hoàng Sa
0 50 100 150 200 Km
Côn Đảo
Trường Sa

The first war of resistance (1945-1954)

tried to set the Khmer ethnic minority against the Vietnamese and to win over the Cao Đài and Hòa Hảo religious sects. In the north, they sought to pit ethnic minorities in mountainous regions against the people of the plains. An extensive political campaign was carried out in an attempt to set up a "national government" headed by the former king of Annam, Bảo Đại, to whom vague promises of autonomy were made.

In France, with the adoption of the Marshall Plan and the ousting of communists from the government, the Ramadier cabinet had resolved to speedily win the war. While "Operation Bảo Đại" was taking place, major military preparations were under way. In May 1947, the French government made its demands known, including the disarming of the Vietnamese armed forces and free movement for the French on Vietnamese territory. On 10 September 1947, France's High Commissioner Bolaert bluntly declared that the military were to have the say.

On October 7, putting into action five infantry regiments, half a brigade of paratroops, several artillery batteries and two engineering battalions, along with 40 aircraft, 800 vehicles and a flotilla of motor launches, the French conducted a major offensive against the Việt Bắc with the aim of destroying the leadership of the resistance. The Việt Bắc, close to being caught in a pincer movement between two armed columns —one moving up the Red and Lô o (Clear) Rivers, the other coming from Lạng Sơn— was to be cleared by airborne troops.

The French command thought the Vietnamese would be taken by surprise. But the battle developed in a manner contrary to French expectations. The column sailing up the Lô River was badly mauled, and the French were deált heavy losses: 3,300 men were killed and 4,000 wounded; 18 planes were shot down; and 38 river vessels and 255 vehicles were destroyed. This was the first major victory for the resistance, and marked the failure of France's blitzkrieg strategy. From then on, the French command had to dig in for a long and costly war and fight according to the strategy dictated by the Vietnamese.

Strengthening of the Resistance

Beginning in 1948, the French, facing the prospect of a long war, sought first to strengthen their rear base by "pacifying" the areas already occupied, in order to extract the maximum material resources and manpower so they could continue to carry out the war. They planned to make "Vietnamese fight Vietnamese" and to "feed war by war." Extensive swoops were conducted, especially in Nam Bộ and southern Trung Bộ. In Nam Bộ, the French command ordered the construction of a complex network of watchtowers along major communication routes. In Bắc Bộ, the French extended their occupation to the provinces of Hà Đông, Hòa Bình, Lào Cai, Sơn La and Cao Bằng. In Trung Bộ, they launched numerous attacks on the provinces of Quảng Bình, Quảng Trị and Thừa Thiên. The French Expeditionary Corps was boosted to 150,000 men, and its expenditure to 300 billion francs per year. The war in Indochina was becoming a heavy burden for France.

The Vietnamese resistance had defined its political and military direction in early 1948. Guerrilla attacks remained the main form of action, while the regular troops tried to switch to mobile warfare. Regular army units were turned into "detached companies" to train and support the regional army and self-defence forces, and to help set up regional branches of power and people's organizations where the enemy was extending their occupation. "Armed propaganda" units infiltrated the enemy's rear base and launched effective resistance. The widening of guerrilla warfare did not prevent the resistance from launching important battles when necessary; for instance La Ngà (2 March), Tầm Vu (19 April), Sóc Xoài (5 August), and Mộc Hóa (September) in Nam Bộ, the battle of Bình Trị Thiên in Trung Bộ, and of Nghĩa Lộ on Highway 4 in Bắc Bộ.

By 1949, armaments workshops had succeeded in setting up production lines making recoilless rifles and heavy mortars, and military operations were being conducted on an ever greater scale. At the end of 1949 and the beginning of 1950, the French command, facing a new situation brought about by the victory of the Chinese revolution, tried to send more reinforcements to Bắc Bộ, strengthen and extend their occupation in the Red River delta, and intensify operational sweeps using mobile groups. Major operations were conducted, particularly on the fringes of the delta, and military posts along the Sino-Vietnamese border were reinforced. The size of the puppet army was boosted to 122,000 men.

But the resistance hit back hard; guerrilla battles flared, fortified villages mushroomed, and enemy stores and communication routes were repeatedly attacked. In 1949-50 more than 200 fortified posts were seized, leaving 10,000 French soldiers dead.

Thus from 1948 to 1950, the opposing sides were about equal in strength, and neither was able to encroach on the other's territory, each trying to reinforce their rear base areas while preparing for a new stage in the war.

For the Vietnamese resistance, economic reconstruction was a central issue. The enemy controlled the industrial centres, part of the rich and populous plains, and the foreign trade routes. The problem was to ensure supplies of food and munitions to the armed forces. The French sought to destroy: a no-man's-land of destruction encircled enemy-held areas. They also blocked the movement of rice, medicines and tools into the liberated zones, sending luxury goods there instead. They wanted to impose the Bank of Indochina piastre on these areas so as to criminate the Vietnamese currency. The Vietnamese resistance on the other hand sought to blockade the towns, and undermine French economic influence. At the beginning the blockade was tight, but it was gradually found that it was more advantageous to control trade between liberated zones and enemy-held regions in order to let certain goods flow in one direction or the other, thereby meeting the needs of the people and the people's armed forces.

The main problem, however, was to increase production in the free zones. Principles and directives were set down in the area of the economy:

- To develop agricultural production as a priority, to encourage handicrafts and small industry;
- To rely mainly on local resources;
- To decentralize and ensure the development of self-sufficiency in each region, limiting as far as possible the exchange and movement of goods, and give broad autonomy to each region;
- To mobilize material resources, manpower and energies under the slogan "all for the front";
- To launch an extensive patriotic emulation campaign aimed at encouraging a spirit of heroic initiative and labour among the broad masses, while gradually introducing democratic reforms aimed at improving conditions for the labouring masses;
- To create State economic departments, nucleus of a future State sector in the nation's economy.

This economic policy brought encouragin results in many areas. In the first place, despite the destruction caused by the enemy and the shortage of manpower, the free zones formerly vulnerable to famine, were now in a position to avert it. The supply of food to the people, armed forces and administrative bodies was ensured. The arms workshops set up in the forests, despite lack of equipment, succeeded in producing a range of weapons. Handicraft workshops produced textiles, paper, medicines, and even certain industrial products such as cast iron, sulfuric acid, small

engines, and other. However, there were huge difficulties; income only met about 20 percent of State expenditure in the years 1948-1950, and the government had to issue banknotes to make up the deficit.

It is important to note that the people in enemy-held areas also made substantial contributions to the resistance by supplying rice, goods and money. The economic war, like the guerrilla battles, spread throughout the enemy's rearguard areas.

Great efforts were made concerning education in the free zones. The literacy campaign that began in 1945 continued on the same scale, remaining a mass movement attracting thousands of people each year. Crash courses were held in workshops and public offices. As from 1946, regular professional courses were organized. By 1950, 1,802 students who had completed their courses were employed in factories and State offices. Higher education establishments (medicine, teachers' colleges, public works) were set up. The first batch graduating in 1950 numbered 1,200. General education spread despite shortages of paper and books. Particular attention was given to the training of cadres from ethnic minorities. Risking their lives, activists went into enemy-held areas to teach the people to read and write.

After several years of effort, the resistance entered the year 1950 with relatively strong armed forces, a reliable rear base, and a State administration that had both the confidence from, and committed to, the people, and prepared for new challenges in every area.

The Border Campaign Victories, A New Franco-American Strategy

The victory of the Chinese revolution and the founding of the People's Republic of China gave strong impetus to the Vietnamese resistance. For China, Việt Nam constituted a rampart protecting its southern borders against the United States which was then showing itself to be particularly aggressive. Early in 1950, the Democratic Republic of Việt Nam was accorded recognition by the People's Republic of China, the USSR, and then by other socialist countries. From then on Việt Nam was no longer as isolated as it had been up to this point.

In the enemy camp a new factor was emerging; more open intervention by the US in Indochinese affairs. On 10 March 1950, a US naval squadron anchored in Sài Gòn, trying by a show of strength to intimidate the population. The response was a mammoth demonstration which forced the American warships to leave. In June 1950, when Washington triggered the war in Korea, a US military mission was sent to Sài Gòn to help the French command. The US gave France considerable financial and material assistance to help it intensify the war. Reinforcements were sent to seal off the Sino -Vietnamese border and reinforce the French garrisons in Lạng Sơn, Đông Khê, Thất Khê and Cao Bằng, situated on Highway 4 running along the northern border.

In mid-September, the Vietnamese command decided to launch an attack on these positions. On September 16, the Đông Khê post was taken, compelling the French garrison at Cao Bằng to withdraw to Thất Khê. Another French column left Thất Khê to meet the one from Cao Bằng. On the way both columns were attacked by Vietnamese forces and the 8,000 men, including commanders, were killed or taken prisoner. The French hastily retreated from Lạng Sơn, Lào Cai, and Hòa Bình. The Sino -Vietnamese border lay wide open and the French plan

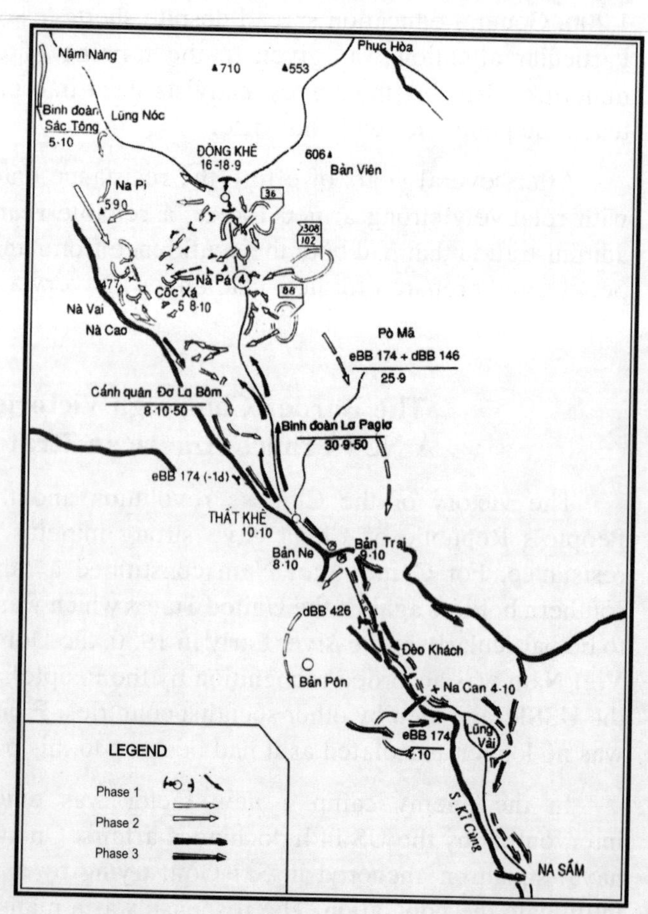
Nậm Nàng
Phục Hòa
710
553
Bình đoàn Sắc Tông
5-10
Lũng Nóc
ĐÔNG KHÊ
16-18-9
606
Bản Viên
Na Pi
590
36
308
102
Nà Pá
4
477
Cốc Xá
5 8-10
88
Nà Vai
Nà Cao
Pò Mã
eBB 174 + dBB 146
25-9
Cánh quân Đơ Lơ Bôm
8-10-50
Binh đoàn Lơ Pagiơ
30-9-50
eBB 174 (-1d)
THẤT KHÊ
10-10
Bản Ne
8-10
Bản Trại
9-10
dBB 426
Đèo Khách
Bản Pồn
Na Can 4-10
eBB 174
4-10
Lũng Vài
S. Kì Cùng
NA SẦM
LEGEND
Phase 1
Phase 2
Phase 3

BORDER CAMPAIGN
(16.9 - 14.10.1950)

to create "autonomous territories" for ethnic minorities in mountainous regions of Bắc Bộ ended in failure.

The border victories threw the enemy into disarray. In France, the anti-war movement, led by the Communist Party, grew in strength. Conflicts intensified within the reactionary parties; some advocated US intervention, others a withdrawal which might help save French domination in Africa. The French government chose to subordinate its policies to those of Washington. General De Lattre de Tassigny, considered to be France's supreme strategist, after a visit to Washington to receive instructions, took over command of the French Expeditionary Corps in an effort to redress the situation.

De Lattre took a series of measures aimed at:

- increasing reinforcements from France in terms of men and military equipment, especially aircraft;
- building up Bảo Đại's puppet army;
- creating a no-man's-land around the Red River delta, with all houses destroyed and concrete bunkers built everywhere; and
- intensifying "pacification" efforts in areas occupied by the French.

These were carried out diligently while the French conducted a wide propaganda campaign aimed at promoting the idea that the French were fighting to "defend the free world" against the communist threat, and to build support for a "national government". In July 1951, the French coerced Bảo Đại into signing a decree on general mobilization. De Lattre showed extreme cruelty in operations conducted against the civilian population, with the aim of creating a ring of bunkers or pacifying rear base areas. Entire villages were burnt to the ground, their inhabitants massacred, and tens of thousands of people herded into concentration camps. De Lattre ordered his troops to systematically destroy crops and food reserves so as to starve the people into submission and prevent food from reaching the resistance. French soldiers were ordered to kill the buffaloes, which were easy targets, and other animals vital in the cultivation of rice. De Lattre also tried to set up reactionary local administrations to control the population.

De Lattre's efforts yielded some results. By the end of 1951 the Red River delta was encircled by a ring of 2,200 blockhouses and bunkers, the ranks of the puppet army had grown to 112,000 men, and the Americans were supplying dozens of aircraft and hundreds of armoured vehicles and artillery pieces. Besides the 55 battalions of occupation troops, the French had based 46 mobile battalions in the Red River delta alone. Franco-American propaganda was full of praise for De Lattre and claimed that he was leading French colonialism to victory. However, in France the mass movement against the Vietnam war was growing. The campaign for the release of Henri Martin, the French sailor who had refused to fight the Vietnamese, gained in size and strength. Actions such as those of Raymonde Dien, who lay down in front of a train carrying ammunition for the French in Indochina, won strong backing from the French public. The Franco-American alliance was not without its problems, with US imperialism beginning maneuvers to oust the French colonialists.

The main obstacle to De Lattre's strategy, however, was the considerable growth in strength of the Vietnamese resistance, not only on the military but also political, economic, and cultural levels.

New Gains by the Resistance

Following the recognition of the Democratic Republic of Việt Nam by the socialist countries and its victory in the Border Campaign, the Vietnamese resistance made rapid advances. An event of great significance took place in February 1951; the 2nd National Congress of the Communist Party. This Congress determined the main directions of the resistance for the next few years. An important decision was taken. The Communist Party of Indochina split into three national parties, each assuming the leadership of the national struggle in its own part of Indochina. In 1930 communists from the three countries had come together within the same party to struggle against a unified colonial administration, the general government of Indochina. Now that the struggle against the French was nearing its conclusion and the three countries would soon recover their independence, it had become necessary for communists from each country to found their own party while maintaining the close ties between the three national movements. The Vietnamese Party took the name *Đảng Lao Động Việt Nam* (Worker's Party of Việt Nam), with Hồ Chí Minh as President and Trường Chinh as General Secretary.

In March 1951, a congress to merge the Việt Minh and Liên Việt Fronts was held, leading to the founding of a broad national front. In the same month a congress was held which proclaimed the unity between the three peoples of Việt Nam, Cambodia and Laos who were fighting shoulder to shoulder against the same enemy, in the struggle for independence and freedom.

The diplomatic and external relations of the Democratic Republic of Việt Nam were constantly expanding. Missions and delegations from

Việt Nam visited China and Korea, attended world youth festivals (Berlin), economic conferences (Moscow), peace congresses (Vienna) and trade union gatherings (Warsaw). At all these international gatherings, the Vietnamese people's struggle for independence was warmly acclaimed and supported in many circles.

In the economic and financial spheres, a whole series of measures gave encouragement to life in the liberated zones as from 1951, helping to boost production to meet the ever-increasing needs of the resistance. An emulation movement was launched in all domains - agriculture, industry, the army, and among the intelligentsia - giving a strong boost to production efforts among the peasantry in particular.

The situation also required that the State assume a greater and greater role in the leadership of the country's economic activities and reform a financial system affected by worsening inflation. In May 1951, the following decisions were taken:

- to establish a National Bank;
- to issue a new currency, a new *đồng* equivalent to 10 former *đồng*;
- to institute a single agricultural tax replacing all taxes, impositions and contributions extracted from the peasantry; and
- to create a Foreign Trade Service.

The proportion of budget expenditure covered by income continued to increase: 23 percent in 1950, 30 percent in 1951, 82 percent in 1952, and 116 percent in 1953. Prices stabilized, with the price index moving as follows: 100 in 1949, 440 in 1950, 464 in 1951 before the issuing of the new *đồng*, 360 for the last months of the year following the issuing of the new *đồng*, 335 in 1952, 115 in 1953, and 92 in 1954. In the Việt Bắc region between 1952 and 1953, the price of rice dropped by 35 percent, that of salt by 55 percent and that of cloth by 30 percent.

Commercial exchanges between the free zones and enemy-held areas, tightly controlled, operated in such a way as to benefit the national currency. The patriotism of the people in both zones and the heroism of the cadres who carried out this work made it possible to win the battle between the two currencies. The national currency strengthened while the Bank of Indochina piastre lost ground, down from a value of 17 francs to 10, then 7 despite substantial American aid.

These economic measures not only helped strengthen the resistance, but formed the nucleus of the State sector of the future socialist economy.

In the area of education, an important turning point was reached. While the literacy campaign continued, greater stress was put after 1951 on further education for cadres, combatants and other people who had learned to read and write, so as to allow ordinary people to assume more and more important responsibilities. In general education schools in 1950, an overall reform program was launched, establishing a standard nine-grade education system with important changes in curricula and methods, so as to train people capable of assuming the revolutionary duties of the time. In 1953, school enrollments in the free zones passed the million mark, and in 1954, the number of higher education establishments reached 1,528. A number of students were sent to other socialist countries for further education.

An important fact to emerge after 1951 was the increasing consciousness among writers, artists and scientists of the need to closely associate their activities with the revolutionary struggle of the entire people. Motivated by patriotism, these people had in 1946 sacrificed their economic well-being to follow the resistance. In the early years of the resistance, many of them clung to out-dated concepts about artistic creativity. In 1948, these problems were aired at a national cultural congress in a talk by Trường Chinh entitled "Marxism and Cultural Issues in Việt Nam." Contact between writers and artists on the one hand, and the People's Army soldiers and common people on the other hand, and their participation in fighting and production, gradually led to profound changes in the outlook of those working in the field of culture. Beside older writers and artists, a new generation born out of the resistance was also emerging.

A new cultural life was born in the liberated zones. Each unit of the armed forces and each village had its own arts group. Writers and artists, both amateur and professional, wrote poems or did sketches, and cinema teams were set up. The award of literary prizes in 1951-1952 made it possible to put in place, alongside those by already well-known authors, new works by young writers and poets. In difficult wartime conditions, these authors were not able to reach great literary heights, but the poems, short stories, fables, reports and occasional novel to be awarded prizes revealed a new wellspring in Vietnamese literature.

While the resistance grew in strength, the Bảo Đại puppet government, despite American intrigue and the efforts of the French, failed to materialize. Power and command of the military effectively remained in French hands while Bảo Đại spent his time in casinos at French seaside resorts.

De Lattre in Difficult Straits

By 1951, the Vietnamese resistance was gaining the initiative despite new equipment at the disposal of the French command. In the south, guerrilla battles continued and the political struggle in Sài Gòn and other cities gathered momentum. The battlefront, however, remained essentially in the north.

In January 1951, popular forces launched an attack in the uplands on the northwestern edge of the Red River delta, took ten enemy positions and wiped out three mobile battalions sent to rescuse them. On March 20, another attack was made in the Đông Triều area, threatening the Hồng Gai coal mining area and the port of Hải Phòng. In May, popular forces attacked the provincial capital of Ninh Bình in the southern part of the delta. On each occasion the French command had to rush reinforcements to the area under attack. De Lattre organized his crack troops into mobile units, but he remained on the defensive.

In France, the National Assembly was scheduled to meet at the end of 1951 to discuss the policies to be pursued in Indochina. The French command, waging a war of reconquest, could not remain cloistered indefinitely behind the Red River delta defensive belt, waiting for the next offensive by the Vietnamese resistance. They had to escape from this passive posture at all costs.

On 14 October 1951, De Lattre sent three paratroops and 15 infantry battalions, supported by seven artillery batteries and two armoured groups, against the provincial capital Hòa Bình, 75 kilometres southwest of Hà Nội, on the Đà (Black) River, in a region mainly inhabited by the Mường ethnic minority. A good deal of propaganda resulted from this seizure of Hòa Bình which Vietnamese forces did not try to defend. The French soon set about building a fortified defence line around Hòa Bình to be guarded by crack troops.

The Vietnamese command decided that De Lattre's drive against Hòa Bình had given it a twofold opportunity, on the one hand to attack and destroy some of the enemy's crack forces outside the delta, and on the other to step up guerrilla activities in the delta itself, which would thus be defended by fewer enemy troops. Three regular divisions with artillery support marched on Hòa Bình, while two other divisions infiltrated into the delta resulting in a two-pronged battle.

On December 10, the Vietnamese attacked Hòa Bình and seized French positions on the Đà River, cutting the river supply route to the French garrison. From then on, all supply columns passing along

Highway 6 were ambushed. The French forces dug themselves in "porcupine" fashion, forming a fortified camp. The Vietnamese forces took a series of strongholds one by one, shelled the Hòa Bình airfield, and harassed the enemy with sporadic sniper fire. It was the first time they had fought a battle of this kind. Every day, the enemy had to deploy 12 infantry battalions and armoured vehicles to escort the supply convoys along Highway 6. Meanwhile, the popular forces stepped up their operations to the rear, inflicting even more serious losses on them than at Hòa Bình. On the night of March 23, the French pulled out of Hòa Bình, losing six companies and dozens of vehicles in their retreat. Between October 14 and March 23, 22,000 soldiers from the French Expeditionary Corps were killed, more than 6, 000 of them at Hòa Bình. De Lattre died of an illness before seeing his efforts fall to pieces.

Following the Hòa Bình defeat, the French Expeditionary Corps was forced on to the defensive everywhere. Guerrilla warfare intensified throughout the country, while each dry season the Vietnamese forces launched large-scale attacks, liberating one important area after another. In October 1952, they liberated the valleys of the Đà and Mã Rivers, an area covering 28,000 square kilometres with 250,000 inhabitants, mostly of the Thái ethnic group. These campaigns involved key regular army units as well as a huge number of *dân công* - supply carriers - who went in the thousands, sometimes tens of thousands, to carry food and munitions to units operating far from their home bases. During the initial stages of the war, the people and the People's Armed Forces had had to destroy roads to block the French advance, but now started to rebuild hundreds of kilometres to facilitate bolder and bolder offensives.

Early in 1953, operating in concert with Pathet Lao forces, the Vietnamese armed forces overran the town of Sam Neua, in upper Laos, liberating a 40,000 square kilometre area with 300,000 inhabitants. The French and Americans then made new efforts to redress the situation.

The Navarre Plan

US aid to France rose to 385 million dollars in 1953, covering 60 percent of expenditure on the war. By 1954, this had risen to 80 percent. American arms supplies totalled 25,000 tonnes per month in 1953, and 88,000 tonnes by July 1954. American missions led by high-ranking officials, including Secretary of State John Foster Dulles and Vice-President Nixon participated directly in working out France's military strategy. Airlifts were organized in France, the Philippines and Japan to supply the French Expeditionary Corps, and American pilots took part in the operations.

In May 1953, a new French commander-in-chief, Navarre, the seventh since 1945, was appointed by the Laniel government. With Pentagon assistance, Navarre had devised a plan for regaining the initiative, wiping out the Vietnamese forces within 18 months, and bringing the war to a victorious conclusion.

Navarre had massed 112 battalions, 44 of these mobile, in the north. With swift, devastating attacks and using large quantities of weapons, these forces would keep the Vietnamese forces on the run and decimate the resistance, which was concentrated mostly in the north. At the end of winter, when the Vietnamese forces would have been worn down by these operations, the French command would transfer its crack units to the south where the Vietnamese regular forces were relatively weak, and a swift victory could thus be achieved in this theatre of battle. Freed from the burden of occupation by the increase in size of the puppet forces, and having reconquered the south, the French Expeditionary Corps would be able to, from the autumn of 1954, concentrate its crack units in the north, win major victories there, and force the Vietnamese resistance to "negotiate."

The new weapons at the disposal of the French command, and the boldness of its strategy, seemed to breathe new life into the French Expeditionary Corps. By the end of 1953, it numbered 250,000 men and the puppet army more than 300,000, the two having between them 26 artillery battalions, 528 aircrafts and 390 vessels. The French command launched attacks from one end of the country to the other: Lạng Sơn near the Chinese border, Ninh Bình, south of Hà Nội, operational sweeps in Bình Trị Thiên, central Việt Nam, and in the provinces of Nam Định and Thái Bình in the heart of the Red River delta.

It appeared as if the French Expeditionary Corps might have regained the advantage. For the Vietnamese resistance, the urgent issue now was that of foiling the Navarre plan.

War and Land Reform

At the end of September 1953, the Politburo of the Workers' Party met, chaired by Hồ Chí Minh. Two strategic directions were discussed:

- Either to deploy the major part of the regular army, to fight the enemy who were striking hard in the northern delta and threatening the liberated zones, or

- To avoid a head-on collision between regular troops and the enemy in the delta where battle conditions favored the latter, and leave regional and local forces there to harass and wear them down, launch the regular forces into areas where the enemy were more exposed, and compel them to scatter their forces and withdraw their troops from the free zones, which they had been temporarily able to occupy.

The attacks launched by Navarre in various regions were seen not as offensives but as operations to forestall preemptive strikes by the Vietnamese resistance. Despite outward appearances the French were on the defensive, and this was therefore the time to attack and destroy them, instead of passively reacting to their initiatives.

The resistance adopted the second strategic direction.

It was decided that the free zones and enemy-held areas would rely mainly on their own forces to counter the enemy. Regular forces were to be used for attacks in mountainous areas, such as the northwest, in Bắc Bộ, and the Central Highlands. Closer coordination with Pathet Lao forces would make it possible to attack the enemy in upper and central Laos. Meanwhile, guerrilla activity throughout the country needed to be intensified.

The theatre of operations thus comprised not only Việt Nam, but Indochina as a whole. It was vital to mobilize millions of people for guerrilla battles, to repair roads, and ensure that supplies reached combat units often stationed hundreds of kilometres from their supply bases. While the majority of the population and the nation's resources were concentrated on the plains, the battlefields were situated in far-off mountainous regions. The scale of operations, the duration of campaigns, and hence the volume of supplies required, the number of people to be mobilized - armed forces as well as *dân công* - surpassed in importance all that had been done previously. The opening of the Yên Bái - Sơn La road for instance, required 2 million man hours, and that of the road linking the 2nd and 3nd Military Regions took 2.6 million man hours.

To overcome the enemy's advantage in aircraft, tanks, artillery and well-trained units, great demands were made on the heroism, tenacity and resourcefulness of combatants and the entire people. The resistance was facing new challenges.

Peasants constituted the bulk of the population, the main driving force behind the revolution, and were making a major contribution to the resistance. Ninety per cent of the fighters were peasants. Now that the resistance required even greater efforts from everyone, the peasantry in

particular, it was important to take more radical measures to improve their situation. Such measures had also become possible, as the political and ideological consciousness of the peasants had been raised by several years of resistance.

From 1946 onward, many measures had been implemented in favour of the peasants, including reduction of land rent, a fair share of communal land, temporary allotment to poor peasants of land left idle or belonging to colonialists, traitors and landowners who had taken refuge in enemy-held areas, reductions in loan interest rates, and the cancellation of some debts. Hundreds of thousands of hectares had thus been allotted to landless peasants. It remained true to say, however, that land-owners continued to possess a good part of the land, allowing them to exploit the peasants, and that village administration remained partly in their hands, thus hindering the implementation of agrarian measures decided upon by the State.

The more democratic measures were applied, the stronger the reaction of the feudalists became, and the more the US stepped up its intervention. As the war spread, reactionary landlords engaged in more anti-State activities, such as founding reactionary parties in the free zones or engaging in spying activities for the enemy. The class struggle became more acute, and the elimination of the feudal class became a necessity in the national struggle.

Until now, with the passing by the State of new agrarian measures, cadres had had to content themselves with explanation and persuasion among land-owners. But experience had shown that many landlords balked at such measures and even opposed them more or less overtly. Only the mobilization of the peasant masses would make it possible to overcome this opposition, and to do eliminate a feudal regime which hindered social progress and national liberation. On 1 December 1953, the National Assembly adopted a Land Reform Law.

"Study sessions" and mass rallies were held in the army and among the population, with peasants telling of their poverty and humiliation, the extortion and the crimes committed against them by landlords and village dignitaries, and iniquities of the former regime. At the end of 1953 in Thái Nguyên and Thanh Hóa provinces, in the heart of the free zone, the first experiments in land reform were conducted. Reductions in land rent and sharing out of land were followed up by poor peasants taking over village administration. For the first time in Việt Nam's history, a thorough land reform program was launched, leading to the abolition of an age-old system and opening up the way for further development of productive forces and liberation of the peasantry.

The mobilization of the masses to achieve land reform sparked great enthusiasm among peasants and soldiers, and gave a boost to the resistance. Hundreds of thousands more peasants joined the army to supply units operating far from their bases, and to build roads through dense forests under fierce bombing by the enemy air force.

"Never before have we seen such a stream of Vietnamese going up to the front. Never before have our young people travelled such long distances, crossing such strange parts in their own country. From the plains to mountainous areas, on large and small roads, along rivers and streams, everywhere the people are coming together, from the rear base men and equipment are pouring towards the front, joining with the army to crush the enemy and liberate the country. The rear base has communicated to frontline soldier its determination to win, its total confidence in the resistance and the enthusiasm sparked by land reform."[1]

Điện Biên Phủ

It was in this revolutionary atmosphere that the Vietnamese command decided its plans for the winter-spring campaign of 1953-54. As had been foreseen, the fierce assaults launched by the enemy into the liberated areas at Lạng Sơn and Ninh Bình brought poor results, and the French forces soon withdrew after sustaining heavy losses.

In November 1953 Vietnamese forces attacked in the northwest, liberating the provincial capital of Lai Châu. The French command was compelled to send relief forces to this region, and on November 20, Navarre ordered the parachuting of six battalions into Điện Biên Phủ, an isolated base deep in the forests of the northwest.

On November 21, in coordination with Pathet Lao troops, the Vietnamese attacked in central Laos where they liberated Kham Muon province and the town of Thakkhet. Navarre rushed several battalions to Laos to reinforce the Seno base. In January 1954, joint Laotian-Vietnamese forces liberated the town of Attopeu and the Boloven Plateau.

For its part, the French command, thinking that the Vietnamese offensive had begun to lose momentum, launched Operation "Atlante," involving 20 infantry battalions, four artillery batteries, and three mobile

1. General Võ Nguyên Giáp, *Điện Biên Phủ, 1960.*

battalions starting from the 5th Military Interzone in Trung Bộ, which included several liberated provinces. By order of the Party Central Committee, only a small number of regular forces remained on the spot to resist the enemy's advance. The bulk of the forces launched an offensive in the Central Highlands, liberating Kontum province. Navarre had to rush in 13 battalions to the rescue of Plây Cu.

While these operations were taking place, both sides were seeking an opportunity to destroy important enemy live forces in the best conditions. Navarre thought he could draw the Vietnamese forces into a trap at Điện Biên Phủ. The Vietnamese command had also resolved to deliver a decisive blow there. The battle was anticipated to take place in January. But Vietnamese forces were advancing in the direction of upper Laos, threatening Luang Prabang. Navarre again had to rush in forces to defend the city and this area of Laos.

By the end of January 1954, therefore, Navarre, who had wanted to concentrate his crack units in the northern theatre, was forced to disperse them to all corners of Indochina. Throughout the winter of 1953 and spring of 1954, guerrilla activities were also being stepped up, particularly in the Mekong and Red River deltas. Highway 5, linking Hà Nội with Hải Phòng and the main lifeline of the French Expeditionary Corpts, was under constant attack. On March 4 and 7, 1954, commandos slipped into the Cát Bi and Gia Lâm airfields and destroyed dozens of aircrafts, dealing the Điện Biên Phủ airlift a stunning blow.

The French, however, remained optimistic. *Carevelle*, the Expeditionary Corps news bulletin, said the following:

"*The Việt Minh command has to move its units and supply them over enormous distances through rugged terrain poorly served by transport routes. A campaign conducted in these conditions can only turn in our favour.*"

Between the plains, where the supply bases of Vietnamese forces were located, and Điện Biên Phủ lay 500 kilometres of exposed track, across mountains and through forests, bombed without respite by the French air force. Food and ammunition were carried on backs, bicycles and boats, and sometimes by truck. In addition, Điện Biên Phủ is a valley surrounded by mountain peaks over 1,000 metres high; artillery pieces had to be hauled up. The Vietnamese also had to move down these peaks to attack fortified positions under heavy fire from enemy artillery and tanks. Supplies and tactical issues remained difficult problems for the Vietnamese command. In February, the French camp received a visit from US General O'Daniel who declared himself

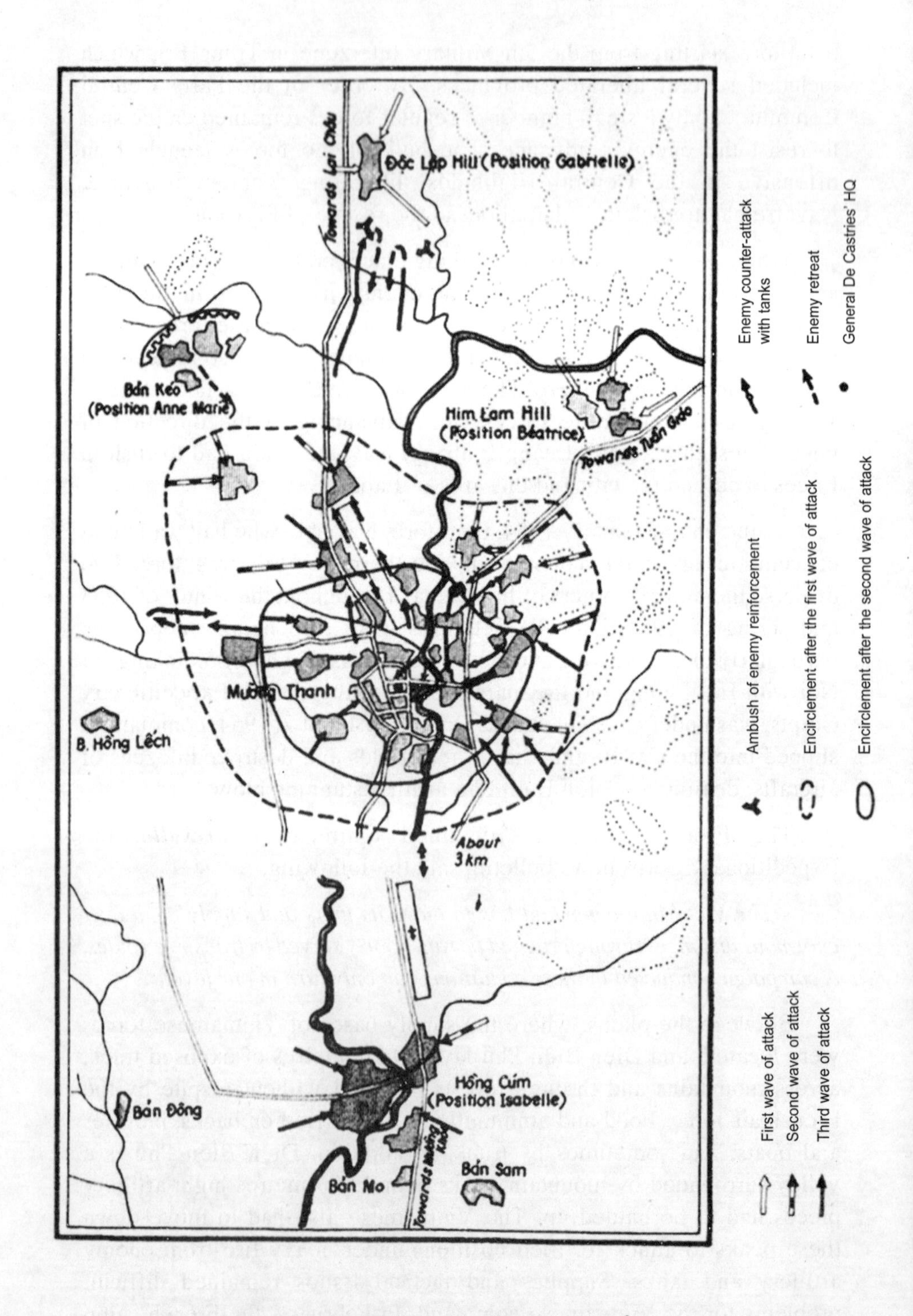
Độc Lập Hill (Position Gabrielle)
Towards Lai Châu
Bản Kéo
(Position Anne Marie)
Him Lam Hill
(Position Béatrice)
Towards Tuần Giáo
Mường Thanh
B. Hồng Lếch
About
3km
Hồng Cúm
(Position Isabelle)
Bản Đông
Bản Sam
Bản Mo
Towards Mường Khoa
Enemy counter-attack with tanks
Enemy retreat
General De Castries' HQ
Ambush of enemy reinforcement
Encirclement after the first wave of attack
Encirclement after the second wave of attack
First wave of attack
Second wave of attack
Third wave of attack

EVOLUTION OF THE ĐIỆN BIÊN PHỦ BATTLE

"enthusiastic" about the prospects for the battle. On March 12, the French command, still optimistic, ordered new units to be landed on the central Việt Nam front at Quy Nhơn as part of Operation Atlante.

On the Vietnamese side, the heroism and tenacity of hundreds of thousands of men and women enabled them to overcome all the difficulties involved in the supply and installation of artillery pieces. On March 13, the Vietnamese command ordered an attack on one of the outer positions at Điện Biên Phủ, Him Lam or "Beatrice." The French were caught unprepared, as they had never believed it was possible to haul big artillery pieces up rugged peaks and camouflage them perfectly, or that Vietnamese gunners could be trained in such a short period of time. Within a few hours, the position was taken. On March 14, the second outer position, Độc Lập (Gabriele) fell. On March 17 the third outer position, the Bản Kéo (Anne-Marie) garrison, surrendered. All the outer defence posts north and northwest of the camp had been captured.

Only the central sector of Mường Thanh and the southern sector of Hồng Cúm remained intact. How would the Vietnamese forces get at them, across a plain swept by fire from enemy artillery and tanks? The Vietnamese forces set about digging a complex network of trenches starting from the surrounding hills and furrowing across the plain, so as to bring the line of attack and encirclement closer to enemy positions. More than 100 kilometres of trenches were dug in this way under enemy fire. The noose was mercilessly tightened around the base supplied by airlift, while on other fronts in the Red River delta and the Central Highlands, the situation rapidly deteriorated for the French.

The French general staff sent General Ely to Washington to seek American aid. With President Eisenhower's consent, a plan code-named "Vulture" was established, which allowed for intervention by the US air force in a bid to save Điện Biên Phủ.

On March 30, with preparations complete, the Vietnamese launched a second offensive aimed at taking the heights defending the eastern part of the central sector. These being the key defensive positions, the battle was fierce. The C1 (Eliane 1) and A1 (Eliane 2) heights changed hands several times. Towards mid-April, the Vietnamese line had reached the central airfield where supplies for the camp were dropped. The enemy launched fierce but unsuccessful counter-attacks in an attempt to retake it. A good part of the food and ammunition parachuted in by the French fell inside the Vietnamese lines. The French air force stepped up the bombing of the Vietnamese lines and roads, but Vietnamese troops clung to their positions and the supply convoys all arrived safely.

On April 15, an American general arrived in Hà Nội to discuss arrangements for Operation Vulture. It was recognized, however, that even the intervention of US bombers would not significantly change the situation at Điện Biên Phủ. Moreover, public opinion in France and other countries prevented the French and British governments from blindly following Washington's war plans. Operation Vulture was called off.

On May 1, the third phase of the offensive began. The A1 and C1 heights as well as other positions, were overrun. On the afternoon of May 7, a final attack enabled the Vietnamese forces to seize the enemy's command post and capture the entire garrison, including General De Castries. They raised a white flag and surrendered. That night, the garrison in the southern sector was captured. Not a single enemy soldier was able to escape.

The French lost their best units at Điện Biên Phủ: 16,200 men altogether including one general, 16 colonels, and 1,749 other officers and NCOs. Throughout the 1953-1954 winter-spring campaign, fighting had been fierce on all fronts, particularly in the Central Highlands, where Vietnamese forces had completely destroyed mobile group 100, which has recently returned from Korea. Guerrilla fighting in the Mekong and Red River deltas, and in Bình Trị Thiên, had reached the scale of regular operations. The losses sustained by the French Expeditionary Corps and the puppet army during this campaign were enormous, totalling 112, 000 men and 117 aircrafts. The defeats at Điện Biên Phủ and in the winter-spring campaign compelled the French government to sue for peace.

The Geneva Conference

The increasing scale of the fighting and French setbacks had by end of 1953 caused deep divisions within French public opinion. Opposition to the war reached traditionally right-wing circles. The strong, pro-American "fight-to-the-bitter-end" element represented by the Laniel-Bidault cabinet became more and more islated. International opinion, deeply concerned, demanded peace.

On 26 November 1953, in an interview granted to the Swedish newspaper *Expressen*, President Hồ Chí Minh declared:

"*If, having drawn the inevitable lessons from these years of war, the French government desires to conclude an armistice and resolve the Việt Nam issue through negotiations, then the people and government of the*

Democratic Republic of Việt Nam are ready to examine the French proposals...The fundamental basis for such an armistice is that the French government must truly respect Việt Nam's independence."

The Laniel-Bidault government, in the face of French and world opinion, could no longer avoid its responsibilities. In February 1954, the French and US governments agreed at a Berlin conference that the Indochina question should be examined at a conference in Geneva in April.

The Geneva Conference on Korea and Indochina opened on April 26. The Americans and the Laniel-Bidault cabinet tried by every means possible to sabotage it, going so far as to deny the Vietnamese resistance any representative status. The US planned to replace the pro-French agents in Việt Nam with pro -American elements who would continue the war, but the resounding victories by Vietnamese forces forestalled all these maneuvers. On May 8, 24 hours after the fall of Điện Biên Phủ, the Geneva Conference on Indochina opened. On behalf of the people and government of the Democratic Republic of Việt Nam, Phạm Văn Đồng spelled out Việt Nam's position.

The Laniel-Bidault cabinet, which was clinging to its policy of war, was toppled by the French parliament on June 8. Mendès France, the new prime minister, had to agree to sue for peace. The Americans tried unsuccessfully to torpedo the conference. On the night of July 20, the agreements putting an end to the Indochina war were signed. Eight states participated in the conference: the Democratic Republic of Việt Nam, France, the Soviet Union, Britain, the People's Republic of China, the United States, Cambodia and Laos, plus the Bảo Đại government.

The principal negotiators were France, Việt Nam and China. The US was there primarily to try to sabotage the conference. As the coasts and ports were blockaded by imperialist forces, Việt Nam was receiving foreign aid exclusively through China, hence the key role it played at the negotiation table.

From May 8 to June 23, 1954, the French delegates in Geneva refused to meet the Vietnamese, but held long negotiations with the Chinese, and the two parties agreed on the main elements of a compromise acceptable to both. The southern part of Indochina, comprising southern Việt Nam and Cambodia, would remain under French influence, while the northern half of Việt Nam and two Laotian provinces (Sam Neua and Phongsaly) would be controlled by the Vietnamese and Lao patriotic forces. China's southern borders would thus be protected by buffer zones controlled by forces that Beijing believed it could easily handle.

The Vietnamese delegation had to fight to see enshrined the principle of respect for the independence, sovereignty, unity and territorial integrity of the countries of Indochina. It was unable to advert partition of the country or secure an autonomous regroupment zone for the Cambodian patriotic forces. Zhou En-Lai had abandoned the Cambodian resistance, presumably because this country had no common border with China.

The signed agreements included military and political provisions. Militarily, it was decided to regroup the forces from each side in two different zones, north and south of the 17th parallel, so as to separate the armies which, given the special nature of the war, had been interlocked like "two combs." A 300-day deadline was agreed on for achieving this regroupment.

Politically, the agreements recognized the independence, sovereignty, unity and territorial integrity of the three Indochinese countries. In no way was the demarcation line along the 17th parallel to be considered as a political frontier. In July 1956 at the latest, free general elections with secret ballots would give Việt Nam a unified government.

Pending reunification, Việt Nam's two zones would refrain from joining any military alliance. No foreign military bases could be set up and no new foreign military equipment or personnel brought into either.

Despite all the limitations imposed on Việt Nam's liberation, the Geneva Agreements did not constitute a great victory for the Vietnamese people. They had freed the northern half of their country, which was to become a powerful rear base from which to continue the struggle for national liberation.

Thus, after nine years of war, French imperialism was compelled to admit the futility of its attempts to reconquer Việt Nam. From these nine years of war, General Võ Nguyên Giáp, commander-in-chief of the People's Army, drew the following conclusions:

"*Our people and army have defeated a powerful and well-equipped enemy because our compatriots and our troops were motivated by a firm determination to fight for and win national independence, for the distribution of land to peasants, for peace, and for socialism. The enemy confronted a united front from all social classes and all political and religious affiliations. Our Marxist-Leninist party headed by President Hồ Chí Minh implemented with mastery the right political and military policies.*

We are, moreover, living in an era in which the imperialists can no longer dominate completely. A whole system of socialist countries with

great political and material strength, and a national liberation movement swelling like a tidal wave are creating extremely favorable conditions for the struggle of oppressed nations. A people's war waged by a people's army may be rightly considered as one of the most decisive achievements, more important than any weapon for the countries of Asia, Africa and Latin America. By liberating themselves, the Vietnamese people are proud to have contributed to the liberation of fraternal peoples.

I believe that in the present era, no imperialist army, however powerful it may be, and no imperialist general, however talented he may be, can defeat a people, even weak and small, who know how to rise up resolutely and unite in the struggle along the right political and military path. Our experience had shown that no illusions should be harboured as to the goodwill of the imperialists. Colonialism in its new form is more dangerous than ever and the people should be prepared to fight it. People should not be overawed by the power of modern weapons. It is the value of human beings which, in the end, will decide victory."

Chapter IX

BUILDING THE INITIAL FOUNDATION OF SOCIALISM AND THE STRUGGLE AGAINST U.S. NEO-COLONIALISM

(1954 - 1973)

The Geneva Agreements on Việt Nam recognized the fundamental national rights of the Vietnamese people: independence, sovereignty, unity and territorial integrity. But the balance of forces between the Vietnamese national resistance on one hand, and the imperialist forces, particularly the Franco-US coalition, on the other, only enabled the Vietnamese people to completely liberate the northern part of their country. Beijing's ambiguous policies also weakened Việt Nam's position.

The agreements stipulated that the southern half of Việt Nam would be handed over to a provisional administration after two years at the most, and that general elections in 1956 at the latest, would give a united Việt Nam a single government.

However, soon after the agreements were signed, Washington, with French government consent, set up a neo-colonialist regime in southern Việt Nam with specific counter-revolutionary aims: liquidating the national revolutionary movement in southern Việt Nam, turning the latter into a military base and colony of the US, and setting up a military and police apparatus to serve as an instrument for the enslavement of the south and reconquest of the north.

For the Vietnamese people, the complete liberation of the northern half of the country made it possible to create a solid basis for the national revolutionary movement as a whole. Partial liberation brought about a unique situation, imposing on the Vietnamese people different tasks in

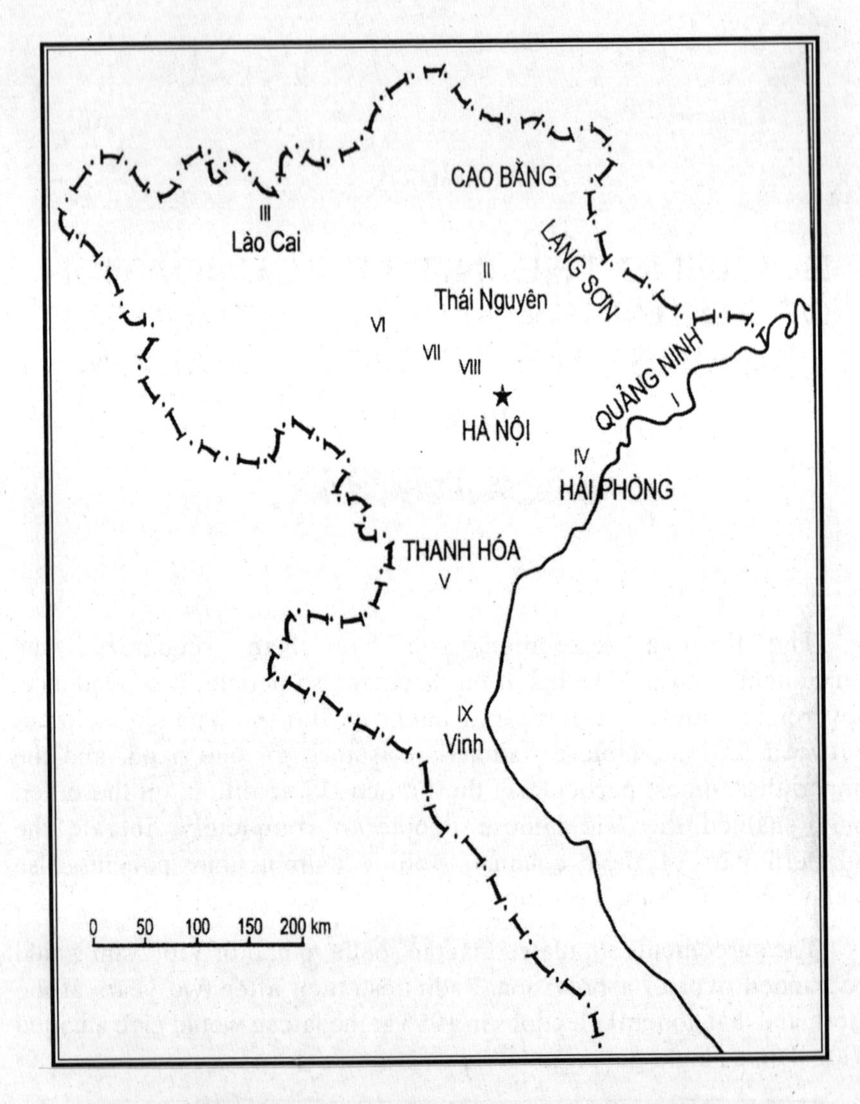
CAO BẰNG
III
Lào Cai
LẠNG SƠN
II
Thái Nguyên
VI
VII
VIII
QUẢNG NINH
I
HÀ NỘI
IV
HẢI PHÒNG
THANH HÓA
V
IX
Vinh
0 50 100 150 200 km

The first industrial establishments in north Việt Nam

I. Quảng Ninh Coal Mine
II. Thái Nguyên Steel Complex
III. Apatite Mine in Lào Cai
IV. Hải Phòng cement factory, shipyard, port
V. Chromium deposits in Cổ Định (Thanh Hóa)
VI. Thác Bà Hydroelectric Project
VII. Lâm Thao Superphosphate Factory
VIII. Thái Nguyên Steelworks
IX. Vinh - Bến Thủy mechanical and wood-processing industries

the north and south. The Vietnamese revolution, one single historical process, found itself confronted with a number of challenges in 1954.

- Achieving the national and democratic revolution in the south;

- Defending the north against any aggression and attempts at destruction and sabotage by the imperialists; and

- Building the foundations of socialism in the northern half of the country which had to rapidly develop its economy and culture to become a powerful rear base for the south which was now in the forefront of the struggle against US neo-colonialism.

For more than twenty years, from 1954 to 1975, the Vietnamese people in both north and south waged a difficult struggle against US neo-colonialism. A thorough renewal of the socio-economic structure and the establishment of the primary political, social and economic foundations of socialism in the northern half of Vietnam was carried out despite US aggression. As the situation developed, the struggle between the Vietnamese people as a whole and the US imperialists became the crucial confrontation of our era. The US imperialists had wanted to make an example of Vietnam, a test of their global strategy, hence their total war using all the means at their disposal. For the Vietnamese people, the challenge was one of the hardest ever faced, but they were aware of fighting not only to defend their independence and freedom, but also for world peace, the liberation of other nations and defence of the socialist camp.

There were three definable stages during the period 1954-1975:

- 1954-1965, the establishment of the initial foundations of socialism in the north, and the southern Vietnamese people's struggle against repression and the neo-colonialist war;

- 1965-1973, the all-out struggle by both north and south against direct US aggression, which ended with the signing of the Paris Agreements of January 1973; and

- 1973-1975, the collapse of the neo-colonialist regime in the south.

Initial Foundations of Socialism (1954-1965)

With the northern half of Việt Nam completely liberated, the immediate question was which road to take; that of capitalism or of socialism. The programme of the Workers' Party (now the Communist Party) of Việt Nam specified that the country, once the national and democratic revolution was achieved, would directly switch to socialism, by passing the stage of capitalist development.

The main obstacle to the establishment of socialism was the backward state of the economy, which was the legacy of centuries of feudalism and colonialism, and had been ruined by long years of war. In 1954, modern industry accounted for only 1.5 percent of total production, and not a single motor could be found in any village of North Việt Nam. The area of land suitable for cultivation was extremely small: one-tenth of a hectare per inhabitant, and the frequency of natural disasters (floods, typhoon and droughts) posed a continuous threat to agriculture. The partition of the country severely disrupted the economy. One year after the liberation of North Việt Nam, annual generation of electricity, for example, totalled less than 53 million kwh, and the proportion of modern industry still in full production was around 3.4 percent.

The Workers' Party, however, asserted that favorable conditions existed for establishing socialism — a strong worker-peasant alliance, the proven leadership of a Marxist-Leninist party trusted by the entire people, and substantial aid from other socialist countries.

Given these conditions, the priority was healing the wounds of war while completing the land reform begun in 1953, turning later to structural change leading to socialism. By 1957, land reform had been completed - despite occasional serious ultra-leftist mistakes committed in the process which were publicly recognized by the Party leadership and rapidly rectified — and total production had reached pre-war levels. In 1958, a period of socialist transformation began, which by 1960 had resulted in:

- The formation of an important State economic sector — industry, domestic and foreign trade, and agricultural and forestry programs — playing a leading role in the national economy;

- The conversion of private capitalist industrial and commercial undertakings into State or joint State-private enterprises, a relatively easy operation given the weakness of Vietnamese capitalism;

- The creation of handicraft cooperatives employing the majority of handicraft workers; and

- The most fundamental component, the establishment of agricultural cooperatives which by the end of 1960 covered about 86 percent of peasant households.

By the end of 1960, North Việt Nam had, for the most part, equipped itself with — at least in an embryonic form — socialist socio-economic structures. With the completion of land reform and the efforts made by a people happy to have recovered their independence, agricultural production made satisfactory progress. With aid from other socialist

countries, new enterprises were set up, the railways destroyed during the war were partially restored, and agricultural hydraulic works were built.

In 1960, economic indices were as follows:

- Population: almost 16 million.

- Arable land: 1,877,100 hectares.

(See table on page 270)

Despite these great changes in the relations of production, North Việt Nam's economy remained underdeveloped due to technical and scientific underdevelopment. Agriculture was still predominant, for the most part based on manual and handicraft labour. The economy was fraught with serious deficiencies:

- Agricultural production — the principal sector of the nation's economy — remained unstable and subject to climatic conditions. The agricultural infrastructure was very basic, as was the level of organization and management of cooperatives and State farms; agriculture was thus unable to constitute a stable foundation for industrial development.

- Heavy industry, still embryonic, was not yet able to supply other economic sectors, particularly agriculture.

- The transportation infrastructure remained rudimentary.

- Skilled workers and management, scientific and technical workers were still few in number and lacked sufficient qualifications.

- Productivity and living standards remained very low.

The 3rd Party Congress held in September 1960 set down general guidelines for economic development and the first five-year (1961-1965) plan for construction of the initial socialist infrastructure. The problem was how to firmly establish a socialist system, and in particular, how to transform a backward economy based on small individual production. To this end, a triple revolution was needed - a revolution in the relations of production, a cultural and ideological revolution, and a scientific and technical revolution, with the latter as the lynchpin. It was vital to mobilize to the maximum all the nation's energies under the Party's leadership, while eliciting any aid available from fraternal socialist countries (the Soviet Union, People's Republic of China and others).

Priority was to be given to the development of heavy industry; this was to be achieved in an appropriate manner as it was also necessary to make greater efforts to develop agriculture as the basis for industrial development. It was also necessary to concentrate efforts on investment,

	1939	1955	1957	1960
Area under cultivation (thousand ha)[1]	2,139.0	2,654.0	2,666.0	2,870.0
Irrigated area (thousand ha)	345.7	922.0	1,427.0	2,202.4
Food production (paddy and subsidiary crops – thousand tonnes) reckoned in terms of paddy equivalent	2,789.0	4,114.0	4,585.0	4,698.0
Electricity (million kwh)	123.0	53.0	121.2	256.1
Coal (million tonnes)	2,789.0	641.0	1,048.8	2,600.0
Cement (thousand tonnes)	283.0	8.5	165.1	408.0
Textiles (million metres)	55.0	8.8	63.1	76.0
Machine tools (units)	0	0	0	799.0
Contribution of industry (handicrafts included) to total value of industrial and agricultural output (%)	–	19.0	33.0	43.8
Contribution of modern industry to total value of industrial and agricultural output (%)	–	3.4	11.2	17.8
Contribution of modern industry to total value of industrial and handicraft output (%)	–	20.2	33.5	40.7

1. Land yielding two crops per year is counted twice.

while seeking to improve the living standards of the people who had endured great suffering during the war. It was also vital not to neglect the nation's defence, since the North was also threatened by the aggressive designs of the US.

Major campaigns were launched to achieve these socialist objectives and improve the organization and management of enterprises, especially the newly formed agricultural cooperatives. While centrally-run industry quickly developed, regional industries, which used handicraft and semi-mechanized techniques, were not neglected, the purpose of both essentially being to serve agricultural development.

Large-scale industrial enterprises came into being: the Thái Nguyên steelworks, the Lâm Thao superphosphate factory, and new power stations. The figures for 1964 were as follows:

- Area under cultivation	2,368,000 hectares
- Electricity	595.2 million kwh
- Cement	600,500 tonnes
- Fabrics	107.2 million metres
- Total food output	5,515,000 tonnes
- Coal	3.6 million tonnes
- Machine tools	769 units
- Contribution of modern industry to the value of industrial and handicraft output	36.7 percent
- Contribution of modern industry to total production	18.4 percent

North Việt Nam's economy began to "take off," gradually taking on the features of a national and independent economy. The general level of development was still of course very low, technically as well as managerially. But the groundwork had been established for future progress.

US aggression compelled the Democratic Republic of Việt Nam to give a new direction to its national economy.

Repression and Neo-Colonialist War (1954-1965)

Washington's interference in Việt Nam's affairs did not date back just to 1954. As early as June 1950, US military mission was already advising the French Expenditionary Corps command.

The US hold over the puppet government and army was gradually tightened despite French opposition. In September 1951, an "economic cooperation" agreement was signed directly between Bảo Đại and the administration in Washington which, putting pressure on the French, gradually installed American agents in the Bảo Đại administration. In 1953, in exchange for the large-scale aid granted to France for the implementation of the Navarre plan, the Americans obtained permission to take part directly in the training of puppet troops. Early in 1954, General O'Daniel came to Việt Nam to lead this mission.

When a French defeat appeared imminent in April 1954 at Điện Biên Phủ, the "hawks", headed by Vice-President Nixon, began to press for US troops to intervene directly in Indochina. Washington proposed massive bombing of the Điện Biên Phủ front by planes taking off from the Philippines and escorted by fighters from the 7th Fleet. The victories of the Vietnamese resistance and their effect on French and international public opinion dissuaded the British government from joining the venture, and Operation Vulture was called off. Some US generals, including Ridgway, former commander-in-chief of US forces in Korea, expressed opposition to the plan, experience having taught them that committing American troops to fight in Asia was to court defeat, or at least risk becoming bogged down in a bottomless quagmire.

Washington tried to prevent the holding of the Geneva Conference on Indochina, then after having failed, concentrated its efforts on undermining it and supporting the preposterous demands of Bảo Đại's agents for the unconditional surrender of the Vietnamese resistance, and on grouping imperialist and local reactionary forces in Southeast Asia into a coalition which would allow them to continue the war. The first scheme failed, and the Geneva Conference closed on 20 July 1954 with the drawing up of agreements putting an end to the war. The Southeast Asia military coalition project had to be put off for a few weeks after the signing of the agreements.

Meanwhile, Washington had managed to persuade the French to accept Ngô Đình Diệm as Bảo Đại's minister (June 1954).

From Repression to War

Washington was not prepared to accept the peace agreements and wasted no time in implementing a new strategy. Its objective was clear, i.e. turning South Việt Nam into a new type of US colony, a political and strategic base from which to dominate Southeast Asia.

In September 1954, a Southeast Asian military alliance (US, Britain, France, Australia, Pakistan, Thailand and the Philippines) was set up under a treaty which included a protocol enabling it to intervene in Indochina. US economic missions and "advisers" arrived to oversee the Sài Gòn administration. These missions and advisers controlled all branches of activity and every project from the drafting of a constitution and the training of the army and police to the carrying out of "agrarian reform" and the school syllabus. In exchange for a number of economic and cultural concessions granted to France, the Americans eliminated all direct French influence. Pro-French religious organizations were brought to heel, some by means of corruption, others by force of arms. For Paris, anti-communism was advantageous primarily in defending French interests.

On 28 April 1956, French troops finally left Việt Nam, but Paris side-stepped its responsibilities with regard to implementing the Geneva Agreements, which provided for general elections to achieve the peaceful reunification of Việt Nam.

US policy in Việt Nam rested on opposing reunification by all available means. Openly violating the Geneva Agreements, Washington poured arms and military personnel into South Việt Nam to set up a huge puppet army, logistics and air and naval bases, and a complex network of strategic communications.

Also in violation of the agreements, the US advised Ngô Đình Diệm to set up a separate south Vietnamese state with a National Assembly and Constitution of its own. A fake referendum was held, enabling them to oust Bảo Đại and put Ngô Đình Diệm in power.

Thus by 1954 the main planks of US neo-colonialist policy had become clear: to do away with the French presence, and take over South Việt Nam; to set up a puppet dictatorship entirely dependent on Washington; to liquidate the national and revolutionary movement in South Việt Nam and eventually to try to reconquer North Việt Nam.

The liquidation of the national and revolutionary movement was the *sine qua non* of US domination of Việt Nam. With the help of the US advisers, the Diệm regime, immediately after it assumed power, applied a policy of systematic terror against the entire southern population. The experience of colonialism and neo-colonialism in the area of repression, fascist methods inspired by those of the Nazis, and the medieval methods used by Vietnamese feudalists - represented by Ngô Đình Diệm himself - were all applied to terrorize the people and eliminate opposition.

A repressive machine controlled the whole country from the capital down to the most remote villages. Massacres, torture, deportations, mass imprisonment and raids... never had the South Vietnamese people experienced such a dark period. In fact, the few years of "peace" between 1955 and 1959 saw more victims in South Việt Nam than the preceding years of war.

During the first years after the signing of the peace agreements, the people avoided violating them by limiting their resistance to political activity such as demonstrations, petitions and meetings. The peasants in particular fiercely defended themselves to avoid being robbed of their land by landlords and village notables. From 1945 to 1954, peasants in many regions had been allotted land by the revolutionary power and had lived under a democratic system. The feudalists had sought refuge in the cities where they lived under the protection of the French Expeditionary Corps. Under the Diệm regime, they returned to the villages to take back their land and re-establish administrative and political control.

The US and Diệm set up an apparatus of repression with strong armed forces and an omnipresent police. Apart from regular troops, the army consisted of security units at provincial and civil guards at village level. Several different secret police services roamed the cities. Any person who had played even a minor part in the resistance against the French was accused of being a "communist" or of "collusion with the communists". The parents of cadres and combatants regrouped to the North were mercilessly hunted down. The charge of "communism" could lead to prison, deportation for an indefinite period, and often to death by torture. The notorious "tiger cages" date back to the beginning of the Diệm regime.

After refusing to hold the general elections provided for by the Geneva Agreements, the Sài Gòn administration intensified its repression, and as opposition grew, the repressive measures became more brutal. Raids conducted by forces of between 10,000 and 15,000 men swept through vast regions; steps were taken to concentrate the population, or resettle whole groups in "agrovilles" in rural areas, and agricultural settlements in mountainous regions.

Except for those surrounding the family of Ngô Đình Diệm, and adventurers prepared to do anything for a few dollars, all social classes and strata were subject to repression including peasants, workers, intellectuals, the patriotic bourgeoisie and those who simply wanted to establish normal relations with the North, ethnic minorities, and non-Catholic religious organizations. Even ministers had to go into exile to escape the police. With US blessing, Diệm, his brother, and his sister-in-law (the notorious

Mme Ngô Đình Nhu) used his power of life and death over the people. For a time Washington thought that US domination in South Vietnam had been achieved, and called Diệm "the Churchill of Asia."

The US and Diệm had of course seriously underestimated the capabilities of the Vietnamese people. From 1860, the people of South Việt Nam had continuously waged a tough political and military struggle against French colonialism. Between 1945 and 1954, this national and democratic struggle had reached its peak, involving all strata of society. From March 1950, while the war against the French colonialists was still raging, hundreds of thousands of people were demonstrating against US intervention. This intervention now needed to be camouflaged, given that it had quite blatant. The anti-national policy of the Diệm family, which wanted to perpetuate the partition of the country, and their bloody repression of the bulk of the population, began to arouse more and more violent opposition.

In May 1959, this repression was given a legal fig leaf. The Sài Gòn National Assembly passed Bill 10/59 which permitted special military tribunals to carry out summary execution without trial of those arrested by the police or during raids. The threat of elimination weighed on the patriotic movement and the people in South Việt Nam as a whole. From political struggle, they gradually moved into self-defence and armed struggle. The first clashes with the Diệm army and police took place in remote villages and mountainous regions. In January 1960, in the Mekong River delta province of Bến Tre, popular forces toppled the Diệm administration in many localities and set up an autonomous people's power. A "chain insurrection" movement swept many provinces and the Diệm regime in rural areas was soon in a state of crisis.

This crisis soon reached the cities and even parts of the Sài Gòn army. On 11 November 1960, officers and a number of units launched a coup attempt. The coup failed, but the regime had been seriously undermined.

Challenging the neo-colonialist regime set up by the US was a vast national and popular movement, bringing together all social classes, ethnic minorities, religious bodies, and political groups within a population which had a long experience of armed political struggle. On 20 December 1960, a number of organizations and opposition and resistance groups joined together to form a National Liberation Front (NLF) with the aim of overthrowing the Diệm administration, ending all foreign intervention, establishing a national coalition government and democratic system, implementing a foreign policy based on peace and neutrality, and proceeding to the peaceful reunification of Việt Nam. Early in 1961, a People's Liberation Army came into being.

The "Special War"

The Kennedy administration, newly in power in Washington, was faced with a dilemma - whether to drop the Diệm regime and the attempt to control South Việt Nam, or wage war against the Vietnamese people. Kennedy chose the second option. With him in power, US global strategy began to be decisively directed towards the Third World which it considered as a hotbed of revolution to be crushed with urgency. The Kennedy-Taylor-McNamara team set up a whole political and military apparatus and even worked out a "doctrine" to conquer the Third World, and to crush or divert the national liberation movements of Asia, Africa and Latin America from their objectives. Washington paid particular attention to "counter-insurgency" techniques and weapons to fight guerrilla and other forms of armed struggle.

The "special war" strategy was born. Classic colonial adventures with direct intervention by US troops were becoming increasingly difficult, and Washington was trying to wage war by proxy. US technical and financial muscle enabled it to maintain a large puppet administration and army, and to equip mercenaries with up-to-date weapons. They thought it was sufficient to direct this army using US "advisers" specially trained for this type of war, in which a complex political and military strategy backed up by ultra-modern weapons technology would enable them to defeat the revolutionary movements of the Third World.

Washington chose to make South Việt Nam a testing -ground for this new "special war" strategy. With preparations complete by early 1962, the US operational command set up its Sài Gòn head -quarters in February with a group of "advisers" — which rapidly swelled to 25,000 by 1964 —to command the Sài Gòn army.

All categories of puppet troops - regular, regional and local - were strengthened, reaching half a million men by 1964. An air force with 500 planes, an armoured corps comprising several hundred land and amphibious vehicles, numerous river units, ultra-fast sub-machine guns, powerful artillery, and numerous electronic devices, gave this army great mobility, considerable firepower, and sophisticated means of information-gathering and detection. For the first time in human history, toxic chemicals were used to destroy crops and natural vegetation.

In terms of both manpower and armaments, Washington concentrated more force on winning this "special war" than France had in 1954 at the time of Điện Biên Phủ. From 1962, the US and puppet command began to conduct operations, averaging several a month and sometimes involving from 15,000 to 20,000 men each.

Washington was pursuing a dual goal, on the one hand destroying the liberation armed forces in lightning military operations, and on the other, forcing the entire rural population to regroup in some 16,000 "strategic hamlets", which were more like concentration camps where, behind the barbed wire, the Sài Gòn regime could impose direct and absolute control.

Helicopters in particular, were used to ensure absolute domination by Sài Gòn troops, enabling them to strike anywhere by surprise and swoop down on trapped guerrillas like "hawks on sparrows", as the promoters of this weapon put it. Mass bombing, endless artillery shelling, spraying with toxic chemicals and indiscriminate terror were employed in order to crush all attempts at resistance and compel the people to join the "strategic hamlets". This ruthless war and the means of mass destruction and slaughter employed resulted in numerous victims and initially, particularly in 1962, caused great problems for the resistance. Around 20, 000 operations were conducted. US aid to the Sài Gòn administration by then totaled 600 million dollars, four times as much as in 1960. Washington aimed to "pacify" South Việt Nam by the end of 1962 (the Staley-Taylor plan).

But the South Vietnamese people and their armed forces rapidly found ways to counter US weapons and strategy. Combining armed struggle with political struggle, building combat villages everywhere, fighting in rural areas as well as cities, on the plains as well as in mountainous regions, and using rudimentary weapons such as booby traps, as well as modern arms captured from the enemy, the people and liberation forces caught the enormous US - puppet military and administrative apparatus in an equally vast net, paralysing it and inflicting severe losses on it. The work of explanation and political persuasion among the puppet forces also succeeded in demoralizing them.

In January 1963 at Ấp Bắc, 80 kilometres from Sài Gòn, the two cornerstones of the "special war" - helicopters and amphibious vehicles - first showed their vulnerability. After Ấp Bắc, 1963 was marked by severe setbacks for the Sài Gòn army. The victories of the liberation forces greatly helped the people in their struggle. Many "strategic hamlets" were demolished or turned into combat villages. Many of these hamlets changed hands several times, the American and Sài Gòn regime desperately attempting to retake one that had been liberated. The entire population, men and women, old and young, in all regions and localities, joined this desperate struggle. By the end of 1963, 80 percent of "strategic hamlets" had been destroyed.

The repeated military setbacks and failure to control the population showed Washington that Diệm was no longer capable of controlling the situation. It was necessary therefore to replace Diệm's civilian dictatorship with a military junta that would directly carry out the orders of the US command. On 1 November 1963, Diệm and his younger brother Ngô Đình Nhu were assasinated, and the US mission installed a military junta headed by General Dương Văn Minh. In 1964, Robert McNamara visited Sài Gòn to work out new pacification plans, and Washington dispatched new equipment for the battle. But the Sài Gòn army and administration, badly shaken, were in a state of continual crisis. There was a succession of coup d'états in Sài Gòn while the US mission searched in vain for a government which would conduct the war effectively, whether a military junta, joint military-civilian government, or dictatorship by a general, old hands or young turks.

For their part, the people and the liberation armed forces, having rapidly mastered the art of armed and political struggle, swung on to the offensive. By early 1965, the failure of the "special war" had become obvious. The puppet army had disintegrated, losing all fighting capacity; the puppet regime was in crisis, the "strategic hamlets" policy had been bankrupt, and the liberation armed forces, far from being destroyed, had become battle-hardened and were able to challenge all US weapons and tactics.

The area liberated by the NLF covered almost four-fifths of the territory and two-thirds of the population, while public opinion in the United States had begun to turn while the international prestige of the US declined. By contrast, international support for the NLF was growing.

Once again, Washington faced a dilemma; either it renounced all further attempts to dominate South Việt Nam and sued for peace, or it continued to escalate the war to try to save at all costs the tottering puppet regime, holding on to Việt Nam and Indochina at all costs.

People's War vs. Escalation and Local War (1965-1973)

At the end of 1964, having foreseen the failure of the "special war", the US command took the first step towards escalation. On 5 August 1964, an aircraft from the 7th Fleet bombed several coastal areas in North Việt Nam. Washington's rationale was quite simple, even simplistic: threatening North Việt Nam through aerial bombings would be enough to bring Hà Nội to its knees, and consequently, to put down the Vietnamese resistance. But the bombers were met with a firm response, while the popular forces in South Việt Nam stepped up their struggle. President Johnson ordered a

further step in escalation. On 7 February 1965, US planes again bombed the DRV, and raids multiplied in the following weeks; on March 6, the first contingent of US marines landed at Đà Nẵng. On April 7, Johnson, while ordering that the bombing be stepped up, put forward peace proposals which amounted to a call for surrender by the Vietnamese forces. In the minds of American leaders, the increasing threat of elimination would eventually force the Vietnamese people to accept US conditions.

But the Vietnamese people did not give in. Washington expanded its military presence. American strategists had anticipated that if the "special war" failed, US forces would have to intervene, using all their firepower so as to create a decisive breach and impose Washington's will. Within a few months, while the bombing of North Việt Nam was intensified, crack American divisions, accompanied by forces from satellite countries (South Korea, Australia and New Zealand) landed en masse in the South. The 7th Fleet warships and aircrafts based in Thailand also took part in the operations. In November 1965, by the start of the dry season, American forces in South Việt Nam had reached 190,000 (more than the French forces in 1954). Together with the Sài Gòn army and forces from satellite countries, the 7th Fleet and US units in Thailand, the whole constituted a war machine 800,000 strong, equipped with several thousand aircrafts and helicopters (450 helicopters for the US Air Cavalry Division alone), and several thousand artillery pieces. Việt Nam as a whole, North and South, was engaged in a total war against the American imperialists.

People's War vs. the Air and Naval War of Destruction

The escalation of the US air and naval war against North Việt Nam had a twofold aim:

- To block all aid from the northern population to the people and combatants in the South; and

- To deal serious, if not fatal, bows at the socialist system in the North, and drive North Việt Nam "back to the Stone Age."

The North Vietnamese people, under the leadership of the Party and the government of the Democratic Republic of Việt Nam, did not limit itself to passive responses to US raids. The national economy and society and culture were reorganized on a new basis.

The question was whether to halt the establishment of socialism and concentrate all efforts on national defence. The general policy drawn up by the Party advocated a considerable strengthening of defence while continuing to promote the former. Despite outward appearances, the US escalation against North Việt Nam, as well as the landing of GIs in the South, were not offensive operations, but operations conceived and conducted by the American imperialists in a losing and passive strategic situation. The raids against the North could only be conducted in the form of "escalation", i.e. very gradually, by probing the terrain and testing the reactions of world opinion. By openly attacking a sovereign member of the socialist camp, Washington was locking itself into increasingly serious political isolation. North Việt Nam was able to ensure its defence while continuing with the establishment of socialism.

Mobilizing the entire population, it concentrated its defence efforts in several crucial areas:

- Setting up an anti-aircraft defence program involving the various branches of the armed forces - missiles, fighter planes, light and heavy artillery, and infantry - which attacked US planes at all altitudes and in every region. Wherever they operated, US aircrafts flew into a deadly net. The omnipresence of local militia, with significant participation from young women using infantry weapons or light artillery pieces, made low altitude flights and dive-bombing raids, which enabled the planes to reach precise targets, very difficult. US naval units were also countered by coastal defences organized along the same lines. All sappers and commandos who landed or were parachuted in were put out of action or promptly captured.

- Maintaining at all costs the transport links supplying the southern front and meeting the economic needs of the various regions. Besides technical units and services, the people helped repair damaged roads, bridges and railways, building new ones and transporting materials, goods and ammunition. All available means were mobilized to this end, from the most up-to-date to the most rudimentary.

- Increasing aid to the South until the final victory. The more bombs and shells the US dropped on the South, and the more GIs they landed, the more aid arrived from the North despite fierce attacks by the US airforce and navy.

The North-South road along the coast was in US hands. It was therefore necessary to build the "Hồ Chí Minh Trail" along the Trường Sơn Range, through dense forests and across high mountains. The Hồ Chí Minh Trail gradually became a complex network of roads, totaling thousands of kilometres in length and accompanied by a small pipeline. The construction of this network and the flow of aid to combatants in the

South, under repeated attack from the US air force, required considerable effort and sacrifice. It was truly an epic feat indeed.

The defence effort and aid to the South were only possible provided the economy held up to the repeated bombing raids. A new economic structure suited to wartime conditions was set up, with the following essential elements:

- Evacuation and dispersal of major factories from towns and industrial centers to villages and forests. The urban population, workers, technicians, and administrative bodies were dispersed among villages. The people followed their machinery and their offices, and lived with the local inhabitants or in temporary barracks. Schools, colleges, laboratories and hospitals were also evacuated and continue their activities in the countryside and forests. Operation *Sơ tán* (evacuation and dispersal) was a complete success. Although major projects were stopped, the country's economic and social activity was never disrupted even for a moment, nor was there the slightest sign of disorganization or panic.

- Development of the economy, especially of regional industries, at the provincial or district level. Each province, consisting of an economic unit of about 1.5 million inhabitants, sought to become self-sufficient in the most essential products and consumer goods by tapping its natural resources, and developing semi-mechanized and eventually mechanized workshops and handicraft industries. Advocated since the 3rd Party Congress in 1960, this policy of regional industrialization was fully implemented as a result of the war.

- Maintenance, thanks to the strict reorganization of domestic trade, of stable prices for basic commodities sold by State-run services such as rice, salt, fabrics and petroleum; these were regularly supplied to the population whose living conditions were not too disrupted by the war.

- Development of communications and transport.

International aid, especially from the Soviet Union, the People's Republic of China and other socialist countries, contributed enormously to the maintenance of economic stability. This aid, however, would have been much more effective if the Beijing government had not gradually changed its policy after 1965.

An important aspect of economic life during the war years was the strengthening of agricultural cooperatives. The important role played by rural workers in defence and communications did not prevent cooperatives from continuing to build hydraulic works, improve the soil and gradually introduce new farming techniques. Mechanization, particularly the installation of pumps and husking and threshing machines, proceeded rapidly. New varieties of rice with short-growth cycles and high yields were introduced, leading to new cropping patterns, more frequent harvests and a gradual shift away from the mono-cultivation of rice to different crops. This was the most important advance in agriculture in North Việt Nam during these critical years. Within just a few years, the rural landscape of North Việt Nam had changed.

The newly-established socialist system was weathering the trials of war, and its structures remained intact. The US air and naval bombardment intensified and gradually reached important industrial areas, hitting major cities such as Hà Nội and Hải Phòng. Yet none of the strategic targets were reached, while the Vietnamese people succeeded in fulfilling both their national and international obligations. Reconstruction work began immediately after the bombing campaign was called off in 1968, and in 1972, after the violent bombing raids during the second escalation, the balance sheet was as follows:

	1964	**1968**	**1971**	**1972**
Total food production	100	84.0	89.2	104.1
Electricity	100	63.2	127.6	92.5
Cement	100	11.6	58.8	25.8
Coal	100	66.7	94.4	47.2
Fabrics	100	78.0	102.2	68.4
Price of one kilo of rice (in *đồng*)	0.04	0.40		0.40
Number of US aircraft shot down between 1965 and 1972			4,181	

Although the socio-economic infrastructure held up, the enormous destruction caused by the bombing did seriously impede the country's economic development, especially in the area of industry.

People's War vs. "Local War"

The landing of the massive US expeditionary corps in South Việt Nam to help the Sài Gòn army completely changed the nature of the war. Against the "local war" strategy applied by the Pentagon, the people and liberation armed forces of South Việt Nam, under the leadership of the NLF and with aid from the North, applied a strategy of "people's war" taken to the highest level.

In November 1965, thinking that it had mustered sufficient force, the US command launched its first dry season offensive. A hundred battalions were dispatched in five directions in Nam Bộ and central Việt Nam with the aim of crushing the NLF regular forces, reconquering a large part of the liberated areas, and driving the Vietnamese resistance back towards remote mountainous areas. Never before had a battle corps had such firepower, mobility, and numerical superiority over its opponents. What could be done in the face of this colossal war machine? Did the Vietnamese people have any option other than unconditionally accepting US conditions? The war was being conducted without mercy, with massive artillery shelling, carpet bombing by B52s, and widespread used of toxic chemicals, napalm and cluster bombs. Right from the first battle, the American propaganda machine was already claiming victory.

The 1965-1966 dry season dragged on. By April 1966, the US command was forced to order its troops to retreat, and admitted that none of its main objectives had been attained. On its side, the NLF published an account according to which 100,000 enemy troops, including more than 40,000 Americans, had been put out of action. The myth of the invincibility of the US war machine was thus exploded.

The failure of the first dry season counter-offensive forced the US command to come to the inevitable conclusion that the means at its disposal were insufficient. It therefore threw in even more American and puppet troops. By the end of 1966, the US armed forces in South Việt Nam totalled 380,000 men and by early 1967, 440,000. With the puppet army and forces from satellite countries, the enemy army comprised more than one million men, 4,500 aircraft and helicopters, almost 3,000 artillery pieces, and 3,500 armoured vehicles. Each month, the Americans fired 1,700,000 shells and dropped 50,000 tonnes of bombs on Vietnamese territory.

Despite this military build-up, the US command had shown more caution in the dry season of 1966-1967, setting less ambitious objectives for its counter-offensive than for the previous one, concentrating its forces in the areas northwest of Sài Gòn, in Tây Ninh province where the NLF was supposed to be headquartered. Greater attention was paid this time to the "pacification" campaign to which units of the puppet army were specifically assigned. Destruction of villages, with displacement of the population and mass killings, became common practice.

Between the end of October 1966 and April 1967, the US successively launched three large-scale operations in the direction of Tây Ninh. The biggest of them, "Junction City", involved nearly 45,000 men, 800 armoured vehicles and several hundred aircrafts. For their part, puppet troops numbering 175,000 assisted by 40,000 "civil guards" specially trained for this operation, sought to "pacify" the region. Never before had the US military effort in South Việt Nam been so great, and bombing raids on the North were intensified.

The Tây Ninh operations failed, and Washington, in the middle of a war, was forced to recall two generals, who had commanded the sector. About 175, 000 US and Sài Gòn troops were put out of action during this dry season campaign, and 1,800 aircrafts and helicopters were shot down or damaged on the ground. The US command had to postpone indefinitely its plan to reoccupy the Mekong delta. Early in 1967, when US and pupper troops were sustaining heavy defeats northwest of Sài Gòn, the liberation forces opened up a new front on Highway 9 near the 17th parallel. General Westmoreland then had to rush the best US and puppet units to this new theatre of operations, leaving the Nam Bộ front exposed. US and Sài Gòn troops completely lost the initiative and had to pull back to ensure the defence of Sài Gòn, the major bases, and communication routes. The rate of desertion from the puppet army increased sharply.

During 1967, Washington attempted to send new reinforcements to Việt Nam, but increasing opposition from American public opinion meant that the US command only received 100,000 reinforcements in 1967 as against 170,000 in 1966. By the end of 1967, the number of GIs in South Việt Nam had grown to 480,000 and in early 1968, to more than half a million, not counting units stationed in Thailand and the 7th Fleet. With a rapid increase in all categories of puppet troops and forces from satellite countries, the US command had 1.2 million men on the South Việt Nam battlefield by 1968.

This huge force, however, was not sufficiently able to hold off repeated assaults by the liberation forces which retained the initiative, attacking US/puppet bases and posts northwest of Sài Gòn on the high plateaus and during regular operations, while guerrilla fighting was stepped up in the Mekong delta.

It was this situation that enabled the people of South Việt Nam and the liberation armed forces to launch their 1968 Tết Offensive. On the night of January 29 and during the following days, armed attacks and popular uprisings took place in 60 cities, provincial capitals and townships and on military bases. The people coordinated their action closely with those of the liberation forces. On the night of January 30, a series of key targets inside Sài Gòn were attacked including the US embassy, "Presidential Palace," headquarters of the puppet General

Staff, a radio station, headquarters of the puppet marines and paratroops, police head-quarters and numerous munitions and fuel depots. The 4th, 5th, 6th, 7th, and 8th Precincts in Sài Gòn were occupied by liberation forces, and the people there promptly organized self-defence units and set up people's committees.

In Huế on 31 January 1968, the liberation forces infiltrated the city, hoisted the NLF banner over the royal citadel, and freed 2,000 prisoners. In response, the US subjected the city to brutal bombardment, almost completely destroying the royal palaces, which are among Việt Nam's most important cultural relics. On February 6, a special communiqué from the NLF reported that the cities of Sài Gòn, Huế, Đà Lạt, Nha Trang, Đà Nẵng and Quy Nhơn, as well as several dozen provincial and district capitals, had been attacked, that everywhere the people had joined in a combined effort with the armed forces, and that 50,000 enemy troops, including 10,000 Americans, had been put out of action, and 1,500 aircrafts and helicopters destroyed, mostly on the ground.

The 1968 Tết Offensive and uprising demonstrated that the liberation forces were capable, at a time when the US/puppet forces had reached maximum strength, of launching closely coordinated attacks everywhere, while the Sài Gòn and Washington propaganda machine kept broadcasting to the world images of an NLF completely crushed by US military power. The resounding victories of the NLF caused deep divisions in world and US public opinion. On 7 February 1968, Walter Lippmann wrote in Newsweek that:

"Johnson-Rusk policy in Asia is crumbling. What is crumbling is the idea that the United States can with its military force determine the order of things on the Asian continent. Washington has had to recall Westmoreland from his command in Indochina, and replace him with General Creighton Abrams."

The Pentagon had not only to name a new commander-in-chief, but also to change its strategy entirely. It was no longer possible to send to Việt Nam the 200, 000 reinforcement troops requested by Westmoreland following the losses of Tết, 1968. Abrams received the order to stick to a defensive strategy, and instead of launching operations to "search and destroy" the NLF's regular units, limited himself to "clean and hold" operations in the areas surrounding the major towns and bases, Sài Gòn in particular.

This did not imply that the Pentagon had abandoned the idea of imposing by force a *Pax Americana* on Việt Nam. Compelled to reduce the scale and number of ground operations, the US command multiplied air and naval bombardments, artillery shelling and spraying of toxic chemicals. The areas surrounding Sài Gòn and other cities, for several dozen kilometres, were practically razed to the ground and every bush was doused with toxic chemicals. The bombing of North Việt Nam became heavier every day.

Meanwhile, the American public was losing patience and Johnson and the Democratic Party had their electoral campaign to think about. The issue on which world and American opinion showed itself to be the most sensitive was the serious escalation against the Democratic Republic of Vietnam, an independent and sovereign state, and member of the socialist camp. On 31 March 1968, Johnson had to declare that from then on the bombing would be conducted on a restricted area of North Việt Nam, that he would not run for re-election, and that Washington agreed to negotiate with the representatives of the DRV government. The latter promptly accepted the proposal, and in May 1968, talks were opened in Paris which lasted until 1973, while military operations continued.

After March 31, the US airforce concentrated its attacks on the southern part of North Việt Nam, from the city of Vinh to the 17th parallel, in the hope of cutting all communications between the North and the South, and terrorizing the people in this region with the systematic destruction of towns and villages. In this area, the population and the communication lines were concentrated in a narrow passage squeezed in between the mountains and the sea. For seven months, the region was subjected to intensive air and naval bombardment of an unprecedented barbarity. But this supreme effort against the DRV proved futile. The elections in the US were drawing near. On November 1, Johnson was forced to order an unconditional cessation of the bombing of the DRV. This last-ditch maneuver, however, was unable to save the Democrats which lost the presidential election, the American people having lost confidence in both Johnson and his party. With his promises of peace, Richard Nixon succeeded in being elected, and the Republican Party returned to office.

Nixon's War

Promises of peace and a policy of war was the line promoted by Johnson in 1964 before his election. Nixon followed exactly the same path. A ruthless advocate of war, he had as early as 1954 called for direct US intervention on the side of the French colonialists. This time,

fully in control, he was determined to win the war. But the situation when he came to the White House in 1969 did not leave him with any more options than it had with Johnson in 1965. Nixon was unable to reinforce the US expeditionary corps, and was obliged to begin to bring the "boys" home. US losses in Việt Nam had reached unacceptable levels for the American people. Expenditure on the war in Indochina had topped 30 billion dollars a year, while social welfare and school development projects were starved for funds. Opposition to the war increased, especially on university campuses across the country. America began to awaken.

How could the war be continued and won, while reducing losses in US lives and expenditures to levels acceptable to the American public, without renouncing, however, the claimed right to impose conditions on the Vietnamese people? Nixon's solution was to "Vietnamize" the war.

The key requirements were to:

- Sufficiently strengthen the puppet army in terms of men and equipment to make it the main fighting force, capable of eliminating the Vietnamese resistance and constituting the main bulwark for a Sài Gòn administration entirely committed to Washington's interests;

- Gradually withdraw US ground forces;

- Maintain in Việt Nam sufficient air power and artillery to give effective support to the puppet army. This US military presence would last as long as proved to be necessary; and

- Make life unbearable for the people by massive air raids and continual spraying of toxic chemicals, thus compelling the population to regroup in towns controlled by the Americans and their agents.

This forced "urbanization" advocated by Harvard professor Samuel P. Huntington, was aimed at turning those parts of South Việt Nam not controlled by US forces into deserts pockmarked by bomb craters, where no vegetation would grow, where no birds would sing, and where, as a consequence, revolutionary forces could not set foot. Millions of rural inhabitants therefore, would be forced to seek refuge in the towns, and would find no other means of livelihood than joining the puppet army and police.

In areas they controlled, the US sought to intensify the pacification campaign with incessant raids, the assassination of activists and suspects, and the imprisonment and deportation of hundreds of thousands of people. The military forces and police intimidated the people without respite,

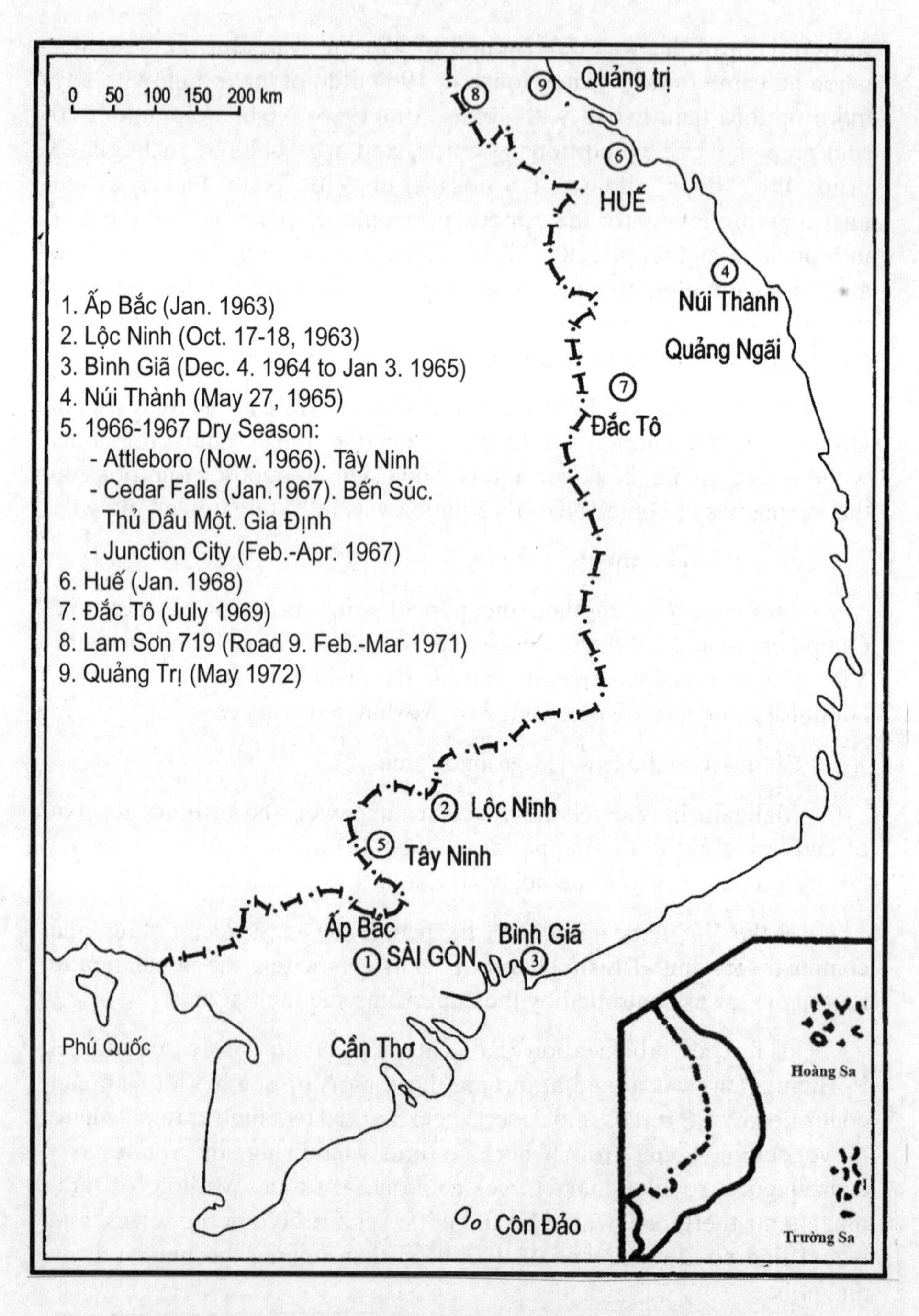
0 50 100 150 200 km
Quảng trị
HUẾ
Núi Thành
Quảng Ngãi
Đắc Tô
Lộc Ninh
Tây Ninh
Ấp Bắc
Bình Giã
SÀI GÒN
Phú Quốc
Cần Thơ
Côn Đảo
Hoàng Sa
Trường Sa
1. Ấp Bắc (Jan. 1963)
2. Lộc Ninh (Oct. 17-18, 1963)
3. Bình Giã (Dec. 4. 1964 to Jan 3. 1965)
4. Núi Thành (May 27, 1965)
5. 1966-1967 Dry Season:
- Attleboro (Now. 1966). Tây Ninh
- Cedar Falls (Jan.1967). Bến Súc.
Thủ Dầu Một. Gia Định
- Junction City (Feb.-Apr. 1967)
6. Huế (Jan. 1968)
7. Đắc Tô (July 1969)
8. Lam Sơn 719 (Road 9. Feb.-Mar 1971)
9. Quảng Trị (May 1972)

Resistances against the US in south Việt Nam
Principal Battlefields

while terror was stepped up. Some 44,000 specially trained pacification agents backed up the regular policy in terrorizing the population.

Nixon applied this barbarous policy at the same time that he was forced to begin withdrawing the GIs, when the resistance in South Việt Nam was rapidly gaining both politically and militarily.

In these conditions, and increasingly as the presidential elections drew nearer, Nixon turned to total war. In 1969, while North Việt Nam was being only sporadically bombed, the quantity of bombs dropped on Laos and especially on South Việt Nam passed the 1968 total to reach 1,389,000 tonnes. This did not include artillery shelling and the spraying of chemicals, the latter covering several million hectares and resulting in virtual biocide. According to US sources, between 1965 and 1973, 10 million rural people were forced by these methods to leave their villages and move to the cities.

Shortly after the 1968 Tết Offensive, the Alliance of National, Democratic and Peace Forces (ANDPF) was formed, bringing together intellectuals and members of the middle class in enemy-held cities for joint action with the NLF. In June 1969, The NLF and the ANDPF held a national congress which established the Provisional Revolutionary Government (PRG) of the Republic of South Việt Nam, which was rapidly recognized by many governments and international organizations. Revolutionary People's Committees were elected in most villages and districts and many provinces. This flowering of the national and democratic movement through all regions and social strata contrasted sharply with the worsening crisis in the puppet regime. The death of President Hồ Chí Minh on 2 September 1969 deeply saddened the whole country, but his passing only strengthened the will of the entire people to carry through the national liberation struggle.

The massive US troop commitment had clearly saved the puppet regime from collapse, but had also emphasized the anti-national character of the agents Washington had placed at the head of the Sài Gòn government. Increasing US economic aid undoubtedly enabled the Sài Gòn regime to survive, but only at the cost of aggravating inflation and ruining local industries. In particular, the forcible conscription of young men sparked daily opposition from those concerned, and from all other strata of the population. Debauchery, corruption and the imposition of the American "way of life" eventually sparked deeply-felt anti-US sentiment, even among those who benefited from American aid.

Expanding the War

Neither intensified bombing and destruction nor the strengthening of troops numbers and armaments in the puppet army could succeed in crushing South Việt Nam's popular forces, much less continued propping up of the Sài Gòn regime. While "Vietnamization" meant prolonging the war in Việt Nam, it also led to its expansion to encompass the whole of Indochina, as the "protection" of South Việt Nam could be ensured only if Laos and Cambodia were integrated into the US sphere of influence. The French colonialists had experienced this earlier themselves.

Losing in South Việt Nam, Nixon lurched into forward flight and launched operations which none of his predecessors would have dared undertake.

In Nixon's mind, "Vietnamization" was to be achieved by "Indochinanization" and eventually by "Asianization"; Indochinese were to fight Indochinese, and Asians to fight Asians. To ensure continued US domination in Asia, Washington would have to provide only dollars and weapons. Only the skin colour of the casualties would change.

In Laos, from 1969 onwards, Washington tried to strengthen the right-wing forces militarily and politically, strengthening "General" Vàng Pao's mercenaries to use them as a spearhead against liberated zones, and introducing Thai troops.

The Americans intensified the bombing of regions controlled by Lao patriotic forces. Up to 600 sorties were made every day, using all types of planes including B52s. Many villages saw their populations forcibly removed by helicopter to be regrouped in refugee camps.

In August 1969, under the command of 12,000 American advisers, 50 battalions with large-scale air support launched an attack on the Plain of Jars - Xieng Khouang area. Fighting lasted until February 1970, when Lao patriotic forces, aided by Vietnamese forces, launched a major counter-offensive and drove the enemy out of the region, inflicting severe losses on them. In this operation, the US command had mustered all the most effective means at this disposal for the first test of the Nixon doctrine: specially trained mercenaries, numerous American advisers, and large-scale air support.

The failure of this operation led to a new push forward. On 18 March 1970, US intelligence engineered a coup d'état against the neutral government of Cambodia. Prince Norodom Sihanouk, who had striven to maintain Cambodia's independence and neutrality, was toppled by pro-American agents - Lon Nol and Sirik Matak. But no sooner had the Lon Nol government come to power then it began to face strong popular resistance. An appeal by Norodom Sihanouk, followed by the April Summit Conference of Indochinese Peoples, to draw up a joint program of action to form a National United Front of Kampuchea (NUFK) and Royal Government of National Union of Kampuchea (RGNUK), greatly encouraged the Khmer people's resistance.

To save the Lon Nol government, the US command on 30 April 1970 launched an attack by Sài Gòn and US troops against Cambodia. Seventy thousand men invaded the country while US and Sài Gòn planes bombed cities and villages. Cambodia in turn experienced all the horrors of American warfare. But the Khmer people put up strong resistance. Most of the countryside, in response to the NUFK appeal, rapidly organized itself in order to deal stunning blows against the Phnom Penh puppet administration. The RGNUK called for help from Vietnamese troops and the coup d'état against Norodom Sihanouk brought entirely unexpected consequences for Washington: in solidarity with the Vietnamese and Lao people, the great majority of the population of a hitherto natural country now became engaged in a determined armed struggle against the US imperialists and their agents.

The reaction of American and world opinion to the invasion of Cambodia forced Nixon to withdraw US ground forces after June, but Washington continued to step up aid in weapons and dollars to support the tottering Phnom Penh regime at all costs. The most important task - military support - was assigned to Sài Gòn troops, who occupied Cambodia where they behaved like true conquerors. The Nixon doctrine appeared in all its barbarity; making Asians kill Asians for the benefit of the US.

Before 1975, as the war unfolded and the Khmer resistance badly needed Vietnamese military aid, Beijing and Khmer Rouge leaders could not openly foster discord.

Nixon's bellicose and adventurous policy brought the three peoples of Indochina closer together, and the most bitter setbacks experienced by the GIs and Washington's mercenaries were related to their mutual support. Isolating the national and local resistance in each country so as to throttle them more easily, and cutting all communications between them, became major US objectives following the serious setbacks of 1970. The liberated zone in southern and central Laos constituted a sort of umbilical cord which the Pentagon set about severing early in 1971.

The southern Laos operation began in February using the maximum firepower available, including 2,000 US aircraft and helicopters, the best Saigon units (paratroops, rangers, the 1st Infantry Division, and armoured units), and powerful US ground forces. A total of 45,000 men were engaged on Highway 9, which runs close to the 17th parallel from the South Vietnamese coast to the Mekong River. With such a huge deployment, of aircrafts in particular, the US command believed it could cut enemy communications, thus preventing the liberation forces from supplying their troops fighting further south, and that the all-powerful US airforce could, if necessary, crush them if they engaged in battle.

With air force protection, helicopters landed Sài Gòn troops on the hills overlooking the highway, while armoured columns swiftly advanced down the road to take Tchepone, the hub of the communications network. But the liberation forces reacted promptly. Fire from anti-aircraft batteries brought down hundreds of helicopters loaded with men and equipment, while enemy posts set up on the mountaintops along Highway 9 were crushed by the liberation forces' artillery. Caught in ambushes and mine traps, the armoured columns were decimated. The battle, begun on February 8, ended on March 22 with the destruction of almost all the puppet forces engaged in southern Laos, and heavy losses for US and puppet troops stationed in the South Vietnamese sector of Highway 9. A total of 23,000 men were put out of action, 730 aircrafts and helicopters brought down, and 1,400 military vehicles destroyed. This was one of the greatest battles to have taken place during the Indochina war since 1945.

For the US command, the gravity of this defeat lay in the fact that it had deployed its key assets, i.e., the crack units forming the strategic reserves of the Sài Gòn army, maximum air support, and carefully-prepared tactics. Washington had wanted to make this operation a test of the policy of "Vietnamization". But the event itself proved to be a failure.

By mid-1971, 11 months before the presidential election, Nixon found himself faced with a less than encouraging situation; resistance by the Vietnamese, Lao and Khmer peoples continued to intensify, while support from socialist countries and other peoples kept increasing and US public opinion reacted more strongly every day.

On 1 July 1971, Mrs Nguyễn Thị Bình on behalf of the PRG put forward a seven -point plan for the settlement of the Vietnamese issue, with two basic conditions: withdrawal of US troops, plus the resignation of the Thiệu government and its replacement with a new administration

that would hold talks with the PRG on the forming of a government of national reconciliation. This initiative, strongly supported by world opinion and 70 other nations, did not spark any serious response from Washington. Nixon, announcing a trip to Beijing, tried to persist with the fiction that the Việt Nam issue could be settled, not between representatives of the Vietnamese people, but between the big powers.

In its editorial of July 19, *Nhân Dân*, the organ of the Workers' Party of Việt Nam, put the record straight:

"Nixon is going astray. The way out is clear, yet he is walking into an impasse. The days when big powers decide the fate of small countries are past and gone forever."

Having secured Beijing's agreement, however, Nixon went ahead with his military and political maneuvers with the aim of imposing his will. On September 21, 200 aircrafts heavily bombed Quảng Bình province in North Việt Nam, and on October 3, Thiệu saw himself re - elected president with, he claimed, 94 percent of the vote. Pacification operations continued, but encountered strong resistance, especially in October, in the western Mekong delta province of Trà Vinh. On October 11, Kissinger tabled a US sponsored peace plan without, however, giving a precise date for the withdrawal of US troops, and demanding the maintenance of the Thiệu government as the sole government in Sài Gòn. Military operations intensified in Laos and Cambodia during the last months of 1971 as well. In South Việt Nam, the pacification campaign in the U Minh region in the west of the Mekong delta ended with 16,000 men killed or wounded. In Cambodia in December, the defeated Lon Nol forces had to call off their "Tchenla-2 Operation" launched in August, the most serious setback so far for the Phnom Penh administration. In Laos, patriotic forces had almost completely liberated the Plain of Jars, wiping out many Vàng Pao and Bangkok units. US aircraft continued to fly reconnaissance and bombing missions over parts of North Việt Nam. Repression was stepped up in Sài Gòn while in Cambodia, Lon Nol was gradually driven into complete isolation. He launched a new coup on 10 March 1972, dissolved the national assembly, and assumed the titles of President of the Republic and Chairman of the Council of Ministers.

For Nixon, 1972 was the year of the presidential election. To achieve re-election, he had to give the impression that he was determined to end the Indochina war, but being a diehard neo-colonialist, he wanted to perpetuate the American "way" in Việt Nam and impose his own conditions on the Vietnamese people. Three years of "Vietnamization" had enabled him to considerably strengthen the Thiệu army and police, which together totaled 1.2 million men and was equipped with one of the most up-to-date air forces, naval and river flotillas, and armoured corps in the world. Three crack divisions (rangers, paratroopers and marines) formed the spearhead of this army, and were trained to destroy enemy regular forces and protect major towns and bases. The US airforce and navy provided significant support to these forces, while the ruthless pacification campaign kept the Sài Gòn -controlled areas in a state of terror. Continual bombing had turned liberated zones into deserts.

More than 70,000 officers had been trained to command this army; they also controlled the political apparatus while engaging in all kinds of trafficking. The model for them was Nguyễn Văn Thiệu himself who, while still a young man, had joined the French army's paratroop force before crossing over to the US, and whose wife and close relatives had amassed huge fortunes in countless deals. This "military-political-trafficking" caste, trained and indoctrinated by the Americans, constituted the true ruling class in South Việt Nam. It was neither a bourgeoisie, nor a native feudal class. It was a pure creation of US imperialism, just as the enormous military and police apparatus which it commanded was created by dollars and the policy of systematically destroying the South Việt Nam countryside. Ruffians and thugs were specially trained to kill and torture, to back up troops, carry out the dirty work and terrorize the population.

With this gigantic machine, Nixon thought he could carry through his "Vietnamization" policy and gradually withdraw American ground forces, all the more so that he could launch fierce bombing raids against North Việt Nam at any moment. Efforts were also made to give a semblance of economic prosperity to areas still under Sài Gòn control. US aid, both military and economic, averaged out at two billion dollars a year - an enormous sum for Việt Nam - but nothing compared to the 30 billion dollars spent annually on the direct intervention of American troops in the war.

Nixon had a certain amount of success; the enormous economic and technical power of the US directed for so many long years against a small country could indeed produce results, and it was not without reason that Nixon confidently entered the election year, especially since negotiations between Beijing and Washington had already brought about substantial agreement.

The confrontation of 1972 was decisive. On the Vietnamese side, answers had to be given to several military issues of prime importance:

- Could the outer defence system set up by the US and Sài Gòn armies be overcome?
- Could the crack units of the Sài Gòn army be wiped out?
- Could supplies be maintained in case of a long, drawn-out offensive?

In a bid to gain some control over the direction of operation, Beijing proposed that China send 200, 000 Chinese troops to Việt Nam. The Vietnamese refused.

The offensive launched by popular forces on March 30 shed vivid light on the situation. By May 1, fortified positions in the northern part of Quảng Trị province near the 17th parallel, those located northwest of Sài Gòn in the direction of Lộc Ninh and An Lộc, and important bases on Highways 14 and 19 in the Central Highlands, one after another fell as a result of attacks by the people's artillery, tanks and infantry. The best Sài Gòn units, in spite of strong support from the US air force and navy, were unable to withstand the assault. Quảng Trị province was completely liberated.

The Vietnamization policy had sustained a devastating defeat, and Washington was obliged to partly "re-Americanize" the war. Key air force and naval units arrived to reinforce those still in Indochina. The fleet of US tactical aircraft and fighter-bombers grew to more than 1,300, and the number of B52s to 200. Washington had to come to the rescue of Sài Gòn, since it was not only the outer defensive perimeter that was threatened, but also the area to the rear, the zones that had already been "pacified". Guerrilla battles were raging and the administrations set up by Sài Gòn in regions such as Bình Định and the western area of the Mekong delta were being dismantled. To help Sài Gòn troops retake the provincial capital of Quảng Trị, the US airforce and navy daily fired 15,000 to 20,000 shells at its citadel, while around 300 aircraft were in operation behind enemy lines.

To save his unsuccessful Vietnamization policy, Nixon ordered a new escalation against the Democratic Republic of Việt Nam. On April 16 B52s destroyed many quarters of Hải Phòng, the second biggest city in North Việt Nam, which was systematically bombed until the end of 1972. The US airforce operated over North Việt Nam in terror raids against the population (carpet bombings of towns and villages) or using pinpoint bombing raids targeting sophisticated weapons (laser bombs) against economic targets, bridges, factories, and so on.

Almost all the towns in North Việt Nam were totally or partly destroyed, and all industrial establishments damaged in Washington's

attempt to systematically destroy the country's industrial economy. Agriculture was also a target, the most important hydraulic installations being subjected to saturation bombing. To top off the escalation, many bombing raids were directed at the network of river and sea dykes, with the aim of causing catastrophic floods at times of heavy rain in July and August.

To supplement the bombing, on May 8, Nixon ordered the blockading of all ports of the Democratic Republic of Việt Nam with thousands of mines so as to stop all foreign supplies from coming in. North Việt Nam hit back. Many American planes were brought down, the supplies were kept flowing and the people remained calm and continued fighting. The Sài Gòn forces only retook the town of Quảng Trị at the cost of a massive and desperate effort. Massive intervention by US forces had of course saved the Saigon army and administration, but Nixon had failed once again to impose his will. In the North, the year 1972 was a dry one, and the raids against the dykes did not bring the expected results. An operation by Vàng Pao's mercenaries to retake the Plain of Jars in Laos failed. Nixon was unable to present any prospects for peace to American electors, and McGovern's nomination as Democratic Party candidate posed a serious threat to him. The intensification of the bombing certainly inflicted serious losses on the Vietnamese people and boosted the stocks of the Thiệu regime, but Nixon remained in an impasse.

On September 11, the PRG proposed a fair and reasonable solution consisting of the withdrawal of US troops and formation of a provisional government of national reconciliation comprising representatives of three parties: the PRG, the Sài Gòn government, and a third group of other political forces in South Việt Nam. Thus neither a communist nor pro -American government would be imposed on South Việt Nam. It became more and more difficult during the election period to keep obstructing the peace plans of the Vietnamese side. Nixon had to resign himself to negotiating as American losses in planes and pilots mounted. Between April and October, 554 US aircraft were brought down over North Việt Nam, and on October 17, the 4,000th US aircraft was shot down, an F111, the latest pride of American technology.

During the first weeks of October, negotiations took place between delegations from the DRV and United States. It was agreed that on October 22 the two sides would initial an agreement in Hà Nội, and that on October 30, the foreign ministers of the two countries would officially sign it in Paris. On October 22, Nixon sent a message to Prime Minister

Phạm Văn Đồng of the DRV. This enabled Nixon to appear before his electors as having already settled the Việt Nam affair. On October 23, after the votes were cast, Washington, under the pretext of difficulties raised by Sài Gòn, went back on the terms of the agreement and the agenda that had already been set. Military operations in the South and bombing of the North resumed, while the US command took advantage of the hiatus to send large consignments of new weapons, especially aircrafts, helicopters and armoured vehicles, to the Sài Gòn army. By the end of 1972 the Sài Gòn air force thus had more than 2,000 planes, making it the third most powerful in the world; US officers passed themselves off as civilian technicians "advising" the Thiệu army. The naval air arm launched fierce attacks on North Vietnamese provinces between the 17th and 20th parallels. Washington then demanded drastic changes to the basic provisions of the agreement reached in October (126 changes were proposed), with the aim of denying the Vietnamese people their fundamental national rights.

Having failed to impose his conditions on Vietnamese negotiators, on December 18 Nixon sent B52 strategic bombers against the major cities of the DRV. From December 18 to 30, 1972, several hundred fighter-bombers and about 150 B52s operated daily over North Việt Nam. Vietnamese anti -aircraft defences brought down 81 American planes including 34 B52s, until then thought to be invulnerable. A wave of protest swept the world. The failure of the B52s to cause panic among the population of North Việt Nam, the huge losses in number of aircraft and pilots, and worldwide indignation compelled Nixon to halt the bombing and return to the negotiating table.

On January 27, the "Agreement on the Cessation of the War and the Restoration of Peace in Việt Nam" was signed in Paris. It stipulated in particular that the United States should respect the fundamental national rights of the Vietnamese people, and that US troops and advisers and all other military personnel of both the US and its allies should be withdrawn from South Việt Nam before March 27. The withdrawal of US forces opened the way for a political settlement. The Paris Agreement implicitly recognized the existence for two administrations and two armies, as well as three political forces which were to work for the implementation of national reconciliation. On February 21 in Vientiane, an agreement between the two Lao parties on the re-establishment of peace and the implementation of national reconciliation in Laos was signed, also guaranteeing the Lao people the exercise of their basic national rights. The United States had to cease all intervention and aggression, end its military presence in Laos and disband the special forces set up in that country. A new provisional government of national unity was envisaged as well as a consultative political council with equal participation from the Vientiane government and Lao triotic patriotic forces.

Thus, in January and February 1973, Washington was forced to recognize, at least in principle, the right of the Vietnamese and Lao peoples to settle their own affairs without American interference. The most important point was the obligation on the US to withdraw all its military forces from South Việt Nam. In view of the systematic nature of the interventionist policy followed by the US in Việt Nam since 1950, and pursued after 1970, this was a major defeat and serious setback for US imperialism. To have geared all its strategy to tutoring the Third World, to have for over 20 years concentrated all its efforts on trying to crush the Vietnamese national movement, to have to recognize the existence of the DRV and that of the PRG in South Việt Nam, to find itself confronted by a battered American nation, a younger generation and an army tormented by doubt, the nation's honour stained for ever by the magnitude of the crimes committed - this setback constituted a bitter failure for the Washington neo-colonialists.

Cultural Development in the Period 1945 - 1975

Thirty years of war and social upheaval did not prevent Vietnamese culture from undergoing continuous development. It was an integral part of the revolutionary movement, one of the essential weapons of national liberation and social renewal.

Never before in Việt Nam's history had cultural activities developed so rapidly in terms of both quantity and quality. The flourishing of literary, musical, theatrical, and artistic works of all genres over the thirty years 1945-1975 surpassed that of several previous centuries, even without counting the birth of new arts such as the cinema.

Eighty years of colonial domination had stifled both traditional culture and the potential for modernization, and of all renewal. With the triumph of the 1945 August Revolution and especially with the complete liberation of North Việt Nam after 1954, and with all the attention given by the Party and government to the development of science and culture, conditions were created for the reassessing of traditions and the birth of a national culture suited to the current era. Việt Nam underwent a true cultural renaissance.

Many social and historical factors were involved:

- Use of the national language as the medium of instruction at all levels in place of French. The national language was quickly updated in many areas, including tens of thousands of scientific and technical terms;

- Complete elimination of illiteracy and rapid spread of education. By 1958, almost every adult in North Việt Nam could read and write, and after 1960, even during the US bombing, one out of three North Vietnamese was involved in some sort of study. The number of intellectuals increased dramatically, while the various strata of the population eagerly took part in cultural activities, read newspapers and books, and went to the theatre and cinema;

- Renaissance of traditional culture and the modernization of contemporary culture were also carried out among various ethnic groups in mountainous areas, and Vietnamese culture took on an increasingly multi-ethnic character; and

- Close contacts were established with other socialist countries including the Soviet Union and others in Europe, China, Cuba, and also with cultural organizations throughout the world. An open-door policy, though hindered by war, was maintained, enabling the nation's culture to benefit from the rich cultural treasury of other nations.

Immense material and human losses due to war and partition hampered this cultural upsurge significantly. Many scientists and artists died in battle, and many art works and historical monuments were destroyed or damaged. Artists, writers, and scientific researchers had to work in very difficult conditions.

Education and Scientific Development

The literacy campaign launched in September 1945 achieved rapid success. With the use of the national language and the elimination of outdated and reactionary notions from syllabuses and textbooks, a new education system took shape. In 1950 in the liberated zones, the education system began to closely link political and armed struggle, production and school education. Teachers' colleges and technical and higher education institutions were set up one after another.

The complete liberation of North Việt Nam in 1954 created conditions for the rapid development of education. The literacy rate in newly liberated areas quickly increased, while schools introduced a

uniform ten-grade system of general education. Infant classes were set up not only in cities but right down to villages level, paid for by agricultural cooperatives. Further education courses, specially designed for activists and qualified people, were offered to literate adults, helping them to raise their educational standards. Many higher and secondary technical schools were opened.

When US aggression began in 1964, North Việt Nam had a comprehensive schooling system from infant level up to university, with further education courses for adults. Each village had at least one first level (primary) school for children aged 7 to 11; most had a second level (junior high) school for ages 12 to 15, and each district had at least one third level (senior high) school for pupils aged 15 to 18.

US aggression posed a great challenge for the Vietnamese school system. Within ten years a new generation had been suitably educated, providing the armed forces with soldiers capably of handling modern weapons - artillery, missiles, radar, jet planes - which had not been in existence at the time of Điện Biên Phủ. Educated politically and ideologically by the new system, the young assumed wartime obligations both at the front and to the rear.

Party and government directives were clear on the following point. In spite of the war, education was to be developed to help the war effort, but also to meet the needs of the future. Schools and colleges from the cities had to disperse to the forests and villages, and village schools had to break up into small units. Each evacuated or dispersed school had to build new premises, shelters and trenches, house teachers and pupils, and set up libraries and laboratories either in people's houses or in temporary compounds. This enormous task was performed successfully thanks to the dedication of the teachers and pupils and the assistance given by the entire people.

For these reasons, educational progress was not interrupted during the war years even in the most frequently bombed provinces such as those situated near the 17th parallel. In 1965, responsibility for higher and vocational education was transferred to a new ministry separate from the Ministry of Education.

In mountainous areas, conditions were much more difficult owing to great ethnic and linguistic diversity, with economic and educational standards lagging behind those of people living on the plains, while the population was more scattered as well. Special commissions developed scripts for the languages of the most important ethnic groups. Pupils in

mountainous regions thus learned both the language of their own ethnic group and that of the Kinh, the common national language.

The following tables illustrate progress made in education:

North Việt Nam	1955	1956	1972
Enrollments in general education (not counting infants' classes)	716,000	2,666,000	4,882,000
Higher education	1,200	26,000	53,000

(not counting the many students learning by correspondence and those studying abroad)

School enrollments across the whole of Việt Nam (north and south) in 1939, under the colonial regime:

General education	University
567,000	600

With regard to scientific and technical research, the legacy of the colonial regime was practically nil in terms of equipment and personnel. The first students at the new colleges and universities did not graduate until 1959 or 1960, and only after that date can one speak of the birth of scientific research in Việt Nam. In 1959, the State Committee for Science and Technology was established in order to lead and coordinate research. In 1967, this committee split into two, the Committee for Natural Sciences and Technology and the Committee for Social Sciences. In fact, the first facilities for scientific research purposes were not really established until 1966. Several dozen specialized institutes were set up, many of them during the war against the US. An Association for the Popularization of Science and Technology attracted many members, with branches reaching down to the level of village and agricultural cooperative. *Khoa Học Thường Thức* (Journal of Scientific Popularization) enjoyed considerable success. The social sciences — history, archaeology, linguistics, ethnography and so on — also saw rapid advancement.

Literature and the Arts

The 1945 August Revolution freed writers and artists from the narrow and suffocating atmosphere in which they had been working under the colonial regime, particularly since the start of the Second World War. Almost all writers and artists left the cities to join the

resistance against the French. Fighting, living among the people, and political and ideological work gradually transformed these artists of the former regime, while new writers and artists trained by the resistance itself progressively emerged on to the cultural scene.

The complete liberation of North Việt Nam in 1954 and the first steps in the establishment of socialism led to a new flowering of cultural life. Exhibitions, conferences and festivals as well as specialized journals and publishing houses multiplied. The State at both central and provincial levels encouraged artistic, theatrical, musical and dance groups, and set up art schools, offices and studios to develop film-making. Amateur theatre companies were formed in factories, villages and army units. Never before had the country witnessed such a ferment of cultural activity.

Despite the partition of the country, the US intervention failed to break the national and revolutionary unity of the artistic movement. Works produced in the period 1954-1975 in the North as well as in the liberated zones of the South sprang from the same sources. Political writings, in particular those of leaders such as Hồ Chí Minh, Lê Duẩn, Phạm Văn Đồng, Trường Chinh and Võ Nguyên Giáp, with their concise style and the finesse of their language, constitute literary works in their own right.

National and revolutionary realities, the tough and heroic struggle of an entire people against aggression and the building of a new society were the main themes used by writers and artists. The era of romantic dreams, of hermetic literature, and of art for art's sake was gone. But while the literary and artistic portrayal of the national struggle was relatively easy, the building of a new society, a new people, and socialism which was only at its beginnings, was expressed with much less ease. In this domain, the transformation of villages, and the problems of the world of the peasant were reflected more often and more easily than those of industry and the workers' world. The problem also arose, especially in theatre and music, of safeguarding the traditional heritage while modernizing it. These were problems pertaining to a developed and growing body of literature and art. It was only in the light of the struggle that the ancestral legacy could be correctly evaluated and only by continuing the nation's traditions could the nation's cultural life be modernized.

The period 1945-1950 was marked by the appearance of shorter works: poems, narratives and short stories. Only after 1950 did the first novels appear. The new guidelines for writers were about creating a national, scientific and popular culture. In the period 1954-1960, the first war of resistance provided the main source of inspiration for literary and artistic works. After that date, short stories, novels and films tackled, with varying degrees of vigour and skill, the problem of establishing socialism, in particular those of agricultural co-operatives, conflicts between the young and older generations, the blunders, disputes, and enthusiasm of activists, and the emancipation of women. From 1965 to 1975, more and more poems, narratives, short stories and films dealt with the struggle against the US in both South and North. It often sufficed just to describe the life and struggle of a combatant to create a good quality work, the reality of the struggle being so rich and moving.

While Tố Hữu remained the leading figure, poets of the pre-1945 romantic generation had undergone profound change. Xuân Diệu, Chế Lan Viên, Tế Hanh, Huy Cận and others now depicted with warmth and skill the heroes and achievements of the advancing revolution. These masters were joined by a host of young poets, often still entangled in clumsy expression, many of them from worker or peasant families, or from minority ethnic groups, such as Nông Quốc Chấn and Bàn Tài Đoàn. From the South came poems by Thanh Hải, Giang Nam, and Thu Bồn, poems which had a profound resonance throughout the country. A generation of child poets was born, Trần Đăng Khoa being the most famous.

Novels, narratives, and short stories flourished. Pre-1954 veterans such as Nguyễn Công Hoan and Nguyễn Tuân kept on producing major works. Many new talents such as Nguyễn Đình Thi, Nguyễn Văn Bổng, Võ Huy Tâm and Nam Cao grew up during the first resistance, and after 1954, younger writers emerged such as Nguyên Ngọc, Nguyễn Khải, Chu Văn, Vũ Thị Thường and Bùi Đức ái. From the South came novels and short stories by Anh Đức, Nguyễn Thi, Phan Tứ and Nguyễn Trung Thành which depicted the arduous struggle with conviction. A new genre of literature for children also appeared, and the Kim Đồng Publishing House specializing in this genre had within 15 years (from 1958) published about 1,000 works.

A tidal wave of change produced by the revolution also swept through music and theatre. A large-scale revival of the national cultural legacy was undertaken, revolutionary songs were written, and symphonic poems were composed for traditional orchestras. European music, however, was not neglected. Composers tackled major musical forms including opera and symphony. Through its development, music made an effective contribution to the development of other artistic sectors such as theatre, cinema and dance.

Dance saw significant development with the revival of national choreographic traditions, particularly those of ethnic minorities, while renovated dance forms were also successfully introduced. All forms of theatre - *chèo*, *tuồng*, *cải lương* and spoken drama - were able to develop, once again by reviving traditional themes and techniques while also assimilating modern ideas.

In spite of material and technical difficulties, cinema was one of the areas which developed most rapidly after 1954 and especially after 1965. Newsreels, feature films of varying lengths, documentary and animated films - all these genres were represented, some works being awarded prizes at international festivals.

The literary movement closely followed the revolutionary movement, setting itself revolutionary tasks; during the war the motto was to "cover the sound of the bombs by singing," so helping to encourage revolutionary heroism among the broad masses. Literature and the arts in Việt Nam proudly fulfilled this mission. However, it was inevitable that we would have to wait for a time of peace for really great works to emerge.

Chapter X

COLLAPSE OF THE NEO-COLONIALIST REGIME

(1973 - 1975)

The Paris Agreement signed in January 1973 forced the United States to recognize the independence, sovereignty, unity and territorial integrity of Việt Nam, and the existence of the Provisional Revolutionary Government with its armed forces and its liberated areas. By 29 March 1973, all US troops had been withdrawn, and for the first time since 1859, no foreign soldier was stationed on Vietnamese territory.

This, however, did not mean that Washington had renounced its primary aim of destroying South Việt Nam's patriotic and revolutionary forces and retaining indefinitely a neo -colonialist regime in Sài Gòn. In Washington's eyes, these aims were perfectly feasible, all the more so as by then Washington and Beijing were working hand in glove to force the Vietnamese people to accept the country's indefinite partition. In this vision, South Việt Nam was to remain under US control while North Việt Nam, exhausted, would easily fall within the Chinese orbit. What could the Vietnamese revolution do in the face of this Washington-Beijing alliance?

The Neo-Colonialist Apparatus

The massive intervention by US forces from 1965 to 1973 had been just an emergency operation aimed at warding off imminent catastrophe. The basic neocolonialist objective remained — setting up a puppet military and police apparatus capable of suppressing the patriotic and revolutionary forces.

This military and police apparatus, carefully built up since 1954, had been considerably strengthened after 1969 in anticipation of the withdrawal of American troops and of several thousand American aircraft. The Sài Gòn army, police and administration had more than doubled in size since 1965.

Their equipment as well as method of operation had been totally overhauled. Tens of billions of dollars had been spent to this effect, the best experts from the US police, advisers tested in colonial wars such as the British General Robert Thompson, and all branches of US science and technology and so on, mobilized to set up a model neo-colonialist regime in South Việt Nam.

At the same time, Washington had done all it could to weaken the patriotic and revolutionary movement in Việt Nam. After 1968, the US command, which had refused Westmoreland's request for an additional 200,000 reinforcements, no longer sought to reconquer areas liberated by the NLF. Such classical military operations, conducted with vast amounts of manpower and material against an elusive enemy supported by the entire people, were too costly for the US forces.

The United States, armed with high technology, was in a position to wage another type of war. Against widespread popular resistance it had the means to apply total war by making life impossible across vast areas and destroying all life in regions controlled by the NLF and the PRG. For years, aircrafts, helicopters and heavy artillery had poured several million tonnes of bombs and shells on to the liberated zones of South Việt Nam. They had fired at anything that moved, and sprayed chemicals wherever they detected signs of plant life capable of feeding human beings. They had razed villages and hamlets to the ground, and aircrafts would immediately arrive to strafe the tiniest column of smoke even if it rose from totally uninhabited regions.

NLF-controlled areas were thus emptied of their inhabitants and transformed into virtual deserts pockmarked by millions of bomb craters, which became stagnant ponds teeming with mosquitoes. It was impossible to find a piece of wood or a brick to rebuild the huts or to cultivate a plot of rice or a garden. Millions of the inhabitants of rural South Việt Nam were thus "urbanized." The fighting was to cease for lack of combatants, the NLF having lost its reserves of militants and armed forces. The US command planned to kill two birds with one stone; those who had once lived in the liberated zone and participated in the struggle under NLF leadership, now streamed into the cities and concentration camps, finding no other means to survive than joining the

Thiệu army and police. In this way the latter were gradually reinforced as the GIs left, bringing their strength to over one million troops and 150,000 police.

Washington had taken care to extend the destruction to North Việt Nam, the great rear base of the Vietnamese revolution. The bombings between 1965 and 1968, then those of 1972 had destroyed almost every industrial establishment, numerous towns and cities, thousands of villages, all the bridges, most of the dams, and hundreds of schools, colleges and hospitals in North Việt Nam. In the last months of 1972, while the B52s were targeting the cities of North Việt Nam, a last-ditch effort was made to introduce a massive number of new weapons into South Việt Nam for Thiệu, who would thus control an airforce with almost 2,000 planes, ahead of France, Britain, Japan and West Germany, and with all the most up-to-date firepower.

In US-controlled cities and rural areas where the bloodiest repression had occurred, repeated "pacification" campaigns ended in the assassination of tens of thousands of those suspected of being NLF activists or sympathizers, and the arrest of several hundred thousand others.

Facing a PRG supposedly weakened by such destruction and the forcible concentration of several million inhabitants who could no longer count on any significant aid from North Việt Nam, itself ruined by intensive bombing, was a Sài Gòn administration with an imposing army and police strongly equipped and trained throughout the years by qualified US advisers. The situation appeared to be more favorable for Washington than in 1954 after the signing of the Geneva Agreements, when the Ngô Đình Diệm regime was still newly installed with a relatively small army and police, US domination in South Việt Nam remained incomplete and Sài Gòn's cadres and functionaries were still inexperienced.

From 1954 onwards tens of thousands of Sài Gòn officers were trained and indoctrinated by the Americans. Most of them were adventurers hungry for dollars, who amassed fortunes and influence thanks to American aid and the war. These officers had gradually taken on important political posts — president and vice-president of the republic, provincial governors, and so on. They had grown enormously rich through plunder in the course of military operations, trafficking in weapons and drugs, and had placed in the hands of their parents and relatives the most lucrative businesses such as import-export, hotels and prostitution. It was to this military, bureaucratic and trafficking oligarchy that Washington entrusted the management of the Sài Gòn regime and its neo-colonialist society.

As for the agents trained to carry out the dirty jobs — torture, killing, assassinations and arson — American intelligence services had recruited these from among the host of demobbed soldiers and delinquents who inhabited the cities. American experts taught them the latest techniques for interrogation and physical and psychological torture. A huge propaganda and ideological and cultural indoctrination apparatus had for years poured out slogans, films and images at the South Vietnamese population, aimed at erasing any trace of national or simply human feeling in themselves, in order to turn them into easily manipulated mercenaries.

*

*   *

Outwardly, the machine seemed to run smoothly. The GIs have gone, it was now sufficient simply to provide this military and police apparatus with weapons, dollars and advisers. It would carry out Washington's policy at much less cost than US forces, and Richard Nixon, then Gerald Ford, sought to find the few billion dollars a year necessary to keep the war machine on course. What would 2-3 billion dollars mean to the US budget and to the nation? The American public had been led to believe that following the withdrawal of the GIs, the US was no longer engaged in the Indochinese quagmire. Extracting a few billion dollars without alerting public opinion and Congress was a straightforward operation for White House and Pentagon professionals.

On 20 February 1975, USAID officials gave Representative Bella Abzug the following figures concerning US military aid to Thiệu:

1972	US$ 2,382,600,000
1973	US$ 2,270,500,000

Thus, in 1973, despite the signing of the Paris Agreement, US military aid had remained practically the same as in 1972, the high point of the war. Weapons supplied by the US surpassed in both quantity and quality those which simply had to be replaced because they had been put out of use. In this way, ultra-modern F5E planes were sent to Thiệu purportedly to replace outdated F5As.

To boost arms deliveries, the Pentagon used methods such as declaring weapons prices at far below their actual value, identifying them as coming under different budgetary allocations and so on. Once an "accounting error" was even found, allowing the discovery of a surplus of tens of millions of dollars which the American services promptly paid over to Sài Gòn.

The pay for Thiệu's soldiers, officers and police was guaranteed by American "economic" aid. The US ambassador in Sài Gòn, Graham Martin, went out of his way to provide Thiệu with an average of 700 million dollars a year for the period 1974-1975, a sum equal to that received by the Sài Gòn administration when half a million GIs were still stationed in South Việt Nam and the war was still at its height. Although weapons and equipment were supplied freely by the US, military expenditure still made up 60 percent of Thiệu's total budget.

Addressing an Asia and Pacific Study Group meeting convened by the US House of Representatives, Fred Branfman disclosed that in fact only 4 percent of the American aid to Indochina earmarked by President Nixon for fiscal year 1974 (12.4 million out of 2,900 million) was intended for reconstruction and development, and another 4 percent or so, 107.4 million dollars, for humanitarian purposes. Ninety-two percent of the aid requested by the administration in 1974 was to be used to continue the war, 72 percent of this for military assistance, while funds granted as economic aid and for "food for peace" also indirectly served war objectives.

Embezzlement of "food for peace" funds destined for other countries, loans exceeding 100 million dollars, and so-called multilateral aid through international organizations were used to boost the Sài Gòn budget. USAID in Sài Gòn confirmed that 83.6 percent of this budget came from American aid.

USAID, which administered the funds, failed to reduce its Sài Gòn staff of several hundred, while American military personnel and technicians, passing themselves off as civilians, took over the repair and operation of equipment (aircraft in particular) for the Thiệu army, and monitored the needs of the Sài Gòn army as operations continued. The so -called diplomatic staff serving at the US embassy in Sài Gòn were boosted by a new contingent of several hundred agents to occupy four consulates in each of the four military regions of South Việt Nam and the "consular offices" scattered throughout the country. The US ambassador had 145 assistants to monitor military operations, while the embassy military attaché (DAO) had at least 50 officers at his disposal.

The "diplomatic" labels were in fact nothing but camouflage for a complete general staff which led and commanded the Sài Gòn armed forces, drew up operational plans, and made decisions on strategy. Thiệu officers received their marching orders straight from American advisors. Nothing had changed with regard to the nature and conduct of the war. Both before and after the signing of the Paris Agreement, the war, which was claimed to have been "Vietnamized," remained an American war.

The War Drags On

The Paris Agreement advocated national reconciliation, and recognition of the third force and of two different administrations in South Việt Nam, each with its own territory. However, well supplied in arms and dollars, and assured of Washington's unconditional support, Thiệu reaffirmed his "four no's" policy: no to communism, no to entente with communism, and no to the partition of his territory. It was evident that the first three were mere statements of principle, but the fourth "no" did not depend on Thiệu's will alone, nor even on those of Nixon and Kissinger. The existence of the PRG, of territory under its control, and of its armed forces, were written in facts, on the terrain, and not simply in the text of the agreements. Neither a stroke of the pen nor a speech could erase it.

Although the US - Sài Gòn command had tried to fill the southern part of the country with 250 military sub -sectors and 10,000 posts, there remained countless localities where the PRG exercised power, forming in the rich and populous plains of central Việt Nam and the Mekong delta areas which dotted the country like a leopard's spots, preventing Thiệu and his Washington overlords from sleeping in peace. This permanent presence of the PRG, its armed forces, activists, and social and cultural organizations close to the areas still controlled by Thiệu, hung like the sword of Damocles over the Sài Gòn regime.

Right after the signing of the Paris Agreement, on 28 January 1973 Thiệu declared, "The cease-fire does not mean the end of the war". And he soon unleashed his columns of infantry and armoured vehicles and his air force against the liberated zones. As early as 29 January 1973, the US News and World Report pointed out that Sài Gòn forces were advancing towards disputed areas and those occupied by the liberation forces, to reduce the area of territory and population under NLF control. While US forces were no longer there to support the Sài Gòn troops, US air bases in Thailand and throughout the Pacific, with 140,000 men serving on them, could still serve as a "deterrent", especially since the Vietnamese people were repeatedly threatened with further attack by the US airforce (for instance the statement by US Defense Secretary James Schlesinger on 18 June 1973).

Immediately after the signing of the Paris Agreement, not content with just keeping his troops in the dark about it, Thiệu threw them against the liberated zones. On January 26, his troops attacked the port of Cửa Việt, Hải Lăng and Triệu Phong districts in Quảng Trị province near the 17th parallel. Southwest of Huế the army sought to retake

Highway 79 linking A Sầu to the former imperial capital. During the first months of 1973, Thiệu troops attacked various regions in Quảng Nam province, the port of Sa Huỳnh in Quảng Ngãi province (February 1973), along Highway 4, in Mỹ Tho province, and in the first days of March, Tống Lê Chân and Rạch Báp in Thủ Dầu Một province.

These surprise attacks in the weeks following the cease-fire announcement, involving considerable firepower, enabled the Sài Gòn army to take back some localities, and in a joint communiqué released in April 1973, Nixon and Thiệu waxed lyrical about the fighting morale and successes of the Sài Gòn armed forces.

These initial successes encouraged Thiệu to boost the scale of operations. He mustered forces the size of a division or more for single operations. From June to September 1973, 70 battalions of Sài Gòn troops attacked Chương Thiện province. From May to November two divisions operated in Bến Cát region, Thủ Dầu Một province, and one division southwest of Phú Bài. These encroachment operations, conducted openly or in the form of localized incursions, were accompanied by "pacification" campaigns in regions more or less controlled by Sài Gòn, particularly in heavily populated ones. Having become the main support for the neo-colonialist strategy since the Vietnamization of the war, pacification was intensified after the signing of the Paris Agreement with the aim of consolidating rear guard areas for the Sài Gòn army and the regime's strongholds.

All localities previously or newly reconquered by Sài Gòn were immediately put under the control of a repressive apparatus consisting of a network of military outposts and sectors with garrisons of regular troops, local security forces and civil guards, regular and special police forces, a puppet administration, undercover informers, and reactionary political organizations.

Also imposed on them was a whole series of "humanitarian", "cultural", "religious", "mutual aid", and other organizations which trapped each inhabitant in their nets. Twenty years' experience and input from numerous experts had helped the US neo-colonialists refine their methods of coercion. After having assassinated or imprisoned militants and sympathizers of the patriotic movement or simply those citizens who came under suspicion, and after having catalogued, filed and terrorized the people, Thiệu's agents press -ganged sections of the population into paramilitary groups and civil defence organizations which were then unleashed against the patriotic forces. The Sài Gòn army thus had cover during operations, and reserves from which to draw recruits.

In places where the Sài Gòn forces could not deploy their political and military machine to recruit in this way, they forced the population into concentration camps or their own sectors. More than 1.5 million people were concentrated thus in 1973 and 1974. Regions held by the PRG were bombed, raided and sabotaged by commando units. Washington's neo-colonialist policy in Việt Nam could only succeed through war; the Thiệu regime could only continue to survive if there was war. Strict implementation of the provisions of the Paris Agreement would have brought disaster for this policy and heralded the end of the Sài Gòn regime.

Decay of the Neo-Colonial System

The Thiệu regime and US neo -colonialist policy faced not only a well-entrenched PRG in liberated zones, but also growing opposition from people in the cities and rural areas under Sài Gòn's control. The signing of the Paris Agreement, the withdrawal of US forces, the policy of national reconciliation clearly defined by the PRG, and the formal recognition of the third force through the agreement all strengthened the broadly-based movement for peace, independence and democratic rights, and for the safeguarding of the nation's culture and customs, which had long been spreading among the urban masses.

Thiệu and his American masters had foreseen all this. In the month preceding the signing of the agreement, Thiệu had taken a series of measures designed to strengthen the system of repression already weighing heavily on the population. A rapid succession of new decree - laws were enacted to further curtail whatever limited freedoms remained.

In August 1972, a decree-law abolished the system of elected village and hamlet heads, and ruled that from then on such notables would be chosen by the administration. Seven thousand officers were appointed to these posts, with 10,000 others assigned to security duties in the villages. Also in August 1972, Decree-Law 007 imposed on the press such drastic restrictions that only 18 out of the 40 existing newspapers were able to continue publication. Many of those which survived were controlled and financed by the administration itself. As of September 1972, newspapers had to deposit 20 million piastres as a security fee which provided for any fines to be paid on actions that did not please the authorities; news reports unfavourable to the regime could earn their writers a five-year jail sentence and 5 million piastre fine. These measures caused the more ethical papers to close down.

Seizures became more frequent, making it impossible for newspapers to cover their costs without government assistance.

A decree-law on local security banned all strikes and demonstrations and authorized the police to open fire on demonstrators. Decree-Law 090 authorized the police to arrest all suspects. Barely one month before the signing of the Paris Agreement, a new decree-law imposed such drastic conditions on political parties that only four of the 20 existing groups were able to survive.

Strict implementation of the Paris Agreement which required the safeguarding of democratic liberties would have been fatal for the Saigon regime. On 28 January 1973, Thiệu issued the following warning in a televised broadcast:

"A cease-fire on the ground means maintaining the status quo. Wherever our administration, our army and our people stand, we reign supreme. All depends on us there. We will apply our laws, our administration; everything will be done as before and there will be no change."

There was to be no national reconciliation or concord, and no entente either with communists or neutralists. The "constitution", with anti-communism as its basic principle, and all fascist laws would remain in force. Washington took care to increase financial and technical aid in order to boost the strength of Thiệu's police force up from 120,000 to 150,000 men.

The Paris Agreement had clearly stipulated that all political prisoners were to be released. Thiệu's response was to massacre a certain number before the cease -fire, then transform others into common law prisoners and cynically declare that no political prisoners were being detained in his jails. Witnesses from the most diverse circles, American journalists and politicians, religious figures of many nationalities, and some of the world's most prominent individuals all argued in vain, evidence and facts in hand, to demonstrate the existence of about 200, 000 political prisoners in Sài Gòn's prisons and detention camps. Thiệu, backed by Washington, continued to deny it.

He also continued to increase the number of arrests and torture not only of supporters of the PRG but also the third force. Students, intellectuals, Catholic priests and Buddhist monks were savagely clubbed in the streets, arrested en masse, deported or tortured. To whoever was willing to listen to him, Thiệu bluntly declared: "No one who dares declare himself a neutralist or pro-communist shall survive more than five minutes" (12 October 1973).

To bolster his rule, Thiệu applied new measures designed to concentrate all power in his own hands. He had already defeated his sole rival in the presidential elections, Nguyễn Cao Kỳ, in 1971.

Elections to the Sài Gòn "Senate" held in August 1973 were an opportunity for Thiệu to eliminate the members who opposed him. He put one of his men, Trần Văn Lắm, at the head of a double ticket presented by the "Democratic Party". Having placed his agents in both houses, Thiệu proposed a modification to the "constitution" which authorized him to stand for the presidential election in 1975 for a five - year term instead of four, appoint members of the Supreme Court (the houses could only put forward names), and appoint the governors of provinces, cities and districts.

Reshuffling his government in October 1974, Thiệu created a series of "commissariats" directly under his authority, adding a "leadership council" of which Thiệu became the president. The council and commissariats settled all important matters in both domestic and foreign affairs over the heads of the ministers and even the prime minister, who thus became a puppet of the puppets. The prime minister, Trần Thiện Khiêm, was unable to conceal his bitterness. A series of demotions affecting 17 generals and promotions - 39 officers became generals - enabled Thiệu to eliminate those suspected of objecting to his personal authority and introduce his most faithful agents into key posts in the army, police and administration. Nguyễn Cao Kỳ's supporters, as well as those influenced by the French, were ousted in favour of people trained entirely in the United States.

Apart from military aid, Washington attempted to bolster Thiệu through substantial economic aid. They wanted to supply Thiệu with a sum equivalent to that received by Sài Gòn during the war years, including the amount spent by American troops in South Việt Nam. It is estimated that 250, 000 jobs were created through the stationing in Việt Nam of the US expeditionary corps, providing the Thiệu regime with about half its foreign currency income (UPI, 27 January 1974). On average, the US granted Thiệu 700 to 800 million dollars of economic aid a year, as disclosed by the US ambassador, Graham Martin.

To get these aid projects through Congress, Washington and Sài Gòn made loud noises about miraculous reconstruction and development plans, Martin evoked memories of the Marshall Plan which he said had enabled Europe to rise from the ruins of the Second World War and start its astonishing economic development. Thiệu, for his part, presented a six-month plan for rehabilitation and reconstruction, then went to

Washington to beg for dollars. Back in Sài Gòn in May 1973, he launched a seven-year plan for post-war economic reconstruction and development (1974-80) with three main objectives: reconstruction, resettlement of displaced persons, and intensive exploitation of natural resources, with particular emphasis on rehabilitation of agriculture and investment in industry and services, while making special efforts to attract foreign capital by offering concessions.

On 26 March 1973, "Peasants' Day," Thiệu called for the implementation of a five -year plan for agriculture aimed in particular at reclaiming half a million hectares left unutilized due to the war, producing 3 million cubic metres of timber for home consumption and export, and catching one million tonnes of fish, double the 1973 figure. Development of agriculture, forestry and fisheries, he claimed, would provide exports valued at 400 million dollars a year, meeting all the country's foreign currency needs.

Thiệu also raised the possibility of holding an international conference which would decide on mobilities for aid to be granted to the Sài Gòn regime to assist economic development. During the first weeks after the signing of the Paris Agreement, Sài Gòn witnessed the arrival of many American, British, French and Japanese businessmen. South Việt Nam has abundant and varied natural resources (rice, rubber, forests, marine products and oil), and a large and skilled work force paid only half as much as, for example, those of Hong Kong or Singapore - always an attractive prospect for foreign capital. The docile nature of the Sài Gòn regime also constituted a good guarantee. The infrastructure network (communications, ports and docks), built due to war requirements, was good.

South Việt Nam could have enjoyed extraordinary economic development given the aid it received from the United States - more than any other country. But from the first months of 1973, the economic situation clearly went from bad to worse. On 21 August 1973, Thiệu himself was forced to acknowledge that "solving our economic and social problems is proving difficult." Many indicators pointed to economic decline: lower industrial and agricultural output, soaring prices and inflation, unemployment worsening daily, and shortages of rice, fuel and consumer goods.

Sài Gòn's industry had stagnated by this time, stifled by imports of foreign goods, especially American and Japanese. Its industrial production accounted for barely 10 percent of total output, and many enterprises simply made semi-manufactured products from imported raw materials.

Many of these industries were in the hands of French businesses or Chinese from Taiwan. In the first three months of 1973, the textile factories produced 2,000 tonnes less than for the same period the previous year. The situation was roughly the same for other sectors such as sugar, cigarettes, and soft drinks. Vietnamese industrialists, caught between soaring prices for fuel and other imported raw materials and the declining purchasing power of currency had to close a large number of their enterprises. By April 1974, about half the total number were forced to close down.

With devaluation going hand in hand with price rises, the situation deteriorated by the month. During 1973, the Sài Gòn piastre was devalued ten times. Whereas the exchange rate in 1955 had been 35 piastres to the dollar, by 5 January 1974, it had shot up to 560. During 1973, prices increased 100 or 200 percent, often more for vitally needed products. On 5 August 1973, the Sài Gòn administration increased the prices of three basic products at one stroke: 55 percent for rice, 60 percent for sugar and 76 percent for petrol. On November 20, the price of petrol rose another 50 percent. On November 23, the Sài Gòn newspaper *Độc Lập* (Independence) wrote:

"To catch up with petrol, the prices of almost all other commodities, especially vitally needed products, are simply rocketing. The price of rice, a precious and costly commodity which remains the chief concern of the people of Sài Gòn, is rising sharply. Immediately after the rise in fuel prices, 100 kilos of rice went up to 54,000 piastres (as against 7,600 at the end of 1972). The price rises have also affected 900 other items."

The budget figure reached astronomical heights, showing in early 1973 a 116 billion piastre deficit; this had increased by a further 78 billion piastres by the end of the fiscal year. The 1974 budget projected an income of 453 billion piastres and an expenditure of 630 billion. The amount of money in circulation shot up from 51 billion piastres in January 1966 to 202.8 billion piastres by January 1973. Foreign currency reserves, estimated at 200 million dollars in 1972, dropped to 100 million dollars during 1973. The official rate of inflation, 65 percent in 1973, reached 16 percent in the first two months of 1974, an annual rate of 96 per ent. In 1974 , the dollar could be officially exchanged for 685 piastres, and much higher on the black market.

Thiệu tried to squeeze as many dollars out of Washington as he could. But Nixon, then entangled in the Watergate affair and the economic difficulties facing the United States, could only get 500 million dollars from Congress in 1972. Thiệu toured Western capitals, but his quest was in vain. He tried to profiteer from the country's resources by

offering extremely attractive terms to oil and another companies, but received only 51 million dollars from American, French, Japanese and Canadian oil companies, and a few million more from other investments.

To balance his budget, Thiệu resorted to raising taxes and duties:

"Since the beginning of 1973, all taxes have increased: commercial tax, licenses and income tax have tripled. Transport tax has increased 15 times, other taxes have doubled, some have quadrupled, for instance that on print shops."

On 1 July 1973, Thiệu instituted a new tax VAT (Value-Added Tax), which applied to all products. According to the Sài Gòn press, over a period of 40 days 1, 200 million piastres were thus extorted from the population. Vehement protest from all social strata caused the Sài Gòn administration to back down and remove the tax from a number of products. On 22 November 1973, Thiệu increased taxes on more than 200 products. Early in 1973, a litre of petrol cost 40 piastres, including a special tax of 20 piastres. One year later, the price had shot up to 240 piastres and the tax to 100. Sugar, taxed at 10 per cent, cost 200 piastres a kilogram early in 1973 and 600 one year later. The same price escalation was true for tobacco, beer, and cigarettes. Rates went up 20 percent, and taxes on small traders doubled. In 1974, Thiệu planned the raising of taxes in rural areas which had until then only provided some 10 percent of the budget.

Drastic measures were enacted against all delays in payment and undeclared revenue. A fiscal investigation department was set up, and tax-collecting commandos conducted actual "military-fiscal" operations and extortions, in which tax-collecting agents plundered huge amounts of money from enterprises and individuals. Sài Gòn newspapers covered the public outcry in full. On 24 June 1974, *Điện Tín* (Telegraph) wrote:

"Now and then the State dreams up a new tax. Whatever he does, wherever he goes, the citizen runs into the tax-collector. You will be rooted out, even if you barricade yourselves at home. Ordinary people toil from dawn till dusk without being able to earn the rice necessary to feed their children, just to enable high-placed lay abouts to wallow in their air-conditioned rooms, cigars in their mouths, racking their brains for ways to invent new taxes!"

The disastrous effects of the economic situation on people's lives was clear. Two and a half million were unemployed by the end of 1974 according to official estimates, and 3.5 million according to other estimates. In central Việt Nam (Đà Nẵng, Quảng Tín, Quảng Ngãi and

Quy Nhơn), about 50 percent of workers were jobless. Hundreds of thousands of abandoned children wandered the cities where begging, prostitution and drug addiction were rife. More and more people, often whole families, committed suicide. The fabric of Sài Gòn society was rapidly decaying.

One did not need great insight to pin down the prime cause of this decay. The withdrawal of US troops had left a huge gap in the regime's resources, but the pursuit of war had always been, and remained, the main cause of economic and social decline and of the general crisis shaking the society of Sài Gòn. For the first time in South Việt Nam, which formerly produced more than enough rice, people could be seen dying from starvation. How could people reclaim half a million hectares, expand forest exploitation, attract foreign investment, and develop local industries if Thiệu, at the instigation of the Nixon-Kissinger-Ford team, was intensifying encroachment and pacification operations and concentrating more and more people away from their native districts? The war was till being masterminded by the Americans, but now that it had been "Vietnamized", its burden from the point of view of manpower as well as finance was increasingly falling upon the South Vietnamese population.

Beginning of the End

The cease-fire, releasing of prisoners, freedom of movement between zones in Việt Nam, democratic liberates, reconciliation and national concord, recognition of the third force and of course, recognition of the existence of the PRG and the liberated areas - all were ignored by Thiệu. As for Nixon, right after the signing of the Paris Agreement, he had declared that he recognized the Thiệu administration as "the sole legitimate government of South Việt Nam". More than 20 years after the Geneva Conference, these words of Nixon's echoed in a sinister way, similar statements made by Eisenhower following the signing of the agreements on Indochina in 1954.

For Nixon, Ford and Kissinger, the only acceptable outcome was crushing, or at least stifling, the PRG, and a neo-colonialist regime obedient to Washington remaining in power in Sài Gòn. It could be expected that after the signing of the 1973 Paris Agreement, events would unfold as they had following the Geneva Conference of 1954. Certainly in the intervening 20 years Washington had had plenty of time to set up a huge military and police apparatus in South Việt Nam. But American leaders were badly mistaken if they imagined that the death and destruction they had sown on Vietnamese territory had so exhausted and weakened the Vietnamese people that they had become entirely powerless.

In 1954, the Vietnamese resistance had had to evacuate all its armed forces and cadres from South Việt Nam and regroup them in the North, leaving a population without weapons or fighters to face an imperialist enemy. In 1975, the RPG was there, with its territories, and its armed forces. The contrast with 1954 was fundamental. The South Vietnamese population, like that of North Việt Nam, had been tested in battle. The threat of US weapons and soldiers no longer intimidated anyone, even coupled with pressure from Beijing.

In the months following the signing of the Paris Agreement, Sài Gòn troops armed with modern equipment were able to launch some surprise attacks and reap some successes, giving them a morale boost. But the PRG, liberation armed forces and the people of South Việt Nam were not willing to stand by with arms folded in the face of repeated violations of the Paris Agreement, violations which posed a serious threat to peace and the security of all.

Tight police control and fascist measures stepped up after January 1975 did not prevent the people in Thiệu -held areas from waging a political and social struggle which surpassed previous actions, in both scale and duration. The signing of the Paris Agreement, the withdrawal of American troops, the presence of PRG and of its armed forces, and the policy of reconciliation and national concord all helped spur the struggle of an urban population which had suffered so much from the state of war and Thiệu's fascist dictatorship. The economic decline increased the combativeness of the masses, given further impetus by the defeats suffered by Sài Gòn troops. Thiệu yet again intensified the arrests and torture. Demonstrations and strikes spread, with the participation of all social strata. Functionaries and military personnel of the Thiệu administration often joined these actions or showed open sympathy with his opponents.

Immediately after the signing of the Paris Agreement, and despite all the efforts of the Americans and Thiệu to stop the text of the accord from being disseminated, a vast movement to release political prisoners was launched. Few people in South Việt Nam did not have a relative, friend or brother detained in one of the many prisons to be found in every province. While the struggle was waged mainly by working people under NLF leadership, other social strata gradually joined the fight, particularly students, intellectuals and religious people, whose political consciousness and spirit of protest had grown as they witnessed what was happening.

The scale of US military, economic and ideological intervention led people who, for years had remained aloof from the national community, to become gradually aware of the need to fight to save the nation, its traditions, customs, and society as a whole from total destruction. The "third force" thus emerged, with more and more frequent demonstrations. In the prisons their force activists joined with revolutionaries, turning Thiệu's jails into strong bases for the policy of national reconciliation. The same changes occurred among Vietnamese residing abroad, particularly in France, where supporters of the PRG and many other groups, including some once overtly pro-American, united to demand strict implementation of the Paris Agreement and to condemn Washington's and Sài Gòn's actions.

Growing opposition compelled Thiệu to reshuffle his government several times and to stop levying VAT on a large numbers of commodities. In June 1974, Thiệu barred members of the administration, army and police from joining political groups. Opposition even spread to the House of Representatives. In July, 58 of its members signed a petition demanding answers from the government on the implementation of the Paris Agreement, on bribery, smuggling and other social evils. Committees and organizations were set up to demand implementation of the agreement and the release of political prisoners.

In July, 300 Catholic priests meeting in the town of Cần Thơ issued a condemnation of corruption in the Thiệu administration. The movement against corruption spread, while Buddhist leaders condemned persecution of their co-religionists by the administration which was thus following in Ngô Đình Diệm's steps, and called for the safeguarding of peace and the implementation of the Paris Agreement. In September, 30, 000 people in Huế came into the streets to demand that Thiệu renounce the use of force and answer charges of corruption leveled against him and his wife.

Significantly, the Catholic church, which had firmly and consistently backed Ngô Đình Diệm then Nguyễn Văn Thiệu, gradually became alienated from the Sài Gòn administration. The bulk of the Catholic faithful became gradually more aware as events unfolded, and no longer obeyed the hierarchy en masse as they had before; young priests openly stood up for national independence and social progress, and joined with revolutionary militants in the prisons.

Boycotts of the news reports issued by the administration, demonstrations by journalists, statements of opposition by lawyers, a march of 5, 000 Catholics in the Sài Gòn suburbs, a 17,000-strong protest meeting in the provincial capital of Quảng Ngãi, and an appeal from 44 "deputies" condemning the government's repression of bonzes, all were ways in which mass anger continued to grow. Washington became increasingly worried. While Thiệu clung to personal power, gradually eliminating all those who disagreed with him, US leaders, for their part, continued to gather together as many reactionary forces as possible under his baton. Pressure was put on Thiệu to remove those who had been most compromised. Under pressure from both popular opposition and the US, in October 1973 Thiệu had to order the resignation of four of his closest ministers, among them Hoàng Đức Nhã, minister for information, who had been disgraced by the press.

This, however, failed to appease public opinion. At the end of 1974, the trial of three newspapers accused of publishing a communiqué accusing Thiệu of corruption alerted public opinion. To prevent all demonstrations the day of the trial - which the tribunal had had to postpone - Thiệu mobilized no fewer than 40,000 policemen and proclaimed a state of siege. A protest demonstration against the trial attracted tens of thousands, violent scuffles erupted, and many prominent personalities were injured. Sài Gòn newspapers, despite seizures and prohibitions, published charges against members of the government. At Christmas, college and high school students demonstrated against the government's education policies, and in January students again took to the streets to demand an end to repression and conscription. For their part, trade unions held a special meeting to fight lay-offs, support the right to strike, and back demands to counter rocketing inflation and increasing unemployment.

Two years after the signing of the Paris Agreement, Thiệu found himself politically more isolated than ever. The movement pressing for the implementation of the Paris Agreement, for peace and national reconciliation was irresistible. The catchphrase, "Down with Thiệu, set up a Sài Gòn government ready to implement the Paris Agreement" was supported by almost all social strata, political groups and religious bodies. More than ever the policies pursued by Washington and its Sài Gòn agents ran counter to public opinion and denied the most deeply - felt aspirations of the Vietnamese people.

*

* *

Strict implementation of the Paris Agreement would have led to political confrontation between the coalition of national forces and pro-American forces. This was something Nixon and Kissinger, then Ford, as well as Thiệu and Sài Gòn's war profiteers, wanted to avoid at all costs. They chose to pursue military confrontation, still believing that the United States' technical and financial supremacy would make up for their political and ideological failings. The moderation shown by the PRG during the first months after the signing of the Paris Agreement had created an illusion, Washington and Thiệu perceiving this as assign of weakness.

The PRG had disseminated the text of the Paris Agreement widely among the population, hoping the other parties, having drawn the necessary lessons from past experience, would eventually resolve to pursue a policy of peace and national reconciliation. PRG negotiators had, on many occasions, made concrete proposals for a cease-fire, release of political prisoners, application of democratic rights, the setting up of a Council for National Reconciliation and Concord with three parties, and for resolving the issues of general elections and demobilization of armed forces on all sides.

At Washington's instigation, Thiệu continued to ignore the PRG's proposals, and continued its encroachment operations against areas under PRG control. The Lê Đức Thọ - Kissinger talks in Paris in May 1973, then the issuing of a joint communiqué in which the signatories pledged to adopt concrete measures for a thorough implementation of the Paris Agreement, did nothing to change the aggressiveness of Sài Gòn forces and US officials. On June 18, James Schlesinger, US Defence Secretary, spoke of possibly resuming the bombing of North Việt Nam.

In July 1973, while reaffirming its will to implement the Paris Agreement, the liberation armed forces command in Công Tum had been forced to issue a warning: if Sài Gòn troops used air force and artillery and large infantry units against liberated areas, they would encounter an appropriate response. Thiệu continued to order encroachment operations in the eastern Nam Bộ province of Chương Thiện, and raids and pacification operations increased in areas under his control. Meanwhile, US reconnaissance planes still flew over North Việt Nam.

In Tây Ninh province, in the Central Highlands, in the Mekong delta and on the plains of central Việt Nam, Thiệu conducted division level operations, while his air force bombed many localities in liberated zones. Washington even sent an aircraft carrier to cruise off North Việt Nam's coast. During this period, the US command also intensified its bombing of liberated areas of Cambodia.

Faced with the enemy's determination to pursue the war, on 15 October 1973, the liberation armed forces command ordered its troops and the population to fight back against all acts of war by the Sài Gòn forces, in order to defend the lives and property of the population and ensure the implementation of the Paris Agreement. The order made it clear that the liberation forces would not be content with only responding where the enemy attacked, but would themselves choose the time and place of retaliation.

Kissinger immediately flew to Beijing and a Sino-American communiqué was released, declaring that in view of the grave situation, it was important that the two sides meet regularly to exchange view on issues of common concern.

Thiệu, far from ordering a halt to his operations, sent bombers deep into liberated areas, and took advantage of typhoons to intensify "pacification." On November 6, liberation forces' artillery issued a stern warning by shelling the Biên Hòa airfield where the enemy bombers were based. Also in November, seven Sài Gòn planes were shot down over Quảng Đức province. In December, while the bombing of liberated areas by the Sài Gòn air force was being intensified, the liberation forces set fire to fuel tanks in Sài Gòn and destroyed munitions stores near Plây Cu.

The year 1974 began with bellicose statements by Thiệu and Schlesinger, while the Pentagon sent Thiệu ultra -modern F5Es. Nixon asked Congress to double military aid to Thiệu. Sài Gòn planes even strafed the headquarters of the International Control Commission and localities chosen for the release of captured personnel. On January 19, Chinese naval units, with the consent of the 7th Fleet, dislodged Sài Gòn troops from the Hoàng Sa (Paracel) Islands off the Vietnamese coast. This was also a challenge to Vietnamese liberation forces, and the establishing of a Chinese position aimed at further expansion towards Southeast Asia. Nevertheless, the response of the liberation forces and the people became stronger every day.

In February, patriotic forces attacked Quảng Ngãi airfield. In March, they inflicted severe losses on Border Ranger Battalion 62 in Kontum province, halving its strength. In April, Tống Lê Chân, the starting point for many encroachment operations, was encircled and shelled and had to be evacuated by the enemy. Thiệu ordered the bombing of Lộc Ninh and other localities for several days, and ordered the indefinite postponement of negotiations at La Celle Saint Cloud. Nixon and Kissinger attempted to persuade the US Congress to substantially increase military and economic aid to Thiệu, using the pretext of a "moral commitment" to the Sài Gòn puppets. This commitment had materialized after the signing of the Paris Agreement in the dispatch of a million tonnes of bombs and shells, 1,100 tanks and armoured vehicles, 300 artillery pieces, 700 aircrafts, and 200 naval and river units. American equipment and dollars had enabled Thiệu to conduct, in little more than a year, hundreds of thousands of encroachment operations, artillery shelling and aerial bombardments.

A large operation was launched in May 1974 in Bến Cát with three divisions supported by F5E planes piloted by Americans, but the response of the liberation forces in the three months from May to July inflicted on Sài Gòn the loss of 8,000 troops, 182 tanks and armoured vehicles and 34 aircrafts. An officer from Sài Gòn's 5th Division declared to *Newsweek* on 13 May 1974 that morale, and not equipment, was the biggest headache for the Sài Gòn command. By the end of the first three months of 1974, the Sài Gòn army had lost 175,000 men, killed or wounded. Desertions multiplied. In these conditions, the harder Thiệu threw his troops against the liberated zones, the greater their defeats and the faster their disintegration, and not even massive inputs of dollars and weapons could reverse the situation. In July and August 1974, on the coastal plains of central Việt Nam, the Sài Gòn forces lost 160 outposts and military positions which served as jumping -off points for attacks against the liberated zones. Đà Nẵng and Biên Hòa airfields were shelled, and the population of 16 villages, two districts and 16 concentration sectors rose in revolt and liberated themselves. The situation was rapidly deteriorating for the Sài Gòn forces, whether in the Central Highlands, central Việt Nam, or in the Mekong delta. The liberation forces gradually eliminated all outposts set up illegally in the months following the signing of the Paris Agreement.

US General John Murray, commander of the DAO in Sài Gòn, admitted that Sài Gòn's losses in 1973 and 1974 were in excess of 100,000 men, while Thiệu himself acknowledged that "we have lost numerous villages, districts and even one city" (AP, 29 January 1975). The PRG for its part claimed 255,000 men killed, wounded, or put to rout on the Sài Gòn side. While Ford and Kissinger tried to persuade Congress to vote on supplementary assistance for Thiệu, *Time* wrote on 17 January 1975 that, according to Western military sources, the morale of the Sài Gòn army, more than any lack of military supplies, would be the decisive factor in the months to come.

The Great Spring 1975 Victory

Instead of implementing the Paris Agreement, Nixon, Ford, Kissinger and Thiệu had chosen to enforce a military solution. But it was in the military area that they were to suffer the heaviest and most bitter defeats. The defeats of 1974 had not diminished Thiệu's aggressiveness, while the liberation forces, encouraged by their victories from December 1974 onwards, successively attacked the military sectors and outposts from where encroachment and pacification operations were being conducted.

In December 1974, the liberation forces launched offensives in several provinces, particularly in Phước Long (capital Phước Bình), northwest of Saigon, on the road leading to the Central Highlands, in the western Mekong delta provinces of Rạch Giá and Cần Thơ, and in Bình Tuy province. The regular forces of the liberation army, fielding powerful weapons, wiped out fortified bunkers and positions while guerrillas attacked administrative and paramilitary organizations. On 6 January 1975, the provincial capital of Phước Long was liberated, 3, 000 Sài Gòn troops were killed or wounded and 650 others taken prisoner, 12 heavy artillery pieces captured, and 10 aircrafts shot down. For the first time, a whole province including its capital was liberated. The loss of Phước Long fanned public opinion in Việt Nam and throughout the world, while Thiệu and the US administration tried to gain credence through a loud but fruitless propaganda campaign.

Early in March, attacks were concentrated on the Central Highlands and the northern provinces of Quảng Trị, Thừa Thiên, Quảng Đà, Quảng Tín, Quảng Ngãi and Quảng Đức. From March 5-9, fighting was intense along strategic highways leading towards provincial capitals in the Central Highlands, Highway 14 —the vital lifeline linking Quy Nhơn with Plây Cu t and Highway 21 linking Ninh Hòa with Buôn Ma Thuột. Important military sub -sectors and posts controlling access to Buôn Ma Thuột were overrun.

On March 10, after a sustained artillery barrage, the liberation forces, ignoring outer defenses, swept into the centre of Buôn Ma Thuột where the enemy headquarters were located. The command's radio stations were quickly neutralized, paralyzing the enemy. The occupation of the airfield and munitions stores completely demoralized the Saigon troops who took to flight. On March 11, the town was liberated. Two thousand men were taken prisoner and 25 artillery pieces and 200 vehicles captured. Helicopters came from Sài Gòn to fly out two American advisors taken prisoner. Puppet General Lê Trung Tường was wounded, and Colonel Vũ Thế Quang killed. Sài Gòn's 23rd Infantry Division was wiped out. The enemy air force proved entirely powerless. Sài Gòn attempted a counter - offensive by massing troops at Phước An, northwest of Buôn Ma Thuột, but this centre was soon overrun by the liberation forces. With Buôn Ma Thuột, the entire province of Đắc Lắc was liberated. The routed Sài Gòn troops did not have time to destroy the huge munitions depot in Buôn Ma Thuột (1.5 km long, almost 1 km wide), which provided obvious proof that the enemy was losing not due to lack of weapons.

The sudden fall of Buôn Ma Thuột came as a painful shock for Thiệu and his Washington bosses. The best Sài Gòn units were easily put to rout, abandoning their equipment, and the people in many villages rose in revolt, completely isolating provincial capitals, leaving the liberation army's regular forces free to launch direct attacks on major centres.

The liberation forces had thus proved capable of attacking major centres in the Central Highlands which were already isolated. The only course of action left open to Sài Gòn was to order a general retreat of forces stationed in Công Tum, Plây Cu, and Phú Bổn (Cheo Reo). The retreat took place in an atmosphere of panic in the direction of Tuy Hòa along Highway 7, regular forces and armoured vehicles mixed up with administrative services, paramilitary forces, soldiers' families and the administration's agents. Sài Gòn soldiers and police forced part of the population to follow them, destroying houses and spreading the rumour that the "Việt Cộng" would massacre anyone who stayed behind. This mass exodus was also being used as shield by the Sài Gòn troops, for the enemy

TÂY NGUYÊN CAMPAIGN

(4.3-3.4.1975)

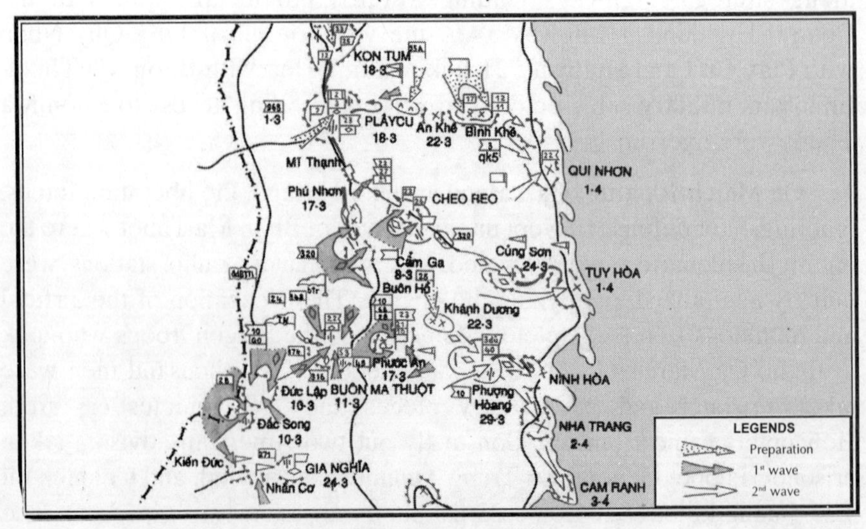
KON TUM
18-3
PLÂYCU
18-3
An Khê
22-3
Bình Khê
qk5
QUI NHƠN
1-4
Mĩ Thạnh
Phú Nhơn
17-3
CHEO REO
Củng Sơn
24-3
TUY HÒA
1-4
Cẩm Ga
8-3
Buôn Hồ
Khánh Dương
22-3
Phước An
17-3
NINH HÒA
Đức Lập
10-3
BUÔN MA THUỘT
11-3
Phượng Hoàng
29-3
Đắc Song
10-3
NHA TRANG
2-4
Kiến Đức
GIA NGHĨA
24-3
Nhẫn Cơ
CAM RANH
3-4
LEGENDS
Preparation
1st wave
2nd wave

command knew quite well that the liberation forces would not fire on the population. Seven thousand soldiers and officers in flight, along with 700 vehicles and 91 artillery pieces, were captured by the patriotic forces.

The Central Highlands were virtually completely liberated by March 19. The outer defence posts of Kiến Đức and An Khê fell on March 22 and 23. In less than three weeks, Sài Gòn had lost an area of 40,000 square kilometres with more than 800,000 inhabitants belonging to 30 different ethnic groups, and important natural resources. The Central Highlands stretch for over 500 kilometres from the 17th parallel southward to within 100 kilometres of Sài Gòn, and borders the liberated areas of Cambodia as well as southern Laos. It was a strategic area of prime importance not only for South Việt Nam but also for Indochina as a whole. Ever since 1954 Washington had wanted to turn the Central Highlands into a strategic base, a political bastion by putting the various ethnic groups against one another, and an economic base of some significance.

In Quảng Trị province, guerrilla actions launched on March 8, coordinated with popular uprising in villages, quickly led to the elimination of many military outposts, the liberation of numerous villages and the isolation of the provincial capital which was finally liberated on March 19. Six hundred and fifty Sài Gòn soldiers were put out of action while many officials, soldiers and policemen of the Thiệu administration surrendered and went over the PRG.

HUẾ - ĐÀ NẴNG CAMPAIGN

(21 - 29.3.1975)

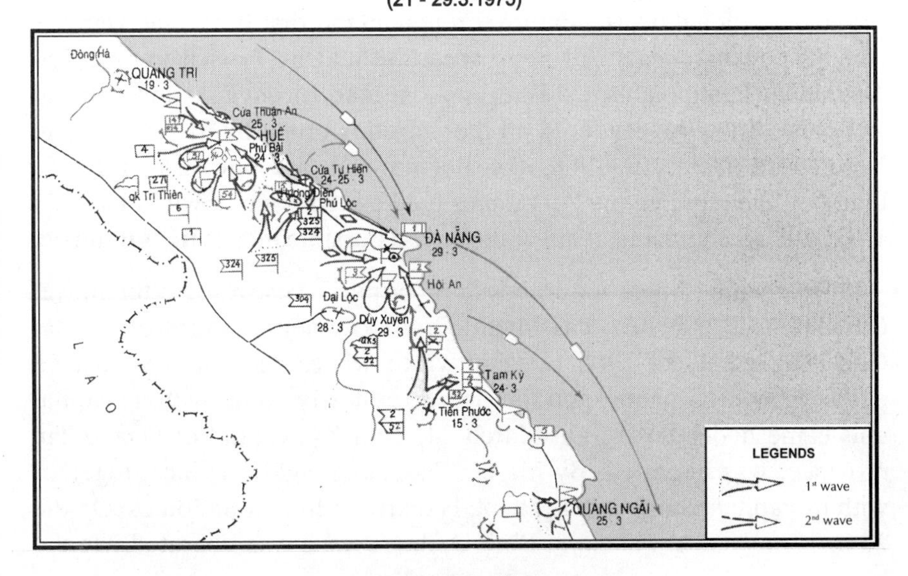
Đông Hà
QUẢNG TRỊ
19 · 3
Cửa Thuận An
25 · 3
HUẾ
Phú Bài
24 · 3
Cửa Tư Hiền
24-25 · 3
Phú Lộc
qk Trị Thiên
ĐÀ NẴNG
29 · 3
Hội An
Đại Lộc
Duy Xuyên
29 · 3
28 · 3
Tam Kỳ
24 · 3
Tiên Phước
15 · 3
QUẢNG NGÃI
25 · 3
L A O
LEGENDS
1st wave
2nd wave

During the same period, the people of Thừa Thiên province, together with the liberation army regular forces, liberated the six districts surrounding the former royal capital of Huế. Huế was thus isolated, with the Huế-Đà Nẵng highway cut, particularly at the Hải Vân Pass. On March 19, liberation forces attacked the command post of the Saigon 1st Infantry Division which defended the city, the Mang Cá military sector and Tây Lộc airfield. On March 22 and 23, the outer defensive positions around Huế were attacked, and on March 24, the Phú Bài airfield was subjected to fierce shelling. On March 25, the liberation forces moved into the city and the enemy hurriedly withdrew to the coastal sand dunes on the other side of the Thuận An estuary. The PRG flag flew over Huế, the former capital of the Nguyễn kings. On March 26, the city was completely liberated with its houses, public services, and monuments almost intact. In their hasty retreat, Sài Gòn troops ran into resistance from the people and some agents, soldiers and officials of the puppet regime who stopped them from carrying out the planned destruction of many facilities. On March 27 and 28, the Sài Gòn forces regrouped on the seashore but failed to board ships sent to take them away, which were being pounded by liberation artillery. Many surrendered, totally exhausted.

The battle of Thừa Thiên-Huế cost Sài Gòn the whole of the 1st Infantry Division; 15,000 men were taken prisoner, among them 100 senior officers, and 1,000 vehicles and 300 artillery pieces were captured.

Thừa Thiên province, with an area of 5,670 square kilometres and 600,000 inhabitants, and its capital Huế, a political, cultural, and historical centre of great significance, constituted together with Quảng Trị an operational nerve centre. Throughout the first Indochina war, the Huế -Đà Nẵng sector had been securely held by French troops. The Americans had transformed Huế into a military stronghold and political and cultural centre, rendered all the more important by its proximity to North Việt Nam. In 1968, the people and patriotic armed forces liberated the city and the Americans paid a high price to win it back. In 1972, the US command again deployed all possible means in its defence.

Meanwhile, liberation forces in other provinces were on the move. On March 20, An Lộc was liberated, 70 kilometres northwest of Sài Gòn. The whole of Bình Long province where An Lộc was located passed into PRG hands, and the province of Tây Ninh, with its capital thus came under threat. On March 24, Tam Kỳ, capital of Quảng Tín province, was liberated. By March 25, Quảng Ngãi province, together with its capital, came under the total control of liberation forces. On the 26th, Tam Quan township in Bình Định province was liberated. On the

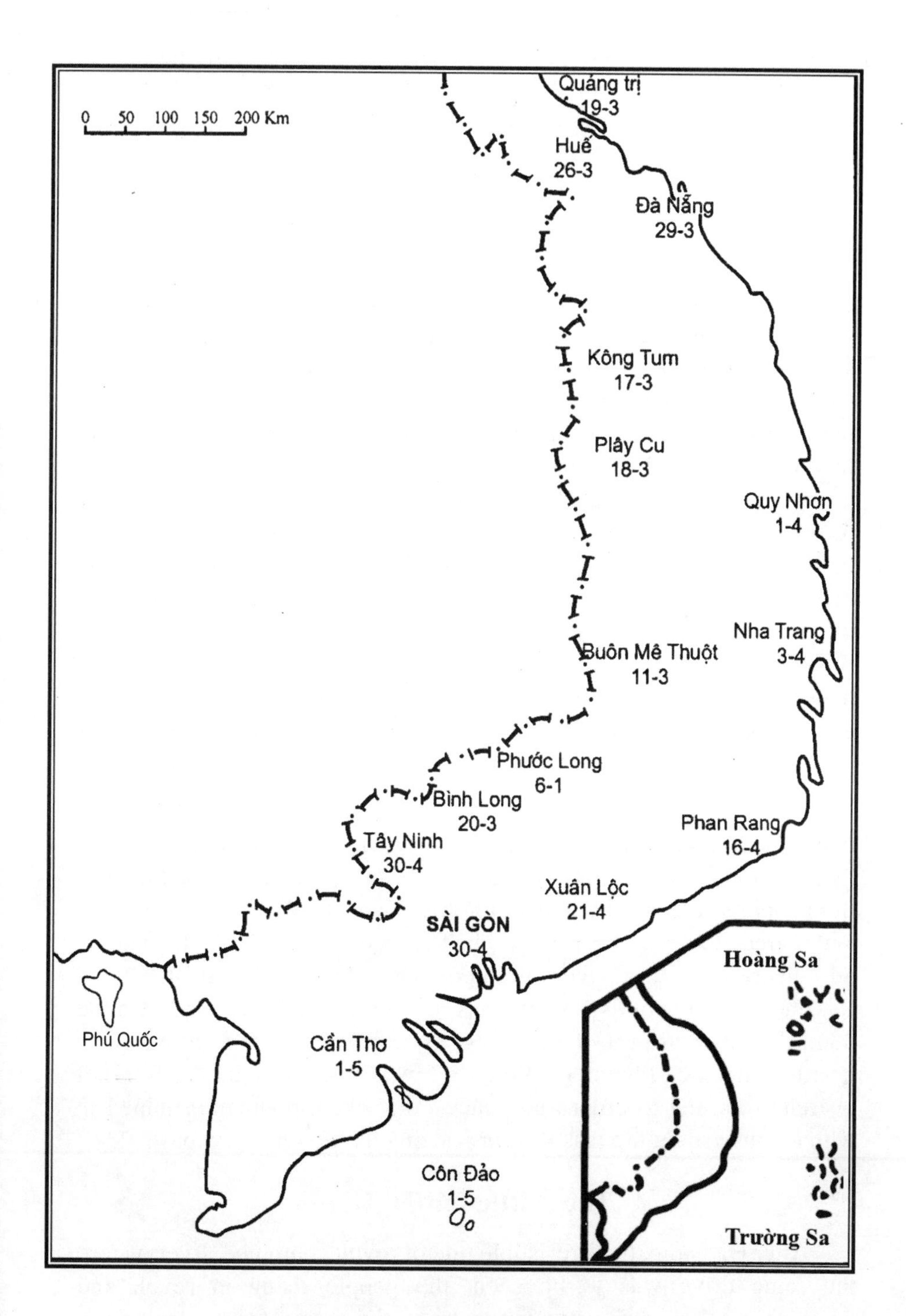
0 50 100 150 200 Km
Quảng trị
19-3
Huế
26-3
Đà Nẵng
29-3
Kông Tum
17-3
Plây Cu
18-3
Quy Nhơn
1-4
Nha Trang
3-4
Buôn Mê Thuột
11-3
Phước Long
6-1
Bình Long
20-3
Phan Rang
16-4
Tây Ninh
30-4
Xuân Lộc
21-4
SÀI GÒN
30-4
Hoàng Sa
Phú Quốc
Cần Thơ
1-5
Côn Đảo
1-5
Trường Sa

The March - April 1975 Campaign

27th, the famous air base of Chu Lai, one of the biggest military bases set up by the US in South Việt Nam fell into the hands of the liberation officers. In the provinces of Bình Định, Phú Yên, and Khánh Hòa along the coast of central Việt Nam, the rural population everywhere, operating in concert with patriotic regular forces, rose in revolt, posing a serious threat to the Sài Gòn administration and army. On the 28th, Bảo Lộc was liberated, thus completely isolating the city of Đà Lạt.

The fall of Huế in the north and Quảng Ngãi in the south, and the liberation of the surrounding rural areas, completely isolated Đà Nẵng, a city and port of special military and political significance for South Việt Nam as a whole. It was at Đà Nẵng that the American had landed their first marines and set up port and military installations which protected and supplied the northern provinces of South Việt Nam and an important part of the Central Highlands. It was to Đà Nẵng that the retreating Sài Gòn troops fell back, in the hope either of holding out there or of fleeing to Sài Gòn by sea. They had forced many villagers and Huế's population to follow them to Đà Nẵng. During the last days of March, Đà Nẵng became a beleaguered city where virtual anarchy reigned. Sài Gòn units disobeyed orders, soldiers plundered shops and houses, and would-be escapers attacked the airfields. The US aircraft carrier Hancock cruised off the coast of Đà Nẵng, while Filipino and Taiwanese ships closed in to rescue the refugees.

On March 25, the liberation forces shelled military positions in Đà Nẵng. On March 28, liberation army units penetrated the city, and on the 29th occupied the airfields. Sài Gòn units mutinied and crossed over to the people's forces. The population took over the defence of the town and searched for Thiệu's agents. The Sài Gòn command, like the puppet administration, was overwhelmed. On March 29, at 15:30, a Revolutionary People's Committee was installed at the city hall. On the 30th, the city and port of Đà Nẵng, as well as the whole province of Quảng Nam, was liberated. Within a few hours, a city on the brink of anarchy returned to order and peace. The whole population joined in with enthusiasm in the task of reorganizing its life on a new basis.

The Battle for Sài Gòn

After Đà Nẵng, the irresistible tide of revolt continued. Everywhere the same drive was to be seen, the people rising in revolt and coordinating their actions with attacks by the armed forces, leading to the routing of Sài Gòn troops, some of whom mutinied and crossed over to the people's side.

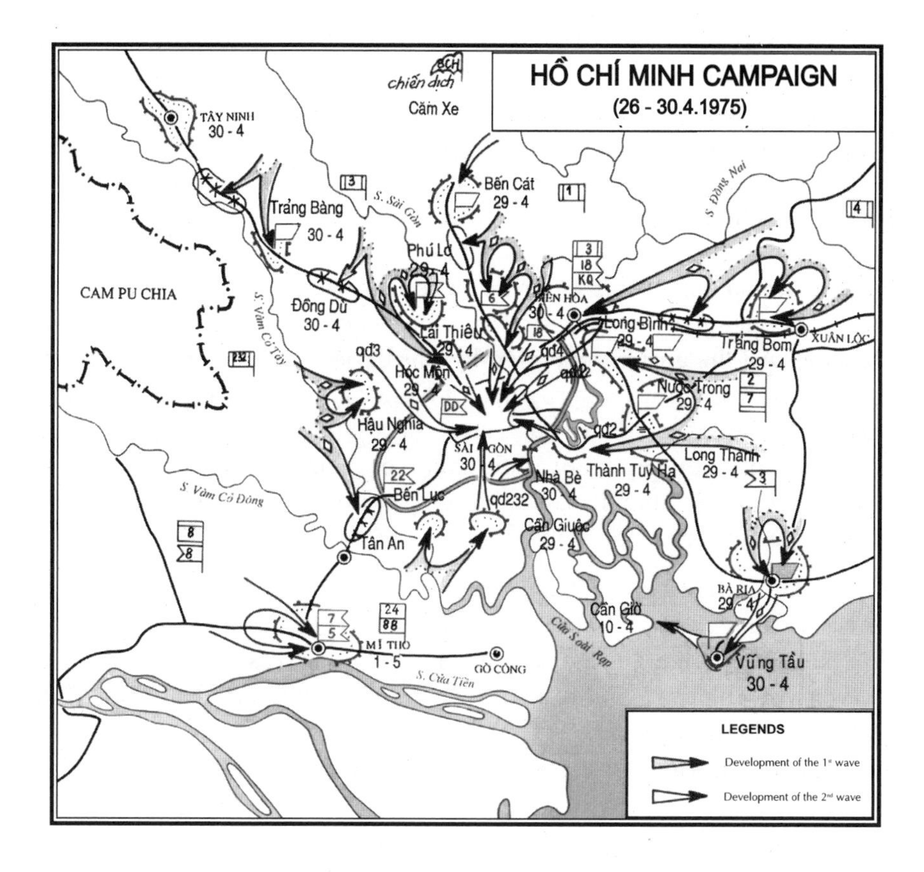
HỒ CHÍ MINH CAMPAIGN
(26 - 30.4.1975)
TÂY NINH
30 - 4
Cầm Xe
Bến Cát
29 - 4
Trảng Bàng
30 - 4
CAM PU CHIA
Đồng Dù
30 - 4
S. Sài Gòn
S. Đồng Nai
S. Vàm Cỏ Tây
Long Bình
Trảng Bom
29 - 4
XUÂN LỘC
Hóc Môn
Hậu Nghĩa
29 - 4
Nước Trong
Long Thành
29 - 4
SÀI GÒN
Nhà Bè
Thành Tuy Hạ
29 - 4
S. Vàm Cỏ Đông
Bến Lức
Tân An
Cần Giuộc
BÀ RỊA
Cần Giờ
Vũng Tầu
30 - 4
MĨ THO
1 - 5
GÒ CÔNG
S. Cửa Tiền
Cửa Soài Rạp
LEGENDS
Development of the 1st wave
Development of the 2nd wave

Five days after the liberation of Đà Nẵng, on April 3, popular forces occupied the province of Khánh Hòa and its capital, Nha Trang. By now, the 1st and 2nd Military Regions of the Sài Gòn army (stationed in four regions) had been eliminated; six divisions had been wiped out; 300,000 men had been put out of action; and military equipment valued at 1 billion dollars had been captured. The Sài Gòn forces were left with seven divisions, and the remnants of various units which had to be tacked together to form new ones.

The defence of Sài Gòn became an urgent problem for the Sài Gòn command. For this purpose, it had four divisions assisted by numerous local forces and important fortified military bases and positions. An outer defence line, under the command of the 3rd Military Region, ran from the town of Phan Rang on the coast of central Việt Nam to Tây Ninh, northwest of Sài Gòn.

Phan Rang, an important port and communications centre for the southern part of central Việt Nam, had three airfields, one of them with a 3,000-metre runway. It was defended by the 6th Air Force Division, and the remnants of routed units coming from northern provinces were regrouped and reorganized there. On April 15, Trần Văn Đôn, defence minister for the Sài Gòn administration, inspected the defence lines. After the liberation of the important base of Cam Ranh, the people's forces switched to launching an attack on Phan Rang. The town was entirely liberated by the morning of April 16. General Nguyễn Vĩnh Nghi, commander of this outer defence line, was taken prisoner along with his colleague Phạm Ngọc Sang, commander of the 6th Air Force Division. All the aircraft operated by this division were captured intact. After the town, the whole province of Ninh Thuận (of which Phan Rang was the capital) was liberated. Three days later, it was the turn of the port of Phan Thiết, capital of Bình Thuận province. Sài Gòn naval units, which tried to save the disbanded troops, were pounded by the people's artillery, which sank one ship.

Following the loss of Phan Rang and Phan Thiết, the defence of Sài Gòn was stepped up; to the east on Highway 1, the 18th Division had to defend the important town of Xuân Lộc, 70 kilometres from Sài Gòn. To the west, on Highway 13, the 5th Division gathered around Thủ Dầu Một, about 40 kilometres from Sài Gòn. On the western section of Highway 1 leading to Tây Ninh were stationed the remnants of the 22nd and 23rd Divisions. Highway 4, a vital lifeline linking Sài Gòn with the Mekong delta, was placed under the protection of two crack divisions, the 7th and 9th, and the southern sector was defended by the 25th Division.

It was at Xuân Lộc that the Sài Gòn command concentrated the bulk of its efforts. This was to be the key battle proving that the fighting morale of the Sài Gòn troops, greatly undermined by the defeats of the previous weeks, could be bolstered. A huge propaganda campaign was conducted for this purpose. But the bombing of Thiệu's residence by pilot Nguyễn Thành Trung, who crossed over to the PRG afterwards on April 8, was an unequivocal sign of this demoralization.

Weyand, chief of the general staff of the US army, was in Sài Gòn to encourage the puppet command and closely watch the progress of operations. The least sign of any improvement in the morale of Sài Gòn troops was scrutinized. General Lê Minh Đảo, regarded as one of Sài Gòn's best officers, and in command of the Xuân Lộc position, swore to defend it to the death.

Without waiting for the distant positions of Phan Rang and Phan Thiết to fall, popular forces attacked the Xuân Lộc front on April 9. A paratroop brigade and armoured brigade were sent as reinforcements,

while Sài Gòn forces tried to hold the fortified positions encircled by liberation forces. Both reinforcement brigades sustained serious losses, while popular forces attacked many points on Highways 1 and 20. Four hundred Sài Gòn troops stationed at Núi Thi mutinied and crossed over to the people's side. Combat group 52 belonging to Sài Gòn's 18th Division was wiped out.

The Sài Gòn airforce was unable to assist the units besieged at Xuân Lộc, as Biên Hòa airfield was under continuous bombardment from the people's artillery. The enemy holding the Xuân Lộc position was also unable to stop the advance of liberation forces, which attacked the Trảng Bom area west of Xuân Lộc. During the siege of Xuân Lộc, on Highway 4 south of Sài Gòn and in the western sector, local and regular forces of the liberation army attacked at many points, liberating numerous localities within a 30-kilometre radius of Sài Gòn.

While the battle for Xuân Lộc raged, the situation in Sài Gòn rapidly deteriorated. Foreign embassies began to evacuate personnel and banks were besieged. Sài Gòn's prime minister Trần Thiện Khiêm was sacked and replaced by Nguyễn Bá Cẩn of whom not even the most sympathetic commentators had heard. Pressure grew on Thiệu to resign.

On April 21, the very day that PRG forces gained complete control of Xuân Lộc, Thiệu tendered his resignation, and in a spiteful speech, poured out his bitterness against American officials whom he accused of having reneged on their promises. Trần Văn Hương, another agent of Washington, succeeded Thiệu. Obtaining supplementary loans from the US Congress and shoring up the morale of the troops, trying to halt the advance of the liberation forces by negotiating - all the political speculation surrounding Thiệu's resignation proved illusory. Paris and Beijing tried in vain to dissuade Vietnamese forces from continuing the fight and put pressure on them to negotiate. The PRG made it clear that the Vietnamese people would only cease fighting if the US withdrew all its personnel and refrained from all further intervention whatsoever in Việt Nam, and if the entire military, police and administrative machine set up by Washington to enslave the Vietnamese nation was completely dismantled.

The liberation forces continued their irresistible advance supported by popular uprisings. Along the coast they liberated Hàm Tân, capital of Bình Tây province, several districts of which had already been liberated during the previous weeks (April 23).

The defensive line east of Sài Gòn now passed through Biên Hòa, 25 kilometres northwest of Sài Gòn, the provincial capital of Long

Thành, 32 kilometres from Sài Gòn, then through Bà Rịa and Vũng Tàu, all the positions being linked by the strategic Highway 15.

On April 26, the PRG reaffirmed its stance, demanding that the US strictly abide Articles 1, 4 and 9 of the Paris Agreement and remove the Sài Gòn administration, instrument of American neo-colonialist policy. It called on the entire population to rise up and fight for the achievement of these objectives. Bargaining began between political groups in Sài Gòn, and on April 27, both houses of the Sài Gòn national assembly met, accepted Trần Văn Hương's resignation and named Dương Văn Minh president of the republic, while Thiệu and Trần Thiện Khiêm fled to Taiwan. But no power was left in Sài Gòn, and the new president and his new ministers had nothing to rule over. Cao Văn Viên, Sài Gòn's last chief of the general staff, fled, to be followed by Nguyễn Bá Cẩn, the outgoing prime minister who did not even take the time to hand power over officially to his successor.

On April 26, at 17:00, the final push for Sài Gòn, named the "Hồ Chí Minh Campaign" began. The liberation forces attacked simultaneously from five directions— east, southeast, west, northwest, and south. From the southeast, they liberated Bà Rịa and Long Thành on the 27th, cutting Highway 15 linking Sài Gòn and Vũng Tàu, which fell in the 28th. As a consequence, all communications between Sài Gòn and the sea were cut.

From the south, the liberation forces attacked Bến Lức on Highway 4 and in neighbouring localities, and on the 28th occupied Phú Lâm, 9 kilometres from Sài Gòn, as well as Hanh Thông Tây in the suburbs of Sài Gòn. The west and northwest, the bases of Củ Chi and Đồng Dù were attacked and, on the morning of April 29, liberation army tanks smashed their way into the command post of the 25th Division. On the same day the capital of Hậu Nghĩa province, Khiêm Cường, 25 kilometres from Sài Gòn, was liberated.

On April 29, aircrafts pounded the big air base and international airport at Tân Sơn Nhất. Rockets and artillery shells also rained down in the airport. The liberation forces arrived on the fringes of Chợ Lớn. To the east, also on the 29th, the liberation forces swept into Thanh Tuy Hà where the largest depots of the Sài Gòn army were located, and seized Cát Lái, Sài Gòn's new port.

On the eastern front, the liberation forces took the city of Biên Hòa, a major military base and airport and location of an important military complex protecting Sài Gòn. The fall of Biên Hòa and the

shelling of Tân Sơn Nhất airport caused panic among the puppet forces and Americans in Sài Gòn. Ford ordered the evacuation of all Americans, something which the White House had deliberately delayed. Eighty-one helicopters were mobilized for this last-ditch operation. Those helicopters unable to land safely had to pick Americans up from the tops of one building after another. Outraged Sài Gòn soldiers fired on the helicopters. The US consulate in the Mekong delta province of Cần Thơ evacuated its personnel using two river craft which made for the sea. Two helicopters from the Sài Gòn airforce strafed the fleeing craft. On April 29, at 15:30, Ambassador Graham Martin left Sài Gòn, ending 25 years of US intervention in Việt Nam (the first American military mission had been installed in Sài Gòn in June 1950). The plan to grant a 327 million dollar loan to evacuate Americans and Vietnamese officials disintegrated of its own accord.

After April 29, there was no Sài Gòn command nor administration left to speak of. General Nguyễn Văn Minh, the commander of Sài Gòn, fled, as did General Lê Nguyên Khang, deputy chief of the general staff. Vĩnh Lộc, the new chief of the general staff, disappeared, as did Nguyễn Cao Kỳ who, a few days earlier, had declared that he would never leave the country. At the general staff and defence ministry, according to foreign news correspondents, officers and non-commissioned officers wandered through the deserted halls. No general was there to answer queries or calls. Nobody observed the 24-hour curfew. At grassroots level, functionaries and policemen left their posts in large numbers, while the population in the city's quarters and streets organized themselves into self-defence and caretaker units to defend their property and public services.

On the night of April 29, liberation forces closing in from several directions, struck at the paratroop base in the heart of the city, occupied Tân Sơn Nhất airport, the Sài Gòn army general headquarters, the Phú Lâm communications centre and other important points. The people, guided by revolutionary fighters who had formerly been engaged in underground activities, occupied public services and disarmed or neutralized the remaining diehards. Puppet troops and policemen put down their arms on the morning of April 30, and, at 11.30, led by a column of tanks, the liberation forces raised the PRG flag over the Presidential Palace. Everywhere Saigonese troops and police surrendered unconditionally to the liberation forces, while the population warmly welcomed the liberators.

At 14:00, the liberation forces entered Chợ Lớn.

The battle for Sài Gòn had ended. The city, completely liberated, returned to the homeland forever, and for the first time since 1859.

On the evening of April 30, Sài Gòn shone with all its lights.

Following the liberation of Sài Gòn, the last units of the puppet army and police quickly surrendered to the people's authorities, and all the provinces and provincial capitals of South Việt Nam were liberated. The whole puppet military, police and administrative apparatus had collapsed.

On 1 May 1975, the workers and citizens of Việt Nam, from North to South, for the first time ever were able to celebrate May Day in a completely liberated country.

Chapter XI

LOOKING TO THE FUTURE

1859: French troops seize Gia Định

1975: Last US soldier leaves Sài Gòn

In recording events during the period between these two dates, the task of the historian is relatively easy. History evolved along a single track. The recovery of national independence: movements, parties, social and religious organizations, personalities on the historical scene, always put the same essential question to themselves - to what extent had they succeeded in promoting the struggle for national liberation? The difference between patriots and those who "sold out the fatherland" can be perceived without much difficulty. Those who claimed to be neutralists or members of the third force were actually political allies of those who fought with weapons in their hands. The only legitimacy recognized by the population as a whole belongs to those who succeeded in ending foreign domination, to the successors of Lý Thường Kiệt, Trần Hưng Đạo, Lê Lợi, Nguyễn Trãi and Quang Trung, not to religion, doctrine or ethnicity.

After 1975, the development of history is more complex, and the historian can no longer be satisfied with any dichotomic vision which was so often put forward during the years of war: national — anti-national, communist — anti-communist, East — West, socialist — capitalist and so on. National and international issues, economic, political, social, religious, cultural and ethnic questions were intertwined at different levels with discrepancies in time and complex interaction, creating an imbroglio for which no schema or model can give an exhaustive explanation.

While emphasizing this great complexity, we do not wish to relinquish all analyses or attempts at rational comprehension. While strongly affirming the modesty of our aims, we are trying however to determine different stages, define a number of issues and highlight the distance covered while always being prepared for some unexpected event to happen which will oblige us to rethink our theses and hypotheses. It matters little. However, a reassessment of events over the past two decades is always useful, the subjects treated being so rich and the issues raised so fascinating.

First of all, the following chronological landmarks can be identified:

- 1975-1976: year of political and administrative reunification, and for the whole nation, a year of "rediscovery" (we shall define this term);
- 1977-1978: first measures taken towards economic reconstruction, many of them ill-timed. Aggravation of economic conditions resulting from war.
- 1978-1979: international crisis due to open conflict with China and Pol Pot's Kampuchea.
- 1980-1985: first attempts at economic reform. Economic and social crises emerges. Disastrous economic situation. Unpopular measures taken.
- 1986-1988: 6th Congress of the CPV. Renovation very much in the news, with new economic and political direction. Freeing up mainly economically; more slowly, culturally.
- 1988-1990: economic reforms of decisive importance in agriculture, development of private enterprises, the law on foreign investment, extension of the powers of directors of state enterprises, gradual abolition of management through government subsidies, troop withdrawal from Cambodia.
- 1990-1992: first results of economic reforms and the open-door policy. Many political, social, cultural and ideological problems remain. The crucial issue for the years to come is which socio-political and ideological structures are to be promoted to ensure economic development without threatening the stability of the regime.

Reunification — Rediscovery

North-south reunification was carried out with drums beating. This included rehabilitation of interzonal communications, in particular of the Hà Nội -Sài Gòn railway, elections to the National Assembly in April 1976,

setting up of a single government for the whole country of administrative structures at all levels down to the most remote rural communes and most isolated villages in mountainous regions and, at the close of 1976, the holding of the National Congress of the Communist Party of Việt Nam (CPV), the ramifications of which were felt throughout the country.

According to some, this political and administrative reunification was premature, even imposed through coercion.

This shows great ignorance of the profound aspirations of the people as a whole, the national consensus being based on two fundamental demands: national independence and peace. These demands could only be met by the departure of all foreign armed forces. For 116 years no party, political or religious organization other than the CPV had been successful in achieving this. No one, not even the most inveterate anti-communist, can deny that Hồ Chí Minh is acknowledged as the founding father of an independent Việt Nam, and that the CPV is recognized as the principal architect of victory. The legitimacy of the new power, truly national in every meaning of the word, is undeniable and admitted by all.

National independence: For over a century, a nation proud of its millenia-long past and a history marked by repeated and resounding victories over foreign aggressors, continuously resisted colonial rule, and people still vividly remembered heroes who fell in the course of the long struggle. Even many of the upper class suffered the daily humiliation inflicted on a subjugated people. Besides communists, those taking part in the struggle included mandarins, landowners, traders, adherents of all religions and eminent intellectuals. Privation, torture undergone together in prison, and many ordeals shared in the course of the long years of armed resistance cemented a lasting alliances among people.

Peace: Between 1939 and 1979, bombs continually rained down and in succession, Japanese, Chinese, French, and US troops — not counting South Korean, Australian and Thai troops operating in collusion with the US — had occupied the country for 40 years, massacred the population, and reduced cities and villages to ashes.

What is worse, these foreign powers had at their disposal huge resources, an enormous military, administrative, financial and propaganda machine, and had succeeded in pressganging millions of youths into their armed and police forces. Saigonese commanding officers forced their men to open fire on their own brothers fighting on the opposite side.

Hundreds of thousands were jailed for long periods and millions of rural people took refuge in the cities, fleeing the bombardments that had

razed their villages and the spraying of defoliants that had destroyed their crops. North-south communications were entirely cut (the US did not allow the tiniest message to get through). Millions of people for years received no news of husbands, children, parents or friends.

With the collapse of the Sài Gòn army, the roads and streets of cities, strewn with helmets, boots, weapons and uniforms of all kinds, offered an extraordinary sight — a pile of odds and ends spreading for several kilometres. Hundreds of thousands of soldiers and police thought of only one thing to get rid of all these signs of the old regime as quickly as possible, to return to their families, and to embrace those who until the previous day had been fighting against them. Hundreds of thousands of "Việt Cộng", also returned from jail or the jungle. The Geneva Agreement of 1954, forced hundreds of thousands of people in the south to move to the north. For 21 years the US occupation prevented them from returning. On the day after victory, they rushed to rejoin their relatives. Millions of peasants returned without delay to their villages, many of them only to find their houses and gardens in ruins. It is difficult for a foreign observer to understand the overpowering emotions of a whole nation who was living through one of the most bewildering moments in its history.

It is understandable that in such circumstances, rapid reunification was the only possible policy, and proposals to perpetuate for many more years the division of the country into two zones, each with its own government and administration, made no sense.

One can also easily understand why the notorious "bloodbath" predicted as inevitable by many foreign observers did not occur. There were not even summary executions of "collaborators" which took place in European countries after the departure of occupying fascist troops. The regime's new policy of national conciliation was not merely a slogan. The new regime was founded on undeniable legitimacy. Internationally, in spite of hostility from the great capitalist powers and China, no one attempted to deny this legitimacy, which compelled recognition as an incontestable historical reality. In 1977, the reunited Việt Nam was admitted to the UN; Western embassies opened one after another in Hà Nội.

Objective Constraints and False Steps

The path taken was not without difficulties. On the contrary, an underdeveloped country could not go through 40 years of war and international isolation without being traumatised. It is important not to

be confused by two opposing opinions — either completely forgetting the terrible and continuing consequences of war (and therefore to overlook the crimes of the politicians and strategists in Washington); or keeping silent about errors and mistakes which would be clearly recognized some years later.

The results of the war included: 26 million bomb craters, 14 million tonnes of bombs and shells dropped; three-quarters of the villages in the south, two-thirds in the north, and all the cities in the north intensively bombed, all bridges in the north destroyed, 10 million rural people driven from their villages. No precise figures can be given regarding the number of soldiers killed or wounded or of civilian casualties including orphans, invalids, victims of social evils (drugs and prostitution), the consequences of foreign occupation and military operations, and of the disintegration of village communities and families. Nor can one forget the ecological and genetic effects of chemicals warfare.

The new regime had to deal with the most pressing issue first: the economy. Two billion dollars in US aid per year ceased which caused a serious economic and social crisis overnight.

Many provinces, especially in central Việt Nam, no longer received imported rice and were threatened with famine. Several million people lost their jobs (the administration, army and police alone accounted for over 1 million unemployed), resulting in the risk of creating dangerous hotbeds of agitation, especially in overpopulated Sài Gòn. The north sent urgently needed food relief to the central provinces and the Soviet Union granted 2.5 million tonnes of food aid for the first two years, 1975-1976. The government and population joined efforts to rehabilitate the most damaged communication routes. In April 1976, the government reconnected 1, 000 kilometres of the Hà Nội-Sài Gòn railway line which had stopped operating in 1945. The resettling of hundreds of thousands of displaced people as well as the provision of first aid and assistance to the war -wounded and the victims of drug addiction and epidemics were ensured. In 1978, the monetary system was unified, enabling easier circulation of food and services between north and south. The first steps in the reestablishment of order were a success and the most serious distortions in society and the economy had been remedied.

A gradual return to normal life was possible if public security could be assured and the threat of civil war avoided. This was crucial. So when US President Gerald Ford proclaimed there would be a bloodbath after the departure of US troops, he knew his intelligence services prepared for it and ensured all necessary conditions for a civil war were in place.

Like millions of other workers, nearly one million soldiers, officers and policemen from the old regime could not find jobs after their rout. The militia belonging to various religions - Catholic integrists, Hòa Hảo and Cao Đài - still existed although they were officially dissolved. In the high plateaus, the French and then the US secret services had for many years been creating FULRO (Unified Front for the Liberation of Oppressed Peoples), bringing together ethnic minority groups to demand the formation of an autonomous territory. Armed and financed by the US, FULRO attempted to launch a guerrilla movement against revolutionary forces after 1975.

The situation was also tense among the two main ethnic minority groups - the Hoa and Khmer. The Hoa of Chinese origin have lived in Việt Nam for a long time. Nationally, they represented one million people. In Sài Gòn they formed a colony apart, a compact group of 700, 000 people concentrated mainly in Chợ Lớn — a Chinatown with its own administration, schools and hospitals. Many Hoa were shrewd traders and served as intermediaries between large French, then US, companies and the Vietnamese population. US aid enabled the businessmen of Chợ Lớn to rapidly set up major enterprises and become the main power brokers in the Sài Gòn economy, in collusion with a number of Sài Gòn ministers and generals. They felt directly threatened by a regime led by a communist party. From the very beginning they tried to undermine the national economy, being all the more dangerous since the nucleus of Hoa businessmen in Chợ Lớn control the entire network of hundreds of retailers down to the most remote villages in the Mekong delta. Another 200,000 Hoa, mainly fishermen, lived at the north near the Chinese frontier. Beijing's hostile policy towards Việt Nam put the Hoa in a difficult situation.

Several hundred thousand Khmer acquired Vietnamese nationality and lived in a number districts in the Mekong delta, keeping their mother tongue and religious traditions.

In spite of political and administrative reunification, the south constituted a real mosaic of diverse regions and groups. Their integration into the new regime gave rise to a number of major problems, further exacerbated by the direct and indirect intervention of two great powers, the US and China, and of a neighbouring country, the Kampuchea of Pol Pot. The Voice of America called overtly for revolt, and US agents trained commandos in Thailand who infiltrated into Laos then Việt Nam. They also gave financial support to émigré organizations in the US to prepare for revenge.

In the months following liberation, some small groups attempted armed struggle without great success. The population did not respond to their appeals. It was important to avoid civil war by every means possible. One security measure was imperative: to dismantle the apparatus set up by Washington which attempted to prolong the war.

The structure of the old Sài Gòn regime was comprised of 70,000 officers and at least an equal number agents of the secret police and torturers, in charge particularly of counter-revolutionary operations. These people who were well trained and indoctrinated had maintained tight control over the population by means of a large military machine, police terror and the conduct of bloody sweep operations and harsh repression. Under the direction of US advisers, their mission was to wage total war against the population aimed at wiping out popular resistance. To this end some even disguised themselves in religious vestments.

While it was possible to let over 1 million soldiers, policemen and officials of the old regime return quickly to civilian life, it would have been impossible to prevent civil war if all these former officers and cadres had had freedom of movement. The decision was made to detain them in "reeducation camps." After some time, those who proved to be of good will and accepted the new regime would be released. In principle, this measure was justified but the government erred in carrying it out indiscriminately. Those who had conducted military operations, mopped up and pounded villages, massacred the population and forcibly recruited physicians, teachers and technicians into the Sài Gòn army were all put in the same basket with officers of the old regime. Worse still, an atmosphere of political suspicion was maintained vis-à-vis all those who had worked in the Sài Gòn Administration. They were dismissed from positions of responsibility at all levels of the new administration, even in technical services. Tens of thousands of families particularly from the middle classes, intellectuals, traders and industrialists had to live for several years in fear of being considered counter-revolutionaries.

As the joy of the first months after liberation faded and economic and social difficulties accumulated due to the cessation of US aid - food shortages, lack of goods and unemployment - and as detention of those in camps was prolonged for both good and unjustifiable reasons, discontent increased in certain circles.

Moreover, a new shadow loomed more and more visibly on the international horizon. The conflicts with the Kampuchea of Pol Pot became increasingly exacerbated, endangering the very foundations of the regime. Proletarian internationalism and combat solidarity with other communist parties constituted one of the essential foundations of all communist parties. At the 4th Congress of the CPV in December 1976, in the course of which the Workers' Party of Việt Nam took the new name of CPV, the presence of delegations from parties in other countries implicitly recognized the legitimacy of the CPV, both national and international. Only the Communist Party of China was absent. Aid and support from China was not only of economic and political significance; the conflict occurring this time with Beijing undermined the ideological basis of the regime. Aggression by the Japanese, then the French and the US had hardly been repelled when a new menace appeared, coming this time from a "fraternal country." The shock was severe for a whole generation of enthusiastic militants who had sacrificed everything for their ideals, for millions of young people dazzled by the glory of their elders, heroes of national liberation and pioneers of a new society, a glory that would rapidly tarnish. The majority of combatants and cadres returning from the forests or the north had won the admiration and esteem of everybody as a result of their strict discipline. They refrained from abusing even the smallest piece of property of the population and demonstrated an affability which sharply contrasted with the manners of earlier armies. But some of them, including those of highest ranks, took for themselves villas, apartments, cars, and other property left behind by those who had fled and became involved in corruption.

Thus, in December 1976, the 4th Congress of the CPV was held in an atmosphere full of hope but also fraught with menace. For the reunified country, the congress had to define general directions for the future, and the bases on which to build a new society and maintain its place in the international arena. The Government achieved positive results during the first months (May 1975-December 1976). However, these measures were only temporary, taken and implemented in an atmosphere of urgency. The general line and strategies adopted in various fields - economic, social, cultural, and international politics - would decide the path to be followed for decades. The leadership of the Party had all the power and all the necessary authority to make decisions of crucial importance.

A few years later, the Party publicly admitted it had committed serious errors at the 4th Congress. The historian can, however, view this question with impartiality. In viewing the circumstances of that time the historian must ask, could it be otherwise? It is always easier to judge after the event, at least initially after the historical drama has evolved through all its sequences; we shall try to identify the principal reasons leading to the adoption of a policy that would prove disastrous, particularly in the economic field.

Between the beginning of the Second World War and 1955 Việt Nam had been entirely cut off from the rest of the world. From 1955 to 1975, the DRV's international relations were exclusively maintained with the socialist countries, mainly with the Soviet Union and China, countries which were themselves technologically backward as compared with the capitalist world, in spite of some spectacular achievements for the USSR. Faced with US aggression, general hostility from capitalist countries (except India and Sweden), and boycotts by neighbouring countries in Southeast Asia, the Việt Nam liberated in 1975 could turn only to the socialist countries.

For the majority of Vietnamese, capitalism only evoked memories of a long colonial past with all its injustices, atrocities, and the horrors of merciless war. Faced with the always menacing imperialist countries, it naturally sought support and assistance from the socialist countries; in contrast to capitalist development, stood the socialist path already explored by the fraternal countries. For backward Czarist Russia, a few decades of a socialist system sufficed to make it a superpower capable of crushing fascism; for the virtually colonized China, the adoption of a socialist path and association with the community of socialist countries had taken it to the status of great world power. If the 4th Congress of the CPV deliberately chose the socialist path to development and rejected all other suggestions to solve the pressing difficulties of the moment, then this was surely quite logical.

From the 1930s to the 1980s, the leaders of the national movement had only lived underground, spending long years in jail and in guerrilla bases, enduring untold privation and suffering, completely cut off from the social and historical changes which radically altered the world as a result of the scientific and technological revolution. Faithfully following the Soviet model of development, they only strengthened the country's international isolation and confined themselves within a rigid ideological framework resistant to change. The great influence of Maoism had increased the negative aspects of an orthodoxy which had sometimes become stifling. This is why they did not realize (as in all other socialist countries at that time) the contradictions in the use as an example of the building of socialism in one country, i.e. the USSR in the 1930s and 1940s, and the work of building the economic community of socialist countries, the SEV (also known by the name COMECON).

The affirmation of proletarian internationalism focused on politics. Economically, the 4th Congress of the CPV envisaged the development of an independent national economy with all the sectors of a modern economy, not participating in the international division of labour, and not being integrated into the world economy, even the economic community of the SEV. Even in Europe, the SEV was not an aggregate of integrated independent national economies. Việt Nam, received substantial aid from other socialist countries, especially from the USSR and China — bilateral aid not multilateral — which covered almost all necessary imports. This important aid and the state of war eliminated the necessity of turning to the world capitalist market. But the delay in getting acquainted with the world market constituted an effective brake on economic development.

However, the most significant errors, as highlighted ten years later by the 6th Congress, were in domestic economic policy.

Errors and Illusions

Errors in thinking that socioeconomic backwardness could be overcome by directly shifting to "large-scale socialist production", by skipping the stage of capitalist development and in consequence liquidating as quickly as possible all forms of private, family and capitalist economic activity. Even cooperatives were considered to be transitory structures, the ideal consisting in placing all economic entities under the administration and management of the State. The result was the establishment of an enormous bureaucratic apparatus which decided everything down to the smallest detail, excessive centralization which left no room for any initiative by provincial leaderships, enterprises, or individuals. Each unit and individual resigned to awaiting from central level financial subsides, raw materials, planned targets, and decisions on wages and price regarding personnel. This system was denounced some years later under the name *bao cấp* (the State universal supplier). The illusion was in thinking that with this regime, one could skip stages and push forward rapid development. The indexes for 1980, the last year of the 1976-1980 five-year-plan, testified to this ambition: 21 million tonnes of food, 10 million tonnes of coal, everything in an optimistic vein. Major projects were on the drawing board: metallurgical complexes, heavy industry a priority, construction of a new capital, rapid transformation of the nation's 500 districts into 500 agro-industrial centres, each provided with modern infrastructure in all respects, massive transfer of people to mountainous regions, and accelerated reclamation of uncultivated land.

As early as 1977, all the apparatuses of the Party and State as well as mass organizations - women, youth, trade unions and Fatherland

Front - were mobilized with a great deal of commotion in a campaign to eliminate private business, to transform capitalist enterprises in Sài Gòn into state or jointly -owned enterprises, to make all the peasants in the south join agricultural cooperatives, and those already existing in the north to be enlarged to commune size. Big State farms were created to serve as vanguard units in agriculture.

Crisis

The year 1978 began in an atmosphere of feverish activity creating currents throughout the country, particularly in Sài Gòn, where there were about 300,000 households belonging to traders and industrialists, large and small-scale, all classified as "capitalists". Besides its economic attributes, this term also had an immoral connotation which gave the campaign of "transformation of the old relations of production" an emotional character which exacerbated anxiety among all strata of the population. The issue was complicated by the fact that the majority of Sài Gòn's "capitalists" were the Hoa in Chợ Lớn, forming a virtual state within a state and controlling, as noted previously, key sectors of the southern Vietnamese economy.

Repeated typhoons in the summer of 1978, causing the loss of 3 million tonnes of rice and affecting 6 million people, considerably aggravated the situation in an economy already deteriorating due to unfortunate measures and erroneous policies, and destabilized by the mass exodus of the Hoa. The rural regions of southern Việt Nam undermined. The accelerating campaign towards agricultural cooperativization, agricultural, industrial, and handicraft production fell considerably, and the black market favoured by the establishment of a double market — a free market along with prices fixed by the State — spread rapidly. The rate of inflation rapidly increased, causing on the one hand rapid impoverishment of many strata of the population, particularly civil servants and workers in State enterprises and, on the other, the rapid enrichment of a number of traffickers and corrupt managers. Popular discontent increased and the legitimacy of the regime began to erode.

The situation was all the more critical as Việt Nam was militarily caught in a pincer movement. In December 1978, while Pol Pot's forces launched a violent attack on the frontier city of Tây Ninh. Chinese armed forces massed on the northern frontier.

In the face of the aggression by Pol Pot, and hostility from the US and Western European powers, Việt Nam tightened its alliance with the

USSR and other socialist countries in Europe. For many years, Việt Nam had vainly tried to reconcile the two "great brothers," the USSR and China. This time, it had no choice if it wanted to safeguard its endangered national independence. In June 1978, Việt Nam became an official member of the SEV (COMECON). In November, a long-term alliance was concluded with the USSR, including military provisions.

Stronger due to this political, economic and eventually military support, the Vietnamese high command was able to implement an appropriate strategy, offensive on the southwestern frontier against Pol Pot's forces, and defensive on the northern frontier facing the Chinese troops. First, it eliminated Pol Pot's threat. In combination with Cambodian popular forces in revolt against the bloody regime of Pol Pot, grouped together as the United Front for National Salvation of Kampuchea, the Vietnamese army launched a large-scale offensive which resulted in the liberation of Phnom Penh on 7 January 1979 and in the crushing of Pol Pot's army which fled to Thailand. A new government was set up in Phnom Penh with the support of Vietnamese armed forces.

Military successes did not prevent the aggravation of economic and societal difficulties. On the contrary, aid in all fields had to be provided to a completely ruined Cambodia which had been devastated by four years of the Pol Pot regime: food, medicine, restoration of communications, medical care, and the resettlement of displaced people. Regions damaged by the Chinese occupation had to be rebuilt.

In August 1979, the Plenum of the Central Committee of the CPV had to admit economic failure and to take measures aimed at guaranteeing the interests of family and individual initiatives, and those of workers hitherto sacrificed for the benefit of the State and collective. Severe criticism was made of "negative" aspects, a euphemism meaning corruption, which rapidly spread to officials of the State and Party.

In 1980, the National Assembly adopted a new constitution founded on the following three principles: the party assumes the role of leader, the State the role of manager, the people the role of master. However, these principles did not lead to drafting a set of laws which would put them into practice and establish a new legality. Notions of citizen's rights, democracy, and legality still remained abstractions, often not understood by leading cadres at all levels or the people.

By the end of the 1976-1980 five-year plan, economic failure was evident: food production stood at 14.4 million tonnes and not 21 million tonnes as expected. Vietnam had to resort to massive imports. This food

shortage undermined the very foundations of economic development. Two figures were particularly significant:

- increase in food production of 1976-1980: 6.45 percent
- population growth: 92.7 percent

Things were no more brilliant in the industrial field:

- 0.1 percent growth
- 1.75 million metres of fabrics as against a 450 milion metre target
- electricity: 3.68 billion kwh as against an expected 5 billion.

The terrible consequences of the war, though real, could no longer explain everything. Some spoke of 'crisis', but the term was carefully avoided in official speeches highlighting errors in implementing general policy, management, administration, and the shortcomings and inadequacies of specific policies. Rectification measures were taken but were unable to stop the impoverishment of the majority of peasants, functionaries and workers. This was all the more so because military expenditure could not be substantially reduced in view of continuing international tension. With Kampuchea looking over its shoulder and hostility from big capital powers, Việt Nam had to devote important resources to national defence. It should also not be forgotten that the country has 3,200 kilometres of sea coast and 7,000 kilometres of land frontier.

In such difficult circumstances, inexperience in economic management had disastrous consequences and manipulation of prices, wages and currencies often brought about results contrary to those expected. Price adjustment in 1981 caused a surge in inflation. Spirited discussions took place throughout the period of preparation for the 5th Congress of the Party held in March 1982. The 5th Congress had a more realistic vision of the situation than the 4th Congress: huge objective difficulties, serious errors, excessive ambitions and bureaucracy.

The 5th Congress could not, however, map out a really new policy. Even with short-term objectives it promoted the stepping up of cooperativization of most peasant households, and the taking of agricultural and industrial products for planned distribution throughout the country to all social strata. The movement towards agricultural cooperativization was aimed at bringing 85 percent of peasant households in southern Việt Nam into various forms of collective undertaking.

Basic socioeconomic structures were not actually dealt with. Some measures or policies had nevertheless brought about certain results; for instance, attention was given to the production of consumer goods,

notably handicraft, hitherto neglected in favour of heavy industry. This boosted the production of a number of articles in common use.

Resolution "Contract No. 100" from the Politburo recognized the temporary allotment of family plots to peasant households, giving them some liberty of action regarding cultivation and the sale of agricultural products, and did increase production somewhat.

These improvements were, however, neither significant nor enduring. Other measures were inappropriate, such as permission given to State enterprises to carry out, in addition to the official plan, a "third plan" oriented towards the free market. The general situation was precarious. The balance of trade showed a large deficit. Earnings from exports covered only one-third of imports (on average 500 million roubles worth of exports for 1.5 billion roubles worth of imports). The most serious distortions were found in the financial area, in prices, wages, and currencies. The retail price index increased from 1 in 1980 to 17.3 in 1985; prices for the same product differed, depending on the sector which produced it. This fact encouraged the growth of the black market, corruption and smuggling. Wages and salaries barely met one third of the minimal expenses for workers' families. Should functionaries and workers be paid only in cash or should they be supplied also with goods according to a complex rationing system? State expenditure far exceeded receipts. Inflation increased; the value of the monetary unit in 1985 was only 0.075 of that in 1981. The more State enterprises, both industrial and commercial, produced, the larger their deficits became. Absenteeism and desertion by workers paralyzed their enterprises. Peasants lost interest in the activities of the agricultural cooperatives, intellectuals could not carry out their functions, and a class of newly rich people, the "neo-bourgeoisie", emerged. Economic in origin, the crisis took on a social character, destroying the fundamental values of society, and gradually creating a state of "anomaly." Party documents revealed that from 1975 to 1985, 190,000 Party members were expelled, mostly for reasons of "morality." In just a few years, 1.5 million emigrated, a diaspora which was a new factor in the history of the Vietnamese nation.

A New Path?

In September 1985, a new financial measure seriously aggravated the state of crisis. It was decided that new banknotes should be issued, the new monetary unit being 10 times the value of the old one. The results were contrary to expectations - a powerful new impetus was given to inflation. The National Assembly session held in December 1985 observed in its report that the economic and social stabilization objectives put forward by the 5th Congress of the CPV, as well as the indices of the 1981-1985 plan, had not been achieved. At the same session, influential members of the government were relieved of their duties, the first time a measure of this kind had been taken, testifying to the serious nature of the economic and social crisis and to the fact that disenchantment was increasingly spreading throughout different social strata.

A new phenomenon emerged. Hitherto, apart from criticism from certain quarters, the population in general were accustomed to accepting policies decided by the leadership without protest. This time, a storm of opinion arose, particularly among the most politicized social strata. Even Party militants and quite a few intellectuals outside the Party were engaged in passionate discussion of economic and social problems and burning ideological issues. Information from the Soviet Union about *perestroika* and *glasnost*, ideas from the 27th Congress of the Communist Party of the Soviet Union (CPSU), and changes in the Party leadership, galvanized the Vietnamese people. The leadership of the CPV affirmed in an official statement "its total support for the internal and external policies adopted at the 27th Congress of the CPSU, considering it an historic turning point in the evolution of Soviet society."

Preparations for the 6th Congress of the CPV throughout 1986 were carried out in an atmosphere entirely different from those before previous congresses. In grassroots Party organizations, mass organizations, trade unions, the administration, and committees of the Fatherland Front, the issues were exhaustively discussed; many suggestions from the rank and file obliged the leadership to considerably modify the draft general report prepared by the Politburo. Never before had political life been so animated, with the discussions and election of delegates to the national congress being backed by a groundswell of opinion.

On 10 July 1986, after the death of secretary-general Lê Duẩn, Trường Chinh was elected to replace him and proclaimed the Party's new policy with the key-word, renovation *(đổi mới)*. This slogan aroused great enthusiasm in the ranks of the Party and population, and breathed new life into the press, which for the first time spoke clearly and frankly about the errors and shortcomings of the regime and social problems, overtly denouncing bureaucratism, corruption and conservatism. On 15 December 1986, the 6th Congress of the Party opened and filled the people with great hope. In its political report, the Party pointed out that "the congress should mark a crucial stage in the renovation of our philosophy, our work methods and our organizational modalities, in accordance with the foundations of Marxism-Leninism and with the requirements of our era, as was expressed in the great ideas of the 27th Congress of the CPSU. Our Party must look straight at the truth and speak the whole truth." The report gives special attention to the errors committed and not to objective circumstances: "serious and prolonged errors regarding the most important specific policies, errors in strategy and in the implementation of programs decided," errors caused by subjectivism, voluntarism and stemming from ideological mistakes, and errors in the policy of organization and promotion of cadres.

The resolution predicts in particular that the period of transition to socialism will be long and fraught with difficulties, and that it will comprise many stages. It affirms the necessity of maintaining the existence of private, individual and capitalist economic sectors with the same legal rights as the public sector. The management of all economic sectors, the public sector included, must no longer be based on purely political criteria, but on profitability. Political and ideological mobilization must be replaced by material incentives. The dogmatic priority of heavy industry was, if not given up, at least attenuated; handicrafts and light industry as well as the production of consumer goods were given an important position. This new economic policy was proclaimed, allowing the implementation of many reforms in the coming years and thereby dramatically modifying traditional structures and opening up the still unexplored path of the market economy.

In 1987 and 1988, in pursuing the new economic policy, measures of vital importance were put in place:

- the very liberal law permitting foreign firms to invest in Việt Nam.
- resolution "Contract No. 10" regarding the allocation of land for 15 years to peasant households to fulfill Resolution No. 100 of 1981, by giving almost full freedom of utilization and commercialization. The allocation of fallow lands hitherto belonging to the State, also led to the rapid transformation of important areas into cultivated lands.

These measures greatly stimulated agricultural production, which had shrunk to alarmingly low levels at that time. Other anti-inflation measures gradually lowered the rate of inflation. The influx of foreign capital gave an impetus to the development of light industry and services in Hồ Chí Minh City and Vũng Tàu. In December 1989, the government presented a positive economic balance to the National Assembly, marked particularly by the possibility of exporting over one million tonnes of rice annually, food production having already exceeded the target of 20 million tonnes. This substantial improvement in agricultural production constituted the fundamental premise for future economic development. The cities, particularly Hồ Chí Minh City, Hà Nội, Hải Phòng, Đà Nẵng and Vũng Tàu were now linked to the world market, and put on a new face with the construction of numerous new buildings: private villas, hotels for tourists, headquarters of foreign firms and banks, and public buildings. There began an ever increasing influx of tourists and Vietnamese emigrants returning to visit their families, with a profusion of goods of all kinds and of different origin, both Vietnamese and foreign. By the end of 1988, the country had irreversibly embarked upon the new economic path opened up by the 6th Congress.

The troop withdrawal from Cambodia at the end of 1989 and the open-door economic policy put an end to international isolation and added an optimistic new note to the balance sheet.

Was it sufficient to renovate economic structures without touching other domains — political, social, cultural and ideological? Theoretically, the 6th Congress enshrined comprehensive renovation; economic renovation must be carried out along with reforming structures and fundamental policies in other sectors. The concept of legality was highlighted and at each session of the National Assembly, numerous laws were debated and adopted. Each sector of the civil and judicial administration and the economic management endeavoured to define in detail the modalities for the application of the new laws. Continuing the momentum of the 6th Congress, in October 1987 the new secretary-general Nguyễn Văn Linh tried to define a new cultural policy. About 100 writers and artists who assembled for this purpose unanimously demanded the liberalization of existing structures and practices and obtained the concurrence of the first leader of the Party. Many previously condemned writers and artists were rehabilitated. A new generation of writers and artists began writing novels, stories, poems, and making films in a new spirit without being over-preoccupied with criteria previously prescribed under the signboard of "socialist realism." Fundamental concepts in the human sciences - history, sociology and philosophy - again began to be questioned and dogmatic affirmations like condemnations without appeal were no longer accepted by many researchers.

Things were, however, not as clear as in the economic field where the sanction of realities - profits, deficit, productivity, competition in the national and international market, inflation and unemployment -

were more visible. How do we assess the long-term negative or beneficial effects of a poem, film, song, or painting? To what extent can an organization or individual be given the authority to decide the fate of a work, often the future of a writer or an artist? These problems throughout history and particularly in Việt Nam at the end of the 20th century unless the use of new mass media technologies confer great acuteness on them.

As early as 1989, the enthusiasm sparked by Gorbachev's policies in the Soviet Union faded and, if the desire for economic renovation and the demand for greater democratization in many circles remained unchanged or wavered, then a clear tendency to withdraw appeared. The motto was launched: "Priority to political stability! No injudicious upheaval!" Passionate polemical arguments about the publication of certain novels and films which were accused by one sector of public opinion of nihilism and destroying all national values and praised to the skies by an other part. The successive changes in socialist countries in Europe and the break-up of the USSR slowed the movement in thought. The leadership of the Party strongly reaffirmed its loyalty to Marxism-Leninism, its unshakeable will to build socialism, according to the "way" opened up by Hồ Chí Minh, and its opposition to any form of pluralism, while promoting a market economy controlled by the State.

The Party reaffirmed all these economic, political and ideological principles at the 7th Congress held in 1991, in a more complex national and international context. On the domestic front, while the general economic situation had improved, serious imbalances and distortions persisted, some becoming even more serious. Corruption, an increase in fraud, smuggling, tax evasion, the influx in of foreign goods, the increase in criminality and the danger of drugs darkened the picture. In 1992, the National Assembly elected a new Council of Ministers and unanimously urged the new government to wage a resolute struggle against corruption. On the international front, while relations with ASEAN, Western Europe and India saw marked development with investment in many domains (in petroleum particularly), the USA obstinately maintained its embargo, and the situation in Cambodia, in spite of direct UN intervention, remained uncertain. With Beijing, the official statements of both sides reiterated the desire to normalize relations. The new group in power, with Đỗ Mười as secretary -general of the Party and Võ Văn Kiệt as president of the Council of Ministers, from 1993 on was able to work for undeniable economic development but had to cope with difficult and complex problems.

The Issues

The task of a historian is not to make short-term political revisions nor to venture into far-reaching predictions, but to provide an historical overview and to pinpoint some issues that are believed to be of vital importance.

Since the French colonial conquest, Việt Nam has gradually been forced to integrate into the international market. This process of staged integration lasted for nearly two centuries and was characterized by a long and large -scale armed struggle which left serious and lasting consequences. One cannot speak of Việt Nam without recalling the "long resistance" started by the patriotic scholars of the 19th century and crowned by the liberation of Sài Gòn in 1975. Forgetting this dramatic history would lead to the world understanding nothing of Việt Nam, and for Vietnamese, denying this past is to set oneself apart from the Vietnamese nation. Now that the historical period of armed struggle is over, the issue is to know whether economic integration into a world market dominated by multinational companies is possible, and where the emergence of Japan as a superpower and the appearance of new "dragons" in Asia has created new opportunities for expansion and prosperity; a new area of strength. Will this integration be successful or will it lead to new disappointments and catastrophes?

To answer this question, one cannot be satisfied with analysis of international data. Domestic conditions also play a role; if not fundamental then at least of equal importance. The colonial conquest, wars and integration into the world market have led to the sometimes brutal, gradual destruction of traditional society. Yet a liberated, independent, reunified Việt Nam must build a new society. In what way and on what basis?

After the August 1945 Revolution, as if on an irresistible tidal wave, many millions of people in all regions and of all opinions, rose in revolt. For many of them, mostly non-Party members, things appeared to be simple. The struggle for recovery of national independence would "naturally" continue through the development of a socialist society.

The Communist Party, which then had 5,000 members, was recognized nevertheless as the incontestable leader of the national movement and Marxism-Leninism the compass indicating the solutions to all problems. Once political power was in the hands of a popular state led by the Communist Party, the Party way was what carried out the necessary socio-historical restructuring under a well-defined plan. It proclaimed:

- Elimination of feudalism, gradual elimination of capitalism, the private economy and the market economy;
- Radical agrarian reform and agricultural cooperativization and eventually the formation of State farms;
- Rapid development of a State sector controlling the whole process of production and distribution of material goods, under a plan governing all aspects of economic activity;
- Integration into the "socialist camp" in opposition to the "capitalist camp."

With the partition of the country into two zones of almost equal size with regard to area and population, one with a socialist regime, the other a capitalist, a true experiment on a historical scale began. Until 1975 it appeared that the northern zone, where not only new economic structures were built but also where the foundations of national culture and ethics were renovated, had prevailed over the southern zone, the economy of which depended entirely on massive US aid and which suffered massive social deprivation. Even though it was clear that living standards in the south were higher, it was argued that this economic growth was built on unsound foundations and had no future.

The problem is seen from the wrong angle if viewed in a context of north-south opposition. With the end of US occupation and reunification, Việt Nam emerged from the war which had isolated it from the international community and joined the group of "third world" countries. And it was faced with similar problems. Political and administrative reunification of the two zones, north and south, under the authority of the same government, was just one aspect of an internal dilemma which was far more fundamental; that of national integration. Like many other third world countries, Việt Nam had regained its independence. It created a centralized state, but did it forge a psychologically unified national state? Vietnamese historians are divided on this question: with its millennia-long history, does the country really constitute one nation, or must it still pass through additional stages to achieve a national feeling of unity? Certainly national feeling has deep roots, as proved by the staunch resistance against all external aggression. However, to declare from this fact that a Vietnamese national community has now been constituted in the present meaning of the term, is still a big step to take.

There is no longer any temporary north-south division to heal, but there is great diversity in the geography, ethnicity, religion and linguistics fields (54 ethnic groups), which makes the country a mosaic, the elements of which must be gradually integrated into a homogeneous national entity.

The creation of a nationwide market based on the construction of a modern communication network constitutes an indispensable premise for this unity, which supposes successful industrialization. Now that peace has been restored, industrialization can be achieved in a few decades. Training in new technologies and the mastering of new scientific data are not insurmountable obstacles for the Vietnamese people and the intelligentsia. National integration calls for the eradication of malaria which for centuries has hindered the use of extensive mountainous regions. It calls for dissemination of a common national language through schooling, and the interaction of various ethnic and religious groups who have been, until recently, secluded within their own community. Inter-ethnic and inter-faith marriages, if not forbidden, were extremely difficult. This national integration must safeguard the languages and cultural values of the different groups in order to avoid serious problems, while resisting separatist tendencies. In the case of Việt Nam, three ethnic groups are particularly difficult to integrate, the Hoa, Khmer, and H'mong. As for religious groups, the Catholics, comprising 7-8 percent of the population, form a solidly based church and have been rightly or wrongly accused for two centuries now of collusion with Western powers.

Thanks to newly regained independence, these diverse groups have been able to integrate themselves more easily into the national community. Culturally, however, Christianity, in spite of its long-standing existence in Việt Nam, retains a character which is generally alien to Buddhism.

Việt Nam lies at a crossroads where, as early as prehistoric times, diverse influences were being exerted, particularly those of China and India. On the foundations of a vigorous and popular culture, a scholarly culture had been formed from the doctrinal syncretism of Buddhism, Taoism and Confucianism. Since Việt Nam established contacts with Europe, which began in the 17th century, new cultural factors arrived to enrich the common heritage: Christianity, experimental sciences and technology, liberal and democratic concepts, and last but not least, Marxism. The assimilation of these cultural elements is one of the essential aspects of national integration, of the formation of a new culture, of the shift from a traditional society to a modern one. We have already mentioned the difficulties in assimilating Christian values. In 1962, we expressed the view that many centuries of influence from Confucianism, essentially of a nationalist character, prepared the ground for the entry of Marxism without excessive difficulty. We can see that ideas from the French Revolution, primarily the Jacobite tradition, were admitted without difficulty by Confucian thinkers and considered on their merits by Marxists as historical precedents in their own doctrine.

In view of the fact that the Communist Party has played a leading role in the struggle for national independence, and that it remains dynamic, Marxism has been incontestably the most powerful catalyst in political and cultural life since the 1930s. To what extent is it in a position to assume exclusively the ideological and cultural direction of the whole nation?

This issue is directly linked to another: what socio-political structures will be compatible with the installation of a market economy? We have seen how the present direction of the Party has rejected any idea of ideological and political pluralism. The same question will still arise even if economic growth brings the country, it is to be hoped, reasonable prosperity. What are the characteristics of Vietnamese socialism? The Vietnamese people no longer have to cope with military aggression, but with a more insidious danger. Economic liberalization and the opening up of the country to foreign capital have led to the birth of a "wild capitalism", the development of which brings with it the risk of ecological disaster, exacerbation of social inequalities, social problems, criminality and drug addiction. "Wild" capitalism has mobilized in its own interests important areas of the State apparatus, transforming it into a veritable mafia, inimical to all forms of democracy, of social justice and ecological protection. Can the Vietnamese people, if not able to prevent the rise of this wild capitalism, at least limit its destructive nature? The battle will certainly be fierce and prolonged. Does it bring the risk of armed confrontation? These questions do not only concern Việt Nam. The solutions depend on very complex factors, both national and international. Since historians are accustomed to seeing these issues bring about, in our era more than in any other, unexpected and unpredictable events, they hesitate therefore to give an answer in one direction or in another. Moreover it is not their role to do this; Vietnamese historians formerly wrote dynastic annals and modestly called them "mirrors." They only recorded the facts, merely to help kings reflect on the problems of government.

Like all mirrors, the one I have presented is perhaps distorted, or biased, to use a term currently in vogue. It is up to each individual reader to make any adjustments and re-interpretations that may be seen as necessary.

January 1993

Year of the Cock

INDEX

A

A1: east of Điện Biên Phủ, a strong entrenched fortification of the French army.

Act 10/59

Act 10/59: issued by Ngô Đình Diệm on May 6th, 1959: "To punish saboteurs and violators of national security and people's life and property, martial law is established." The act was divided into two parts. The first part (5 points) specified people to try and named the death penalty (Act 21, issued on July 4th, 1959, allowed the guillotine) and a life sentence of hard labor as punishments. The second part (16 points) allowed of drumhead court-martials with freehanded power to sentence without the possibility of appeal.

An Lộc: belonging to present Bình Phước Province.

An Nam: Meaning "The Pacified South"; this name was adopted in 679 by the Tang dynasty when they ruled over Việt Nam. Under French domination, An Nam referred to Central Việt Nam.

Anh Đức: See Bùi Đức Ái

Ấp Bắc: Ấp Bắc was a small hamlet with a population of 600 in Tân Phú commune, Cai Lậy district, Tiền Giang province, 15km from Mỹ Tho City. The Ấp Bắc battle took place on 2nd January 1963. The South Vietnamese Liberation forces defeated the helicopter and armoured vehicle operation of the American and Sài Gòn forces.

B

Ba Đình: (See Đinh Công Tráng)

Ba Đình: belonging to Nga Sơn district, Thanh Hóa Province.

Bà Rịa: now belonging to Bà Rịa-Vũng Tàu Province.

Bắc Bộ: North Việt Nam, or the northern provinces, from Ninh Bình Province to the Chinese border.

Bắc Sơn: Bắc Sơn District, Lạng Sơn Province.

Bạch Đằng: Bạch Đằng Port is where the rivers of the Thái Bình River system of the Northeast Mountains empty into the East Sea, seperating Thủy Nguyên District of Hải Phòng City from Hưng Yên

District of Quảng Ninh Province.

Bạch Hạc 20

Bạch Hạc: modern Việt Trì of Phú Thọ Province. The converging point of three rivers: Black, Lô and Red rivers.

Bãi Sậy 145

Bãi Sậy: The military base of the Bãi Sậy Uprising (1885 – 1889), set up by Nguyễn Thiện Thuật to fight the French as part of the Cần Vương (Save the King) Movement. Bãi Sậy was a swamp located in Mỹ Văn and Châu Giang districts, now part of Hưng Yên Province, 30 km east of Hà Nội.

Bản Kéo 257

Bản Kéo: a range of entrenched fortifications the French built in Điện Biên Phủ town to protect the French military bases in the center (1953-1954).

Bàn Tài Đoàn 302

Bàn Tài Đoàn (1913–): a writer from the Dao ethnic group. His real name was Bàn Tài Tuyên, born in Quang Thanh Commune, Nguyên Bình District, Cao Bằng Province.

Bảo Đại 192, 212, 216, 219, 225, 240, 245, 248, 259, 271-272

Bảo Đại (1913 – 1997): the last king of the feudal Nguyễn Dynasty. Bảo Đại was the imperial name of Nguyễn Vĩnh Thụy, starting in January1926.

In September 1945, he was invited to be a consultant for the Provisional Government of the Democratic Republic of Việt Nam. He was a member of the First National Assembly of the Democratic Republic of Việt Nam.

On March 1946, he was appointed to Chong Qing, China following the friendly policy of the Democratic Republic of Việt Nam's government with Chiang Kai-shek's administration. However, then he left for Hong Kong and did not go home.

In 1949 the French colonial administration took him back to Việt Nam to act as Head of State backed by France.

In October 1955, Ngô Đình Diệm pushed Bảo Đại out of office and into exile in France, where he died in 1997.

Bát Tràng 68

Bát Tràng: an 800-year-old pottery village in Gia Lâm District, a suburb of Hà Nội.

Bến Cát 310, 323

Bến Cát: now belonging to Bình Dương Province.

Bình Trị Thiên 15, 241, 251, 258

Bình Trị Thiên: now divided into three Provinces: Quảng Bình, Quảng Trị and Thừa Thiên-Huế.

Bình Định Vương 72

Bình Ngô Đại Cáo 81, 84

Bình Sơn tower 68

Bình Sơn Tower: located in modern Tam Sơn, Lập Thạch District in Vĩnh Phúc Province.

Bình Than 87

Bình Tuy 324

Bình Tuy: in the present eastern region of South Việt Nam.

Bồ Đề 68

Bồ Đề: now part of Long Biên District in Hà Nội (on the east side of the Red River).

Bùi Đức Ái 302

Bùi Đức Ái (1938 –): a writer with the pen-name of Anh Đức. He was born in Bình Hòa Commune, Châu Thành District, Long Xuyên Province, now called An Giang Province.

Buôn Ma Thuột 325-326

Buôn Ma Thuột: the capital of Đak Lăk Province.

C

C1 257-258

C1: an entrenchment in the hills east of Điện Biên Phủ, a French stronghold.

Cả river 17, 90

Cả River: 531 km long; from its source in upper Laos, it flows across Nghệ An Province before emptying into the Hội Estuary (Nghệ An).

Cẩm Phả 141

Cẩm Phả: in Cẩm Phả town, a famous coal mining area in Quảng Ninh Province.

Cần Thơ Province

Cần Thơ Province: belonging to Cần Thơ Town and Hậu Giang Province now.

Cần Vương 143, 161

Cao Đài 179-180, 203, 222, 240, 341

Cao Đài Religion: established in 1926 by Ngô Văn Chiêu (1887-1932), a civil servant under French domination, in Kiên Giang Province. The center of Cao Đài Religion is in Tây Ninh Town, Tây Ninh Province.

Cao Thắng 146

Cao Thắng (1864 – 1893): the right hand man of Phan Đình Phùng, leader of the Hương Khê Uprising. He commanded the attacks on the French. On November 21st, 1893, he was killed in a battle in Thanh Chương District, Nghệ An Province.

Champa 41-42, 51-55, 65-66, 109-115, 117-118

Chế Bồng Nga 115

Chế Lan Viên 302

Chế Lan Viên (1920–1989): a great poet of Việt Nam. His real name was Phan Ngọc Hoan. He was born in Nghệ An Province but his native land is in Cam Lộ District of Quảng Trị Province. In 1937, he published his first collection of poems called “Điêu tàn” (Withering)

Chi Lăng Pass

Chi Lăng Pass: belonging to Lạng Sơn Province, located on National Highway 1A from Hà Nội to Lạng Sơn.

Chinh Phụ 122-123

Chợ Lớn (Big Market)

Chợ Lớn (Big Market): Districts 5 and 10 of Hồ Chí Minh City now.

Chu river 45

Chu River: originates from Hua Phan in Sam Neua in Upper Laos. It is 325km long and runs parallel to the Mã River in Thanh Hóa;

25km from the East Sea, the two rivers join.

Chu Văn 61, 65, 213, 302

Chu Văn (1920 –1994): a writer. He was born Nguyễn Văn Chử in Trực Nội Commune, Thái Ninh District, which is now Đông Quan Commune, Đông Hưng District of Thái Bình Province.

Chu Văn An 61, 65

Chu Văn An (1292 – 1370): a famous educator. Born and raised in Thanh Liệt, Thanh Trì District of Hà Nội, he was appointed the principal of Quốc Tử Giám (the Imperial University) in Thăng Long by King Trần Minh Tông.

Chu Văn Tấn 213

Chu Văn Tấn (1910 – 1984): born into a Tày ethnic family in Phú Thương, Võ Nhai District, Thái Nguyên Province, he was a commander, a political commissar, a secretary of the Việt Bắc Interregion (1954-1957) and then the Việt Bắc Military region (1958-1976). He joined the Revolution in 1934 and became a member of the Việt Nam Communist Party in 1936. He led Bắc Sơn's Guerilla Unit (or National Salvation Unit I). He was the captain of the National Salvation Unit II starting in September 1941, and became the leader in 1944. After the August Revolution in 1945, he became the Minister of Defense of the Provisional Government. From 1956 to 1975, he was the secretary to the Party Committee, the Chairman of the Administrative Committee of the Việt Bắc Autonomous Zone, a member of the Việt Nam Workers' Party Central Committee during the second and third terms, and a deputy from the Third to Sixth National Assemblies. He was promoted to the rank of 3-star general in 1959.

Chương Sơn Tower

Chương Sơn Tower: located on Ngô Xá Mountain in Ý Yên District of Nam Định Province. Built in 1108 under Lý Nhân Tông and destroyed by the Chinese Ming Dynasty in the 15th century.

Cổ Loa 17, 21-22, 41

Cổ Loa: now belonging to Đông Anh District of Hà Nội, 20 km north of the city center.

Cochinchina 134-135, 137, 139-140, 143, 149-151, 155-156, 165, 168-171, 173, 175, 179-180, 186, 188, 191-192, 196, 205, 208, 210, 214, 216, 230-233

Củ Chi 333

Củ Đai

Củ Đai: Củ Chi District of Hồ Chí Minh City.

Cù Mông 110

Cù Mông Pass: about 500m above sea level, situated in the mountains of Tuy Hòa District, Phú Yên Province, southern region of Việt Nam.

Cúc Bồ 41

Cúc Bồ: belonging to Hưng Yên Province

Cung Oán 122-123

Cương Mục 65, 91, 93, 128

D

Dạ Trạch: now Dạ Trạch Marsh of Mỹ Văn District, Hưng Yên Province

Diên Hựu Pagoda: now Một Cột (One Pillar) Pagoda in Ba Đình District of Hà Nội. It was built in 1049 and repaired in 1105.

Dương Văn Minh (1916–2002): President of the Republic of Việt Nam (1963 and 1975), a general of Sài Gòn's military forces; born in Mỹ Tho, or modern Tiền Giang Province.

Đ

Đà River: originating from Vân Quý (Yun Gui) plateau of Vân Nam (Yunnan) Province in China. About half (570km) of its length (1010km) runs through Việt Nam across Lai Châu, Sơn La and Hòa Bình. It meets the Hồng River at Bạch Hạc (Việt Trì, Phú Thọ Province).

Đại La: presently Hà Nội.

Đại Việt Party: also known as the Đại Việt National Revolutionary Commissioner Association, set up on March 11th, 1945; a pro-Japanese organisation.

Đặng Tất (? – 1409): a famous commander of Trần Giản Định, who founded the posterior Trần dynasty. He was born in Can Lộc in modern Hà Tĩnh Province. After the collapse of the Trần Dynasty, he was highly appreciated under the Hồ Dynasty. When the Ming Dynasty attacked the Hồ king, Đặng Tất pretended to surrender so he could hold his post while he prepared his forces to resist the Ming army and restore the Trần Dynasty. Later, in 1409, Trần Giản Định ordered his assistants to kill him.

Đặng Thị Huệ (? – 1782): the imperial concubine of Trịnh Sâm, who by her beauty and intelligence, so distracted Trịnh Sâm that he paid no attention to court affairs. When she gave birth to their first child, Trịnh Cán, she persuaded Trịnh Sâm to name him the Crown Prince, instead of the queen's son, Trịnh Khải.

Đặng Trần Côn 122

Đặng Trần Côn (18th century): a poet, born in Nhân Mục Village (Mọc Village), Thanh Trì District, Hà Nội. He passed the inter-provincial exam and became an education officer in Tường Phủ. Later, he became the chief of Thanh Oai District (now in Hà Tây Province).

Đề Kiều 146

Đề Kiều (1691 – 1760): Lê Hữu Kiều

Đèo Ngang

Đèo Ngang: 2650 m long; located at the border between Hà Tĩnh and Quảng Bình Provinces at the 18th parallel north.

Điện Biên Phủ 145, 236, 254-255, 257-259, 271, 275, 299

Điện Biên Phủ: Điện Biên Phủ Town is now the capital of Điện Biên Province.

Đinh 41-42, 84, 102, 144

Đình Bảng 212

Đình Bảng: a commune of Từ Sơn District, Bắc Ninh Province.

Đinh Bộ Lĩnh 42

Đinh Bộ Lĩnh (924 – 979): Born in Hoa Lư in modern Ninh Bình Province, Đinh Bộ Lĩnh put down twelve revolts, unified the country, and renamed it Đại Cồ Việt. In 965, he ascended the throne as Đinh Tiên Hoàng, and set up his capital in Hoa Lư, where he was born. In 979, he and his son Đinh Liễn were poisoned by his military aide Đỗ Thích.

Đinh Công Tráng 144

Đinh Công Tráng (1842 – 1887): Originally, he was chief of Tràng Xá canton, now Thanh Tân Commune, Thanh Liêm District, Hà Nam Province. When the French attacked South Việt Nam for the second time in 1882, he joined Hoàng Tá Viêm's army and defeated Henri Riviere's troops at Cầu Giấy (now Cầu Giấy District in Hà Nội) on May 19th, 1883. Henri Riviere and some other French officials were killed. In 1886, when the anti-French movement in North Việt Nam was suppressed, Đinh Công Tráng went to Thanh Hóa with Trần Xuân Soạn to continue fighting. He and some patriotic intellectuals set up the Ba Đình base (in Nga Sơn district, Thanh Hóa Province), for which he was a hig-ranking military leader. In 1887, French forces attacked Ba Đình Base. On January 20th, 1887, the insurgent army had to withdraw and move to the mountains. After that, Đinh Công Tráng went to Nghệ An and Hà Tĩnh provinces to contact Phan Đình Phùng, the leader of the Hương Khê Uprising. On the way, he was captured by the French. He died on October 6th, 1887.

Đinh Tiên Hoàng 102

Đọ 13, 25

Đỗ Mười 353

Đỗ Mười (1917 –): an important Vietnamese statesman. Born in Thanh Trì District, Hà Nội City, he joined the revolutionary movement at an early stage. Throughout his life, he held many important posts in the State government and the Party: Minister, Vice-Prime Minister,

Chairman of the Council of Ministers, and General Secretary of the Central Committee of the Việt Nam Communist Party (7 and 8 tenures).

Đồ Sơn 94

Đồ Sơn: Đồ Sơn Peninsula in Đồ Sơn District, Hải Phòng City.

Đoàn Thị Điểm 122

Đoàn Thị Điểm (1705 – 1748): a Vietnamese woman poet, whose real name was Hồng Hà. Originally of the Lê family, her family name was changed by her father to Đoàn. Her father was born in Giai Phạm Village, which was later changed to Hiếu Phạm Village, Văn Giang District, Kinh Bắc Prefecture (now Hưng Yên Province). Đoàn Thị Điểm translated *Chinh phụ ngâm* (Lament of the Soldier's wife) by Đặng Trần Côn from Hán into Việt Namese. She also wrote *Truyền kỳ tân phả* (Strange Stories in New Versions) in Hán script in 1811.

Độc Lập 257, 315

Độc Lập: a hill northeast of modern Điện Biên Phủ Town. Starting in 1953, French colonialists built a base here to protect the group of fortresses in Điện Biên Phủ. This base fell on March 15th, 1954.

Đốc Ngữ 146

Đốc Ngữ (? – 1892): the leader of the resistance to the French invasion of North Việt Nam. Born in Xuân Phú Commune, Phúc Thọ District, Hà Tây Province, his real name was Nguyễn Đức Ngữ and he worked as a boatman ferrying people across the Red River. When the French attacked North Việt Nam for the first time in 1873, he joined the Sơn Tây army in what is now Hà Tây Province. After many battles and victories, he was appointed an army commander. He took an active part in the Giếng Bridge Battle in 1882, when the French attacked North Việt Nam the second time. Đốc Ngữ's insurgent army quickly expanded after 1890 and they carried out extensive activities along the banks of the Red and Black rivers. French troops killed him on August 7th, 1892.

Đống Đa 104

Đống Đa: in Đống Đa District, Hà Nội.

Đồng Đậu 17

Đồng Đậu: Đồng Đậu Commune in Vĩnh Lạc District, in modern Vĩnh Phúc Province

Đồng Dù 333

Đồng Dù: belonging to Tây Ninh Province.

Đông Dương Cộng Sản Đảng 182

Đông Dương Cộng Sản Liên Đoàn 182

Đồng Khánh 143

Đông Kinh Nghĩa Thục 161

Đồng Nai River 15, 19, 112

Đồng Nai River: 635 km long; from its source on the Lâm Viên plateau in Lâm Đồng Province, it flows across Lâm Đồng, Đồng Nai Provinces and through Hồ Chí Minh before discharging into the East Sea.

Đông Sơn 17-19, 30-31, 38, 67

Đông Sơn: now belonging to Đông Sơn District, Thanh Hóa Province

Đường Kách Mệnh 178

G

Gia Định 98, 100, 102, 106-107, 134, 336

Gia Định: the area around Hồ Chí Minh City.

Gia Lai-Kon Tum and Đắc Lắk

Gia Lai-Kon Tum and Đắc Lắk: now divided into four Provinces: Gia Lai, Kon Tum, Đắc Lắk and Đắc Nông.

Gia Long 8, 107-108, 125, 127

Giang Nam 302

Giang Nam (1929 –): a writer. His real name was Nguyễn Sung. Other names included Châu Giang, Hà Trung and Lê Minh. He was born in Ninh Bình Commune, Khánh Ninh District, Khánh Hòa Province.

Giấy Đáp Cầu

Giấy Đáp Cầu: on the bank of the Cầu River in Bắc Ninh Province.

Gò Công 137

Gò Công: Gò Công Town in Tiền Giang Province.

H

Hạ Hồi 104

Hạ Long 15, 41

Hạ Long: Hạ Long Bay, now belonging to Quảng Ninh Province.

Hải Thượng Lãn Ông 129

Hải Vân Pass 110-111, 328

Hải Vân Pass: about 496m above sea level, on the 16th parallel between Đà Nẵng City and Thừa Thiên-Huế Province. "Hải" means sea and "Vân" means cloud.

Hàm Nghi 143-146

Hàm Nghi (1872 – 1947): the eighth emperor of the Nguyễn Dynasty, who ruled only one year from August 1884 to August 1885. His real name was Nguyễn Phước Ưng Lịch. After his older brother, Kiến Phúc, was murdered, Tôn Thất Thuyết, a high-ranking mandarin who was strongly anti-French-minded in the Nguyễn Court, put Hàm Nghi on the throne. Living in exile, he married a French woman, and bore two daughters and a son. He was good at painting and profoundly knowledgeable about French culture. He died in Algeria.

Hàm Tử 55, 84

Him Lam 257

Him Lam: a mountain village, north of modern Điện Biên Phủ Town, that served as a French military base in Điện Biên, built between 1953 and 1954. By then the French called it Beatrice. The base was set on five 50m-high hills, 200 m to 300 m away from each other and 2 km far from the center. Although solidly built and defended, this base was the first to fall in the Battle of Điện Biên Phủ on March 13th, 1954.

Hồ Chí Minh 176, 201, 209, 215, 219, 221-223, 225, 227, 229, 231-233,

Hồ Chí Minh (19-5-1890 – 2-9-1969): He was born in Kim Liên Commune, Nam Đàn District, Nghệ An Province as Nguyễn Sinh Cung. Since then, he had many names. When he went to school, his name was Nguyễn Tất Thành. In mid-1919, he changed his name to Nguyễn Ái Quốc (Nguyễn the Patriot). In 1928, he became Hồ Chí Minh.

Growing up in a poor but traditional Confucian family, Nguyễn Tất Thành felt great anguish at his country losing its independence and being ruined by French colonialists. From an early age, he cherished a desire to liberate his homeland.

In June 1911, he worked on a French ship in order to go abroad and find a way to save his country. He traveled to many European, African and American countries before he settled in France in 1917. In 1919, Nguyễn Ái Quốc entered the French Socialist Party. In 1920, at the Congress of Tours, he applied for membership in the Communist International and took part in the foundation of the French Communist Party. In 1921, he helped establish the Colonial People Union and became the editor-in-chief of *Le Paria* newspaper. In 1923, he traveled to the Soviet Union, joined international communist organizations, attended the Fifth Congress of the Communist International and was nominated as an officer of the Orient Department, directly in charge of the Southern bureau.

In late 1924, he traveled to Guangzhou, China to look for Vietnamese patriots, awaken and educate them, and then select a few to join the Việt Nam Association of Revolutionary Youth, the forerunner of the future Communist Party. He published a newspaper called The Youth and wrote *Đường Kách mệnh,* which means The Path of Revolution. In May 1927, he traveled to the Soviet Union.

In July 1928, he went to Thailand to work in the Vietnamese community there for over a year. In 1930, he returned to China and called a conference for the purpose of establishing the Việt Nam Communist Party by combining the three domestic Communist organizations. At this conference (3 February 1930) in Hong Kong, the attendees passed the Party's brief political program and tactics.

In June 1931, British colonialists arrested Nguyễn Ái Quốc in Hong Kong. With the help of international organizations (the Anti-Imperialism Union for National Independence, and the International Red Cross) and the British lawyer Frank Loseby, he was released in the spring of 1933. He then returned to the Soviet Union.

From 1933 to 1937, he studied at Lenin University, worked at the International Communist Party's Research Institute for National and Colonial Issues, and attended the Seventh Congress of the

Communist International as a consultative delegate.

From 1938, he returned to China to guide Việt Nam's revolution and prepared to return to Việt Nam. On January 28th, 1941, he went to Pắc Bó in Cao Bằng Province. There, together with the Central Committee of the Đông Dương Communist Party, he guided the campaign for Việt Nam's independence from France.

On May 19th, 1945, Hồ Chí Minh established the Việt Minh Front. On December 22nd, 1945, he founded the Armed Propagation Brigade for the Liberation of Việt Nam and nominated Võ Nguyên Giáp as its leader.

On August 16th, 1945, he held the National Congress in Tân Trào, Tuyên Quang Province, to announce the plan for the August Revolution, which would begin on August 19th, 1945, to seize power from the French. At the Congress, he was voted the Chairman of the Việt Nam National Liberation Committee.

After the success of the August Revolution, on September 2nd, 1945, on behalf of the provisional government, Hồ Chí Minh publicly read the Declaration of Independence, an act which founded the Democratic Republic of Việt Nam. He was a member of the First, Second and Third National Assemblies, the Chairman of Việt Nam Workers' Party (Communist Party) during Terms Two and Three, and the President of the Democratic Republic of Việt Nam from 1945 to 1969. He was a brilliant thinker, an important figure in Vietnamese history, and was recognized as a World Great Man of Culture by UNESCO.

Hồ Chí Minh City 351-352

Hồ Chí Minh City: the new name of Sài Gòn-Gia Định City (including Chợ Lớn). Sài Gòn City was established on 15th March 1874. Chợ Lớn was incorporated into it in the early 20th century. On July 2nd, 1976, the Sixth National Assembly of the Socialist Republic of Việt Nam officially changed its name.

Hồ Chí Minh Trail on the Sea

Hồ Chí Minh Trail on the Sea: A supply line on the sea from the North to the South of Việt Nam during the war 1954-1975.

On 23th October 1961, Group 759 (or Unnumbered Flotilla) under Việt Nam's Navy was founded with the task of transporting secretly war materiel from the North to the South. (It was changed into Group 125 on 24 January 1964).

After the first failure in this effort in 1959, in July 1961 the Vietnamese leaders decided that groups of boats should start from the southern provinces, receive weapons in the North and then would be back to the South. Thus, the flotilla of Bến Tre started its journey on 11st June 1961, followed by that of Cà Mau on 7th August, and that of Bà Rịa on 18th August. All the journeys were successful.

With the experience drawn from these trials, Group 759 sent its Ship "Phương Đông" 1 to Cà Mau in the South on 14th September 1962 and the journey was also successful. This strategic supply route started running smoothly. Up to 1963, 1,318 tons of weapons had been carried to Military Zone 7, 8, 9 in the South; up to February 1965, 5,000 tons had been carried to the South with 88 journeys of ships and boats from 4 to 100 tons. However, on 15 February 1965, the Sài Gòn and American forces detected the route and they took measures to prevent it.

In such circumstances, the leaders of North Việt Nam diverted the route to the international seas, sometimes to the territorial waters of the Philippines, Malaysia and Indonesia.

The route stopped in 1973.

Hồ Nguyên Trừng 69

Hồ Nguyên Trừng: the first son of Hồ Quý Ly. In 1401, his younger brother, Hồ Hán Thương, came to the throne, and he became Co-Prime Minister. His specialty was in manufacturing different kinds of weapons. He improved two types of guns and various warships. In 1407, he was arrested by Ming invaders and brought to China.

Hồ Quý Ly 65, 69, 76

Hồ Quý Ly (? – ?): As a famous reformer in Việt Nam's history; his forefathers were from Quỳnh Lưu in modern Nghệ An Province. Two of his aunts were King Trần Minh Tông's imperial concubines and both became the mothers of Trần kings. Under his cousin King Trần Nghệ Tông, Hồ Quý Ly was appointed an ambassador and got married to Princess Huy Ninh. Because of his excellence in many fields and political knowledge, he earned the confidence of the king. In 1395, Nghệ Tông died and Hồ Quý Ly rose to power. In 1400, he overthrew the Trần Dynasty and set up the Hồ Dynasty, which only lasted for seven years. He moved the capital to Tây Đô in Thanh Hóa Province and renamed the country Đại Ngu. In 1401, he abdicated the throne for his younger son, Hồ Hán Thương. He and his son were arrested by the Ming invaders and exiled to China in 1407.

Hồ Tông Thốc 65

Hồ Tông Thốc: well-known for being intelligent and hard-working, he was the first doctoral laureate of a court exam under the Trần Dynasty. He became a member of the Court Academy, and a member of a delegation to China.

Hồ Xuân Hương 122-123

Hồ Xuân Hương: a famous woman poet of the 18th century. There are still many myths surrounding her life and literary career. Her exact birth and death dates and native land are unknown.

Hòa Hảo 222, 240

Hoa Lư 42, 114

Hoa Lư: now belonging to Hoa Lư District, Ninh Bình Province, 90km south of Hà Nội.

Hoàng Diệu 141

Hoàng Đình Bảo 97

Hoàng Đình Bảo (? – 1786): born in Phụng Công Commune, Yên Dũng District in present-day Bắc Giang Province, his real name was Hoàng Đăng Bảo. After passing the inter-provincial examination, he was given Trịnh Doanh's daughter in marriage. In 1774, he joined the Trịnh army and participated in the attack on Phú Xuân. Because of his great success, he was promoted higher and higher. He even allied himself with Trịnh Sâm's imperial concubine, Đặng Thị Huệ. In 1782, when Trịnh Sâm died, Hoàng Đình Bảo helped Đặng Thị Huệ put her son Trịnh Cán, the younger son of Trịnh Sâm, on the throne. The rightful heir and the son of the queen, Trịnh Khải staged a coup to overthrow Trịnh Cán. In the midst of this upheaval, Trịnh Khải's soldiers stoned Đình Bảo to death.

Hoàng Đức Nhã 320

Hoàng Đức Nhã: Minister of Information under Nguyễn Văn Thiệu's Sài Gòn regime.

Hoàng Hoa Thám (Đề Thám) 146

Hoàng Hoa Thám (1858 – 1913): born in Dị Chế Village, Tiên Lữ District in modern Hưng Yên Province. He later migrated to Sơn Tây and Yên Thế, which is now in Bắc Giang Province. In 1885, he took part in the insurgence against the French, which was under the leadership of Hoàng Đình Kinh (Cai Kinh). Cai Kinh gave him the name Đề Thám. When Cai Kinh died, Đề Thám became the leader of the Yên Thế Movement against the French invasion. In 1890, Đề Thám's army established a system of fortified positions in Hố Chuối Valley. There, in December 1890, Đề Thám's 100,000 soldiers defeated three attacks of French troops. The Đề Thám Insurgence caused much damage to French forces. Đề Thám's headquarters became a meeting place for many patriotic intellectuals, such as Phan Bội Châu and Phan Châu Trinh, who were also anti-French-minded, wanted to gain national independence, and wanted to discuss how to coordinate wars and create interactive support among movements. Starting in January 1909, the French attacked Yên Thế, and by the end of the year, they had besieged Đề Thám. Ba Cần (Đề Thám's third wife) was captured and many soldiers killed. The Yên Thế insurgence gradually declined. On February 10th, 1913, Đề Thám was murdered by a traitor.

Hoàng Lê Nhất Thống Chí 128

Hoàng Sa 322

Hoàng Trọng Phu 163

Hoành Sơn 21

Hòn Gai 491

Hòn Gai: in Hạ Long City of modern Quảng Ninh Province.

Hồng Cúm 257

Hồng Đức 77

Hồng River

Hồng River (Red River): originating from Yunnan, China, and

entering Việt Nam at Hà Khẩu, Lào Cai Province. The river is about 1126 km long; the section in Việt Nam is 556 km long. It runs through Lào Cai, Yên Bái, Phú Thọ, Vĩnh Phúc, Hà Nội, Hải Dương, Hưng Yên, Hà Nam, Nam Định and Thái Bình Provinces before emptying into the East Sea at Ba Lạt Estuary, the border between Thái Bình and Nam Định Provinces. The Red River, together with the Thái Bình River system in the East, forms the triangle of the Red River Delta, which covers an area of 16,654 km2.

Huy Cận (1919 - 2005): a writer. Huy Cận was his pen-name. He was born Cù Huy Cận in Ân Phú Village, Hương Sơn District, Hà Tĩnh Province.

Huỳnh Thúc Kháng (1876 – 1947): a revolutionary writer, whose real name was Huỳnh Hanh. He had many pen names including Sử Bình Tử and Xà Túc Tử. He was born in Tiên Bình Village, Tiên Phước District of modern Quảng Nam Province to a poor Confucian family. In 1904, he sat for the court exam and won the doctoral laureate title, but didn't want to enter the government. He was friends with patriotic Confucians such as Phan Châu Trinh and Trần Quý Cáp, and actively participated in the Duy Tân (Reform) Movement in Central Việt Nam. In 1908, when the anti-tax movement broke out in Central Việt Nam, Huỳnh Thúc Kháng was arrested and exiled by the French to Côn Đảo Prison, where he would stay until 1921. In prison, he learnt French by himself. In 1926, the French organized the People's Representative Assembly in Central Việt Nam, for which he became the chairman. He used his position to struggle for independence. Two years later, he resigned after a disagreement with the French Resident Superior in South Việt Nam. He turned to journalistic activities. In 1927, he began publishing the newspaper *Tiếng Dân* (Voice of the People) as its director and editor-in-chief. The newspaper opposed oppression and tyrants in rural areas. It promoted a progressive ideology and the legitimate aspirations of the people. On March 9th, 1945, Huỳnh Thúc Kháng refused an invitation to join the Japanese cabinet after a coup d'etat. In 1945, when Việt Nam re-gained its independence, he joined the Vietnamese government as Minister of Home Affairs (1946). He was also the acting President while President Hồ Chí Minh was busy with a negotiation in France. In the second resistance war against the French (1945-1954), he was the government envoy to the inter-region composed of Quảng Nam, Quảng Ngãi and Bình Định provinces.

K

Khái Hưng (1896 – 1947): a writer. His real name was Trần Khánh Dư, and he was born in Cổ Am Village, Vĩnh Bảo District, Hải Phòng City.

Khúc Hạo 41

Khúc Hạo (? – 917): Khúc Thừa Dụ's son, who succeeded him as governor. When the Liang Dynasty ousted the Tang Dynasty, they offered Khúc Hạo the post of An Nam governor. While in this post, he carried out many progressive reforms.

Khúc Thừa Dụ 41

Khúc Thừa Dụ (? – 907): the leader of an insurgence that occupied Tống Bình Citadel (modern Hà Nội) in 905, which housed the headquarters of the Tang Dynasty. After the successful insurgence, the Tang Dynasty assigned Khúc Thừa Dụ as governor of the region, which formerly was held by a Chinese man from the China Empire.

Kiến An 94, 181

Kiến An: now a suburban district of Hải Phòng City.

Kiếp Bạc 58

Kiếp Bạc: belonging to Côn Sơn - Kiếp Bạc in Chí Linh District, Hải Dương Province.

Kiều 86, 119, 125-127, 146

Kinh 45, 49, 65, 77-78, 86, 94, 128, 161, 300

Kinh Bắc 94

Kinh Bắc: now called Bắc Ninh Province.

Kinh Thi 65

L

Lạc Long Quân 20

Lạc Việt 19-21

Lai Châu 78, 216, 230, 254

Lai Châu: now two Provinces: Điện Biên and Lai Châu

Lam Sơn 72, 81

Lam Sơn Thực Lục 81

Lao Bảo 203

Lao Bảo: belonging to modern Quảng Trị Province, on road number 9, along the Việt Nam-Laos border.

Lê 5, 42, 45, 55, 61-62, 65, 71-82, 88-90, 93, 96, 98, 101-102, 104, 114-115, 120, 123, 125, 127-129, 140-141, 163, 192, 301, 310, 321-322, 325, 331, 334, 336, 350

Lê Chiêu Thống 101-102

Lê Chiêu Thống: a grandson of emperor Lê Hiển Tông. His real name was Duy Kỳ. In 1786, emperor Hiển Tông passed away, and Nguyễn Huệ put Kỳ on the throne with the reign name of Lê Chiêu Thống. In the court in Thăng Long, there were power conflicts during his reign, which resulted in Lê Chiêu Thống asking the Qing Dynasty for help in 1788. The Qing Dynasty sent troops to recover his post and invade Việt Nam. But in 1789, Quang Trung's troops defeated the Qing troops, and Chiêu Thống went into exile in China.

Lê Duẩn 301, 350

Lê Duẩn (1907 – 1986): Born on 7

April 1907 in Hậu Kiến Village, Triệu Đông Commune, Triệu Phong District, Quảng Trị Province. He joined the Tân Việt Party (a Communist organization) at the age of 21. In 1929, he joined the Vietnamese Revolutionary Youth League. In 1930, when the Vietnamese Communist Party was founded, he joined it. In 1931, he was a member of the Propagation and Training Section of the Northern Executive Committee of the Party. He was arrested in Hải Phòng and sentenced to twenty years in jail (in Hà Nội, Sơn La and Côn Đảo). In 1936, he was set free under the pressure of the French Popular Front. In 1937, he became the secretary of the Central Committee of the Indochinese Communist Party (latter renamed the Việt Nam Communist Party). In 1939, he became a member of the Central Committee of the Party. In 1940, he was arrested in Sài Gòn, sentenced to ten years in prison, and exiled to Côn Đảo Island. When the August 1945 Revolution succeeded, he was liberated and started leading the resistance war against the French in South Việt Nam. At the Second Congress of the Vietnamese Workers' Party (Việt Nam Communist Party), he was elected to the Politburo and the Central Committee. From 1946-1954, he held the position of secretary of the Southern Regional Party Committee and later the secretary of the Central Bureau for South Việt Nam. After the Geneva Accords were signed in 1954, he stayed in the South to lead the revolutionary movement. In 1957, he was sent to Hà Nội. In 1960, at the Third Congress of the Việt Nam Workers' Party, he was elected the First Secretary of the Central Committee. In 1976, at the Fourth Congress of the Party, which was renamed the Việt Nam Communist Party, he was voted the General Secretary. In 1982, at the Fifth Party Congress, he was elected General Secretary for the second time. He was a deputy of the Second and Third National Assemblies.

Lê Đức Thọ 321

Lê Đức Thọ (1911 – 1990): a statesman and diplomat, who negotiated at the Paris Conference and led the war of liberation in South Việt Nam. He was born in Địch Lễ, Mỹ Lộc District, which is now Nam Vân Commune, Nam Định Town in Nam Định Province, with the name Phan Đình Khải. At a young age, he became a member of the Indochinese Communist Party. He was arrested many times, and spent time in Côn Đảo, Hỏa Lò, Sơn La and Hòa Bình prisons. In late 1944, he was released and continued his revolutionary activities. From 1948 to 1954, he held key posts in the Southern Party committee and the Central Bureau of the Việt Nam Workers' Party in the southern region. In 1955, he returned to North Việt Nam and served in the Politburo of the Việt Nam Workers' Party. In 1968, he was chosen to be a consultant for the Democratic Republic of Việt

Nam's delegation at the Paris Conference. After the Paris Agreement was signed, Lê Đức Thọ was nominated as the Head of the South Việt Nam Department for the Party. In 1975, he helped plan the general offensive that liberated South Việt Nam. He was in charge of the Party's organization and personnel for the Politburo of the Việt Nam Communist Party for many years.

Lê Duy Mật 93, 96, 120

Lê Duy Mật (? – 1769): Son of Emperor Lê Duy Tông.

Lê Hiển Tông 101

Lê Hoàn 42, 45, 114

Lê Hoàn (941 – 1005): the first king of the Anterior Lê Dynasty, from modern Thanh Hóa Province: As a General of the Đinh Dynasty, he pronounced himself king of Đại Cồ Việt (King Lê Đại Hành), ousting Đinh Toàn, the rightful heir to the throne. In 981, he defeated the invasion by the Song Dynasty. The Anterior Lê Dynasty lasted for 29 years.

Lê Hồng Phong 192

Lê Hữu Trác 128-129

Lê Hữu Trác (1720 – 1791): a medical expert and famous writer, born in Liêu Xã Village, Mỹ Hào District, Hưng Yên Province, to an aristocratic family with many doctors. Also known as Hải Thượng Lãn Ông (the Lazybones of Hải Thượng). He was the seventh son of Minister Lê Hữu Mậu. The 66-volume tome *Y tông tâm lĩnh* (Medical Essentials) published in 1886, presents his 40-year medical experience. It is considered medical encyclopedia of the 18th century.

Lê Lợi 71-76, 79-80, 102, 336

Lê Lợi (1385 – 1433): He was born to Lê Khoảng, a commander in the region, in Lam Sơn Village of modern Xuân Lam Commune, Thọ Xuân District in Thanh Hóa Province. In 1407, the Chinese Ming invaded Đại Việt. They enticed Lê Lợi to enter the government, but he refused. In 1416, he organized a revolt, assembling forces and setting up headquarters, and chose sixteen leaders who took an oath to him. In early 1428, Lê Lợi ascended the throne as the first king of the First Lê Dynasty and changed his reign name to Thuận Thiên. He died on August 22nd, 1433, and the Lê Court honored him with the name Lê Thái Tổ—the founder of the Lê Dynasty.

Lê Quát 62, 65

Lê Quát (14th century): a student of Chu Văn An and a developer of education. He was born in Phủ Lý Commune, Đông Sơn District, Thanh Hóa Province, and was a schoolmate of Phạm Sư Mạnh. He passed the entrance exam of the Court Academy. Because he was intelligent, efficient, honest and experienced, he quickly got promoted. He closely followed Confucianism and wished to develop and improve education.

Lê Quý Đôn 98, 120, 127-128

Lê Quý Đôn (1726 – 1784): a great scholar, famous militarist and political activist of the 18th century. He was born in Diên Hà

Village, Diên Hà District of Sơn Nam Town (now Hưng Hà in Thái Bình Province). He entered the government during the Lê - Trịnh period. He wrote nearly forty works in several fields of the social sciences: geography, history, culture and literature. Doctor Bùi Huy Bích (1832 – 1890) wrote about him: "A person like him only appears once in a thousand years." Phan Huy Chú (1782 – 1840) remarked: "By nature, [Lê Quý Đôn] was an industrious author. He was profound and knowledgeable of classics and history, and his command of historical references was sufficient and clear".

Lê Thánh Tông (1442 – 1497): His name was Lê Tư Thành. He was the fourth son of King Lê Thái Tông and Ngô Thị Ngọc Dao. In 1459, Nghi Dân, King Thái Tông's first-born son killed Lê Nhân Tông, and his mother to usurp the throne. In 1460, some commanders including Nguyễn Xí, Lê Niệm deposed Nghi Dân and enthroned Lê Tư Thành. He ruled the country for 35 years.

He was not only a good king, a renowned man of culture and poet but also the pioneer in the reform of the feudal government as well as the career of building and developing the country in terms of economics, politics and culture.

Lê Trấc

Lê Trấc (1307-1339): His real name was Lê Thực, also known as Tấc. His work *An Nam chí lược* is rich in materials about the geography, history and culture of Việt Nam.

Lê Văn Huân (1876 – 1929): was born in Trung Lễ Village, which is now in Đức Trung Commune, Đức Thọ District of Hà Tĩnh Province. After his father died, his mother brought him up and educated him. In 1906, he took the inter-provincial exam and became the first category winner. Starting from 1907, he actively participated in the Duy Tân (Reform) Movement. He and Ngô Đức Kế organized Triều Dương shop in Vinh City, Nghệ An Province, an economic and financial foundation for the Đông Du (Go East) Movement. In 1908, he participated in the anti-tax movement in Nghệ An and Hà Tĩnh provinces, for which he was arrested and sentenced to nine years in Côn Đảo prison. In 1917, he was released and returned to Nghệ Tĩnh. He founded the Phục Việt Society along with other intellectuals. In 1927, they reformed it into the Việt Nam Revolutionary League and then into the Tân Việt Revolutionary Party. In September 1929, the Tân Việt cells disintegrated. Key leaders of the organization, including Lê Văn Huân, were arrested. He was kept in Vinh Prison and then moved to Hà Tĩnh where he went on a hunger strike in opposition to the jail system. He died in prison.

Lê Văn Hưu (1230 – 1322): the first

Việt Nam historian. He was born in Phủ Lý Commune, Đông Sơn District, Thanh Hóa Province. In 1247, he became the first winner of the court exam held by the King. He was assigned to work in the Court Academy, and later became the Minister of Justice. In 1272, he offered the King his book Đại Việt sử ký (Complete History of Đại Việt) written in thirty volumes.

Lịch Triều Hiến Chương 128

Linh Xứng 66

Linh Xứng Pagoda: built in the period of 1085-1089 under the direct supervision of Lý Thường Kiệt in Ngô Xá, Vĩnh Lộc, Thanh Hóa Province, which is now in Hà Ngọc Commune, Hà Trung District, Thanh Hóa Province.

Lô River 236, 240

Lô River: originating in Guangxi Province in China, it flows across Hà Giang, Tuyên Quang and Phú Thọ provinces, and meets the Red River at Việt Trì. The Lô River is 470 km long, of which 275 km is in Việt Nam.

Lộc Ninh 294, 322

Lộc Ninh: belonging to present Bình Phước Province.

Long Biên 37

Long Biên: formerly Bắc Ninh, now belonging to Long Biên District in Hà Nội

Long Thành 332-333

Long Thành: now belonging to Bà Rịa-Vũng Tàu Province.

Lon Nol

Lon Nol: A general of the Cambodian Royal Army. He staged a coup that overthrew King N. Sihanouk on March 18th, 1970.

Lương Văn Can 161

Lưu Trọng Lư 200

Lưu Trọng Lư (1912 – 1991): a poet with many different pen-names including Hy Ký and Lưu Thần. He was born in Bắc Trạch Commune, Bố Trạch District in modern Quảng Bình Province.

Luy Lâu 38

Luy Lâu: now belonging to Thuận Thành District, Bắc Ninh Province

Lý 5, 40-47, 49-52, 57-59, 61-62, 65-68, 76, 78, 84, 86-87, 117, 125, 128, 336

Lý Bí 40

Lý Bí (? – 548 AD): also known as Lý Bôn, he was the founder of the Vạn Xuân State. As a descendant of Han Chinese immigrants, he was born in Thái Bình (which belongs to North Sơn Tây Town in modern Hà Tây Province).

Lý Công Uẩn 43

Lý Công Uẩn (974 – 1028): the first king of the Lý Dynasty. He was born in the Cổ Pháp region of Đình Bảng Commune, Từ Sơn District in modern Bắc Ninh Province. When he was three years old, his mother sent him to the Lục Tổ Pagoda (now called Thày pagoda, Hà Tây Province), begging the monks to raise him. Vạn Hạnh brought up and educated the intelligent and handsome child, and when he grew up, he became a minor mandarin in the court of Lê Đại Hành. In 1009, the Anterior Lê

Dynasty declined, and Lý Công Uẩn was enthroned by Vạn Hạnh and other courtiers, as king Lý Thái Tổ.

Lý Nguyên Cát 66

Lý Nguyên Cát: according to legend, he was ethnically Chinese, but served in the Yuan army. In 1285, he was arrested by Trần soldiers. He had once been a an opera artist and was hightly appreciated for his talent; he made a significant contribution to the popularity and expansion of Vietnamese *tuồng*, a kind of theatre at the time.

Lý Tế Xuyên 65

Lý Tế Xuyên (14th century): an advocate of culture during the Trần Dynasty. He was the librarian of the Royal Court Book House before becoming a mandarin.

Lý Thái Tổ 43

Lý Thái Tổ (974 – 1028): the reign name of Lý Công Uẩn, the founder of the Lý Dynasty.

Lý Thái Tông 45, 49-50

Lý Thánh Tông 43, 61

Lý Thường Kiệt 44, 50-52, 336

Lý Thường Kiệt (1019 – 1105): He was born Ngô Tuấn in An Xá Hamlet, Quảng Đức District, now known as Cơ Xá Hamlet, Gia Lâm District, Hà Nội. His contemporaries praised him: "He was not only wise, generous and kind, but also good-hearted, simple and diligent... Knowing that prosperity was the first priority of the people, and that agriculture was the foundation of any country, he did not neglect any crops. He was talented, but not boastful. He took care of the old... used his military power to wipe out dishonest and cruel gangs, used his wisdom and justice to settle lawsuits... helped three dynasties with their political affairs [and] put down revolts at the border... His merits were very great".

M

Mã River 15, 73

Mã River: 512 km long, it flows through Sơn La Province, passing Laos and Thanh Hóa Province before emptying into the East Sea.

Mạc 65, 82, 122

Mai Thúc Loan 41

Mai Thúc Loan (? – 722): Born at Mai Phục Village, Thạch Bắc Commune, Thạch Hà District of modern Hà Tĩnh Province, his insurgence succeeded in 722. He proclaimed himself Mai Hắc Đế (meaning Black King because he had a dark complexion), but soon after, his army was attacked by 100,000 Chinese troops. The insurgency was defeated and had to withdraw to the mountains, where Mai Thúc Loan died of illness. The insurgency failed.

Mai Xuân Thưởng 144

Mai Xuân Thưởng (1860 – 1887): an anti-French resister. He was born in Bình Thành Village, Tây Sơn District in modern Bình Định Province, where he earned his bachelor's degree in 1834. In 1885, he recruited people to the Cần Vương (Save the King)

Movement of Emperor Hàm Nghi. He was awarded the title of Marshal. He organized an intensive resistance war against the French in Bình Định. French troops surrounded his base and urged him to surrender. He took his troops to a remote area to make a strategy for coping with the enemy. In retaliation, the French, with the help of some Vietnamese henchmen, captured Mai Xuân Thưởng's mother. Thưởng stated, "A shogun can be beheaded but will never surrender".

Mang Cá 328

Mang Cá: in Thừa Thiên-Huế now.

Mê Linh 20, 39

Mê Linh: the ancient land between Sơn Tây Town in Hà Tây Province and Tam Đảo, Mê Linh District, Vĩnh Phúc Province.

Mekong River 15, 139, 155, 170, 205, 228, 274, 291

Mekong River: meaning "Mother River" in Laos. From its source in the Tibetan highlands of China, at 5000m above sea level, it flows 4500 km across Myanmar, Laos, Thailand, Cambodia and Việt Nam. In Việt Nam it flows 230 km to the East Sea. At Phnom Penh, the river splits into several branches. The two biggest branches enter Việt Nam through Hồng Ngự District of An Giang Province, forming the Tiền and Hậu Rivers. At Cần Thơ city, the Tiền River divides into nine branches before emptying into the sea, creating the Mekong, or Southern Delta, which covers an area of 39,568 km2. The Vietnamese people call it Cửu Long, which means "nine dragons".

Minh Cầm 16

Minh Cầm: Hà Tĩnh Province.

Móng Cái 145, 164, 216

Móng Cái: now belonging to Móng Cái District, Quảng Ninh Province, it is located in Northeastern Việt Nam. The District is bordered by China in the North and by Việt Nam's Tonkin Gulf in the East.

Mường Thanh 257

Mỹ Sơn 110

Mỹ Sơn: now belonging to Quảng Nam Province. Built in the 4th century, this was the Holy Land of the Chămpa Kingdom. Between the 7th to 13th centuries, Mỹ Sơn was extended and became the most important architectual complex of Chămpa Kingdom. There were totally 70 works of which only 20 items still exist now. On December 4th, 1999, UNESCO recognized Mỹ Sơn as a world cultural heritage site.

Mỹ Tho 7, 100, 118, 205, 310

Mỹ Tho: Mỹ Tho City, the capital of modern Tiền Giang Province.

N

Nam Bộ 25, 100, 118, 226-228, 230-232, 235, 241, 282-283, 321

Nam Bộ: South Việt Nam, or the southern provinces, spreading from Đồng Nai Province to Cà Mau, including the entire

Mekong Delta.

Nam Cao 200, 302

Nam Cao (1915–1951): a writer. Nam Cao was his penname. Born in Đại Hoàng Village, now belonging to Nhân Hậu Commune, Lý Nhân District, Hà Nam Province, his real name was Trần Hữu Tri.

Nam Dược Thần Hiệu 69

Ngang Pass 19, 110

Ngang Pass: about 2560m long, National Highway 1A winds up and over this mountain pass, which now lies along the border between Hà Tĩnh and Quảng Bình provinces.

Nghệ Tĩnh 190-191, 201

Nghệ Tĩnh: the joint name of Nghệ An and Hà Tĩnh provinces.

Nghĩa Lộ 145, 203, 241

Nghĩa Lộ: no longer exists. Formerly, one part belonged to Lai Châu Province and the other part belonged to Lào Cai Province.

Ngô Đình Diệm 192, 208, 271-273, 306, 319

Ngô Đức Kế 163, 176

Ngô Đình Diệm (1901 – 1963): known primarily as the leader of the Southern regime during the American War, who undermined the Geneva Accords. He was born to a high-ranking Mandarin family of the Nguyễn Dynasty in Đại Phong Village, Lệ Thủy District, Quảng Bình Province. In 1920, after his graduation from the Mandarin College of the Nguyễn Court, Ngô Đình Diệm became a mandarin in various provinces of Central Việt Nam. In 1933, King Bảo Đại chose him to be Minister of the Interior in the newly-founded Cabinet and concurrently filled an important role as a privy counsellor in the Nguyễn Administration. Due to his conflict with Phạm Quỳnh, a French supporter, Diệm resigned from office in 1934.

After the August Revolution in 1945, revolutionary forces strictly controlled him until he was taken to America for training in 1950. In 1954, backed by the United States, he became the Prime Minister of Bảo Đại's government; yet he then deposed President Bảo Đại in October 1955 to take power in South Việt Nam. After that, he made every effort to prevent national unification, undermine the Geneva Accords and hinder the revolution.

On November 1st, 1963, Ngô Đình Diệm and his younger brother Ngô Đình Nhu were killed in a coup staged by his opponents with the help of the American advisers.

Ngô Đức Kế 176

Ngô Đức Kế (1879 – 1929): a revolutionary journalist and educator. He was born in Trảo Nha Village, in modern Đại Lộc Commune, Can Lộc District, Hà Tĩnh Province, to a Confucian family. In 1887, he earned his bachelor's degree. In 1901, he earned a doctoral degree, but decided not to join the government. He stayed in his home village to work for the community. He set up a school to raise the people's intellectual standards and to make the country prosper. He sympathized with the Đông Du (Go East) Movement. Because of his participation in the anti-tax movement in Central Việt Nam in 1908, the French arrested him and sent him to Côn Đảo. He was set free in 1921. In 1922, he went to Hà Nội to pursue journalistic activities and set up the *Giác quán thư xã* Publishing House in 1926. He died in 1929.

Ngô Quyền 41-42, 56

Ngô Quyền (899-944): born in Đường Lâm Commune, Sơn Tây District, Hà Tây Province. His father Ngô Mân was a local chief under Khúc Thừa Dụ reign. He was chosen to be Dương Đình Nghệ's inferior general and married the latter's daughter.

Later, he was appointed as the leader of the Ái region (belonging to present Thanh Hóa). In 937, as his father-in-law was murdered by Kiều Công Tiễn, one of Dương Đình Nghệ's generals, he took troops there to chastise Kiều Công Tiễn. Tiễn was so filled with terror that he ordered his people to ask the King of Nam Hán (Southern Han, China) for help. Hán's King delegated his son (Hong Cao) to lead the invading troops. On hearing about that, Ngô Quyền led his army to the North to kill Kiều Công Tiễn. No sooner had the heroes heard of the news than they brought their troops back and together with Ngô Quyền, they were ready to resist the invaders.

Ngô Sĩ Liên 65, 82, 127

Ngô Sĩ Liên: a historian, born in Chúc Lý Village, Chương Đức District (now Chương Mỹ District in Hà Tây Province). He earned his doctoral degree in 1442 and became a mandarin in the Academy of the Lê Dynasty.

Ngô Tất Tố 200

Ngô Tất Tố (1894 – 1954): a writer, journalist and researcher of philosophy and literature; born in Lộc Hà Village, Tiên Sơn District, Bắc Ninh Province.

Ngọc Hà 46

Ngọc Hà: an area in Ba Đình District, Hà Nội.

Ngọc Hân 101

Ngọc Hồi 104

Ngọc Hồi: now belonging to Thanh Trì District, Hà Nội.

Ngọc Lũ: 18

Ngọc Lũ: now belonging to Bình Lục District, Hà Nam Province.

Nguyễn 3-4, 7-9, 65, 72-74, 79-84, 90, 92-94, 97-108, 118-120, 123, 125-128, 133, 135, 138-142, 145-146, 161-163, 175-180, 182, 193, 200-201, 208, 210, 216, 226, 233, 291, 293, 302, 313, 319, 328, 331-334, 336, 352

Nguyễn Ái Quốc 176, 178-179, 182, 201, 210

Nguyễn Ái Quốc: see Hồ Chí Minh.

Nguyễn Án 128

Nguyễn Án (1770 – 1815): a poet, writer and district chief of the Nguyễn Dynasty, born in Từ Sơn Prefecture, Kinh Bắc Town (now in the outskirts of Hà Nội). His works consist of both poems and historical accounts.

Nguyễn An Ninh 175, 177, 179, 193

Nguyễn An Ninh (1900 – 1943): He was born in Mỹ Hòa Commune, Hóc Môn District, Gia Định Province (now Hồ Chí Minh City) to a patriotic Confucian family. After graduating from secondary school, he went to Hà Nội for higher education, and then to France. He earned his Bachelor of Arts degree in 1920. While studying, he wrote for some French newspapers in South Việt Nam. In France, he made contact with Phan Châu Trinh, Phan Văn Trường, Nguyễn Ái Quốc and the Paria Group (Outcasts Group). After earning his B.A. degree, he traveled around Europe to learn more about it. He returned to Sài Gòn and delivered speeches against imperialism at the Southern Study-Encouragement Society, and he was warmly welcomed by agricultural intellectuals. In Sài Gòn, he published the newspaper *La Clôch Fléchit* (The Bell with Cracked Sound) to encourage the people's claim for democracy and freedom. The first issue printed the "Eight Claims of the Vietnamese People," which Nguyễn Ái Quốc had sent to the Versailles Conference in 1919. After seven issues, the paper was banned. Nguyễn An Ninh was arrested and imprisoned. At the beginning of 1926, he was set free and returned to France. After that, he continued his patriotic activities, wrote newspapers, and translated progressive books from French into Vietnamese. In 1928, he was arrested again and sentenced to three years' imprisonment. After being released, he again participated in the patriotic movement. He was arrested two more times (in January and October 1939) before he died in Côn Đảo Prison, with heart wholly devoted to the Communist Party and revolution.

Nguyễn Ánh 7-8, 100-101, 106-107

Nguyễn Ánh (1762 – 1819): Founder of the Nguyễn Dynasty and the grandson of Nguyễn Phúc Thuần. His reign name was Emperor Gia Long.

Nguyễn Bá Cẩn 332-333

Nguyễn Bỉnh Khiêm 82-83, 180

Nguyễn Bỉnh Khiêm (1491 - 1585): He was born at Trung Am Village, Vĩnh Lại District, which is now Vĩnh Bảo District of Hải Phòng City, to a Confucian family. Despite being a good student, he did not take the exams to become a mandarin. In 1535, however, at the age of 45, he followed the advice of his friends and family and took the court exam. He became the First doctoral laureate and a mandarin of the Mạc Dynasty. When his request to execute some corrupt officials was not approved by the king, he resigned and returned to his homeland to take up the teaching career. Later, the Mạc Dynasty appointed him Minister of the Interior and honoured him as Trạng Trình (Wise Man named Trạng Trình); the common people called him Doctor Trình. He left behind a wide range of valuable literary and philosophical works.

Nguyễn Cảnh Chân 72

Nguyễn Cảnh Chân (? – 1409): Trần Giản Định's famous commander. He was born in Ngọc Sơn of Nam Đàn District, Nghệ An Province. He took part in the government of the Trần Dynasty and later held an important role under the Hồ Dynasty. He was killed along with Đặng Tất by Trần Giản Định's assistants in 1409.

Nguyễn Cao Kỳ 313, 334

Nguyễn Cao Kỳ (1930 –): a lieutenant-general and the commander of the Sài Gòn Air Force (1964 – 1975). He was concurrently the Vice President and Prime Minister of the Republic of Việt Nam from 1965 to 1967. In 1975, he emigrated to the United States, where he still lives. He was born in Sơn Tây of modern Hà Tây Province.

Nguyễn Chích 73

Nguyễn Chích (1382 – 1449): a famous general of the Lam Sơn insurgency.

Nguyễn Công Hoan 200, 302

Nguyễn Công Hoan (1903– 1977): a writer, born in Xuân Cầu Village, Văn Giang District, Bắc Ninh Province (now it is Châu Giang District, Hưng Yên Province).

Nguyễn Cư Trinh 99

Nguyễn Cư Trinh (1716 – 1767): a famous Southern writer, politician in the time of Nguyễn Lords, born in Đạm Am Village, Thiên Lộc District, Đức Quang Prefect, Nghệ An Town (now Can Lộc District in Hà Tĩnh Province). As an intellectual government official of the Nguyễn Lords period, he positively impacted the people's lives. He advised the Nguyễn Lords to dismiss corrupt mandarins and helped to reclaim Gia Định - Sài Gòn (now Hồ Chí Minh City).

Nguyễn Danh Phương 94

Nguyễn Danh Phương (? – 1751): the leader of a peasant insurgence in North Việt Nam. He was born at Tiên Sơn village, Yên Lạc District, Sơn Tây region (currently Hợp Thịnh Commune, Tam Đảo District, Vĩnh Phúc Province). In 1739, he took part in the Đồ Tề rebellion. After it failed, he continued his revolutionary career in Vĩnh Phúc, Thái Nguyên, and Tuyên Quang provinces. In early 1751, Lord Trịnh crushed the peasant insurgence in North Việt Nam.

Nguyễn Đình Chiểu 138

Nguyễn Đình Chiểu (1822 – 1888): a poet and physician. He was born in Tân Thới Village, Bình Dương District, Gia Định Province, now Hồ Chí Minh City, into a poor Confucian family. In 1843, he passed high school exams in Gia Định, and went to study in Huế. He opened a school in his hometown. In 1850, he wrote *Lục Vân Tiên*, a versified novel about his love for justice and dislike for fraudulence. He also wrote many poems praising the soldiers fighting the French.

Nguyễn Đình Thi 302

Nguyễn Đình Thi (1924–2003): a writer, poet, dramatist and music composer. He was an artist of versatile talent, a veteran in Việt Nam's modern literature and art.

Nguyễn Du 119, 125-127

Nguyễn Du: His pen-name was Tố Như. He was born in Tiên Điền Village, Nghi Xuân District in modern Hà Tĩnh Province to an aristocratic family. His father was Doctor Nguyễn Nghiễm, the highest-ranking mandarin in the Lê-Trịnh period. Nguyễn Du was a mandarin in the Lê Dynasty. In 1965, he was recognized as a World Great Man of Culture.

Nguyễn Gia Thiều 123

Nguyễn Gia Thiều (1741 – 1798): a poet and a writer, born in Liễu Ngạn Village, Siêu Loại District (now Thuận Thành District, Bắc Ninh Province) to an aristocratic family. His mother was Trịnh Cương's daughter. Nguyễn Gia Thiều was very knowledgeable of literature and arts; He was put in charge of millitary affairs in Hưng Hóa prefecture (the present North West region). In 1786, the Tây Sơn uprising succeeded in overthrowing the Trịnh lords and fought against the invading Qing troops. The Tây Sơn leaders invited him to join the government, but he refused and asked permission to return to his native land.

Nguyễn Hải Thần 226

Nguyễn Hải Thần (1878 – 1959): also called Nguyễn Cẩm Giang, an anti-French revolutionary. His real name was Vũ Hải Thu, and he was born in Đại Từ, now in Hoàng Mai District of Hà Nội. As a winner of an inter-regional civil exam, he was called Bachelor Đại Từ.

Hải Thần went abroad to Japan as part of Phan Bội Châu's Đông Du (Go East) campaign to study at a College in Tokyo (1904-1909). After that, he went to China and joined the Việt Nam Restoration Association (1912-1924). In 1937, he founded and became the leader of the Association of Việt Nam Revolutionary Allies. In 1945, Thần followed Chiang Kai-shek to his home in Việt Nam and became a member of the provisional coalition government on January 1st, 1946. Later, he was voted to the First National Assembly and held the position of Vice Chairman in the coalition government (March 1946). When Chiang Kai-shek's troops withdrew, Hải Thần followed them and lived in exile in China. He died in Guangzhou in 1959.

Nguyên Hồng 200

Nguyên Hồng (1918–1982): a writer. He was born Nguyễn Nguyên Hồng in Nam Định Town, the capital of Nam Định Province.

Nguyễn Huệ 99-104, 106-108, 118, 126

Nguyễn Huệ (1753 – 1792): Younger brother of Nguyễn Nhạc.

Nguyễn Hữu Cầu 94, 126

Nguyễn Khải 302

Nguyễn Khải (1930 –): a writer. His real name was Nguyễn Mạnh Khải, and he was born in Nam Định Province. His father was a district chief under the French administration.

Nguyễn Lữ 99, 106

Nguyễn Lữ (18th century): Younger brother of Nguyễn Nhạc and

Nguyễn Huệ.

Nguyên Ngọc 302

Nguyên Ngọc (1932 –): a writer. He was born as Nguyễn Văn Báu in Thăng Bình District, Quảng Nam Province. His other pen names included Nguyễn Trung Thành, Nguyễn Kim.

Nguyễn Nhạc 99-100, 102, 106

Nguyễn Nhạc (? – 1793): leader of the Tây Sơn uprising, and the first emperor of the Tây Sơn Dynasty. His ancestors were from the Hồ family, who originally lived in Thái Lão Village, Hưng Nguyên District in Nghệ An Province (just outside modern Vinh City). In his father's generation, the family moved to the Tây Sơn Hạ region, Quy Nhơn Prefecture (now Kiều Mỹ Hamlet, Bình Thành Village, Tây Sơn District, Bình Định Province). Nhạc was the eldest son; next were Nguyễn Huệ and Nguyễn Lữ.

Nguyễn Quang Bích 145-146

Nguyễn Quang Bích (1832 – 1890): a revolutionary and a winner of the court exam in 1869; born in An Ninh Commune, Tiền Hải District, Thái Bình Province. In 1882, he became the chief of Hưng Hóa Province. In 1883, the French attacked Hưng Hóa, and he led his soldiers to protect the citadel. When the citadel was lost, he disobeyed the Court's order and led his troops to the northwest mountains to set up a base for long-lasting resistance against the French. He supported the Cần Vương (Save the King) Movement of Emperor Hàm Nghi, organized a rebellion, and caused many troubles to the French. Before he died in 1890 of terrible sickness, he asked his relatives to adopt the date on which the Hưng Hóa Citadel was lost to the French as his death anniversary date. He left behind many valuable literary works.

Nguyễn Quyền 161

Nguyễn Sĩ Cố 65

Nguyễn Thái Học 179

Nguyễn Thái Học (1904 – 1930): the leader of the Yên Bái Uprising against the French. He was born in Thổ Tang Village, Vĩnh Tường District, Vĩnh Phúc Province. He studied Chinese, Vietnamese and French at the French-Vietnamese School, Vĩnh Yên, Vĩnh Phúc Province, and then at Hà Nội Teachers College and the Hà Nội Business College. In 1926, he wrote to the French Governor to demand that the latter expand industry and commerce in the region, set up a technical college and allow Vietnamese people to open schools. He also requested that the Governor reform the local administration and allow freedom of speech. That same year, he dropped out of school and began his political activities. In 1927, he founded the Nam Đồng Publishing House in Hà Nội and the Vietnamese Nationalist Party, of which he was elected chairman. The Party's mission was to unify the Vietnamese people, irrespective of class or religion, and use violence to gain independence for Việt Nam. In 1930, his Party organized uprisings in Yên Bái and Phú Thọ provinces.

He personally led the Yên Bái Uprising on February 10th, 1930, but it failed. Nguyễn Thái Học and his twelve comrades were arrested in Hải Dương and on June 17th, 1930, they were executed in the town in Yên Bái Province where the uprising took place.

Nguyễn Thi 302

Nguyễn Thi (1928 – 1968), a writer with many pen-names, including Nguyễn Thi and Nguyễn Ngọc Tấn. His real name was Nguyễn Hoàng Ca. He was born in Quần Phương Thượng Commune, Hải Hậu District, which is now Hải Anh Commune, Hải Hậu District of Nam Định Province. He died on the front in Southern Việt Nam during the American War (1954-1975).

Nguyễn Thị Bình 291

Nguyễn Thị Bình (1928 –): former Foreign Minister of the Provisional Revolutionary Government of the Republic of South Việt Nam, former Minister of Education and former Vice President of the Socialist Republic of Việt Nam.

Nguyễn Thiện Thuật 145

Nguyễn Thuyên 65

Nguyễn Thuyên (13th century): Born in Thanh Khê Commune, Nam Sách District in modern Hải Dương Province, he became a mandarin of the Trần Dynasty, and was the Minister of Justice during Trần Nhân Tông's reign. His pen-name was Hàn Thuyên.

Nguyễn Trãi 73-74, 79-82, 84, 336

Nguyễn Trãi: Nguyễn Trãi was born in 1380 in Nhị Khê Village, Thường Tín District, present-day Hà Tây Province. He passed the court exam in 1400 under the Hồ Dynasty, and held the post of *Ngự sĩ đài chính trưởng* (supervisor of the King's activities). When the Ming troops invaded Đại Việt from China, he refused to cooperate with the invaders. He hid at Đông Quan citadel for over ten years before moving to Thanh Hóa Province. Where he joined the Lam Sơn Resistance (1418-1428). After the victory, Nguyễn Trãi resigned and lived like a hermit on Côn Sơn Mountain. In 1442, Nguyễn Trãi was accused of murdering the king in partnership with his concubine Nguyễn Thị Lộ. He was sentenced to execution along with three generations of his family. In 1464, King Lê Thánh Tông cleared Nguyễn Trãi of his accusation. As a scholar, poet and master strategist of the 15th century, Nguyễn Trãi was honored as a World Great Man of Culture by UNESCO in 1980.

Nguyễn Tri Phương 141

Nguyễn Trung Ngạn 65

Nguyễn Trung Ngạn (1289 – 1370): a famous mandarin, politician, militarist and poet of the Trần Dynasty. As an infant in Thổ Hàng Hamlet, Thiện Thi District (now Ân Thi District of Hưng Yên Province), he was known as an intelligent prodigy. When he was fifteen, he ranked second in the court examination, and held many different positions in the Royal Court. In 1314, he was sent as an ambassador to the Yuan Emperor. As a mandarin, he was known to be just in his rulings. Later, in 1337, he began researching the history of the nation.

Nguyễn Trung Thành 302

Nguyễn Trung Thành: a pen-name of writer Nguyên Ngọc.

Nguyễn Trung Trực 135, 139

Nguyễn Trung Trực (1838 – 1868): His other name was Nguyễn Văn Lịch (Quản Lịch), born in Tân An Prefecture, Định Tường Province (now Long An Province). He had a good command of the language Hán, and engaged in both farming and fishing. He drastically resisted the French invasion of South Việt Nam. In 1867, the French occupied South Việt Nam. After the Huế court surrendered to the French, they gave Nguyễn Trung Trực a title and assigned him a post in the Central part of Việt Nam. He refused to go and stayed in the South to organize the resistance war, establishing bases at Hòn Chông. At dawn on June 16th, 1868, his troops attached the Kiên Giang military post of the French (now Rạch Giá City), and wiped out the French troops stationed there. Then, he withdrew to Phú Quốc Island, and soon after, the French attacked the island. In September 1868, he was captured. The French executed him on November 27th 1868, at Rạch Giá.

Nguyễn Trường Tộ 140

Nguyễn Trường Tộ (1830 – 1831): an intellectual and diplomat from a poor Catholic family. Born in Bùi Chu Village, Hưng Nguyên District, Nghệ An Province, he was hard-working, intelligent, despite starting going to school late. He preferred a pragmatic method of learning and disapproved of the system of formal examinations. In 1856, a French Catholic priest named Gauthier invited him to teach Hán script for the Church at Đoài Village (Nghệ An). He accepted, and while he was there, they taught him French, and took him to visit Singapore, Hương Cảng (Hong Kong), Rome and Paris to study social and natural sciences. In 1861, he returned to Gia Định (Sài Gòn) after the French occupied it. He worked as an interpreter, helping the Huế Court negotiate with the French. Once he informed the mandarins of a French plot to use Vietnamese henchmen to cause riots in Bắc Kỳ (North Việt Nam). During that time, he pressured the Court to modernize the country, broaden diplomatic relationships with other countries, and send people to developed countries to study scientific and technical subjects. The Nguyễn Court sent him to France to hire professors, technical experts and procure machines and books for a new Western-style technical college. While there, he sent the court a very important petition requiring reform of the country. However, the Nguyễn Court did not accept his proposal and he was called back to Viet Nam. Even back at home, Nguyễn Trường Tộ continued sending his proposals on reform and economic strategy to the Court.

Nguyễn Tuân 302

Nguyễn Tuân (1910–1987): a great

Vietnamese writer, born at Mọc Village, or Nhân Mục, belonging to Nhân Chính Commune, Thanh Xuân District in Hà Nội.

Nguyễn Tường Tam 226

Nguyễn Văn Bổng 302

Nguyễn Văn Bổng (1921– 2001): a writer. His other pen-names included Trần Hiếu Minh, Lê Nguyên Trung, Vương Quế Lâm and Phương Nguyên. He was born in Đại Quang Commune, Đại Lộc District, Quảng Nam Province.

Nguyễn Văn Thiệu 293, 319

Nguyễn Văn Thiệu (1923 – 2001): President of the Sài Gòn government (1967-1975). He was born in Bình Thuận. In 1948, he joined the French army. In 1954, he served in Ngô Đình Diệm's administration. He became a lieutenant general in Sài Gòn military in 1965. He took part in three coups (1963: against Ngô Đình Diệm; 1964: against Dương Văn Minh; 1965: against: Nguyễn Khánh), the last of which put him in power. In April 1975, he fled to Taiwan when the Liberation troops marched into Sài Gòn. After that, he lived in exile in Great Britain and the USA.

Nha Trang 111, 156, 284, 330

Nha Trang: Nha Trang Coastal Town is now the capital of Khánh Hòa Province.

Nhất Linh 200

Nhất Linh (1906 –1963): a poet. He was born Nguyễn Tường Tam in Cẩm Giàng District, Hải Dương Province.

Như Nguyệt 50-51

Như Nguyệt River 51

Như Nguyệt River: now called Cầu River and the natural border between Bắc Ninh and Bắc Giang provinces. It flows across Bắc Cạn, Thái Nguyên, Bắc Giang and Bắc Ninh provinces, and just 40km north of Hà Nội before joining the Thái Bình River system.

Nông Quốc Chấn 302

Nông Quốc Chấn (1923–2002): a write from the Tày ethnic group. He was born at Nạ Cọt Village, Ngân Sơn District, Bắc Cạn Province, and became the Deputy Minister of Culture and Information of the Socialist Republic of Việt Nam later in life.

Nùng Trí Cao 50

Nùng Trí Cao (? – 1053): His father Nùng Tôn Phúc, the leader of the mountainous Thảng Do District (now called Cao Bằng), led his troops to kill other neighboring leaders, occupy land, and set up a kingdom with himself as emperor. King Lý Thái Tông led his troops to repress the rebellion. Tôn Phúc was arrested and killed, but Nùng Trí Cao and his mother escaped. Later, he returned to Thảng Do District to set up the Đại Lịch State. King Lý sent his army to put down the revolt. Both Nùng Trí Cao and his older brother were arrested. King Lý later forgave him and allowed him to go back to his former district and manage some of the neighboring districts. But Nùng Trí Cao was not content with his lot and occupied the neighboring regions. In 1052, he proclaimed himself Emperor. He

then led his army to attack Hua Nan (now part of China). He occupied Yang Zhou (Guangxi, China) and brought his troops to the foot of Guang Zhou Citadel (Guangdong, China). The Song Dynasty mobilized the army to resist and Nùng Trí Cao was completely defeated by 1058. Cao fled to Da Li (in Yunnan now), but was captured and killed.

O

Óc Eo 15

Óc Eo: now belonging to Vãng Thê Commune, Thoại Sơn District, An Giang Province

P

Pắc Bó 209

Pắc Bó: belonging to Hà Quảng District, Cao Bằng Province near the Việt Nam-China border.

Phạm Đình Hổ 128

Phạm Đình Hổ (1762 – 1839): an author of poems, historical accounts and monographs, born in Đan Loan Village, Đường An District, which is now Cẩm Giàng District of Hải Dương Province.

Phạm Hồng Thái 176

Phạm Hồng Thái (1895 – 1924): a revolutionary factory worker. He was born on May 14th, 1895, to a poor Confucian family in Do Nha Village, which is now Hưng Nhân Village, Hưng Nguyên District, Nghệ An Province. In 1920, he started working at the Trường Thi Railway Factory and the Bến Thủy Lamp Factory, both in Vinh City. After participating in a strike, he was fired. Then, he managed to find a job at the Chợ Chu zinc mine in Bắc Cạn Province. There, he organized a strike and was fired again. Then, he went to Hải Phòng to work in a cement factory. In 1924, Lê Hồng Phong, Lê Thiết Hùng and he traveled to Thailand, and then to China. In Guangzhou, he joined the Vietnamese patriotic organization Tâm Tâm Xã (Union of Hearts). To make a resounding statement of the Vietnamese revolutionary movement, he devised a plot to assassinate the Indochinese Governor Merlin when the latter visited Guangzhou. He detonated a bomb at a hotel party, where Merlin was present but Merlin was only slightly injured. Afterward, being chased by the French police, he threw himself into the Zhou Jiang River.

Phạm Huy Thông 200

Phạm Huy Thông (1916 –1988): a poet and specialist in Vietnamese history. He was born in Đào Xá Village, Ân Thi District, Hưng Yên Province.

Phạm Ngọc Thạch 214

Phạm Ngũ Lão 56

Phạm Ngũ Lão (1255 – 1320): a famous general of the Trần Dynasty. Born into a farmer family in Phù Ủng Hamlet, Đường Hào District (now called Ân Thi District in Hưng Yên Province), he was interested in martial arts and literature. He was both a scholar and a warrior and as such was highly appreciated by the kings of the Trần Dynasty.

When he died, King Trần Minh Tông mourned him.

Phạm Quỳnh 192

Phạm Sư Mạnh 65

Phạm Sư Mạnh (14th century): a famous mandarin of the Trần Dynasty. Born in Hiệp Thạch Hamlet of Hiệp Sơn District in what is now Hải Dương Province, he was intelligent, hard-working, and cherished by his teacher Chu Văn An. He passed the court exam during Trần Minh Tông's reign (1314-1329), and was selected to be a mandarin. Later, he was sent to the Yuan-Mongol Emperor as a representative of the Trần Dynasty. He was an expert in literature, poetry and history.

Phạm Văn Đồng 259, 296, 301

Phan Bội Châu 161, 163-164, 176-177

Phan Bội Châu (1867 – 1940): a revolutionary, leader of the Duy Tân Movement, and founder of the Việt Nam Restoration Society. His real name was Phan Văn San, alias Sào Nam, and he was born on December 26th, 1867, in Đan Nhiễm Village, which is now in Xuân Hòa Commune, Nam Đàn District, Nghệ An Province, into a poor Confucian family. From an early age, he was famous for his intelligence, industriousness in school, good performance in exams. He was close to the common people and an ardent patriot. In 1882, on hearing that the French had attacked North Việt Nam, he wrote the Appeal *Bình Tây thu Bắc* (Fight the French and recover the North) in Chinese characters. In 1885, the Huế citadel was lost to the French, after which, Phan Bội Châu organized a group called *Sĩ tử Cần Vương* (Confucian scholars for the King's rescue) in support of the Cần Vương (Save the King) Movement. In 1900, he was the top winner of an inter-provincial exam, and began his revolutionary career. In March 1909, the Đông Du organization was dissolved. Phan Bội Châu was expelled by the Japanese government, and had to go to China. In 1911, he established the Việt Nam Restoration Society in China to "drive off the French enemy, restore the nation and set up the Nationalist Republic of Việt Nam". On December 24th, 1913, he was imprisoned by Chinese military forces, and released four years later. He studied the Russian October Revolution of 1917 and wrote articles on Vladimir Lenin. In 1924, he transformed the Việt Nam Restoration Society into the Việt Nam National Party, modeling it after Sun Yat-sen Chinese Nationalist Party. During this time, he kept in touch with Nguyễn Ái Quốc (Hồ Chí Minh) to get advice on improving the Vietnamese Nationalist Party. However, he was arrested soon after by the French on his way from Hang Zhou to Guang Zhou (China). From 1926 on, he was isolated from the national struggle. Yet, he wrote books and articles to raise the people's intellectual standards. He left behind 800 poems, several novels, and valuable research works when he died on October

29th, 1940 in Huế.

Phan Chu Trinh 161-163, 176-177

Phan Chu Trinh (1872 – 1926): a revolutionary and contemporary of Phan Bội Châu. He was born Tây Hồ in Tây Lộc Village, Tiền Phước District of modern Quảng Nam Province. After he had gained success in a court exam, in 1901, he was appointed to the Ministry of Rites in the Huế court. Under the influence of bourgeois democratic thought, he resigned and initiated the Duy Tân (Reform) Movement with Huỳnh Thúc Kháng and Trần Quý Cáp. So began his life of patriotic activities. In 1906, he went to Japan to meet Phan Bội Châu. They disagreed on the strategy for gaining national independence: Phan Châu Trinh advocated for non-violent and open struggle, while Phan Bội Châu preferred violent revolutionary uprisings. Phan Châu Trinh returned home and wrote to the Indochinese Governor to criticize the domestic policy and condemn the Huế' Court. In 1907, the Đông Kinh Nghĩa Thục Institute invited him to Hà Nội to deliver speeches in support of the Duy Tân Movement and reform. In 1908, he and many other patriots were arrested and exiled to Côn Đảo Island. Three years later, after his release, he requested a permission to go to France, so as to urge the French Human Rights Association to demand the Indochinese colonial government to carry out reform in politics and respect human rights. During World War I, he was imprisoned by the French government for 15 months. From 1917 to 1923, in Paris, he maintained contact with patriots like Phan Văn Trường and Nguyễn Ái Quốc (Hồ Chí Minh). In 1925, he returned to Việt Nam to carry out revolutionary activities in the traditional way. He died in Sài Gòn on March 14th, 1926.

Phan Đình Phùng 146, 162

Phan Đình Phùng (1847 – 1895): An anti-French revolutionary. He was born in Đông Thái Village, now Đức Phong Commune, Đức Thọ District, Hà Tĩnh Province, and earned his doctoral degree in 1877. He was appointed chief of Yên Khánh Province, now Ninh Bình Province. Then, he became a counselor in the Huế court. In 1885, he spoke out against Emperor Dục Đức and supported putting Hiệp Hòa on the throne. He was dismissed and sent back to his village. In 1887, Tôn Thất Thuyết took Emperor Hàm Nghi to Hà Tĩnh. Phan Đình Phùng was invited to support the Cần Vương (Save the King) Movement and set up an anti-French base in the mountains between Hương Sơn and Hương Khê districts of Hà Tĩnh. After he died, the French excavated his grave, burnt his body, mixed the ashes with gun powder and shot into the La River in Hà Tĩnh. For the Việt Namese, this was an act of ruthless revenge.

Phan Rang 330-331

Phan Rang: now belonging to Ninh Thuận Province.

Phan Thanh Giản 137, 139

Phan Thanh Giản (1796 – 1867): a mandarin and revolutionary. Born in Bảo Thạnh Village, Bảo An District, Vĩnh Long Province (now Ba Tri District, Bến Tre Province), he earned his doctoral degree in 1826 and became a mandarin for three Nguyễn kings. He held many important positions, and was famous for his uprightness and morality. When the French invaded Nam Kỳ (South Việt Nam), he and Lâm Duy Hiệp, on behalf of the Huế Court, negotiated with the French, and signed on 5th June 1862 the Treaty which gave three southeastern provinces over to France. Afterwards, Phan Thanh Giản was appointed to the negotiation delegation charged with getting the provinces back. The negotiations failed. He returned home and became the Administrator of three southwestern provinces. The French sent troops into these areas to threaten the local leaders. After estimating the situation and the balance of forces, Phan Thanh Giản handed Vĩnh Long Citadel (now Vĩnh Long Province) over to them and told the mandarins in An Giang and Hà Tiên (now Kiên Giang) provinces to follow suit (1867). Soon after, however, he realized his mistake, started fasting, told his children not to cooperate with the French, and poisoned himself. He was a great cultural activist, with many valuable literary and historical works. Emperor Tự Đức ordered his name to be removed from a doctoral stele.

Phan Tứ 302

Phan Tứ (1930 – 1995), a writer, whose real name was Lê Khâm. He was born in Quế Châu Commune, Quế Sơn District of modern Quảng Nam Province.

Phan Văn Trường 175

Phan Văn Trường (1876 – 1933): Born in Đông Ngạc Village, also called Chèm Village, Từ Liêm District, Hà Nội, he was an interpreter in the Resident Superior's office. Later, he went to France and taught at the School of Far East Languages. Here, he also earned his Bachelor of Arts degree. In 1914, he was drafted into the French armed forces, but then arrested for his involvement with the Vietnamese resistance movement. In 1917, after being released, he became a millitary worker in Toulouse until the end of war. In 1919, he set up a law office in Paris, and earned a doctorate with the thesis "Brief Scientific Research on Gia Long Law". During this time, he joined political activities, and became one of the most famous members of the Group of Vietnamese patriots in France. He had a close relationship with Nguyễn Ái Quốc (Hồ Chí Minh). He sympathized with Marxist – Leninist doctrine and the Russian October Revolution. In 1923, he returned to Việt Nam. In Sài Gòn, he actively participated in the campaign for democracy and opposed the reactionary policies of the French colonial government. Due to these activities, he was put in prison. He died on 23rd April 1933 at his native village.

Phát Diệm 144

Phật Tích pagoda 67

Phật Tích Pagoda: also known as Vạn Phúc Pagoda, this pagoda was built under Lê Thánh Tông's reign. It is located on Phật Tích Mountain (or Lan Kha Mountain), now belonging to Phượng Hoàng Commune, Tiên Sơn District, Bắc Ninh Province.

Phay Khắt 210

Phay Khắt: belonging to Nguyên Bình District, Cao Bằng Province.

Phổ Minh 68

Phổ Minh Pagoda

Phổ Minh Pagoda: also known as Tháp Pagoda (meaning Tower Pagoda), it was built during the Lý Dynasty and extended in 1262 during the Trần Dynasty. It is located in Tức Mạc Hamlet, Lộc Vượng Commune, Nam Định Town, Nam Định Province, about 90 km east of Hà Nội.

Phú Bài 310, 328

Phú Bài: now belonging to Thừa Thiên-Huế. Phú Bài Airport is located southeast of Huế City.

Phú Quốc 100

Phú Quốc Island: in the Gulf of Thailand, now belonging to Kiên Giang Province. The island has an area of 585km2, and is 50km long and 25km wide. There are 99 mountains with a height of about 600m, and 70% of the island is forested.

Phú Xuân 98, 100-102, 106

Phùng Hưng 41

Phùng Hưng (? – 789): He was born in Đường Lâm Commune, Ba Vì District of modern Hà Tây Province. When he died, the people honoured him to Bố Cái Đại Vương (the Father King of the Vietnamese Nation).

Phùng Nguyên 17, 30

Phùng Nguyên: now belonging to Phú Thọ Province

Phước Long 324

Phước Long: belonging to present Bình Phước Province.

Q

Quân Trung Từ Mệnh Tập 81

Quảng Đà 325

Quảng Đà: belonging to present Quảng Nam, Quảng Ngãi, Northern Trường Sơn and Northern Tây Nguyên.

Quảng Đức 322, 325

Quảng Đức: Part of present Quảng Ngãi province and the entire present Quảng Nam province.

Quảng Nguyên 51

Quảng Nguyên: now belonging to Lạng Sơn Province.

Quang Trung 7, 102, 104-105, 336

Quảng Yên 155, 196, 213

Quảng Yên: in present Yên Hưng District, Quảng Ninh Province.

Quốc Âm Thi Tập 81

Quốc Dân Đảng 179-181, 188, 200

Quốc ngữ (Romanized Vietnamese script)

Quốc ngữ (Romanized Vietnamese script): Introduced in the first half of the 17th century by the Jesuit missionary Alexandre de Rhodes

(1591 – 1660).

Quy Nhơn 100, 102, 106, 115, 257, 284, 317, 325

Quy Nhơn: Quy Nhơn Town is now the capital of Bình Định Province.

Quỳnh Văn 14-16

Quỳnh Văn: now belonging to Quỳnh Lưu District, Nghệ An Province (North Central Việt Nam).

Rạch Gầm - Xoài Mút

Rạch Gầm - Xoài Mút: located on the Tiền River (part of the Mekong River system), part of which crosses modern Mỹ Tho City.

Rạch Giá 139, 324

Rạch Giá: Rạch Giá Town is now the capital of Kiên Giang Province.

S

Sa Đéc 191

Sa Đéc: Sa Đéc Town (Sa Đéc Province in the French colony) now belongs to Đồng Tháp Province on the Mekong River Delta.

Sa Huỳnh 19, 33, 310

Sa Huỳnh: belonging to Quảng Ngãi Province (Central Việt Nam)

Sài Gòn - Chợ Lớn

Sài Gòn - Chợ Lớn: the joint name of the two areas of Sài Gòn City before 1976. Now, Hồ Chí Minh city includes both; Chợ Lớn (Big Market) comprises Districts 5 and 10.

Sóc Trăng 191

Sóc Trăng: now Sóc Trăng Province on the Mekong River Delta.

Sơn Tây 17, 94, 96, 181

Sơn Tây: now belonging to Hà Tây Province.

Sơn Tinh 20

T

Tân Việt 179, 182

Tao Đàn 81

Tây Đô citadel 69

Tây Đô Citadel: In An Tôn, now Thanh Hóa Province. One wall of the building is still standing, called Hồ Dynasty's Wall.

Tây Nguyên 155, 163

Tây Nguyên: the rich, red, mountainous, forested region spreading from western Thừa Thiên-Huế Province to Lộc Ninh of Bình Phước Province. The Trường Sơn mountain range runs from Quảng Bình Province to Bình Phước in Southeastern Việt Nam, reaching almost 1000m above sea level. Tây Nguyên, or Central Highlands, now contains Kon Tum, Gia Lai, Đắc Lắc, Đắc Nông and Lâm Đồng provinces.

Tây Sơn 5, 7-8, 89-90, 97, 99-107, 119, 125, 127

Tây Sơn: including Tây Sơn Thượng (Upper Tây Sơn) of Gia Lai Province and Tây Sơn Hạ (Lower Tây Sơn) of Bình Định Province.

Tế Hanh 302

Tế Hanh (1921–): a writer. His real name was Trần Tế Hanh. He was born in Bình Dương Commune, Bình Sơn District, Quảng Ngãi Province.

Thái Bình River system

Thái Bình River system: three merging rivers, Cầu River, Thương River and Lục Nam River, originating from the North East mountainous area and Việt Bắc. Thái Bình River flows from Phả Lại, Quảng Ninh to four estuaries. The Red River and Thái Bình River form the Northen delta of Việt Nam.

Thái Phiên 165

Thái Phiên (1882 – 1916): a revolutionary, born in Nghi An Village, Hòa Phát Commune, Hòa Vang District of Quảng Nam Province. In 1906, he participated in the Đông Du (Go East) Movement to encourage young students to study abroad. Starting in 1908, he was responsible for the finances of the Duy Tân (Reform) Society of Phan Bội Châu. Starting in 1912, he worked with the Quang Phục (Việt Nam Restoration) Society to gather patriots, including Emperor Duy Tân (1900-1945), in Central Việt Nam for an uprising against the French. Their plot was discovered, however, and Thái Phiên and the Emperor were arrested southeast of Huế. On May 17th, 1916, the French colonial government executed him.

Thăng Long 43, 46, 52, 54-55, 76, 90, 94, 102-105, 107

Thăng Long: meaning "soaring dragon"; the name given by King Lý Công Uẩn in 1010 to his new capital established at La Thành, now Hà Nội.

Thanh Hải 302

Thanh Hải (1930 – 1980): a writer. His real name was Phạm Bá Ngoãn. He was born in Phong Bình Commune, Phong Điền District, Thừa Thiên-Huế Province.

Thanh Niên Cách Mạng Đồng Chí Hội 178

The Hồ Chí Minh Trail or Trường Sơn Route

The Hồ Chí Minh Trail or Trường Sơn Route: This was a strategic supply route from the North to the South during the anti-American war (1954-1975), running along the East-West flank of the Trường Sơn mountain range through the territory of Việt Nam, Laos and Cambodia. It was based on the North-South communication line during the anti-French resistance (1945-1954). From 1954 on, it was also called the Unification Route.

The development of the Trail was started on 19th May 1959 under the charge of Group 559, the Ministry of National Defence. It started from Tân Kỳ (Nghệ An province) and from Khe Hó (Vĩnh Linh, Quảng Trị province).

The Trail included the following routes:

* The communication route, about 3,000 km long, starting from Bãi Hà, Quảng Trị province to the Eastern region of the South (Bình Phước province nowadays).

* The gasoline pipe line. It was started in June 1968, from Khe Hó (Vĩnh Linh, Quảng Trị province to Lộc Ninh (Bình Phước province) in the Eastern region of the South.

It was 1,339 km long, had 46 stores with a capacity of 17,050 tons and 113 supply stations.

* The transportation route for bicycles, horses, elephants and humans.

* The transportation route for cars. It had 5 main axes (5,530 km in total); 21 branches (4,019 km in total) and 440 detours (4,700 km in total). There was a system of hidden roads (called route K, 3,140 km in length) for cars to run even in the day time. Two of the 5 main axes ran along the eastern side of Trường Sơn (Việt Nam) and the other three, along the western side (Lao, Cambodia).

* The water route made up of streams, rivers, rivulets; about 500 km in length. It was intended for boats, canoes, rafts, etc.

The entire Trail was built with the efforts of young volunteers and military engineering personnel who spent about 10 million working days digging 21 million cubic metres of earth and rock, and building 13,418 m of bridges, and 10,000 culverts.

The adversary dropped on the Trail 1,340,000 tons of bombs with 33,460 B-52 sorties, and millions of mines; sprayed over it toxic chemicals and "artificial rains" (valued at US$ 21 million); built an electronic bar to prevent the circulation and carried out 120 big sweeps to destroy the Trail.

Thế Lữ (1907 – 1989): a poet, writer and activist for the Vietnamese stage. Born in Phù Đổng Village, Tiên Du District (Tiên Sơn District now) of Bắc Ninh Province, as Nguyễn Thứ Lễ, his penname was Lê Ta.

Thu Bồn (1935–2003): a writer. His real name was Hà Đức Trọng. He was born in Điện Thắng Commune, Điện Bàn District, Quảng Nam Province.

Thu Bồn River: 205km in length, flowing from Kon Tum Province through Quảng Nam Province to Đà Nẵng City, where it reaches the East Sea.

Thủ Dầu Một: now belonging to Bình Dương Province.

Thuận An River: in modern Thừa Thiên-Huế (Bồ River flows out to Thuận An estuary).

Thuận Châu: belonging to Sơn La Province.

Tố Hữu (1920 – 2002): a poet. His real name was Nguyễn Kim Thành (another name: Lành), and he was born in Phù Lai Village, Quảng Điền District, Thừa Thiên-Huế Province. He started to write poems when he was only sixteen years old, and became a great poet of Việt Nam during the 20th century. He was also a patriot and revolutionary. In 1938, he joined the Indochinese Communist Party, for which the French arrested him in April 1939. He escaped from prison in 1942 and continued his revolutionary activities. He was the Deputy Prime Minister and a Member of the Politburo of the Việt Nam Workers' Party.

Tôn Đức Thắng 177

Tôn Đức Thắng (1883 – 1980): He was born in a poor family of farmers in Mỹ Hòa Hưng Village, Long Xuyên Province (now An Giang Province). In 1910, after graduating from a vocational college, he worked in a French naval workshop in Sài Gòn. In 1912, he organized a strike with the students of his college and the workers of the Ba Son ship-repair factory. He fled to France afterward because he was wanted by the French government. At first, he worked in a marine factory, then became an engineer for the French navy and participated in a political campaign in the French armed forces. In 1919 near the Black Sea, he joined French workers and sailors in support for the USSR when fourteen imperial powers sought to wipe it out. The French Navy assigned him to a ship that would attack on Sevastopol (Russia). Yet, in celebration of the October Revolution, he ran up the flag of the Communist Party. Soon after, he resigned from the navy and took a job at a car-making firm. In 1920, Tôn Đức Thắng returned to Việt Nam with the repatriating Vietnamese soldiers after the First World War. In Sài Gòn, he formed secret trade unions and led a successful strike of Ba Son workers in August, 1925. In 1926, he joined the Vietnamese Revolutionary Youth League. In the following year, he was appointed to its Southern Executive Committee. In 1929, he was arrested by the colonial government, sentenced to twenty years of hard labor, and exiled to Côn Đảo. When the August 1945 Revolution succeeded, he was freed by the new revolutionary government. From 1945 to 1969, he held many important Party and State offices. After President Hồ Chí Minh passed away, he became President of the Democratic Republic of Việt Nam (later the Socialist Republic of Việt Nam), a position he held until his death.

Tôn Thất Thuyết 142-143

Tống Bình 40-41

Tống Bình: a previous name of Hà Nội.

Tống Duy Tân 146

Tống Duy Tân (1837 – 1892): born in Bồng Trung Village, which is now Vĩnh Tân Village, Vĩnh Lộc District, Thanh Hóa Province. He earned his doctoral degree in 1875 and was appointed as the chief of Vĩnh Tường District, now Vĩnh Phúc Province. Recognizing that the Nguyễn Dynasty was powerless against the French, he resigned from his post and returned to his hometown to open a school. Later, Tôn Thất Thuyết appointed him education officer of Thanh Hóa Province and later the chief of the mountain regions of the province. In 1885, in support of the Cần Vương (Save the King) Movement, he set up an anti-French base at Hùng Lĩnh in his province. His insurgent army fought for six years before retreating in 1891-1892 to the mountains in Bá Thước, now in Thanh Hóa Province.

Tốt Động: belonging to Chương Mỹ Commune of present Hà Tây Province.

Trà Kiệu: in present to Quảng Nam Province.

Trà Vinh: belonging to present Trà Vinh Province now.

Trần Cao Vân (1866 – 1916): a revolutionary of profound knowledge and understanding of literature. He was born in Tư Phú Village, Điện Bàn District, Quảng Nam Province. He joined the Cần Vương (Save the King) Movement in its early stages. After that, he moved to Bình Định Province to become a teacher. In 1898, he and Võ Trí led an uprising against the French, for which he was put in prison for 11 months. When released, he opened a school in Phú Yên Province. Because of his continued revolutionary activity in Bình Định and Phú Yên provinces, the colonial government arrested him again and sentenced him to death. The sentence was later reduced to three years in prison. During the anti-tax demonstration in Central Việt Nam, he was arrested, sentenced to hard labor, and exiled to Côn Đảo island for six years. After being set free, he joined the Quang Phục (Việt Nam Restoration) Society, and in 1916, participated in an unsuccessful uprising in Huế. He was executed with Thái Phiên.

Trần Đăng Khoa (1955 –): a poet, born in Hải Dương.

Trần Di Ái: an uncle of Trần Nhân Tông. In 1281, he, together with Lê Mục and Lê Tuân, was sent as an envoy to the emperor of the Yuan-Mongol Dynasty. Trần Di Ái surrendered to them and was chosen to be "An Nam Quốc Vương," or An Nam's King. Mục became a court mandarin, and Tuân became a Minister.

Trần Duệ Tông (1341 – 1369): died young from illness, leaving no

son to continue the dynasty.

Trần Hưng Đạo 49, 54-56, 58, 64, 102, 336

Trần Hưng Đạo (1231 – 1300): He was honoured as Hưng Đạo Royal Highest Trần Quốc Tuấn (Trần Hưng Đạo). Even now people worship him as a saint.

Trần Huy Liệu 175, 216

Trần Huy Liệu (1901 – 1969): born into a patriotic Confucian family at Vân Cát village, Vụ Bản District, Nam Định Province, he was a famous journalist, cultural researcher and historian. He started to write poems and articles when he was seventeen. Trần Huy Liệu took part in political activities in the patriotic and democratic campaign from 1925 to 1926. In March 1926, he participated in the foundation of the Sài Gòn Youth Party. He was the editor-in-chief of East France Times from 1925 to 1927, and a member of the Việt Nam Nationalist Part in Nam Kỳ (South Việt Nam) at the same time.

In August 1928, he was arrested and exiled to Côn Đảo Prison, where he was introduced to Communism. In 1935, he was released from prison and exiled to North Việt Nam. He continued his activities and was admitted to the Đông Dương (Indochinese) Communist Party, appointed to public activities. He became the editor-in-chief of the News, an important public newspaper of the Party in Hà Nội. In 1939, he was arrested and exiled to Sơn La Prison in Nghĩa Lộ until 1945, when he escaped and returned to Hà Nội. There, he started working for the National Salvation newspaper of the Việt Minh Front. At the National Congress in Tân Trào, Tuyên Quang in August 1945, he was elected Deputy Chairman of the National Liberation Committee and the Minister of Information and Propagation of the Provisional Government.

After the August Revolution in 1945, Trần Huy Liệu led the delegation that recognized Bảo Đại's abdication. During the anti-French Resistance War (1945-1954), he held several important posts in the Resistance Government.

When the war ended (1954), he turned to cultural and academic pursuits. He became the manager of the Literature, History and Geography Research Department, and then director of the History Research Institute, Vice Chairman of the State Scientific Commission and Commission of Social Sciences. He was honored with the Humbold Medal and was invited to be a correspondent member of the German Democratic Republic's Academy of Sciences. He left behind many valuable works of historical research.

Trần Ích Tắc 55

Trần Ích Tắc: a son of King Trần Thái Tông, who became Chiêu Quốc Vương (King Chiêu) in 1267. He was intelligent and diligent in his study, particularly good at classics and history. In 1285, however, he betrayed his country by surrendering to the Yuan-Mongol emperor, when he invaded Đại Việt. In exchange for his easy surrender, Kublai Khan made Trần Ích Tắc the king of An Nam. The Yuan-Mongol troops held Đại Việt for only a short time, and when they were forced to retreat back to China, Trần Ích Tắc followed them into exile and never returned to his country.

Trần Khánh Dư 56

Trần Minh Tông 45

Trần Nhân Tông 46, 54, 59, 64-65

Trần Nhân Tông (1258 – 1308): the third king of the Trần Dynasty. In 1293, he abdicated the throne for his son and became the King-Father. Some years later, he left the court to live at the Yên Tử Pagoda on Yên Tử Mountain in modern Quảng Ninh province and established the Trúc Lâm (Bamboo Forest) Zen sect.

Trấn Ninh 96

Trấn Ninh: in present Hà Tĩnh Province.

Trần Phú 179, 182, 191

Trần Phú (1904 – 1931): an orphan born on 1 May 1904 in Đức Phổ District, in present-day Quảng Ngãi Province (his ancestors came from what is now Đức Sơn commune, Đức Thọ district, Hà Tĩnh Province). He was raised and educated by his relatives. In 1922, he finished the College of Elementary Education in Huế, after which he was appointed to the elementary school Cao Xuân Dục in Vinh City. In 1925, he joined Phục Việt (Việt Nam Recovery) the Restoration Society (also called the Hưng Nam, then Tân Việt Revolutionary Party). He was sent to Laos to carry out revolutionary activities at the Pak Hin Pun mine. In July 1926, he was sent to Guangzhou, China, to meet the leaders of the Vietnamese Revolutionary Youth League and discuss its merge with the Tân Việt. There, he met Nguyễn Ái Quốc, was trained in Marxist-Leninist doctrine, and briefed on the Russian October Revolution. He was admitted to the Communist Party before returning to Việt Nam. In the spring of 1927, he went to study at the Oriental University in Moscow. He became the secretary of a Vietnamese Communist group studying there. In April 1930, he returned again and drafted the Vietnamese Communist Party's Political Thesis. This Thesis was approved at the First Plenum of the Party's Provisional Central Committee at Hương Cảng (Hong Kong, China) in 1931. Also at this conference, he was elected the Party's General Secretary, and the Party was renamed the Indochinese Communist Party. In March 1931, he chaired the second Plenum of the Provisional Central Committee, which rectified the wrong tendency in the Party's activity. On April 19th, 1931, he was arrested by the colonial government. In August 1931, he suffered a terrible illness and died soon after in Sài Gòn (Hồ Chí Minh City now).

Trần Quang Khải 55

Trần Quý Cáp 163

Trần Quý Cáp (1870 – 1908): a patriot and follower of the Duy Tân (Reform) Movement. He was born in Bất Nhị, Điện Bàn district, modern Quảng Nam Province. He earned a doctoral degree in 1904. Under the influence of the thoughts of Khang Hữu Vi and Lương Khải Siêu from China, he showed a patriotic spirit very early. He vigorously opposed the traditional system of examination and initiated an advanced method of learning. In 1905, he went to Nam Kỳ (South Việt Nam) with Phan Châu Trinh and Huỳnh Thúc Kháng to call up people to join Duy Tân Movement. In 1906, he was put in charge of education for Thăng Bình Prefecture in Quảng Nam Province. He used this position to spread the Duy Tân Movement. Later, the French government forced him to become an examiner for Diên Khánh District, Khánh Hòa Province. In 1908, the anti-tax movement in Quảng Nam Province broke out. The French acused him of being involved in it and executed him in Diên Khánh on 3th May 1908.

Trần Quý Khoáng

Trần Quý Khoáng (? – 1414): the leader of a resistance against the Ming forces. He was a grandson of King Trần Nghệ Tông. In 1409, he led a resistance in Nghệ An Province. In April 1409, he ascended the throne and led an insurgence against the Ming forces. He was captured by the Ming in summer 1414 and exiled to China. One the way he committed suicide.

Trần Thái Tông 59

Trần Thiện Khiêm 313, 332-333

Trần Thiện Khiêm: Prime Minister of the Sài Gòn government under President Nguyễn Văn Thiệu. He fled to Taiwan together with Nguyễn Văn Thiệu in April 1975.

Trần Trọng Kim 208, 212, 216

Trần Trọng Kim (1882 – 1953): an educator and Vietnamse literature and history researcher. He was born in Kiều Lĩnh Village, Đan Phố Commune, Nghi Xuân District in what is now Hà Tĩnh Province, and wrote under the penname Lệ Thần. After Japan's coup d`état overthrowing the French on September 3rd, 1945, Trần Trọng Kim became the Prime Minister of the government set up by Japan.

Trần Văn Hương 332-333

Trần Văn Hương: Prime Minister of the Sài Gòn government after Nguyễn Văn Thiệu and Trần Thiện Khiêm fled to Taiwan.

Trần Xuân Soạn 143

Trạng Lợn 124

Trạng Quỳnh 124

Triệu 39-40, 65, 84, 309, Trịnh 82, 90-94, 96-101, 104-105, 107, 120, 123-124, 127-128, 164

Trịnh Doanh 94

Trịnh Kiểm 82

Trịnh Kiểm (1502–1570): He led a resistance against the Mạc Dynasty. After his father-in-law, Nguyễn Kim, died, King Lê

Ngãi Province. In 1850, he was appointed commander of a company of the local armed forces. In 1853, when the French forces occupied the Gia Định Citadel, Trương Định recruited people to fight against the French. In 1861, he built his resistance base at Tân Hòa (Gò Công province). Trương Định's insurgent army launched many attacks on the French at Gò Công, Tân An, Mỹ Tho, Chợ Lớn, etc. In 1862, in defiance of the Nguyễn court's order to move to An Giang Province, he stayed in Gia Định to become the Chief of the "Annihilating French Invaders Movement". His army launched many attacks on the French troops in various provinces. On February 25, 1863 the French army with many big-sized warships attacked and occupied the Gò Công base. Trương Định's forces withdrew to the three eastern provinces of South Việt Nam. In 1864, the French forces raided Trương Định's headquarters. Heavily wounded, Trương Định killed himself on August 20th.

Trương Hán Siêu 63, 65

Trương Hán Siêu (? – 1355): a famous writer and politician of the Trần Dynasty. He was born in Phúc Thành village, Yên Ninh district (now Yên Khánh distric, Ninh Bình province). In 1308, he was invited to work at the Academy. He took part in many political affairs and was highly appreciated by the King.

Trương Phúc Loan 98-99

Trương Phúc Loan (? – 1774): an important government official in the Nguyễn Lord period. In 1785, Lord Nguyễn Phúc Khoát died. Phúc Loan put twelve-year-old Nguyễn Phúc Thuần on the throne because he could easily be controlled. Phúc Loan was appointed Minister of Economics and was known to be corrupt, dishonest and greedy.

Trương Quyền 139

Trương Quyền (1844 – ?): Leader of an anti-French uprising. His real name was Trương Huệ, and he was the son of Trương Định. Trương Quyền participated in his father's uprising, leading the "Army of the eldest brothers." After his father died in 1864, he took his army to Tây Ninh, where he set up a military base in cooperation with Pokumbo army from Cambodia. In 1866, he commanded a series of battles against the French army at Thuận Kiều (Bà Điểm, Hóc Môn District, Hồ Chí Minh City nowadays), Củ Chi, Hóc Môn (Hồ Chí Minh City nowadays), Trảng Bàng (Tây Ninh), Long Trì (Tân An, Long An). The Trương Quyền Pokumbo army attached Trà Vang (Tây Ninh and An Cá post, killed a French platoon, and six French officers. Trương Quyền fell in battle.

Trường Sơn 111, 143, 279

Tự Đức 140-142

Tự Đức (1829 – 1883): the reign name of Nguyễn Hồng Nhậm, also called Dục Tông, the fourth emperor of the Nguyễn Dynasty. He reigned for 36 years.

Từ Hải 126

Tú Mỡ 201

Tú Mỡ (1900–1976): a satirical poet. Born in Hà Nội, his real name was Hồ Trọng Hiếu.

Tuệ Tĩnh 69

Tuệ Tĩnh (1330 – ?): a researcher of Southern medicines and treatments. He was born as Nguyễn Bá Tĩnh in Cẩm Giàng District, Hải Dương Province, and orphaned at an early age. He was raised at a Buddhist temple, and although he passed the court exam, he did not enter government. He chose to spend his time researching into Vietnamese medicine.

V

Vân Đồn 46, 56, 94

Vân Đồn: an archipelago with over 600 islands in Bái Tử Long, Quảng Ninh Province. About 50 km southeast of Hạ Long City, it was a bustling "border" trading port during the 11th and 12th centuries.

Vạn Hạnh 47, 63

Vạn Hạnh (? – 1116): Born in Cổ Pháp (Đình Bảng, Từ Sơn district, Bắc Ninh province nowadays). He was an intelligent man who had good knowledge of Confucianism, Buddhism and Taoism. He was initiated into monkhood at the age of 21, at Lục Tổ pagoda. In 981, the Chinese Song sent troops to invade Việt Nam. Vạn Hạnh gave the Court valuable advice in the strategy of resistance. Therefore, Vạn Hạnh commended deep respect of King Lê Đại Hành and the Court. When small, Lý Công Uẩn, the founder-king of the Lý dynasty, was brought up by Vạn Hạnh. Later, Lý Công Uẩn became a mandarin in the Lê Court. When king Lê Long Đĩnh died in 1009, Vạn Hạnh and the high-ranking mandarins decided to enthrone Lý Công Uẩn to give birth to the Lý dynasty. Then, the new king conferred on Vạn Hạnh the title of Quốc sư (National Master). When Vạn Hạnh died, the king himself attended his funeral as a token of respect.

Văn Lang 19-20

Văn Tiến Dũng 213

Văn Tiến Dũng (1917 – 2002): born in Cổ Nhuế, now belonging to Cầu Giấy District in Hà Nội, he became a member of the Indochinese Communist Party in 1936. After being arrested by the French, he escaped from prison in 1944. In January 1945, he was sentenced to death by French colonialists in absentia. The Communist Party appointed him to direct the preparations for a revolution against the French in Hòa Bình, Ninh Bình and Thanh Hóa provinces. In December 1946, he was elected the Director of the Political Bureau of the Vietnamese People's Army, and the Vice Secretary of the Central Military Commission. In early 1948, he became a lieutenant general of the Vietnamese People's Army, the political commissar and also the Commander of Military Zone III. From November 1953 to May

1978, he was the General Chief of Staff of the Vietnamese People's Army, who led the Road 9 – Southern Laos Campaign (1971), the Quảng Trị Liberation Campaign (1972), and the Tây Nguyên Liberation Campaign (1975). He was the Commander of the Hồ Chí Minh Campaign, which liberated Sài Gòn – Gia Định.

In April 1974, he was promoted to the rank of 4-star General. In May 1978, he was elected the First Deputy Secretary of the Central Military Commission. In February 1980, he became the Minister of Defense. He was elected an alternate member of the Central Committee of the Vietnamese Workers' Party in February 1951, an alternate member of the Politburo in March 1960, an official member of the Politburo of the Party in March 1973, an official member of the Central Committee of the Communist Party of Việt Nam (CPV) in December 1976, a member of all the National Assemblies from the Second to the Seventh (1960 to 1986), a member of the Politburo of the CPV in March 1982, and a member of the 6th Central Party Committee of the CPV. He was assigned the task of summarizing war experiences and the military history of Việt Nam.

Vạn Xuân 40

Vàng Pao 289, 292, 295

Vàng Pao: from the Mèo ethnic group; a pro-US general in Laos. He now lives in exile abroad.

Viên Chiếu 63

Việt 1, 3-8, 11, 13-17, 19-21, 35, 37, 40-43, 49-52, 54-57, 61, 63, 65, 71, 74, 77, 79, 82, 84, 90, 99-100, 102, 104, 106, 109-110, 112-115, 117-118, 121, 127, 129, 131, 133, 139-143, 145-146, 150, 152, 154-155, 163-165, 167, 169, 172, 175-179, 181-182, 185, 188-189, 196-199, 201, 203, 205-206, 208-217, 219-222, 224-225

Việt Bắc 20, 145, 237, 240, 247

Việt Bắc: in North Việt Nam before 1954; it included the present provinces: Hà Giang, Cao Bằng, Lạng Sơn, Bắc Cạn, Thái Nguyên and Tuyên Quang.

Việt Cách 225-226, 231

Việt Cách - Việt Quốc: a name for the Đại Việt National Revolutionary Commissioner Association, used before the August Revolution in 1945. The association was based in China and supported Chiang Kai-shek and Vietnamese political activities in China.

Việt Cộng 326, 339

Việt Cộng: the name Americans and the pro-American Sài Gòn government gave to the revolutionary forces fighting for reunification.

Việt Điện U Linh 65

Việt Minh 201, 208-217, 220, 222, 225, 230, 246, 255

Việt Minh: the short name of the Việt Nam Federation of Independence, established on May 19th, 1941.

Việt Nam Quang Phục 163

Việt Nam Workers' Party

Việt Nam Workers' Party: the name

given to the new Party of Việt Nam at the Second Congress of the Indochinese Communist Party in January 1951. Before, the Communist Parties of Laos, Cambodia and Việt Nam were combined. This name change marked the separation of the parties. In 1976, at the Fourth Party Congress, the Việt Nam Workers' Party decided to change its name to the Việt Nam Communist Party.

Việt Sử Cương Mục 65

Vinh - Bến Thủy 190

Vinh - Bến Thủy: the joint name of Vinh City, a coastal town at the mouth of the Lam River. Some years ago, the Trans-Việt Nam Highway had to cross the river by ferry, but now, Bến Thủy Harbor includes a bridge, connecting Nghệ An and Hà Tĩnh provinces.

Vĩnh Long 191

Vĩnh Long: now Vĩnh Long Province on the Cửu Long (Mekong) River Delta.

Vĩnh Yên 94, 210

Vĩnh Yên: belonging to Vĩnh Phúc Province.

Võ Huy Tâm 302

Võ Huy Tâm (1926–1996): a writer. His pen-names included Hà Tuyến, Anh Tuấn and Phu Mỏ. His real name was Võ Huy, and he was born in Gia Hòa Commune, Mỹ Lộc District, Nam Định Province.

Võ Nguyên Giáp 210, 213, 229, 232, 254, 260, 301

Võ Nguyên Giáp (1911 –): the famous revolutionary general and mastermind of the Điện Biên Phủ Campaign in 1954. He was the Minister of Defense of the Democratic Republic of Việt Nam and the Socialist Republic of Việt Nam from 1946 to 1977, Commander-in-chief of Việt Nam's National Military and Civil Defense, Deputy Prime Minister from 1978 to 1992, and has been a top-ranking General and a member of the Việt Nam Communist Party since 1948.

He was born in Lộc Thủy, Lệ Thủy District, Quảng Bình Province, and became a history teacher at Thăng Long High School in Hà Nội. After taking part in revolutionary activities since 1925, he joined the Communist Party in 1940. In 1930, he was arrested by the French. Then, in December 1944, he was assigned by Hồ Chí Minh to set up the Armed Propagation Brigade for the Liberation of Việt Nam.

On August 4th, 1945, he became the commander of the Việt Nam Liberation Army. At the Second Conference of the Đông Dương Communist Party, he was voted member of the Central Committee, a member of the Standing Executive Committee. In 1946, he became the Minister of National Defense for the Provisional Government. He led the Biên Giới and Điện Biên Phủ campaigns in 1950 and 1954, respectively, and, together with the Politburo of the Central Committee of the Việt Nam Workers' Party, he led the resistance against the Americans and the Southern regime in North

Việt Nam, commanding significant campaigns, such as the Hồ Chí Minh Campaign.

Võ Nguyên Giáp wrote many books on military affairs. He was a member of the Second, Third and Fourth Politburos of the Central Committee of the Việt Nam Workers' Party, and the Việt Nam Communist Party during terms Two through Four; a member of the National Assembly from the first through seventh terms. He was awarded the most medals of any military man in the State, and was the most famous general in modern Vietnamese history.

Võ Nhai 204, 210

Võ Nhai: belonging to Võ Nhai District, Thái Nguyên Province.

Vũ Trọng Phụng 200

Vũ Trọng Phụng (1912-1939): a writer, born in Hảo Village, Mỹ Sơn District, Hưng Yên Province. He lived in Hà Nội for most of his life.

Vũ Trung Tùy Bút 128

X

Xuân Diệu 200, 302

Xuân Diệu (1916 – 1988): a poet born in Trảo Nha village, Can Lộc District, Hà Tĩnh Province. One of his pennames was Trảo Nha, but his real name was Ngô Xuân Diệu.

Xuân Lộc 15, 331-332

Xuân Lộc: Xuân Lộc District, now belonging to Đồng Nai Province (in South-Eastern Việt Nam).

Xuân Lộc: Xuân Lộc town, Đồng Nai Province now.

Xương Giang 87

Y

Yên Bái 13, 17, 180-181, 188, 200, 252

Yên Thế 146-147, 149, 160, 163

Yên Thế: belonging to Yên Thế District, Bắc Giang Province.

NHÀ XUẤT BẢN THẾ GIỚI
Trụ sở chính: Số 46 Trần Hưng Đạo, Hoàn Kiếm, Hà Nội
Tel: 0084.4.38253841 – Fax: 0084.4.38269578
Chi nhánh: Số 7 Nguyễn Thị Minh Khai, Quận I, TP. Hồ Chí Minh
Tel: 0084.8.38220102
Email: marketing@thegioipublishers.vn
Website: www.thegioipublishers.vn

LỊCH SỬ VIỆT NAM

Tác giả
NGUYỄN KHẮC VIỆN

Chịu trách nhiệm xuất bản
GIÁM ĐỐC - TỔNG BIÊN TẬP
TS. TRẦN ĐOÀN LÂM

Hiệu đính: Karl Tagenfeldt
Judy Naegeli
Biên tập tiếng Anh: Phạm Trần Long
Bìa: Nguyễn Trung Dũng
Sửa bản in: Quang Minh
Trình bày: Trung Tâm Chế bản và In

In 1.000 bản, khổ 16 x 24 cm tại Xưởng in Công ty TNHH MTV Nhà xuất bản Thế Giới - Nhà 23 ngõ 62 phố Nguyễn Chí Thanh, quận Đống Đa, Hà Nội.
Số ĐKXB: 1514-2015/CXBIPH/12-103/ThG cấp ngày 10/06/2015.
Quyết định xuất bản số: 304/QĐ-ThG cấp ngày 10/08/2015.
In xong và nộp lưu chiểu quý III năm 2015.